Here and There in Mexico

Frontispiece: Mary Ashley Townsend, from *Down the Bayou, the Captain's Story, and other Poems* (Philadelphia: Lippincott, 1881, 1895)

Here and There in Mexico

The Travel Writings of
MARY ASHLEY TOWNSEND

Edited by
RALPH LEE WOODWARD, JR.

THE UNIVERSITY OF ALABAMA PRESS
Tuscaloosa and London

2 4 6 8 9 7 5 3 1
02 04 06 08 09 07 05 03 01

Typeface: Adobe Caslon

∞

The paper on which this book is printed meets the minimum requirements of American
National Standard for Information Science–Permanence of Paper for Printed Library
Materials, ANSI Z39.48-1984.

Library of Congress Cataloging-in-Publication Data
Townsend, Mary Ashley, 1832–1901.
Here and there in Mexico : the travel writings of Mary Ashley Townsend / edited by
Ralph Lee Woodward, Jr.
p. cm.
Includes index.
ISBN 0-8173-1058-4 (alk. paper)
1. Mexico—Description and travel. 2. Mexico—Social life and
customs. 3. Townsend, Mary Ashley, 1832–1901—Journeys—Mexico. 4. Authors,
American—19th century—Biography. I. Woodward, Ralph Lee. II. Title.
F1215 .T69 2001
917.204′81—dc21
00-010162

British Library Cataloguing-in-Publication Data available

Contents

Editor's Preface

Mexico, a century ago! At peace and bursting with economic development after years of political disorder and economic decline. For a North American visitor exotic, foreign, and rich in ancient tradition, yet racing to modernize in imitation of its northern neighbor!

Here and There in Mexico is the account of an observant and sensitive Louisiana woman, Mary Ashley Townsend.[1] She was a poet, a novelist, a newspaper columnist, and a mother, who made several trips to Mexico during the last two decades of the nineteenth century. She recorded her observations in her newspaper columns, in diaries, and in letters, and around the turn of the century she wrote a manuscript that presented a composite picture of part of Mexico. The manuscript, published here for the first time, ends abruptly without including all of the places she had visited, cut short by her accidental death in 1901. Written as a single journey, it incorporates impressions and insight from her several trips in her descriptive and lyrical prose. She reveals a wry sense of humor and keen powers of observation in an account that tells us of the political, the economic, the social, and the

---

1. The biographical information in this preface is based on the *Dictionary of Louisiana Biography*, 2 vols., edited by Glen R. Conrad (New Orleans: Louisiana Historical Association, 1988), s.v. "Mary Ashley Townsend," and on a paper presented by Mary Ashley Townsend's granddaughter, Cora Stanton Jahncke, to a meeting of the Quarante Club in New Orleans on an undetermined date. The paper is in Collection 19, Stanton-Townsend Papers, in the Special Collections Division of the Howard-Tilton Library, Tulane University, New Orleans.

cultural sides of Mexico at the end of the 1800s. It vividly describes flora and fauna, architecture, and people, their work and attitudes, at play, dancing, and singing, as well as observations on fashions, society, manners, cooking, and more. Her descriptions of the living quarters and habits of Mexicans of all classes make it especially valuable for social historians of the period.

Born Mary Ashley Van Voorhis in Lyons, Wayne County, New York, on September 24, 1832, the daughter of James G. and Catherine (Van Wickle) Van Voorhis, she grew up in a comfortable family of Dutch descent in upstate New York. In 1853 she married a cousin, Gideon Townsend. Mary and Gideon lived in Fishkill, New York, and Clinton, Iowa, before moving to New Orleans in 1860, where they raised a family of three daughters. Mary had a solid education in New York and in addition to English spoke Spanish and French fluently, and she also translated a number of poems from Spanish and German into English. Although frail as a child, in adult life she enjoyed excellent health and carried on a physically active life. She was a tall, blue-eyed, slender woman with dark hair, noted for her gracious manners. Yet her travels in mountainous Mexico were often by horseback, on which she covered forty or fifty miles without undue fatigue.

Mary Ashley Townsend had been to New Orleans before her marriage, when she visited a sister there in 1850. She had begun to write as a child, but it was during that visit to New Orleans that she wrote her first published work, printed in that year in the Fishkill *Standard* under the name "Xariffa." After returning home, she sent a poem to the New Orleans *Delta*, again under the pseudonym "Xariffa." After her move to New Orleans her poems and articles appeared regularly in the Sunday *Delta*, under the title "A letter from Xariffa." She also wrote, under the name Mary Ashley, for the New Orleans *Crescent*, a newspaper established by William Walker, later known as the "grey-eyed man of destiny" who took over Nicaragua in 1857 before being defeated by a united Central American army. In that same year, Townsend published her first and only novel, *The Brother Clerks: A Tale of New Orleans* (New York: Derby & Jackson, 1857). "Xariffa" also published beyond New Orleans, in the New York *Courier* and New York *Tribune*, as well as in literary journals in Boston and elsewhere. A series of letters entitled "Life in a Trunk" described her summer travels throughout the United States and honed her talents as a perceptive observer.

Her poems reflect a reverence for nature and the outdoors. "I have a passionate love of flowers myself," she wrote, "and when I witness it in others, there is a chord responsive touched on the human harp of one thousand strings, which plays within this breast."[2] She also wrote several popular poems related to the Civil War, including her often reprinted commemoration of "A Georgia Volunteer." The last poem she wrote, in fact, commemorated Robert E. Lee on his birthday and was written at the request of the United Daughters of the Confederacy for their celebration of Lee's birthday on January 19, 1901.[3] Her work eventually appeared in various anthologies and in three volumes of her own.[4] She became a role model for liberated women in the South. Her most popular poem, reprinted many times, was a sensitive love song, "Creed."

> I believe if I should die,
> And you should kiss my eyelids when I lie
> Cold, dead, and dumb to all the world contains,
> The folded orbs would open at thy breath,
> And, from its exile in the isles of death,
> Life would come gladly back along my veins.
>
> I believe if I were dead,
> And you upon my lifeless heart should tread,
> Not knowing what the poor clod chanced to be,
> It would find sudden pulse beneath the touch
> Of him it ever loved in life so much,
> And throb again, warm, tender, true to thee.
>
> I believe if on my grave,
> Hidden in woody deeps or by the wave,
> Your eyes should drop some warm tears of regret,
> From every salty seed of your dear grief,

---

2. Jahncke, 9.

3. Ibid., 15–19.

4. *Xariffa's Poems* (Philadelphia: J. B. Lippincott, 1870); *Down the Bayou and Other Poems* (Boston: J. R. Osgood, 1882); *Distaff and Spindle: Sonnets* (Philadelphia: J. B. Lippincott, 1895), with many subsequent editions of these works, some of which have slight variations in the titles.

Some fair, sweet blossom would leap into leaf,
To prove death could not make my love forget.

I believe if I should fade
Into those mystic realms where light is made,
And you should long once more my face to see,
I would come forth upon the hills of night
And gather stars, like fagots, till thy sight,
Led by their beacon blaze, fell full on me!

I believe my faith in thee,
Strong as my life, so nobly placed to be.
I would as soon expect to see the sun
Fall like a dead king from his height sublime,
His glory stricken from the throne of time,
As thee unworth the worship thou hast won.

I believe who hath not loved
Hath half the sweetness of his life unproved;
Like one who, with the grape within his grasp,
Drops it with all its crimson juice unpressed,
And all its luscious sweetness left unguessed,
Out from his careless and unheeding clasp.

I believe love, pure and true,
Is to the soul a sweet, immortal dew,
That gems life's petals in its hours of dusk;
The waiting angels see and recognize
The rich crown jewel, Love, of Paradise,
When life falls from us like a withered husk.[5]

Townsend's granddaughter described her marriage in idyllic terms:

Gideon Townsend was a poet himself but discontinued writing after his marriage. In Mrs. Townsend's diary, shortly after she married, she wrote on April

5. This poem, reprinted many times, appeared first in the New Orleans *Picayune*,
November 1, 1868.

1, 1853, "found a little book in Gideon Townsend's trunk full of sweet thoughts dedicated to Mary since eight years ago. I was deeply touched and shed a few bright tears." They were always lovers. Mrs. Townsend never wrote a poem she did not first submit it to her husband, and she was wont to say, if he were pleased, she was satisfied. He was an able critic of her works and an unfailing admirer."[6]

In New Orleans the Townsends lived first on Canal Street, but then moved to Carondelet near Lafayette Street, and later farther out to Carondelet and Jackson Avenue, and finally to 3923 Carondelet. Their home became a meeting place for both local writers and those from other places, including Oliver Wendell Holmes, Eugene Field, Joaquín Miller, Horace Fletcher, Joseph Jefferson, and George Cable. One guest wrote:

We sat in the rich and artistic drawing-room of "Xariffa's" beautiful home in Carondelet Street in this City. Never had a fine and refined home a more gracious and graceful mistress. When she crossed her long apartments, her gown trailing in a little frou-frou and whisper of silk about her tall form, her large, nervous hands outheld in welcome, her soft hair brushed back and braided in a golden-brown coronet above a brow that makes one feel it is thought-crowded, there is something so inexpressibly dignified and noble in her bearing that one seems to fully realize for the first time what a thoroughly high-minded and good woman this woman poet is.[7]

She came to be known as the "Poet Laureate of New Orleans" and was a regular at ceremonial occasions in the city. Her granddaughter chronicled such occasions:

There was no public occasion of any importance that her pen was not called upon to perform. She was appointed on January 1, 1880, to write the annual address of the "Carriers" for the New Orleans *Times-Democrat;* on May 10, 1881, the poem dedicated to the Army of Northern Tennessee on the occasion of the unveiling of the statue of Stonewall Jackson; February 28, 1881, the

---

6. Jahncke, 5.
7. Ibid., 6. Jahncke does not identify the writer.

poem dedicated to the Louisiana Press Association; April 7, 1887, the poem on the unveiling of the statue of Albert Sidney Johnston; February 13, 1888, the poem on the occasion of the Confederate Cavalry Reunion at the Washington Artillery Hall; January 27, 1894, the poem for the laying of the cornerstone of Tulane University; and March 5, 1889, the poem on the occasion of the opening of the Howard Memorial Library. She was appointed the official poet of the New Orleans Cotton Centennial Exposition on the opening day in 1884, and also wrote the poem for the opening of the Woman's Department of the Exposition, of which Julia Ward Howe was President. On February 17, 1879, she was appointed Poet Laureate of Rex. And on April 10, 1874, she was appointed to write the poem of the Dedication of the Confederate Monument at Greenwood Cemetery.[8]

She was one of the founders, in 1886, of the Quarante Club, forty women organized for "literary study and improvement." Elected president of the club in 1888, Townsend was reelected for seven consecutive years, until she resigned in November 1894, "owing to expected frequent trips to Mexico."

She developed a deep love for Mexico during her first trip there in 1881, when she spent the winter with her daughter, Cora, who married a Mexican, José Rascón. From Mexico she sent back letters entitled "Travels in Mexico" to the New Orleans *Picayune*. Thereafter she visited Mexico frequently, gaining a deep knowledge of and sympathy for the country and its people. On one of several visits to Mexico, the Liceo Hidalgo, the foremost literary club in Mexico City, honored her with election to membership, the only woman from the United States at the time to be so honored. And she owned a home on beautiful Lake Chapala, near Guadalajara. Many of her poems and sonnets breathe of the tropic beauty of that country. As early as 1882 she had discussed the possibility of a Mexican volume with her publisher, J. R. Osgood of Boston,[9] but although she published many newspaper columns on her travels in Mexico, the book was still in progress in the spring of 1901. Nearly seventy years old, she was once more en route to Mexico when the train on which she was traveling had an accident near Houston. Townsend

8. Ibid., 14–15.
9. J. R. Osgood to Mary A. Townsend [Boston], August 7, 1882, in Collection 19, Manuscripts Division, Special Collections, Howard-Tilton Library, Tulane University, New Orleans.

suffered serious injury and after several weeks of suffering she died in Galveston at the home of a daughter, Daisy Townsend Lee.

After a brief description of Mexico in general and of ways of getting there, Mary Ashley Townsend's charming account describes the sea voyage from New Orleans to Tampico and then south along the Mexican coast to Veracruz. Going ashore there, she describes in rich detail that port and surrounding areas. Subsequent chapters describe a trip inland to Jalapa, and then to Orizaba, Puebla, Cholula, and, finally, the capital city of Mexico, the environs of which occupy much of the latter half of the book. Although her descriptions of places and sights are fascinating, much more valuable are her perceptive and observant comments on people and their manners. She points out both vices and virtues with considerable candor. She is not hesitant about expressing some hostility toward the Roman Catholic Church and the Spanish Inquisition but still admires the churches and cathedrals and the art found within them. She frequently notes the condition of women, their activities, hospital care, children, and other social aspects. She comments on the Indians at length, throughout the work, as well as about the life-styles of the elite. Her comments range over literary figures, politicians, generals, entrepreneurs, historical sites, customs, and manners. Her detailed description of Mexico City in the late nineteenth century is especially insightful, for she deals with both commoner and elite. Reflecting the values of the era of Porfirio Díaz, who dominated the country from 1876 to 1910, she emphasizes Mexico's order and progress and the safety of the country for foreigners. Her style is decidedly poetical. Her sometimes flowery, rather longish sentences are characteristic of her own era but are laced with Mexican Spanish, occasionally incorrect, but clear enough if slightly corrupted. Townsend also voices strong ideas about economic development, reflecting both her U.S. capitalist biases and sympathy for the indigenous masses. Her sympathy for labor reflects an understanding of the economic benefits of higher wages in driving an economy. In this respect, her views may reflect more about attitudes in the United States at the end of the nineteenth century than matters relevant to Mexico. Despite a sympathy for Mexico's Indians and poor people, she does not entirely suppress a sense of Anglo superiority and the racism so common north of the border at the end of the nineteenth century.

Accompanying the handwritten original were a number of illustrative photographs and other illustrations; however, after a century most of the photographs are badly faded or otherwise damaged and they have not been included in this edition. Far better images are found in Townsend's lyrical and poetical prose, in which she inspires our imagination to see, to feel, and even to smell so many scenes in Porfirian Mexico. The descriptive and literary quality of her writing is remarkable and ranks *Here and There in Mexico* among the more notable foreign descriptions of the country in the late nineteenth century. The travel account was a popular literary genre in the United States and Europe in the nineteenth century, as travelers described their visits to the rest of the world. An early classic of such works on Mexico was Madame Fanny Calderón de la Barca's *Life in Mexico, During a Residence of Two Years in that Country* (London: Chapman and Hall, 1843), based on the letters of a Scotswoman, Francis Erskine Inglis, married to a Spanish diplomat.[10] Townsend's work continues in the tradition established by that work and compliments nicely several other travel accounts of the last decades of the century.[11] Her observations of and sympathy for both the elite and the lowly of Mexican society make it an especially valuable window on the period. Her greater coverage of the environs of the capital city also distinguishes her account from most of the others of the period.

10. This work has been republished several times, including a heavily annotated edition with new material from the author's private journals, edited by Howard T. Fisher and Marion Hall Fisher (Garden City, New York: Doubleday & Company, 1966).

11. Among the more notable of the late nineteenth-century travel accounts are Howard Conkling, *Mexico and the Mexicans, or Notes of Travel in the Winter and Spring of 1883* (New York: Tantor Brothers, 1883); Thomas U. Brocklehurst, *Mexico To-day: A Country with a Great Future, and a Glance at the Prehistoric Remains and Antiquities of the Montezumas* (London: John Murray, 1883), which focuses especially on pre-Columbian ruins; Reau Campbell, *Travels in Mexico* (New York: C. G. Crawford, 1890); and Fanny Chambers Gooch [Iglehart], *Face to Face with the Mexicans: The Domestic Life* (New York: Fords, Howard, & Hulbert, 1887). The last-named work, like Townsend's, makes a special effort to explain the Mexicans to a North American audience, but deals with different areas of the country than does Townsend. In the first decade of the twentieth century several more interesting accounts appeared, notably Ethel Brilliana Harley Tweedie's *Mexico as I Saw It* (New York: Macmillan, 1901); W. E. Carson's *Mexico, the Wonderland of the South* (New York: Macmillan, 1909); and, especially useful for its description of Mexico on the eve of the Revolution of 1910, Charles Malcomb Flandrau's *Viva Mexico!* (New York & London: D. Appleton & Co., 1910). For a detailed and scholarly examination of one region of nineteenth-century Mexico based on foreign observations, see Alfred H. Siemens, *Between the Summit and the Sea: Central Veracruz in the Nineteenth Century* (Vancouver: University of British Columbia Press, 1990).

As editor of this work, I have attempted to preserve as closely as possible the language and punctuation of Townsend's original handwritten manuscript. I am indebted to my dear late wife, Sue Dawn McGrady Woodward, who transcribed the first draft of this work from the original manuscript. I have added information sparingly, either in brackets within the text or as footnotes, to clarify a meaning, to correct a factual error, or to identify persons mentioned. In a number of cases, Townsend preferred not to identify certain personages, providing only an initial or a blank for the name. All the explanatory and bibliographical footnotes are mine. I am also deeply grateful to Dr. Wilbur Meneray and his staff at the Special Collections Division of Tulane University's Howard-Tilton Library in New Orleans for their assistance to me in this project. That division is the repository and owner of this manuscript and has granted permission for its publication. The Special Collections Division also holds a vast collection of papers relating to the Townsend and Stanton families, including Mary Ashley Townsend's diaries, letters, articles, and other papers relating to her Mexican travels. Thanks are also due to Janice Chatelain-Woodward for her encouragement and assistance, as well as to Nicole Mitchell and Mindy Wilson of the University of Alabama Press, to my copy editor Kathy Cummins, and to Mike McCracken and Clayton Brown of Texas Christian University.

Ralph Lee Woodward, Jr.

HERE AND THERE IN MEXICO

I

⊛

General Remarks Concerning Mexico

*A few answers to many questions. General remarks concerning Mexico; its area, topography, climate, flora, fauna, soil and productions. Situations of the hot lands (*tierras calientes*), of the temperate regions (*tierras templadas*), and of the cold lands (*tierras frias*). Hints about starting for Mexico. Money matters. Weight of luggage allowed each passenger. Customs Officers. Duties for every state. Diligence rates. The kind of clothing required. The kind of weather to be expected. Temperature of the City of Mexico. Pulmonary complaints in that locality. Medical attendance. Oaxaca and its superior advantages for all lung diseases. Ignorance of the Spanish language not a serious impediment to the journey. Politeness of the Mexicans. Their willingness to welcome and advance American enterprise. Some of the characteristics of the men [and] of the women. The land of tomorrow. The climatic influences which make it so. The readiness with which a foreigner falls under the spell. The form of government. The Constitution. How the Supreme governmental powers are vested. Mexican suffragists. The ballot box. The locomotive as a peace maker.*

Probably no other country on the face of the globe presents, within the same territorial limits, such a variety of soil, climate, agricultural and mineral wealth as our noble Sister Republic. Much as its original boundaries have contracted, it still covers a magnificent area; equal in extent to that of the

United Kingdom, and France, Spain and Portugal put together. It has the productions of every clime, and the climates of every zone. It is nature's "Horn of Plenty" filled with precious metals, rich gems, priceless minerals and exhaustless quarries. Its soil is capable of producing anything that can be raised elsewhere on the earth, and these products are swift of growth and bountiful of harvests. Its flora and fauna are marvelously rich and varied, its fruits delicious and of endless variety. No other country seems so perfectly adapted for self sustenance. If completely severed from all outside inter-course, Mexico would scarcely miss the rest of the world, so richly capable is it at supplying all the wants of its people from its own unlimited resources. A Mexican can find any grade of temperature, the most diverse and mag-nificent scenery, an almost boundless choice of the earth's products, without crossing the boundaries of his own land. He needs not to go to the Pyrenees for mountain scenery, nor to Italy for sunny vales; nor to the south of France for general climes, nor to the Alps for peaks of perpetual snow. The sea upon his right-hand and his left, matchless mountains are always with him, and the exquisite valleys open on every side to provide their feasts of beauty and abundances. Is he a scientist? From her buried cities to her loftiest hill tops, his country offers him unequaled range of study. Is he poet or romanticist? Her diversity of races, her history and her legends afford him inexhaustible sources of inspiration. Is he a painter? The whole land is full of pictures for him. Is he an agriculturist? All that he can desire in the way of climate and of soil are there, and he may drive the plough where neither winter's cold nor summer's heat afflicts, and sow his seed where unending spring makes the land as fair as Calypso's fabled isle.

The highlands are admirably adapted to the cultivation of wheat, barley, corn and oats. The latter grain is scarcely, if at all, cultivated. I do not remem-ber to have seen an oatfield in the country, other products deriving as a thor-oughly satisfactory substitute. Strawberries there is no lack of in this region; the markets in the City of Mexico are provided with them all the year.

The temperate regions produce an infinite variety of fruits, flowers and vegetables, besides coffee and cane, while the hot lands unite the rich pro-ductions of the temperate domain to innumerable tropical products of in-computable value, and a marvelous prodigal vegetable growth which lends to the land both grace and color.

Some of the misapprehension which exists regarding Mexico climatically is occasioned by the fact that those who speak of it forget to state that the Republic and its Capital both bear the same name. Thus, they say Mexico is excessively hot, Mexico is extremely cold, Mexico is neither hot nor cold; Mexico is superlatively beautiful, Mexico is arid as a desert. Contradictory as these statements appear they are all true as, in the area of about eight hundred thousand square miles which the territory of Mexico comprises, all of these features may be found due, principally, to its peculiar configuration conceded to be the most remarkable of any country in the known world. There are regions which are hot with torrid heat, others which are cold. There are regions which, deprived of rains and rivers, are dry and productive of but thorny and fibrous plants; where dust abounds, and the landscape is uninteresting. In other localities rain is abundant, vegetation rich, and the scenery beautifully picturesque. But the City of Mexico and the lovely valley in which it is located, points which the generality of travelers to that country desire to visit first, and then tarry in longest, are of a uniformly delightful climate at all times of the year, scarcely any warmer in summer than in winter and never cold enough for a fire at any season.

If one will call to mind the topography of Mexico he will remember that it lies, not unlike in shape to a huge cornucopia, between the Gulf of Mexico and the Pacific Ocean. Its northern edge is ribboned by the Río Grande, and its southern limit is the peninsula of Yucatan. The Gulf laves its eastern border, the Pacific bathes its western coast and the shore of its most southern states. Its magnificent mountain system is apparently a continuation of the Cordillera of the Andes which, after marching the entire length of South America enters Mexico on the extreme south and there bunches itself, so to speak, for a race across the continent. There it divides into two branches which diverge eastward and westward, though maintaining their general direction toward the north, following the coast-line on each shore of the Republic. The eastern range sinks into lowlands and is lost as it approaches the Gulf near the northeastern boundary, but the western branch continues its course, crossing the most northern limits of Mexico into the United States.

Between these diverging mountain chains is supported an immense extent of elevated table land, varying from seven to eight thousand feet above the sea level and not unlike in outline to a gigantic letter V. This plateau is intersected by lofty peaks, spurs, and ranges of lesser hills, but stretched away toward the north for a distance of more than fourteen hundred miles, widening always as it extends, and giving a natural roadway for the entire distance.

Its geographical position places a great portion of Mexico within the torrid zone in latitudes one associates with the splendid flowers and foliage, the precious gems and regal products and burning skies of the tropics. But, such is its extraordinary geological construction, such the wonderful upheaval of its grand mountain chains and vast central table lands, that the effect of its situation is counteracted by the regions of rarified atmosphere into which it is lifted. Its low coasts on either shore are perpetually washed by the salt seas which it separates. For the most part these lie within the tropics exposed to intense heat and producing all that marvelous bounty of animal and vegetable life peculiar to such latitudes.

A short distance back from the shore, however, the land begins to rise; the heat diminishes as the ascent increases, and such is the grade going west, from tropically hot Vera Cruz, that within a distance of 269 miles or a day's journey by rail, the City of Mexico is found at a height of 7,500 feet above sea level in a climate deliciously cool and equable the year through. In making this ascent from the sea, one enjoys not only variety of climate, but he has the opportunity to observe that entire range of vegetation which attends him from the sea to the summit. He passes from the *tierras calientes* or hot lands, to the *tierras templadas* or cool lands, and from the latter to the *tierras frias* or cold lands. Even in many portions of the latter, snow or frost are almost unknown. The *tierras frias* are those lands comprised within an elevation greater than 6,500 feet. The *tierra templada* or temperate region lies at a height of from 4,000 to 5,000 feet, and the *tierra caliente* or hot district, comprises the low lands on each coast, and all those portions which do not rise to a greater height than 2,000 feet above the sea. It is a land replete with enticement and enchantment for the mere travelers, and for one bent upon more serious pursuits, its future seems so bright, so promising that the grave political stumbling blocks to her progress, which still exist, are scarcely sufficient to deter him from uniting his destinies with hers.

When one is about to start for Mexico from the United States, he will find it to his advantage to provide himself with a supply of Mexican dollars to defray current expenses for the first portion of his trip. These he can buy, at this time, for greenbacks at sixteen percent discount. He should also carry with him, to cash when required, drafts on New York, which now command in our Sister Republic from twelve to fifteen per cent premium. He will spare himself annoyance by looking at tariff rates before packing his trunks, as his luggage will undergo rigorous scrutiny by the customs officers at whatever point he may enter the country, and also, as he passes out of one Mexican State into another. He should also bear in mind that luggage goes by weight in Mexico, the railways allowing sixty pounds to each passenger, and charging a trifle less than five cents for every extra pound. The diligences allow but twenty-five pounds, and charge more in proportion than the railways for any amount of weight exceeding this limit. The quality of clothing to be taken depends upon what part of Mexico one intends to visit. For the coast lands which for the most part are hot, summer wear. Thin woolens, etc. are needed. Penetrating the interior from the coasts, or from the Texan border, such clothing is needed as one wears in early spring or late autumn in the United States. A light wrap or overcoat for the daytime, and extra wraps and rugs for night travel should be taken. These necessities must be provided for the high table land and *for the City of Mexico* which, owing to its elevation above the level of the sea, as I have already said, has very nearly the same temperature both winter and summer; the mercury rarely rising above 70° nor falling below 62°.

In different parts of the country can be found any degree of Fahrenheit desired; but in the city, and on the upper table lands, an even temperature exists all the year around, and but two seasons are talked of—the wet and the dry. The rainy season begins about the middle of May and continues until October. It ordinarily consists of a rain fall beginning about the same hour, and lasting about the same length of time, every day. After this shower the sky clears. The sun shines. The streets dry rapidly and pleasure and business resume their regular routine. As the rain may be expected near the middle of the day and never disappoints, and as it may be counted upon for ceasing early in the afternoon, the Grand Paseo, which is the principal drive, and other points for fashionable gatherings, lose none of their afternoon brightness and attraction during the wet season. Meanwhile, vegetation flourishes so luxuriantly under the benign moisture that the whole land becomes glorified by the increase of verdure and grace and beauty.

Upon the country roads the wet season works some mischief which does not much affect city streets and railways. The highways then become almost impassible. Even the diligence travel, which is over the best made roads in the country, is difficult, and often seriously interrupted. The transportation of heavy machinery or any weighty merchandise, where railway conveyance does not exist, becomes almost impossible. The slippery mud and watery holes prove too much for even the proverbial patience of the donkey, and in no country is it more necessary to make hay while the sun shines than in Mexico. During the rainy weather, fevers, such as thrive on dampness and rapid increase of vegetation, prevail to a greater or lesser extent on the table lands, though never attaining a virulent nor an epidemic type.

The dry season, extending from October until May, is one of sunshine and out of door delight. The dust is then the chief drawback to travel, but that annoyance is neutralized by the beautiful scenery, the peculiar blue skies and the clear atmosphere. The climate of the City of Mexico is regarded by many as especially favorable to persons suffering from pulmonary complaints. The open air life to which the temperature invites has something to do with creating this impression, but it is a false one. It is not the proper place for a consumptive to seek relief or cure in; there being certain properties in the atmosphere which tend to aggravate rather than heal lung diseases. There is, however, always this advantage for the visitor to the City of Mexico who does not find it agrees with his health. He can reach any climate he desires from that point in a very short space of time, and by means of a railway or other chosen conveyance adopt the temperature to his case with as much ease as he could warm or cool the water in his bath. Should illness assail, as excellent medical attendance can be obtained there as elsewhere and the Mexican physician possesses the advantage of having any desired climate close at hand to act as a potent adjunct to his skill.

For all pulmonary diseases, it has been acknowledged, by many men prominent in the medical faculty, that Oaxaca combines more positive advantages than any other state in the Republic. Its climate is as near perfection as can be found in the world, excellent food is easily obtained, luscious fruits abound, the air invigorates, the scenery delights, historical vicinities keep the interest awake and enlivened, while the people are noted for hospitality and kindness. The superiority of this locality over others has been tested with such satisfactory results that the establishment of sanatoriums for consumption, in or near the city of Oaxaca, has been seriously considered by eminent physicians in the southern United States. Oaxaca at this writing can be reached by a branch road, a portion of which is a tramway leading southeast from the Vera Cruz and Mexican railroad at the station of Apizuco. It is also accessible from the Pacific coast, and from its high table lands both the Gulf and the Ocean, between the blue water of which it lies, are plainly discernible.

No one need deprive himself of the pleasure and benefit of a trip to Mexico from a dread that ignorance of the Spanish language would seriously mar enjoyment or comfort. English is spoken by railway officials and in many hotels, and of late years has been very generally studied by the better classes. The Mexicans are naturally linguists, and toward students of their own tongue they are unfailingly courteous and helpful. French is widely spoken throughout the country, and the language of politeness is practiced by all, high and low, throughout the land; a language which is understood by instinct whether the individual to whom it is addressed is accustomed to use it or not.

Indeed, courtesy in the true sense of the word is a characteristic of the nation, and nowhere has a stranger to fear a rudeness or a departure from the rules of high breeding less than in Mexico. From my own observations and the experiences of personal friends, I am led to conclude that the distrust and jealousy with which Mexicans are supposed to regard Americans and American enterprises amongst them, does not exist. It may have at one time gained a footing in Mexico, the natural product of political prejudice, but it is a thing of the past. The Mexicans welcome and encourage enterprise, and rejoice at whatever tends to the welfare of the country, the development of her resources, and the consequent benefit of her people. There are instances in which foreigners who thought to take advantage of Mexicans in business matters have been surprised at their sagacity and intelligence and unwillingness to be imposed upon, and, disappointed in their schemes, have sought to establish for the Mexicans a reputation for suspicion, ill humor and any other quality into which business capacity, discernment and capability for self-defense can be construed. Approached with fairness, they are always as ready for fair dealing as any people on the face of the earth. They are hospitable in the extreme and generous to a fault. The men are intelligent, warm hearted and brave; the women bright, modest, devoted to home and possessed of a most winning sweetness of manner.

True, Mexico at first is too much *la tierra de la mañana* for an American full of energy and national go aheadativeness. He finds the Mexican characteristic of putting off until tomorrow what ought to be done today very try-ing. Fresh from the land of railways and telegraphs, he forgets how long Mexico has lived without their animating influence, and he frets at first un-der the absence of constant electric news—the want of punctuality in all matters, and that air of activity, bustle and hurry which marks American life. But, under the bright skies, and in an atmosphere where hurry is incom-patible with health and comfort, the foreigner speedily falls into the putting off habit himself, and yields to it, as a sort of natural law, rather dreading the day when telephone bells and increased telegraphic communication shall bring the rest of the world so close that its perpetual babble must murder the reposeful quiet of today. If he is from the States he readily makes up his mind that, after his own country, of course, an American is not likely to find any land in which, nor any people among whom, he can dwell with more pleasure and true contentment and find his business projects more cordially favored, if he himself be all right, than in Mexico with the Mexicans.

The form of government, as everyone knows is like our own, Republican. The Constitution closely resembles that of the United States and is very nearly the same as that promulgated at the close of the War of Independence in 1824. That clause, however, in the old Constitution stipulating that the Roman Catholic should be the National religion to the absolute exclusion of all others, was materially modified in that adopted in 1857, under the Juárez administration, and subsequently amended in 1873. Roman Catholic influ-ence is still very strong throughout the country, but the grasp of the Church is loosened and can never, probably, regain its old hold upon the nation.

The Supreme Power of Government is vested in the Legislative, Judicial and Executive branches into which it is divided. The President is elected by universal suffrage to serve for a term of four years. His salary is about forty eight thousand dollars.

A Congress, renewed every two years and divided into a Chamber of Deputies and a Senate, represents the Legislative Power. For the Chamber of Deputies, one member is elected to represent each forty thousand inhabi-tants, or fractions of that number exceeding twenty thousand. A Deputy must be twenty five years of age. The Senate is composed of two Senators for each state. They are elected by the people for the term of two years, and no one can fill this office who is not thirty years of age.

The Supreme Court, numbering seventeen members and a president, constitutes the Judicial Power. The Chief Justice of the Supreme Court is also Vice President of the Republic, and in case of the death or removal of the Executive, assumes the Presidential chair. Provision is thus wisely made for filling the office of Vice President from the chief court of the nation.

Amongst the masses in Mexico there exists a general indifference, almost amounting to apathy, concerning the rights of suffrage. Working the governmental wires is a power vested in the few, and the people at large are not educated up to a knowledge of the value of their votes, nor the lofty principles involved in self government. They are passive and without ambition. The Powers that be have, therefore, everything of this kind much their own way and, evidently, the ballot box is managed and manipulated, much as it is in other free countries where it is one of the great institutions. But whatever political drawbacks may exist, Mexico is progressing. She is rapidly ridding herself of the numerous ills that grew out of her long subjection to other Powers and her sudden freedom from them. The character of the people, which for so long seemed to partake of the volcanic nature of their own mountains ready for outbursts and eruptions on the slightest provocation, is gradually tranquillizing and toning down, and the *pronouncement*[1] is dying a natural death. The people realize the fact that constant insurrection is simply national suicide. Each white man is no longer so eager to be the one white man in power and is more ready to submit with dignity and patriotism to the edicts of the chosen Chief Magistrate. The people have become convinced that any ruler is better than any revolution. The readiness with which news can be transmitted and troops conveyed from one point to another, has, no doubt, had a great deal to do with silencing discontent and lessening the tendency toward internal disturbances. An insurrection has none of the old time chances for ripening and disseminating itself, and augmenting in numbers, as it can now be quickly made known to the authorities, and by them be snuffed out in its incipiency. The gospel that steam and electricity preach is the gospel of peace. It has taught the Mexicans self command, and with it they have gained self respect, and consequently, increased esteem of other nations. Moreover, railways and telegraphs have opened new avenues for the thoughts and energies of the people, besides arousing in them the spirit to keep pace with the marvelous progress of their day and generation.

---

1. Throughout much of the earlier part of the nineteenth century in Mexico, the *pronunciamiento,* or declaration of revolt, by military or political chieftains characterized the frequent changes of government by insurrection or other unconstitutional methods.

2

❋

Existing Routes to Mexico
by Sea and Land

Existing routes to Mexico by sea and land. Steamer from New York. Time made by that line. The Morgan line from New Orleans and its attractions. The Mexican steamer from the Crescent City and its advantages. Price of Gulf trips. Time of starting. Time between Mouth of Mississippi and Vera Cruz. Leaving the steamer after its arrival in front of the City of the True Cross. Steamers on the Pacific Coast. Land routes. Different railways to be taken. The Mexican Central. Distance to City of Mexico from El Paso. Time made. Elevations. Scenes and cities. Advantages some localities offer to Labor and to Capital. Santa Rosalia and Lerdo. The Laguna region. Fresnillo. Zacatecas. Aguas Calientes. Lagos. Anecdotes. León. Silao. Guanajuato and its silver products. The Castilla de Granaditas. Skulls of patriots. Historical associations. Statuettes of clay and of ore. Salamanca. Zelaya. The Barrio. Uncompleted roads. The way we chose.

There are several pleasant routes by land and by sea from which the traveler may choose one to go from the United States to the City of Mexico. By sea one can take the steamer which leaves New York once a week for Vera Cruz *via* Havana and the ports on the coast of Yucatan and Campeche. This trip upon good steamers can be made in twelve days. From New Orleans, and this is the shortest and best sea route, a steamer of the Morgan line leaves every fifteen days starting from Morgan City. To reach this steamer the passenger is ferried across the Mississippi river and takes the cars awaiting him on the opposite side. A run of something over four hours through a pleasant country carries him to the Steamer lying in Atchafalaya Bay. There, in the neighborhood of scenes which Longfellow has immortalized in *Evangeline*, the traveler goes on board, generally with the prospect of a delightful sail down the bay to the Gulf. The next afternoon he is at Galveston, with an opportunity afforded him of going ashore for a look at the handsome town and a drive on its beautiful and justly famous beach. At noon he re-embarks and sails direct for Vera Cruz, which he reaches on the third day after leaving Galveston, wind and weather permitting. The rate of passage by this route is thirty to forty dollars.

An A–No. 1 steamer also leaves New Orleans every twenty days. The vessel is owned by Mexican cotton spinners and manned by Mexican seamen. She is an excellent ship of eighteen hundred tons burthen, and fitted up with electric lights, commodious state rooms and every modern appliance of comfort. The price of a first class ticket is forty dollars in gold, for second class thirty dollars. No round trip ticket is sold. The vessel, the passenger can take at the levee near the Old Cathedral and the French market. At eight o'clock A.M. sharp he is off. The day is passed sailing down the Mississippi between plantations devoted to the cultivation of cotton, rice and sugar, past the forts St. Philip and Jackson, and through the famous jetties into the Gulf. This steamer does not go to Galveston but touches at Tampico and Tuxpán on the Mexican coast. Vera Cruz is reached the fourth day after leaving the mouth of the river. Arriving there, the vessel will come to anchor at the island of San Juan de Ulúa, which is almost covered by its ancient fort. The traveler will find himself about a mile and a quarter from shore, the extensive rocky shallows intervening to prevent a nearer approach to the mainland by steamship. He may go ashore at once in one of the many small watercraft which will swarm around his steamer; or, the weather being rough or any other cause existing, he may remain on board until time arrives to go ashore for the outgoing train bound for the Capital. From Vera Cruz, a trip of twelve hours by rail takes him to the Great City, passing by the old towns of Córdoba and Orizaba and through scenery not exceeded in grandeur and beauty by the most famous parts of Switzerland. Stopping off a day at Córdoba, and another at Orizaba, will enable the tourist to see coffee and mango groves, orange orchards and sugar lands, to say nothing of such picturesque surroundings as old convents and churches, quaint dwellings, the peasantry and the markets, and many places of historical interest connected with Mexico's chequered past.

On the Pacific coast, steamers constantly ply between San Francisco and the sea-ports on the western Mexican slope.

By land starting from the East, North, West or South in the States; one may take either the Gould, Huntington, or the Atchison, Topeka & Santa Fé line of railway. Of course, the best one to take depends upon the location of the starting point, and the part of Mexico one desires to visit. Starting from Laredo, or Eagle Pass, or El Paso, or Benson on the border, there is a railway line which penetrates the Mexican Republic, making four railroads in all leading into that country from its northern boundary. Having reached by rail any one of the above mentioned points, the traveller will find the altitude above the sea and the influence of the trade wind, produce a peculiarly pleasant climate, not too cold in winter, not too warm in summer, especially on the upper table lands.

The Mexican Central Railway, before reaching some of the principal cities along its line, passes through lonely and desolate looking regions which require only population and enterprise to make them richly remunerative. The States of Chihuahua, Durango and Zacatecas have, outside of their rich mining districts, fine lands for cattle, sheep and goats, while other portions are remarkably fertile and well adapted for agriculture in general, and cotton in particular.

Chihuahua, the first city along the line and capital of the State of Chihuahua, is on the Chibusean river near its junction with the Sacramento. It is a quaint old city which has come in contact with the world, as one may say, only within the last two years. It contains 12,000 inhabitants. Capital and American enterprise have already infused new life and energy into this town, to which historical interest attaches as being the place where the hero-priest [Miguel] Hidalgo, the first Liberator of his country, was shot by the Spaniards on the 30th day of July 1811. The climate is cool and dry. The elevation above the sea is 4633 feet.

Santa Rosalia and Lerdo are the next cities one reaches by this route. They are small towns, comparatively speaking, Lerdo having about ten thousand inhabitants. They may be counted on to become flourishing cities of the future, on account of their climate, some remarkable hot springs in the vicinity, and their proximity to the great mining district of *Parral*, and also to that of the Laguna region where cotton is raised successfully, where the grape flourishes and the lime grows, and where the productiveness of the soil and attractiveness of the location offer great inducements to the American agriculturist.

Fresnillo is in the state of Zacatecas and contains 15,000 inhabitants. It was once rich and prosperous on account of its remunerative mines. It is today ruined by water which has overflowed and filled up its sources of wealth and, added to this misfortune is a lack of capital and suitable machinery to work its ores.

Next, comes Zacatecas; and here may be said to begin that portion of the high table land which is well populated and well worked. Zacatecas contains 30,000 inhabitants and a great commercial center. It is beautifully situated in a notch of the mountains, 8,000 feet above the sea. Its streets are narrow and crooked, but some of its buildings are remarkably handsome and of peculiar interest. Its climate is cool and dry. Its wealth is derived from its mines, it being a very old mining city, and still extremely rich in silver mines. The valley in which it lies is irregular and uneven, and surrounded by mountains. Its mean temperature is from 60° to 65°. The mines are worked in the same way they were a hundred years ago, horse power being chiefly used. The introduction of machinery here would richly reward the enterprise.

Aguas Calientes, 6120 feet above the sea has at present 22,000 inhabitants. It has a charming climate, remarkable hot springs, rich vegetation and fine fruits. It has a milder temperature than Zacatecas, and the surrounding scenery is very interesting. Wheat, corn and red peppers are raised in the vicinity. The cultivation of the peppers is extensively carried on and is extremely remunerative. The railroad, which is being constructed from Tampico on the Gulf coast to San Blas almost exactly opposite on the Pacific coast, will pass through this town.

The tourist next arrives at Lagos [de Moreno], a thriving place adorned with many orange and lemon trees. It is in the State of Jalisco and contains 13,000 inhabitants. It is traversed by a stream, *el río de lagos,*[1] has a fine cathedral, a cotton and flour mill run by water. It is a manufacturing town, and in its vicinity are excellent farming lands which can be bought at very reasonable rates per acre. For some reason it has become the habit of neighboring

1. River of Lakes.

towns and the surrounding country to make Lagos the butt of many jokes and satires. When a man would politely call another a fool, he tells him, he is like the Alcalde[2] of Lagos. Tradition has it that, once upon a time, the Alcalde of that place, on a Sunday morning, walked into church with great dignity carrying his hat in one hand, and his baton of office in the other. To his dismay, when the holy water was proffered him, he had no hand that was unoccupied and so plunged his whole head into the sacred vessel! It was at Lagos that, some cacti having grown on the top of a lofty church, it was decided that the only feasible way to destroy the plants was to hoist oxen up there to eat them off! In spite of all this, Lagos is a busy and attractive place.

León, in the State of Guanajuato, is a large city containing 120,000 inhabitants. Saddles, hats, shoes, *chaquetas* and *calzones* (jackets and trousers) of leather are manufactured here on a large scale. León supplies all of the central and northern part of the Republic with these goods, which are remarkably cheap considering that they are made entirely by hand. Its central location will give this place great prominence in the future, and the absence of machinery offers fine opportunities for the mechanic and hardware merchant. Very good lands can be bought in the neighborhood of León for from $5 to $10 per acre. Wheat and corn are raised extensively in the precincts. An American has established a depot for agricultural implements and has found ready sale, notwithstanding the high prices asked. León is situated 6,500 feet above the sea. Its climate is mild and dry, and very favorable for persons suffering with throat or lung trouble. Peaches, apples, figs and pears are to be had here in their season, also grapes. They are moderately good though not equal to American fruits of the same kind. What cultivation and "budding" may do to improve them remains to be seen. León is the headquarters of the central division of the Mexican army.

The road then passes through Silao which has a population of 15,000. At this point there is a branch road to Guanajuato, the Capital of the State of Guanajuato. The city is situated in a rugged and particularly picturesque locality. It contains 52,000 inhabitants and is noted for its silver mines. The mountain gorges, at the junction of which it is located, force its streets into a hilly and irregular line, with streams flowing among them. In its surrounding mountains are some of the richest silver mines known to the world.

2. Mayor.

[Alexander von] Humboldt, in 1803, stated that from them was produced one fifth of all the silver of the globe. It is estimated that their present annual yield is about five millions of dollars. Historical interest attaches to it as being the place from which Hidalgo obtained the final money aid for carrying on the war he had inaugurated. The *Castillo de Granaditas* or *Alhóndiga* which has served at different times the purposes of granary, market and fortress, is a square, massive stone edifice into which the Spaniards, upon the entrance of Hidalgo and his troops in 1810, retired taking with them all their most valuable effects. They supposed the building to be impregnable. The nationalists besieged it. There was loss of life on both sides, but the Alhóndiga finally fell into the hands of Hidalgo together with an amount of treasure exceeding in value five millions of dollars. There is an iron hook upon each corner of this building, and it is said, after the capture and execution of Hidalgo and his three chieftains—[Ignacio] Allende, [Juan de] Aldama and [Mariano] Abasolo in Chihuahua in 1811, that their heads were severed from their bodies and brought to Guanajuato and affixed to these iron hooks.[3] There they remained for ten years, bleaching upon the house top, until the final emergence of Mexico from under Spanish control. If this be true, those whitening skulls held aloft above the people may have had a more powerful influence in bringing about the ends the patriots desired than even the living warriors, sword in hand.

There is greater variety displayed in the architecture of private dwellings in and about Guanajuato than is found in other cities of the country. The nature of the ground has something to do with this, but the exercise of independent individual taste has more. The town was among the earliest built by the Spaniards and dates from 1554. The main portions and its public edifices are of the usual style. Its streets are thronged and busy, its mining works novel and attractive, the wild picturesqueness of the locality, together with the agreeable climate, renders the place one of especial interest for the visitor.

3. Townsend is slightly in error here. The Spanish captured Abasolo at Acatita de Baján in 1811 and took him to Chihuahua, but after he denied any responsibility for the uprising, he was condemned to exile and died at Cádiz, Spain. Allende and Aldama were, in fact, executed in Chihuahua and their heads hung on the corners of the Alhóndiga in Guanajuato along with those of Hidalgo and Mariano Jiménez, also executed in Chihuahua in 1811. See *Encyclopedia of Latin American History and Culture*, 5 vols. (New York: Scribner's, 1996), 1:3, 59.

The Indians there excel in making figures or images by molding rags so as to represent the different classes of people in the country. Silver figures are also molded here by hand which are afterwards colored by some enamelling process so that the hair, eyes, flesh tints and dress are accurately given. Thus, a statuette is produced which is wonderfully life like in color and expression, and is an exact representation of the type it portrays. By applying quicksilver to the pulverized ore, a sort of pliable metal paste is formed, from the amalgam of which the images can be shaped with ease. By exposing these to a certain degree of heat the mercury evaporates leaving only the silver which, though porous, is pure.

Taking up the Central railway line again from Silao, the train runs through rich farming lands under cultivation; the houses of the ranchero and hacendado adorned with orange, lemon and fig trees meet the eye on every hand. Irapuato containing 15,000 inhabitants comes next. The people here are chiefly agricultural, although the place boasts of several factories. There are some fine public buildings, and a noted convent was at one time established here known as *La Eusiñanga*. This building is exceptionally fine. Salamanca containing 10,000 inhabitants follows. It is surrounded by scores of ranchos and haciendas and its population is largely made up of agriculturists. Zelaya succeeds Salamanca. It is a quaint town with a large Cathedral, baths with a swimming tank attached, manufactories, churches, and other handsome public buildings, and a beautiful plaza, on one side of which stands the church of *El Carmen* and on the other the Convent of San Francisco, a notable edifice designed by a native Mexican architect. The town was founded in 1570 and is a bright, attractive looking place. Near Zelaya is a very handsome stone bridge thrown across el Río de Laja. In the State of San Luis Potosí, Charcas, Venado, and Montezuma follow. They are all thriving little towns of about the same size at present, with a population of from four to eight thousand.

San Luis Potosí comes next and is the most important city on this line between Laredo and the City of Mexico. But of this city, as well as of Querétaro, I shall speak later.[4] My object for the present has been only to lay before the reader, as distinctly as I could, the different paths by which he

---

4. Because of her death before completing this work, Townsend does not in this volume return to discuss these places in detail.

might journey through a beautiful land. They are numerous, but as of old it was said, all roads lead to Mexico. Nor, would I have the reader suppose that these lines of travel lead through one uninterrupted grandeur of Eden, where the flowers always bloom and the orange trees grow. They do not. Much of the loveliness of the scenery depends upon the time of year, whether it is winter or summer, whether it is seed time or harvest, whether the soil is fertile or not, whether it is dusty or damp.

Our little party, consulting about the route to be chosen for our second trip to Mexico, selected the river and Gulf line of travel starting from New Orleans, as affording us the day trip down the Mississippi, and a peep at some of the Mexican ports on the Gulf coast between Bagdad and Vera Cruz. In order to be fresh for an early start in the morning, we parted for the night—trusting to the alarm clock "to wake and call us early."

3

Down the Mississippi from New Orleans

A misty moisty morning. The outlook. Off for the ship. Street scenes in New Orleans. On board. The last man. Out in the stream. Fellow passengers. Scenes on the levee. Admonitions regarding Mexico. Their effect. Cost of the trip via the Gulf. Its pleasures and what is thrown in for "lagniappe."[1] *The first summons to dinner. The cabin boy. Distance of the forts below New Orleans. Quarantine station. The sailor's prophecy. The jetties. Distance from New Orleans to mouth of river. Crowds of gulls. "Nasty weather outside." Statement showing the value of the jetties to commerce. The river pilot takes his departure. Letters home. Across the bar into the teeth of a gale.*

The "alarm" of the clock on the mantel sounded at 5 A.M. Now, five o'clock comes altogether too early in the morning to be welcomed by those who are constitutionally inclined to "interview" Somnus at least as late as seven. The little clock seemed to know it, and with that total depravity said to "belong to inanimate things," it did its duty with a vicious delight, and woke us all up, with apparently that same satisfaction as certain individuals whose chief aim in existence seems to consist in making others uncomfortable. That clock whizzed and whirred, and rattled and buzzed as if it had been born and brought up with that terrible maxim, "Early to bed and early to rise." It

1. *Lagniappe* is a word commonly used in Louisiana to signify something extra, often something given to customers by businesses. Although it appears to be of French origin, it is a word not present in modern French.

ceased as soon as it had made itself as maliciously disagreeable as it possibly could, and when not a shadow of a chance remained for anyone of us to obtain "a little more sleep and little more slumber."

To spring up, throw aside the curtains and look out of the window was to behold a cloudy sky, wet streets, drenched roofs, and a scene taken for all in all, too repelling to put one in a good humor with anything, and particularly with the inventor of alarm clocks. Milkmen were dashing past in oil skin suits, sloppy market women were trudging along with that show of stolid indifference to the weather which women who go regularly to market soon acquire, and newsboys with their wet hat brims flapping over their foreheads were running hither and thither, thrusting their damp journals under doors and through shutters, and sending their sharp shrill cries out through the heavy air with a vigor no amount of water could smother.

I turned away, glad to let the humid folds of lace sweep down between me and the uninviting prospect, and hurried to Cora's[2] room to assure myself that she, too, was fully alive to the situation. She was not. Wakened she had been by the malicious little demon in the clock case and then, with a sublime indifference to Mexico, the United States and everything else in this mundane sphere, she had quietly settled herself for another nap. With serene satisfaction I led her from her pillow to the window. Her expression of countenance at once became as dolorous as the most malignant heart could have hoped for, and she looked away over the wet roofs and toward the misty steeples with eyes which might have touched the heart of Old Probabilities himself.

However, when people are awake and out of bed, they generally deem it their bounden duty to dress, if they have any clothes, and to breakfast if they have any appetite. Fortunate enough to have both, we dressed and broke our fast. How sleepy everything in the house looked at that hour in the morning! The furniture, as the early gas light struck it, seemed to rouse itself and make an effort to sit up straight; and the portraits on the walls plainly showed they had not closed their eyes all night. We sipped our coffee and tasted our toast without any of the appetite we had supposed ourselves so abundantly provided with. Parting hours produced heartaches that choked down all hunger aches. We entered the carriage which, with its reeking roof, awaited us at the

---

2. Cora was the author's daughter.

curbstone. The driver cracked his wet whip, the damp horses started, and through the splashy streets of New Orleans we drove briskly out of the American part of town into the narrow streets of the old French Quarter, down to Jackson square and out upon the cotton and sugar laden levee beside which our vessel lay moored.

We hurried on board. Everything about us looked dismal indeed. The decks were wet, the awnings dripping, and the saloon was filled with people each one of whom the rain had rendered a "damp, moist unpleasant body." A canary bird sat muffled up in its feathers in a gilded cage, playing the part of a forlorn bachelor, and an invalid wrapped in his cloak sat in a corner and gazed at the bird. Two little, flaxen haired girls dressed in dark blue were taking a sorrowful leave of their father and mother, and a lonely woman with eyes that seemed full of mournful memories stood and watched them wistfully. A bride and groom, each with a most repentant expression of countenance, sat peering out of different windows as if looking regretfully into that past which comes not back again; and a stranger with flashing black eyes, wrapped in a sarape and wearing a broad brimmed sombrero, paced up and down looking like some bandit chief whose last raid had been unsuccessful.

Suddenly, the gong sounded, indicating that the time had come to ease-off. Its effect was like that produced by the turn of a kaleidoscope. Everything underwent a change. Those who were coming, came; those who were going, went. The canary shook himself and stood up trim and sprightly, the invalid rose and looked out of the window; the lonely lady with mournful eyes watched the little blondes in blue until they reached the shore, then drew her veil close and went below. The bride and groom glanced at each other, and their look of repentance melted into one of supreme resignation, while the bandit-looking individual who had paced the floor so impetuously, stooped with a gentle smile and caressed the ship's cat! Those who were in the cabin went on deck, those who were on deck entered the cabin; bells rang, men shouted, the plank was being drawn in. At this moment, dashing across the levee at break-neck speed came a man. His heavy boots flew through the mud; his hands, gesticulating wildly, seemed playing at fisticuffs with the weather, while his rapid pace had rendered him too breathless to utter a sound. In the pockets of his thick overcoat, one on each side as if hung there for ballast, were two suspicious looking black bottles, parting gifts, probably, from some anxious friends. When his hands were not waving in air, they affectionately clasped the necks of these balance weights. An order was given on shipboard, the plank was re-adjusted, the panting individual rushed across it, and came on board with a leap. Alas! for him he had not calculated distance or his rate of speed. To stop instantly was impossible, and he dashed himself sideways against the cabin. There was a crash and a pungent odor. "Oh my bottle of old rye!" he gasped just as, thrown back by the force of the blow, his other side came in contact with the bulwark! Another crash, another pungent puff of spiritous manifestation, "*and* my brandy!" he moaned. Then dripping whiskey on one side and brandy on the other he walked forward, carefully picking his pockets of bits of broken glass.

Once more the bell rang. Men shouted, the plank was raised, a strip of water began to grow between us and the shore. The engines, slowly working, seemed heaving profound sighs at the prospect of the long, laborious journey before them. Fairly out in the stream, under way and flags afloat, our gun was fired. It seemed to blow off all the hats on shore, for simultaneously with the report we saw them fly from their owners' heads to the owners' hands and wave in last adieu. As we steamed down stream past the dripping docks, the vapory streets, the cathedral towers and further spires, all looking in the mist like phantom spires and towers, the men of war anchored in mid-river before the town dipped their colors while ghost-like forms appeared upon their decks. We could see hands wave and point, like the hand of the dead old Dane in Hamlet. On the levees men shouted inaudibly and shapes hurried hither and thither as voiceless and as noiseless to us, among the engine's pulses and the rush of waters, as though they were mere optical illusions. Cora and I repaired to our staterooms. There, we sat down side by side and laughingly compared the numerous conflicting notes of advice we had received prior to starting on this and our former trip to Mexico. Such warnings lie in wait for all who venture to leave the United States for the Mexican Republic. The officious friend who has never been there, but "who knows all about it," ever pours into the departing ear the most appalling statements. Happy is he who turns to them a deaf ear and pins his faith to the old adage which declares "seeing is believing." Cora and I found in the first place, according to our advisers, we were to be devoured by fleas. These were to begin their assaults in Vera Cruz, continue then wherever we went, and whole colonies of them were to insist upon accompanying us home. Whatsoever the fleas left of us, if anything at all, chinches (oh, horror!) we were assured would finish. We might expect to return home with bones picked nearly as clean as would be those of two helpless canaries exposed upon an ant hill. Then we were warned and re-warned to venture nowhere in Mexico by ourselves. We must call for an armed guard if we wished to cross a street to buy a shoe button. Without a numerous escort we must never dare to ride anywhere, or to take a drive. If we disregarded the admonition we were surely to be kidnaped, and, if our throats were not cut, hidden away in some wild mountain fastness never again to see "the home of the brave and the land of the free."

We had been advised to take nothing of much value or elegance in the way of wearing apparel, as to do so would simply be to throw it into the pack saddle of most unscrupulous highwaymen. We had been commiserated because we were venturing to a country where refinement and civilization were as yet in an embryo state; where at every turn we were to be annoyed by the lack of the most common comforts; where we must expect to eat on bare tables without knives, forks or spoons; where we must freeze in the bleak, frosty weather, and again, where we must perish in the intense heat of a winter in the tropics. We had been seriously asked if we were not afraid to go to a country where more than half of the people were savage Indians and all of them were black! The last individual who had parted from us on the levee had said, "you are going to a land of vermin, villains and vagabonds. Vale!" Even the excellence of the alliteration could not soften the amazing hue of such a picture. That anyone of ordinary intelligence could paint it, was a fact which forced one to the conclusions, that of no country had so much been written and so little read as of Mexico. Such an inference was sufficient to nip any idea of book making in the bud, had it prevailed at the outset with anyone of our party.

Fortunately for our peace of mind we were enabled to listen unappalled to the numerous predictions, personal experience having taught us the untruth and injustice of such admonitions. We knew that a trip to Mexico was one of the most novel and delightful to be attempted in America, involving no more danger nor discomfort than pertains to any long journey, and especially charming as a winter pleasure tour. The cost of the trip is not so much as one from New Orleans to New York, counting in sleeping car expenses, and not much more than to St. Louis or Cincinnati from the Crescent City by river, whilst the time required for those journeys is about the same. The Gulf trip gives one the benefit of sea air, and the charm of novelty at the coast stops is thrown in for *lagniappe*. One experience of the kind had but doubled our zest for another, and our gold eagles went for it more willing winged than for any other bit of travel we had ever undertaken. Nor did we fail to carry with us such purple and fine linen as we possessed that we might fitly appear amongst a people in every way worthy of our best, materially and intellectually.

When the sound of the dinner gong went vibrating through the ship, it was a summons we were not inclined to disregard. To those who go down to the sea in ships via the Mississippi river, the first meal on board is an event of no little interest. Men are aware it is likely to be their last for some time to come, and they apply themselves to it with an earnestness which characterizes a pleasant duty not soon to be performed again. Then, it is the first opportunity to see their fellow passengers all together and to learn who are to be their fellow sufferers in the near future. Perhaps too, there is a mournful satisfaction in doing justice to the ship's cook, and at the same time laying up treasures for that marine deity who seldom fails to demand tribute just outside the bar at the mouth of the river, which bar might be justly called Neptune's toll gate.

In the spacious dining salon we found some forty or fifty passengers assembled; among them an old lady of eighty-four years going from her home in Illinois with her son's family to settle somewhere along the Mexican Central Railroad where the son had some property. Travel made easy has become so familiar to people in the United States that [neither] sex, age, nor previous condition now debars anyone from its pleasures or benefits. There were also one or two ladies bound for the Mexican coast towns, and a number of the sterner sex bound no one seemed to know whither and not to care. We found the table neat and bountifully spread. Among the cabin boys waiting on the table one in particular attracted attention. The "boy" was probably forty years old. His hair, slightly gray, was parted in the middle and arranged with a precision that added severity to a countenance already severe. His features, marked with an air of profound and even stern meditation, never relaxed and were framed in a faultless pair of mutton chop whiskers. His attitude was one of military exactness. He held salver at a "present arms," and wore his white apron with the dignity of a Grand Master. A more solemn face was never seen not even on the shoulders of a fashionable undertaker. Its expression suggested dirges, requiems and a general High Mass singing through his brain for the fish, flesh, fowl and other sacrifices offered up to the altar of appetite represented by the bounteous table. To laugh I am sure was never written on the programs of his life, and had he been a native of the Sandwich Islands where, Mark Twain asserts, the costume consists of a smile, he could never have appeared *en grand toilette,* for the oldest inhabitant aboard that ship had never seen him wear a smile during his entire term of service. To speak, he deemed a superfluous use of the English language. His communications with the fellow servants were carried on by signs, and he performed the necessary duties of his position like a soldier going through the manual. During the entire meal from the turtle soup to toothpicks his imperturbable countenance underwent no change. No *bon mot* brought a twinkle to his eye, and, had an explosion taken place, doubtless he would have calmly conformed to circumstances and gone up with composure unruffled clasping his salver to his breast.

Upon returning to the decks we found the weather, which had been fickle all day, settled into a raw blustery chilliness. A strong wind was blowing and a dull grey sky hung overhead. We passed the Forts Jackson and St. Philip lying almost opposite each other, at a point on the river known as Plaquemine Bend and situated seventy-eight miles below New Orleans. They are objects of interest in themselves and from historical association. Their green turf and aspect of careful neatness lent to them an air of cheerfulness and peace quite at variance with the purpose for which they were erected.

The Quarantine station was next passed, a point not of any interest to a ship going out with a clean bill of health, but a terrible bugbear to vessels coming in during the danger period of infection. As we rapidly approached the mouth of the river the sky grew more lowering, and multitudes of sea gulls flew frantically about indicating, one of the sailors remarked, "nasty weather outside"; it being only when the weather outside the mouth of the river is very "nasty" indeed that these birds flock inland in such immense numbers.

The entrance to the jetties brought all the passengers on deck. The stupendous work disappoints sight-seers who fancy they are to find much of it visible above water. The little that can be seen conveys no idea whatever of the magnitude and value of the noble work which has linked the name of

Captain Eads with one of the most important enterprises of the world. Statistics declare that since the construction of the jetties the depth of water in the channel at the bar has increased from 12 and 18 feet to 26 and 30 feet. The export of grain has increased from 400,000 bushels to 48,700,000 bushels whilst foreign steamers, arriving and cleared, from 82 vessels of a tonnage of 107,900 have increased to the number of 402 steamers of 655,000 tonnage. These figures give an idea of the value of the jetties to commerce and the wealth of nations. The mouth of the Mississippi is one hundred and seven miles below the city of New Orleans and twenty-nine miles below the Forts St. Philip and Jackson.

Cora and I wrote penciled letters home to be sent back by the pilot. The shores on either side, as we neared the sea, flattened down almost even with the water's edge. The handsome plantations, the groves of orange, the spreading Live Oaks were seen no more. Reeds and sedge grass, rusty and sear, rattled in the autumnal wind. It rained drearily, and out before us lay the Gulf, every wave showing its white teeth as if in haste to find us in its jaws. We swept out of the jetties, our river pilot left us, we could see his little boat reeling away in the distance and we found ourselves in the very clutches of a "Norther."

4

✹

Across the Gulf to Tampico

Northers on the Gulf. Infrequency of disasters. Seasickness a mere matter of will. How it was proven to be so. How it gradually swallowed up our party. Good recipes for mala de mar. *The ship's Captain and* La Paloma. *The lamp lighter. Our stewardess and her arrangement. "The total depravity of inanimate things." Second day's storm. Deep sea fishing and a word about the fisherman. Our Jonah. Tales of a Gulf traveler. Lazing along the coast. Entering the tropics. The Tampico bar. Its difficult and dangerous passage a serious impediment to travel and commerce. A long delay. The coming out of the lighter. Jonah and other Tampicoans cast overboard in a chair. They make their way in the lifeboat to safety on the Tug. A new passenger comes on board and we "go rolling on."*

The north wind which prevails upon the Gulf of Mexico from October until April renders the voyage to Vera Cruz more or less rough. That it is not especially disastrous is proven by the very rare occurrence of wrecks in these waters, no loss of life from such causes having been known since the steamers began running ten or twelve years ago.

In the short winter days the vessel does not reach the mouth of the river much before sunset and goes plunging forward into deepening seas and deepening darkness. Truly had our sailor prophesied when he said, "there will be nasty weather outside." The groups gathered on deck seemed visibly and mysteriously impressed by it. Two gentlemen were talking of orange culture.

In the very middle of a sentence both turned deadly pale, as if the orange did not agree with them; both left for parts unknown. Another was standing by the rail, a snatch of song upon his lips. Suddenly the song died a natural death after the manner of most songs under such circumstances. A friend was talking to me of Mexico where, he said, the sweetest days of his child-hood and early youth were passed. Even while he spoke a look of dismay overspread his face. He clasped his hand to his forehead and vanished mut-tering about something which required his immediate attention. A French gentleman with courteous bow and suave manners came to exchange a few words about the absurdity of seasickness, since it could easily be prevented by a mere effort of will. Before a reply could be made, he hurriedly apolo-gized for being *obliged to go and look after his companions.* He went rapidly, and he came no more. Mr. L. and I stood chatting. He thought seasickness also a "mere matter of will," so did Mr. T. who, the moment he had asserted as much, in the most precipitous manner plunged off to leeward. The rain blew against Cora's heavy plaid, against her braided hair, against her serge gown, as we went rolling on. She too believes seasickness to be a mere matter of will, and stands outside talking to [the] ship's physician. She has studied the subject well—*on land*—and is convinced it is a controllable illness. The wind is increasing, and the seas every minute grow deeper and deeper. Looking at them as they hollow themselves out, or rear themselves up or foam and froth in our wake, I seem to hear these prophetic gulls at the river's mouth like veritable witches shouting to the sea:

"Like a hell broth, boil and bubble
Double, double, toil and trouble."

I see Cora's cheek growing whiter and whiter. Some passenger just rushed past her, holding with both hands to his hat brim. An expression of anxious doubt crosses Cora's face, then suddenly without a moment's warning she comes running in, dashing past Mr. T. and me as we stand at the stateroom door. Like death she is no respecter of persons. She thrusts Mr. T. one way and me another and falls headlong upon the leathern lounge, and with a moan straightens herself thereon with her face turned toward the ceiling. The ship's physician has followed her and throws over her the plaid she dropped in her flight. Where is her boasted will? Why does she not exert it?

Fortunately we have been given a stateroom on deck. I set wide the door, open the little window to obtain all the fresh air possible, take a chair and a notebook and prepare to exert *my* will. The Captain passes, sees me sitting braced against the wall and scribbling to keep my courage up. He utters a word of sympathy for Cora, says in a cheery voice "brava" to me, and passes on humming a little Mexican air called "La Paloma." It is now quite dark. A man comes in to light the lamp. I implore him not to do so with a horrible dread flashing over me that it may be a kerosine oil lamp, and that the odor of kerosine is apt to appeal too strongly to seasick sensibilities. He departs and into our room *sans cérémonie* darts the stewardess who, with great haste and much rattle and clatter, begins to arrange two tin receptacles along the edge of the berths. Ah! I know them! They are the contribution boxes! Shakespeare says:

"How oft the means to do ill deeds
Make ill deeds done."

The next day was Sunday. The rain had fallen all night and the sea was still very rough. Cora had not been able to leave her sofa and I occupied the lower berth and held her frightened little hand. Neither of us had undressed. That, in a very early stage of the proceedings became an impossibility. Through our open door and window we took in every now and then during the night with fresh air a taste of salt spray as we shipped a sea. We could occasionally obtain a glimpse of the veiled and misty moon as the tempest driven clouds swept over it, and by the faint light we could see the waves shaking their white manes angrily and making frantic efforts to gain the deck. Our staunch vessel behaved nobly although forced to dance industriously with the many waves which claimed her for a partner during the night. She dipped and rose, and curtsied and bowed, swung corners and went through grand right and left in most approved style. The wind came roaring over the water with a frightful noise, leaped on board, sprang into the rigging and whistled there maliciously. It slid down the ropes with mysterious pattering feet, rushed over the roof of our cabin, then with a shriek, leaped to the deck, rushed forward and plunged into the sea! A row of capstan bars just under our windows, which had been made close prisoners when the storm came on, broke loose in the midst of the tempest and for a few minutes had a gay time. It was diverting to fancy them out there, each hopping up and down on one leg, having a *pas seul* on the quarter deck in the rain. They were quickly discovered and immediately forced to conform to ship discipline. Now and then, by the faint light a low, white figure would creep silently over the doorsill, noiselessly approach and look piteously up at us snow white and so very still. Was it the ship's ghost? Ships were said sometimes to be haunted. I reached out my hand, timorously I must confess, and laid it on the sea wet form of the ship's cat!

Toward morning the rain ceased. About eight o'clock the sky cleared and the sun shone out. The first face we saw was that of our Captain. Cheerful and smiling, he was pacing the deck and humming his favorite little air. He paused and looked in to say the weather was "getting better" and to express regrets at our illness. Cora and I were a forlorn looking pair. If anything is calculated to make one weak and lowly, and wholly indifferent to such mundane things as "bangs" and back hair, it is twelve hours of seasickness. Cora had been very energetic in this line and I, being of a very sympathetic nature, had been much moved by her example. Our next caller was the doctor laden with bay rum, lemons and ice. He wore a refreshing lounging suit of white duck, deer skin slippers and white cap with its visor of exquisite tortoise shell. With him came the stout stomached, kind hearted stewardess bearing the most disgusting lot of "nice things to eat" such as hot meats in rich gravies, steaming vegetables and game swimming in melted butter. A roll of the vessel carried her off, thank heaven, dishes and all. As the sea continued too rough for her to climb the cabin stair again, the solemn faced cabin boy came in her stead. He always presented himself immaculate as to apron and jacket, dignified as to bows, parsimonious as to words and funereal as to expression of countenance. Bracing himself he would silently await orders. These he obeyed with surprising alacrity and handed in whatever he brought, with the air of a general surrendering his sword.

Left again alone, the inanimate things in our roomy deck cabin exerted themselves in the most extraordinary manner to amuse us. The chairs slid to the door and back arm in arm, slippers performed most marvelous feats and some volumes of Humboldt which had been placed on the upper berth kept leaping off as fast as replaced, showing great activity in the book market. Our satchel advanced slowly from under the bed and went gracefully through a waltz, and the bottle of Florida water performed such surprising gymnastics it finally broke its neck. Combs, brushes, oranges, lemons, lumps of ice, hats, gloves and current literature moved about in one mad medley not one of which having apparently any regard for that society we call "*our set.*"

Towards sunset, the seas having somewhat subsided, I attempted to rise and make a toilet, but ———! Many things are said to be good for seasickness. The following recipes I can recommend from personal experience: Take a low seat and put yourself in the proper attitude to button up a pair of French boots. If the boots are a little hard to button the result will be all the more speedy. To kneel down before your trunk and endeavor to place the key in the lock is also very efficacious. To bow down to your washstand with a view of bathing your face acts as well as a tumbler of hot water and mustard. The next best thing is to have hot dishes sent from the table to fill your room with the odors of the best French cooking. The aroma of this will make you feel nobly independent of such vulgar necessities as eating and drinking for a long time.

The next day, Monday, found our seas still uneasy but by no means stormy. The sky was grey and the air cool. There were no evidences at table that morning that our steamer carried any disciples of Epicurus. Nearly all the chairs were empty and those which at first were occupied were speedily vacated one after another by passengers who no doubt went to exert their will.

During the day a gentleman fishing over the ship's side caught a bit of Gulf weed which he gave to me. It was a tiny marine plant of a russet green, thickly crusted with minute shells. The angler was the gentleman in sombrero and sarape who had reminded me of a bandit when I first went on board. I learned subsequently that he was Colonel E. A. Lever, an American by birth and a relative of the great novelist, Charles Lever. He had served in the United States war on the northern side, winning a Captaincy while yet a mere boy. Afterwards, he had gone to Mexico and there fought on the Liberal side through the War of Reform.[1] Finally, having always had a predilection for literature, he adopted it as a profession, published one or two novels and a work on Central America[2] and was besides the very able Central American correspondent of the New Orleans *Times-Democrat.*

1. The War of the Reform (1858–1867) was a major civil war in Mexico in which Liberals headed by Benito Juárez triumphed.
2. Col. Edward A. Lever, *Central America; or the Land of the Quiches and the Chontales* (New Orleans: E. A. Brandao & Co., 1885).

Besides the disciple of Isaac Walton,[3] one other passenger appeared upon deck. He was a short, fat, puffy Frenchman. He wore slippers, a pair of trousers of a bilious hue and wide enough for smokestacks, a pea jacket of remarkable breadth and brevity, and a queer little, rusty felt hat. His shirt collar was high and had an affinity for the wearer's ears, and upon his nose sat a pair of spectacles with one white glass and one blue one. Through the white lens his glance was smiling and serene; through the blue one threatening and severe. His complexion was ruddy and the general expression of his countenance that of patient good nature. He walked the deck incessantly with a cigar which he never lighted between his teeth and both hands in his pockets. His eyebrows were shaggy and bristled over his glasses like *chevaux de frise*. His beard was unshorn and, like Santa Claus, "he shook when he walked like a bowl full of jelly." The sailors regarded him with suspicion and superstition. They declared him to be a "Jonah," and said we could have neither smooth seas, nor favoring gales, until this objectionable personage was landed. He belonged in Tampico and for four months had been striving to get there.

Tampico, like all Mexican Atlantic ports has a very poor harbor. A dangerous reef stretches between the shore and the ship's anchorage, and, as there are only eight feet of water on the bar which intervenes, the passage is extremely difficult if winds be adverse. When a steamer arrives, a tug comes out, weather permitting, to take in passengers and freight destined for this place. Alas! for that freight and those passengers if another "norther" be blowing. The steamer may ride in full view of the shore for hours, unable to anchor; or she may amuse herself by plying up and down in front of the port, waiting for the winds to come to order. The tug and the steamer will constantly signal each other; but the little boat dares not come out and the big boat cannot go in. The steamship has orders to delay itself a certain length of time but, if contrary winds prevail too long, away she goes, carrying off the passengers destined for Tampico to the next port, Tuxpán. This being similarly situated, very probably the traveler is carried on to Vera Cruz, to be sent back by return ship. Possibly, the returning vessel meets precisely the same fortune, and the luckless seafarer brings up again at New Orleans. Such had

3. The author refers here to Isaak Walton (1593–1683), author of *The Compleat Angler* (London, 1653), a discourse on the pleasures and stratagems of fishing and one of the most frequently published works in English literature.

been the fate of the person in question. For four months he had been oscillating, like a pendulum, between New Orleans and Vera Cruz. Once arrived in sight of the shores of Tampico, he had been sent in a small boat from the steamship and put on board a schooner lying at anchor. There he supposed he could safely remain until the lighter could with safety come out. With a happy heart and a quiet conscience he laid himself down to sleep. Alas! While he slept in blissful unconsciousness, the sailors forgot him. Favoring gales sprang up which enabled the schooner to up anchor and put to sea. When our friend awoke, he was out of sight of land, and well on his way to Galveston. In that port he embarked on another schooner bound for Tampico; which schooner by stormy gales was driven past its destination and its passenger landed next upon the mole at Vera Cruz. Here passage was provided for him on a steamer of the line bound for New Orleans, and once more smiling and hopeful, he started for Tampico. There, the malicious "norther" caught him again. No landing could be effected, and once more this sailor in spite of himself went on his course towards the Mississippi. Now again had the undaunted man started for home. No wonder the sailors regarded him with superstition. No wonder he so incessantly walked the deck and spoke not, nor yet did he smile. We found ourselves uttering fervent wishes that the Gulf, then comparatively calm, might not become rebellious again before this *per force* traveler should reach his destination.

Our English friend Mr. C——ds. was proof against all seasickness. He regularly took his meals, his salt bath, his constitutional and his rest. His sketch book was always convenient and he produced with great rapidity remarkable pictures in water color. Sea water color, Cora said. He would have been the life of the party had there been any party left but all its members, Alas! had suffered "a sea change into something new and strange."

Among those who were not sick at all was the old lady aged eighty-four. She appeared at table as punctually as the coffee urn and soup tureen, going to and from the dining saloon without accident, notwithstanding the rolling of the ship made it difficult for the youngest and the nimble to keep their footing. The ship's physician declared that the aged are always exempt from *mal de mer*.

All that night we went loafing along the coast. The engines could scarcely be said to work. Like idle school boys they played along the road. On account of their dangerous harbors it is necessary to make all the coast ports by daylight.

We entered the tropics with a strong, cold wind blowing and our thickest wraps in requisition. The seas were very lonely. Their vastness and solitude constantly were impressed upon one. Not a sail had we seen since we left the mouth of the river. Between the ocean and the sky, those two types of immensity, our ship seemed to swing like a bird which soars and swoops between the meadows and the clouds.

The next morning, Tuesday, land was in sight when we awoke. We were before Tampico. A stiff norther was blowing and the sky as dull as lead. Our unfortunate Frenchman stationed himself at the rail and looked patiently anxious. The ship rolled dismally and it was almost impossible to maintain one's equilibrium. Facing shoreward we could see the angry white breakers curling on the bar, a long irregular line of land and a mountain of remarkable shape and isolation at some distance inland. The most powerful glass, however, could not induce the town to make its appearance. The reason was easy to understand, when once found out. Tampico lay nine miles from shore on its own deep river. It is said to contain five thousand inhabitants and to be a very thriving place. Passing travelers are not likely to contradict anything they are told of this town unless they be told it is in sight from the ship.

About eleven o'clock we anchored. The little steam tug signaled that the harbor bar was impassable; so we lay rolling in the bay trying to possess our souls in patience while our old man of the sea paced the deck incessantly "chewing the cud of sweet and bitter fancy" in the shape of his never lighted cigar. He looked wistfully at the shore where, he said, four months ago he left a wife and now—*ciel*—where might that family be. I fancied as he spoke that I saw a tear twinkle down from under the white lens of his spectacles. Cora said to him, "What a dreadful country to live in!"

"Oh," he replied in quick defense of his home, "ze land no bad, it is ze water mam'selle, ze water. One time I come over and I all ze way hold tight to ze gunnel of ze schooner so no go over. For seex nights and for seex days we joomp about in zite of zat be-yew-ti-full land but nevare get nothing on it but our eyes—noting—nevare! But zat, mam'selle, was because of ze water; ze land very *agreeable;* it is ze water zat is bad."

Besides this unhappy man we had on board a lady, the same one whose

mournful eyes and gentle face had attracted my attention when we left New
Orleans. She had two little children in Tampico and looked landward with a
troubled countenance. She walked about in meek anxiety and a brown me-
rino dress. She kept her prayer book in her hand from which she read at
intervals as if to derive thence new hope and courage, then lifting her eyes
she would gaze off over the waves saying plaintively, "Oh, now! if it were *only*
the Lord's will that I should land!"

It was not until four o'clock in the afternoon that the signal came from
the lighter that she was about to cross the bar. She did it gallantly, only un-
shipping her rudder in the passage. This caused a little fluctuation of hope in
the hearts of the hapless Tampicoans, but the damage was soon repaired.
The seas were still too heavy for the little steamer's coming alongside. She
stopped when she had approached within hailing distance and was ordered
to stand off. The poor Frenchman cast troubled glances at her, first out of the
blue eye and then out of the white eye, and then out of both together with a
gaze that was pathetic. He seemed to measure the tossing seas which lay
between him and her. Finally, he gathered together his luggage, which consisted of an umbrella, and stood by the rail awaiting results.

Our life boat was lowered, and a chair lashed in a rope. Our little sad-
eyed lady in her brown dress was swung over the ship's side, seated in the
chair, and safely lowered down to the tossing, leaping, plunging little boat.
She made the descent courageously, with all the bravery that characterizes
women where affection beckons from the other side of peril. Next, with
much more trepidation went our "Jonah" closely hugging his umbrella to his
heart as his rotund body swung out and descended to the life-boat. Safely
seated there, he cast one last white and blue glance up at the steamer, took
off his hat and bowed. A look of inexpressible relief and satisfaction swept
over his face at his safe departure from our decks; a look that was reflected
on the face of every sailor on board. The next moment the little boat was
away among the billows, now rising on the crest of the wave, now sweeping
down utterly lost to sight in the liquid valleys of the deep. The men pulled
with a will, and in a short time reached the tug. The passengers went on
board. Through the glass we could see the little, fat Frenchman give a shrug
of satisfaction and walk aft alone while the meek little lady was caught in a
pair of manly, outstretched arms and fervently embraced. The life boat came
back, bringing us one passenger from Tampico who came on board swearing

he never would be caught crossing that bar again might the witches fly away with him rather.

Our anchor was lifted, a salute whistled and once more we were under way, our sailors declaring that now Jonah was gone we were sure to have fair winds and peaceful waters for the rest of the way. With this assurance our passengers summoned up courage to leave their staterooms. Dinner was partaken of with reawakened interest in such mundane matters as pertain to what we shall eat and what we shall drink and wherewithal we shall be clothed. Fresh toilets and fresh faces gladdened the decks. The strength of the norther was really spent but we still rolled from side to side with most uncomfortable monotony in the ground swell and, looking through a port hole, we seemed now to slide down, down the sea and now to slide up, up the sky.

5

❁

Tuxpán to Vera Cruz

We anchor in front of Tuxpán. Boats from shore. The boatmen and birds. Fustic and fruits. Cedar oars. The Consul's steam launch. The city of Tuxpán. Its harbor and its inhabitants. Climate, soil and products. Advantages and disadvantages for settlers. The vanilla bean. The way in which it is cultivated, cured and packed. Its value as a commercial commodity. The natives as laborers. The hundred days system. Valuable springs and mines in and about Tuxpán. Need of capital and machinery in this locality. Distance between Tuxpán and mouth of Mississippi River. Distance of Tuxpán from Tampico and from Vera Cruz. We sail away. A pineapple eaten in the climate where it ripened. Moonlight and music. The sixth day out. Skirting the Mexican shores. The summit of the snow peak. Dreams of historic events. The Pilot. The anchorage. The water, hackmen. Getting ashore. The National Express. A sudden "Norther," on the first blast of which we take to small boats and are safely landed at the mole.

The following day just before breakfast we anchored before Tuxpán. The sun was shining, the air was balmy, and the seas like a mirror. We were enabled to approach the shores much more closely than yesterday morning. Still, it required a considerable stretch of fancy to enable one to see the town which, like Tampico, modestly kept itself quite out of sight. The atmosphere was clear, and the thick verdure of the shore was a relief to our sea weary eyes. A little steam launch, gaily painted and floating the Mexican colors, came out to us, and a row boat, bearing both the Mexican and American flags and manned by six natives in mighty hats and meager small clothes, brought out the U.S. Consul for this port and Tampico. This boat, and its oarsmen plying their great cedar oars, presented a very picturesque aspect.

A schooner laden with cedar also came alongside. The cedar was in slabs. It is usually exported in logs and sent to Havana and other ports to be converted into chests, cigar boxes, etc., etc. It is esteemed as one of the most valuable products of this coast where immense cedar forests yield an almost unlimited supply. Fustic, a species of dyewood and remarkable for its great weight, was also sent on board our steamer. May no drowning man have a plank of Fustic thrown him. It sinks as readily as lead. Upon the bow of the schooner were brilliant tropical birds of various kinds, in cages, and parrots were promenading the deck with one wing cut and toeing in according to their usual ungainly fashion. Oranges, pineapples and other fruits less familiar to our eyes were there in abundance. The cargo, the natives in their peculiar dress, the orders and conversations in a strange tongue, the songs of the birds all served to remind one how near he always is to the unknown. It was difficult to realize how close to New Orleans lay this strange land and strange people so different in garb and language, manners and mode of life.

When the schooner had discharged her cargo into our hold she was rowed away by six natives each wearing a long, crowned, white hat with a very broad brim. Each wielded one of the great wooden oars which he plied with both hands. These oars are made of cedar and consist of a long pole with an oval paddle riveted to one end. The blade is about a foot and a half long and the handle about ten times as long as the blade. They look heavy and unwieldy, yet in the hands of the natives, who manage them with great dexterity, they seem light enough. If I do not mistake, the same sort of oar is used by boatmen on the Nile. The Consul was introduced to us. We found him very intelligent and agreeable, ready to give information, and earnest and enthusiastic in the interests of the coast colonies. As the steamer was to be delayed for some time taking on freight, he proposed to take our party and one or two others to shore in his steam launch.

The city of Tuxpán is situated on the Tuxpán River, nine miles from its mouth. Across country, or as the crow flies, the distance is lessened by a league. The river has a depth of from five to six fathoms for a long distance from its mouth, and is navigable for small steamers for about twenty leagues.

The banks of the river with ornamental cultivation and pretty dwellings would be beautiful. Time and money, the twin kings of commerce, will someday convert them into gardens as fair as those of the Gulf. Like Tampico, Tuxpán has about five thousand inhabitants in the immediate settlement, but in the canton or district the population amounts to twenty thousand; among whom are only about two hundred and fifty foreigners. These, who came here to "make a local habitation and name" are most of those men who left the States after the war, determined to find some spot on the green earth where they could rear a vine and fig tree of their own, untrammeled by any of the complications which might grow out of the late differences. Tuxpán seemed to offer every advantage. The soil is productive, the climate delightful, the fruits abundant and the natural products of the earth wonderfully plentiful and of steady market value. As has been said of another clime, they have but "to tickle the land with a hoe and it laughs with a harvest." The city is laid out at the foot of verdant hills and in the midst of magnificent tropical groves. As in many such places, beauty in the dwellings and principal buildings is made subservient to comfort and means and those of Tuxpán are of simple construction. The chief drawback to the progress of the town is lack of capital. The people need capital to improve their harbor, to build roads and buy machinery and to develop the great natural resources of the country.

One hundred thousand acres of land surrounding Tuxpán is owned by a stock company, which with an exaggerated idea of its prospective value, seems disinclined to sell at any price to the would be settler. This company is said to have purchased the land for the sum of fifteen thousand dollars from owners who had it originally from the Spanish viceroys. The shares were divided into sums of twenty-five dollars each. Those Americans who first arrived here found a few owners willing to sell and purchased of them a share, with the right to cultivate all the land they were able to work, in addition to their purchase, free of rent. The settlers soon found, however, that it was not possible to obtain a secure title to their land, and their improvements were liable at any time to be swept from them under a Constitution always subject to the prejudices of the majority, and in this case the majority was very likely to prove inimical to the foreign settler. Under these circumstances the planter erects only such buildings as necessity requires and waits for the good time coming when he can feel himself the undisputed owner of the land he tills. The government of Mexico invites immigration, but local influence as in this case sometimes militates against it.

The crop of Tuxpán sugar for the previous year would, I was assured, have amounted to a million of pounds. Most of it was left ungathered in the fields for lack of machinery to grind the cane. Three thousand barrels of molasses, the product of one season, could not be sent to market for the lack of barrels. With an abundance of material at their own doors of which to make the barrels, the place possessed no coopers. Thence, barrels had to be brought from Galveston, at a cost to the Tuxpán planter of four dollars and a half apiece, making his molasses too costly when freight, etc., was added to the expense for any profit to be gained. The lumber for sugar boxes (here, as in Cuba, the sugar is all put up in boxes, in preference to barrels) had also to be brought from Galveston for need of sawmills in Tuxpán, making it cost the planter half a cent a pound merely to box his sugar. Matters of this kind are now looking a little brighter. There is an abundance of wood in their own forests suitable for sugar boxes. Coopers are finding out there is an opening for them at Tuxpán, and, with the establishment of steam machinery, together with the plentiful supply of cypress the country affords, it is claimed that a Tuxpán barrel can be made as good, and as cheap as anywhere else in the world. There are now, also, several sugar mills erected, or in process of erection, and the planter begins to experience the cheering encouragement which follows in the path of Progress. Nature certainly has been most generous in her endowment of this part of the country. No dangerous epidemics devastate it, and it produces many of the most valuable commodities spontaneously. Medical and dye stuffs, furniture wood and fruits abound here. The sugar cane, once planted, needs no replanting for from fifteen to twenty-five years. It grows to the height of eighteen or twenty feet, and proportionately thick. A cane plantation is, in fact, a sugar forest. The planter leaves it in his field during the wet season, and grinds it in the dry months.

Immense fields of cane were to be seen in full blossom presenting a beautiful appearance. The flower is feathery, or downy rather, in its texture, of a pinkish tinge and resembles somewhat the bulrush blossoms which boy vendors gather in Louisiana swamps to sell in New Orleans streets in autumn.

Like the cane, the cotton, once planted, produces for several years without replanting and becomes quite a tree. Coffee, tobacco and the choicest prod-

ucts of the tropics grow almost for the asking. The vanilla bean flourishes
with but very little care. It only requires room to root, and a tree to climb. It
will even grow without a ground root, being a parasite; but in this case there
are certain trees such as the Liquid Amber which it requires and which are
peculiarly adapted to its support. It is a vine, with a strong leathery stem, a
thick, glossy green leaf, and innumerable tendrils by which it clings to and
climbs up the trees left standing for its sustenance. It blooms and beans in
the third year, and fields of vanilla in favorable seasons yield from four hundred to one thousand dollars per acre. It is a self sustaining product, and asks
no favors of hoe, or spade, or plow when it once gets a start. As it is an article
of no small importance in commerce, the cultivation of vanilla will someday
be a source of great wealth to Tuxpán. I saw a small package bought of one
of the natives by a young gentleman of our party for which he paid seven
dollars a pound. He seemed to be a judge of the bean and stated he had never
seen any that was better in flavor or quality. He declared himself familiar
with it, in all its stages and varieties, and regarded his "sample" with quite an
air of triumph, averring that the same quality in the States would be worth
one dollar per ounce.

The value of the bean depends much upon the time it is gathered and the
manner in which it is cured. Many pull it in September and October when,
although then five or six inches long, the bean is not fully ripe, and must
therefore be sold at a low price on account of its inferior quality. If left on the
vine until the latter part of November, or early December, it arrives at full
maturity, and the perfection of its size and flavor. It is then gathered with
care, and if the weather is sufficiently fine is spread out upon mats in the sun;
but, if the weather does not admit of this, the beans are placed in gently
heated stone ovens where the warmth changes them from a pale green to
a deep, rich, purplish brown. The heat also develops the oil they contain,
which, upon pressure, can be seen to exude from the bean. While still warm
they are taken from the ovens, packed in blankets, and thrust into tight tin
cases where they are left for a time to undergo a sweating process. From the
blankets they are again exposed to the heat of the ovens or the sun, then
again to the blankets and the sweat, until all have attained the required uniform color. The beans are then spread in a very dry room upon shelves of
canvas or loosely woven matting, in order that they may have the benefit of
a free circulation of air. This extracts from them all watery particles, which,

if allowed to remain would cause them to mould and become sour and so be a dead loss to either seller or buyer.

When these processes are finished the beans are thrown into large cases to be assorted according to size and quality. The farmer who cultivates the vanilla seldom cures it, but sells the crop when gathered. Those who cure it are obliged to buy it as it is offered in the market in the raw state. Adepts in the important matter of assorting the beans are few; which fact is a loss and inconvenience to him who cures them. There are about fifteen different classes of the bean, which the packers sell in bulk at one general price. When the beans are finally all assorted, they are neatly tied in bunches of fifty beans each, and firmly packed in tin cases which contain from two to three thousand according to size. These cases are lined with tin foil, and to this lid a ticket is affixed showing quality, size and quantity. Five or six of these are then put into a cedar chest, which is usually lined with zinc and hermetically sealed. The cedar cases are then sewed in *petates,* straw mats, and these again are covered with a coarse bagging in order that they may resist the wear and tear of transportation on mules or donkeys.

In this manner all the Mexican vanilla goes to its market in Europe and the United States, where it is worth from nine to twenty-five dollars per pound; a thousand beans weighing from seven to ten pounds. Formerly France was the principal market for vanilla, but of late years American enterprise has so far diverted the trade that merchants come from Europe to make their purchases of the bean in New York. A few years ago the value in Tuxpán was from sixty to seventy dollars per thousand beans. Today they are worth from one hundred and thirty to one hundred and eighty dollars per thousand. This is chiefly attributable to the fact that while the demand for the bean has increased, the cultivation of it has declined, or, at least not augmented in proportion to its increased consumption. The Consul, to whom I was greatly indebted for many courtesies and much information upon points connected with Tuxpán, stated that the natives were indolent and would only do a certain amount of work in a year. The labor of a hundred days they estimate as fully adequate for the supply of all their wants for a twelve month; and beyond the gratification of their immediate or most pressing necessities they seem to have no ambition. Lucrative as the cultivation of the vanilla is, and doubly valuable as it might be made, they take no further interest in it than the means it may afford them for nine months of comparative idleness for the three devoted to light labor. Immigration would lend redoubled activity to this enterprise and call into existence others of equal value. The Consul entertained the opinion that tobacco would ultimately be the most remunerative product of this part of the country, the climate and soil being particularly well adapted to its cultivation. Petroleum springs, it is said, exist near Tuxpán while in some of the neighboring mountains are mines of precious ore. One, the San [*sic* Santo] Tomás mine, was opened and worked for a time, yielding richly. The absence, however, of necessary capital and machinery caused the works to be abandoned.

Tuxpán is located one hundred and twenty-five miles north of Vera Cruz and ninety miles south of Tampico. Notwithstanding all its great natural advantages it has been in a measure overshadowed by its right and left neighbors, the city of the True Cross on the one hand, and Tampico on the other. The latter, I am told, has surpassed it in trade and growth, although its harbor is no better. Tuxpán claims that one great advantage to its location is that it does not lie within the region of Revolutions. It has escaped unscathed all the troubles of this kind which have agitated the country within the last twenty years, and the yellow fever is unknown here. Tuxpán lies in the State of Vera Cruz and less than six hundred miles from the mouth of the Mississippi River.

Late in the afternoon, with our hands full of flowering cane and long ropes of the vanilla vine, we saw the little Tuxpán boats depart for the shore, and heard our own engines once more breathing hard at their work. After getting under way, we were served with ripe pineapple, the first we had ever enjoyed in its native clime. It was luscious! So far superior was it in flavor and fragrance from the hard, unripened fruit of the kind which is sold in the United States we could scarcely believe it the same product. The process of preparing it was also quite different to that we were familiar with. It is set before one, of a deep, rich color, almost as mellow as a peach, and diffusing an aroma as delicate as it is delicious. The skin is dexterously taken off with a very sharp knife. After being peeled, it is placed upright, upon a dish, and held steady by its green leaves which have been left intact. With the other hand, he who served it picks it to pieces, such is its ripeness, with a fork, leaving the core bare to be thrown away. It is deliciously juicy and sweet enough to require no sugar. Some pour old sherry over it, regarding the flavor of the wine as an agreeable addition to that of the pineapple.

The afternoon was charming. No wind, no rolling. It was an ideal day in the tropics. The sunset was one of the most magnificent I ever beheld and I have never failed to see the sunset when health and weather permitted. After all, there may have been something propitious in getting rid of "Jonah"!

In the evening there was moonlight. The seas were still serene; the air was balmy. Guitars were brought out and there was music and singing upon the deck. The breeze blew from the land and came freighted with delightful odors richly suggestive of "those isles where the mango apples grow." Gazing out over the purple seas, their velvety softness brightened by the moonbeams, it did not seem possible that a norther could tear them to pieces with tempests in the space of an hour and convert them into mad restlessness and confusion.

Thursday, the sixth morning after leaving port, the weather having detained us at Tampico, we found the rugged line of Mexican coast in full view. Like the shining shield on the lofty roof of the ancient temple of Minerva, rose high above all surroundings the snow peak of Orizaba, that landmark which, looming up some twenty leagues inland, the mariner beholds when sixty miles out at sea. It is the first land he descries when approaching Mexico from the great deep, and it is the last he beholds as he sails away to foreign ports. One of our sailors declared it could be seen on a clear day sixty *leagues* out at sea and, considering what a prominent and conspicuous object it is, he was perhaps not much "out of his reckoning." At any rate we could not refute his testimony by any experiences of our own.

The morning was cloudless, the sky a soft, opaline tint, deepening to rose near the horizon. Out of the sea the sun was rising, and over the mountains the moon was going down. The snow peak took on a tinge of pink which changed to amethyst, then paled to dazzling whiteness. One beholds with profound emotions of awe and wonder this stupendous mountain overlooking land and sea as it has done for untold ages. It is an extinct volcano rising 17,400 feet above the level of the sea. The single, snow summit [is] visible from the Atlantic coast. It has not been in a state of eruption since 1545, during which year it threw out ashes, stones and smoke. The region of perpetual snow is found in that latitude at 15,090 feet, and all of Orizaba projecting above that line is constantly covered with its frozen mantle.

Suddenly, murky clouds began to gather about its base. They grew denser and concealed its foot hills; then, lifting themselves higher and higher veiled its icy summit with a cold, blue haze. A fresh breeze sprang up. The water leaped and sparkled beneath us and took on a most exquisite, greenish hue, which a sailor informed us is never seen when out-at-sea or off soundings. Our artists took out their sketch books and made water color sketches of the coast. How the sight of the shores recalled memories of records long since read as we gazed upon them. There, Prescott[1] states, on April 21st, 1519, Cortez landed with all his forces on the very spot where now stands the "modern city of Vera Cruz." It required but a small stretch of the imagination and the "modern city of Vera Cruz" vanished. In its place, a bald, desolate beach, its monotony relieved here and there by some hillock of sand drifted up by bygone northers and many a fierce winter wind; the barks of the daring conquistador sat upon the waters. The foot of the invader for the first time dented the soil. His picturesque tents, composed "of stakes firmly set in the ground and covered with boughs and mats, and cotton carpets" rose to view. The colors of the Spanish King fluttered in the wind that swept toward the Aztec vales. The natives, allured by the arrival of the strange ships and the strange people, came down to the shore to offer welcome and assistance. The Conquest of Mexico had commenced!

It was nearly noon when the pilot came on board to take us into harbor, and between one and two o'clock when we dropped anchor beside the walls of San Juan de Ulúa with its venerable turrets, its low prisons and its many historic associations. Numberless little boats came speeding out toward us. The scene became lively and novel; the tumbling water, the gay barks, the tawny boatmen, and the quaint and quiet city sitting calmly on the shore like some grand old dame gravely waiting to grant us audience. The Fort, founded on the little coral island which it almost covers, lies about two miles from shore and passengers and luggage are landed by means of small boats. As the "northers" prevail upon the Gulf from October until April the traveler may possibly reach his anchorage when one is blowing and so be compelled to remain on board until it subsides. As it is a most unusual thing for the blow to continue longer than six hours, the passenger who finds him-

---

1. Townsend refers to William Hickling Prescott (1796–1859), *History of the Conquest of Mexico: With a Preliminary View of Ancient Mexican Civilization, and the Life of the Conqueror, Hernando Cortés*, 3 vols. (New York: Harper and Brothers, 1843), with many subsequent editions.

self arrested by Boreas[2] may count upon being released at the expiration of that time.

As I have before stated fifty dollars is the price of a ticket by steamer from New Orleans to Vera Cruz. The tourist, when he finds his vessel anchored in front of the latter city, looks about him with a feeling of astonishment that so small a sum has sufficed to transport him so far. Not far in the sense of distance traversed perhaps, for it is less than a thousand miles; but very far in the transition from modern sights and sounds to scenes which date from the Conquest, and which are merely the gates leading to buried cities and ruined temples of an antiquity so remote no man as yet has been so bold as to register the period of their birth. In the roadstead, for the harbor can be called nothing else, glistens the old castle of San Juan; on the shore the ancient city of Vera Cruz with its seven great domes and numerous towers, its solid Moorish architecture and its glimpses of graceful palm trees rises against its background of sand hills, looking like a little picture clipped from "Scenes in Old Spain." Although one has never been led to suppose Vera Cruz a large city, one is surprised to find how small a town it really is, and what a diminutive aspect it presents from the great commercial harbor of which it is the portal. Three steamers are unloading their cargoes, and the French, Italian, German, Spanish and Norwegian flags flying at mastheads indicate many foreign merchant vessels in port. Still, one sees nothing on the shore of hurry, or bustle, or business. All is silence and quietude, so far as the eye can judge, and now that the steamer is at her mooring, the visitor to Mexico naturally wishes to be set on land at once. He must curb his impatience, however, until the health officer has been on board, and the commander of the port had paid his visit.

While these formalities are going on, one sees numerous little row boats with awnings over them and manned by the natives hovering about, at some distance from the ship, watching an opportunity to come alongside and secure passengers. This they dare not do until the doctor and commander have taken their departure, nor can any passenger leave the vessel while a Government officer remains on board. Such is the courtesy of the port, and the respect exacted. Of course, it seems to many of the impatient, seasick, travel-

---

2. In Greek mythology, the personification of the north wind.

worn passengers that the port officials might expedite matters, and cut ceremonies short if they chose; but, they do not choose. "Dressed in a little brief authority," they exercise it to the utmost and take their time, although no one can leave, no matter how urgent his business or eager his impatience, while these government boats lie at the foot of the ship's stairs.

So soon as it is possible for the water hackmen to board a steamer, they do so with a rush. They solicit patronage—hat in hand—not clamorously, but persistently. Their manner is humble, not arrogant. Their tone is pleading, not insolent, while their gestures are graceful and their general appearance highly picturesque. At the same time they have a sharp eye for the main chance and are eager to get all that is possible for their service. No regular tariff established by law exists, and every passenger makes his own bargain. The usual rate, however, is a dollar and a half a head for each passenger and his luggage to be taken ashore and carried, either to the hotel or to the depot, by the native boatmen.

These fellows come on board, most of them barefoot, dressed or only half dressed, with the sarape over the shoulders or without, some with long trousers, some with trousers only to the knee, all with a huge sombrero of straw in the hand or on the head, and all as dirty a set as one could care to see. Many of them are handsome types of the native Indian, of fine stature, with gentle faces, lithe and graceful figures. They have an abundance of shining, coal black hair, into which, alas! their fingers go too often and too industriously. They are skillful in the management of their boats, accidents to luggage or to passengers being almost unknown, although frequently the debarkation is made in very rough weather. In addition to these *boteros*, a National Express has very recently been established by Carvallo and Hoffman of Vera Cruz. They agree "to receive and deliver by passenger train luggage from on board to its destination in the city of Mexico, including freight per railroad at the rate of $9.80 for each 100 kilograms (two hundred pounds), $11.70. *From wharf* to Mexico, including freight per railroad, at $9.80 for each 100 kilograms (or two hundred pounds), $10.70." This express company has its agencies in Mexico and Puebla, and its establishment will be of great convenience to the traveling public.

I was summoned from my quiet station at the rail by someone who came in haste to say a "norther" was coming up rapidly and we had better go ashore immediately or we might not be able to land for many hours. The approach

of "el norte" had hastened the departure of the port officials and we were at
liberty to follow. Hand luggage was hurriedly gathered together, trunks were
identified and the snug little staterooms which had known us so long abandoned. Already the water was rough enough to rock the little boats like egg
shells at the ship's side. I ventured to enquire why they had no steam launch
here as at Tuxpán and Tampico?

"Because Cortez did not" was the slow response from a German resident
of Vera Cruz as he signed to a *botero* to take him ashore.

One of the largest and most substantial boats, manned by four oarsmen
and a pilot was summoned for us to the foot of the ship's stairs. I was handed
to a seat in the stern, Cora given a place just opposite me, and between us, at
the helm, our ponderous pilot stationed himself. The other members of our
party followed together with a number of our fellow passengers until our
boat contained eleven persons besides the four human propellers and the
pilot. These boatmen were all dressed in suits of fresh, white linen, consisting
of a shirt and loose trousers with a bright sash or *banda* about the waist.
Broad brimmed hats covered their heads, and their feet were bare. A word of
command was given, the oars all fell as one and we shot away from the vessel's side managing to ship a sea as we did so which literally threw cold water
on the whole party. I was drenched, Cora with her lap full of brine and her
hat brim similarly endowed shook a small Niagara out of the pockets of an
old gentleman next to her, laughing heartily meanwhile at her own appearance and mine. Our English friend calmly winked a small billow out of each
eye and calmly remarked that enough material for a fine skating rink had
gone "down his neck." Our spirits were not in the least dampened by the
mishap. As no danger whatever attended it we considered ourselves quite
fortunate in being served with this outside slice of a norther in a small boat
as "an experience." By it the trip across the bay was rendered just exciting
enough to be delightful. The sun was now obscured, the water beautifully
green and every wave tossed a white cap.

The men pulled rigorously, and our pilot incessantly shouted to his *mu-
chachos* in stentorian tones, directing, upbraiding, approving and cheering
them as they urged the boat through the ever roughening water. We could
hear the roar of the surf ahead. Every wave grew higher than the last and a
crowd gathered on the mole to watch the approach of our own and numerous
other boats speeding swiftly shoreward. As we rode on the wave tops we

could see the long line of milky foam we had yet to cross breaking upon the beach. A few more strokes and we are in its midst. We mount a wave, and now another, and still one more. We are on the very crest of the surf. We seem to quiver there an instant, like a bird poising itself for flight, then shoot down the billowy slope like a gull descending on its prey. We are in the foaming, sparkling, swirling shallows. The boat leaps forward under the impulse of the eight strong, brown arms. The keel grates, the pilot shouts. Instantly, at his signal, every sailor is in the sea. Out at the stern goes, too, the sturdy helmsman. They are thigh deep in water, for they are short men. They wait just a breath. In comes the wave. The pilot pushes, the men pull, the blade of smooth, spreading water slips under our keel, and with great skill our gallant little boat is brought broadside against the steps of the mole.

6

❀

Vera Cruz

Entering the city gates. Custom house formalities. Luggage and how to dispose of it. No Yellow Fever during winter months. Historical reminiscences. Antique appearance of the town. The number of inhabitants. Street scavengers in feathers. The Church of Our Lady of the Assumption. The Casa Municipal. *The* Lonja Mercantil. *The city railroad and car drivers. Few carriages. Amusing signs. Hygiene as neglected in many public houses. Our hotel and the room we occupied. Strange beds. Trunks at sea, and we on shore. A Vera Cruz breakfast. Mexican dishes and tropical fruits. Ice from an ice house in the clouds. A run to the Gulf. The library in the old church of San Francisco. Its light house tower. Other public edifices. Building material. Water works. Public fountains. Banks. Politics of the State. Literary men. The Plaza. Almond trees and cocoa palms. The* Zopilote—*a study.*

Once landed at the old mole, which is crowded with merchandise, the tourist passes up its length and enters through the rusty but massive iron gates of the city wall which, on the water side, have not been destroyed. It was near these gates when the French, under General Baudin in 1839, attacked the city that General Santa Anna lost his famous leg which was buried and resurrected and reburied with so much pomp and parade. Passing within these gates, it needs no second glance around to impress one with the fact that he is in a "strange country," strangely quaint, strangely picturesque, and strangely interesting. Everything is old, yet everything is new. The people he sees, the clothes they wear, the language he hears, something in the very air around him and the skies above him reiterate to him this fact.

Making his way to the customhouse, which is said to be built of Massachusetts granite, the traveler will find the officials courteous, if rigorous, and opens his trunks for examination. He may then safely entrust them to the *botero*, who will see them taken to the depot and will return with the proper checks to the owner. This business transacted, many hours yet remain at one's disposal, as the train does not leave for the City of Mexico until night. If the passenger prefers to do so, he can remain on his Steamer until the hour approaches for the cars to leave, when he can go ashore and at once to the Depot. It is a common thing to regard Vera Cruz as a dangerous gate through which one had best make his escape to heights beyond with all possible speed. We learned by pleasant experiences that no necessity exists for this. No yellow fever is there in the winter months and nothing else especially deleterious to the health of strangers, and a visit of two or three days in the town and its environs will richly reward one for the time thus spent. It is not the *Villa Rica de la Vera Cruz,* which Cortez first founded, and which the trusting natives hastened to help him build. That was about five leagues further up the coast and was abandoned by the Spaniards after an occupation of three years. They then established themselves, still upon the coast but further south, near the mouth of the Antigua River, and paradoxically named the new city, old Vera Cruz—Vera Cruz Vieja. For reasons which have not come down to us, they subsequently deserted this location. Afterwards, Don Gaspar de Zúñiga, Conde de Monterey, the ninth Viceroy of New Spain, founded the present City of Vera Cruz opposite the island of San Juan de Ulúa on the spot where Cortez and his followers first landed. The original name of the City of the True Cross was never relinquished, but the last town to bear it was not founded until fully half a century after the first debarkation of the Conquerors, and its city charter was not granted until 1615, when Philip III conceded to it the requisite privileges.

The town impresses one with its air of antiquity, although it cannot boast of age exceeding three centuries. Its domes and towers look hoary, and the houses with their arches and balconies of stone look at once ancient and enduring. Probably, no new dwelling within the limit of the old walls has been erected in the last one hundred years.

The visitor is assured that Vera Cruz contains 24,000 inhabitants. He may receive the information with an incredulous shrug, or retort that this must include those hapless number who populate the cemeteries. Yet he will probably be wrong in his hasty conclusions, and his informant quite correct in his statement. The town is so compact, and its dwelling so capacious, one receives a false impression of its population. That which most astonishes one, as he enters the town, is to find it occupied by multitudes of large, ugly, black birds which closely resemble our turkey buzzards. They sit on the railings of balconies, on window ledges, line the edges of the flat roofs, and cluster about the church towers. They fly down into the streets, promenade there with impunity, and hold undisturbed possession of the town. These are the famous *zopilotes*,[1] identified with the country since its earliest records. Doubtless the very creatures that nowadays investigate the visitor with such scrutinizing eyes are the lineal descendants of buzzards which picked the bones of Montezuma's men and regaled themselves upon the fallen followers of Cortez. They are the street commissioners of Vera Cruz and assist in keeping the city wonderfully clean. Their lives are protected by law, and woe betide them who dare to lay violent hands upon or to slaughter any of the tribe of zopilote. They work without salary, save such as they make by pickings and stealings. They know, as well as any modern politician, that a poor office can be made to yield a fat revenue, and they also know how to make it seem to the world that the honor of the position is its own exceeding great reward. It must be acknowledged that they do their duty. They allow nothing to be wasted, nothing to be lost. I suspect if anyone throws away his reputation in Vera Cruz a zopilote gets it and, if a man loses his heart, all he has to do is to get out a search warrant and go through the zopilotes.

After a walk of some duration, hunger turns the footsteps of the tourist toward his hotel to dine. He will be comfortably if not sumptuously served with native dishes and a dessert of excellent fruits and sweetmeats. When the inner man is thus satisfied, it may be his good fortune to be shown to a room which fronts the pretty public square (*La Plaza*) with its fountain and its palms. Here, on the stone balcony which overhangs the *Calle Central*, or main street, he will look out upon the tiled dome and picturesque tower of the parochial church of *Nuestra Señora de la Asunción*. On his left, he will see the tower of the *Casa Municipal*, against which the tropic palm leaves stand

---

1. Buzzards.

brightly out in the sunshine. He will see the gay *caballero* canter past, the beggar in picturesque tatters, and herds of laden donkeys. After a brief rest, he will find there is yet time enough to visit one or two other places of interest, and he will hurry away to the old Church of San Francisco, and visit the *Lonja Mercantil* (the Chamber of Commerce) with its spacious parlors and handsome library where, among other valuable works, is a superb edition of "Lord Kingsbury's Mexican Antiquities."

A street railroad is in operation, running through the main street from one end to the other of the town, and the two ends are not more than a mile apart. These cars resemble our own in structure, and passengers find ingress or egress at each end. Perfectly level as the road is, the cars are drawn by two mules abreast. The driver is a native in the garb of the country, and wears on his breast a small brass horn suspended from a cord passing around his neck. Whenever he arrives at crossings, or chief public places, he blows his horn vigorously. The mules which drag the cars wear no bells. Very few carriages are to be seen, and there is very little use for those. They seem superfluous in a town whose size admits of it being so easily walked all over.

Then, returning to his hotel, the visitor will read with amusement the various signs of the little shops and the pulquerías such as "The Seven Daughters of Eve," "The Poor Devil," etc. When he has regained his balcony, he will find the little plaza illuminated with more than fifty gas lamps, a continuous stream of promenaders going around and around its broad marble walk, and groups of people seated about on stone benches. The ancient towers of the Cathedral rise beyond, the moonlight glitters on the tiled domes. In the distance a band is playing selections from *Gounod*. It is like something one has witnessed in a theater. One almost expects to see the flowers flash into lights by some weird necromancy and to see *Mephistopheles* and *Martha* and Faust and Margarita glide before him in "the garden scene."

Yet, with all this novelty and beauty and enchantment, there is an utter lack of attention to some of the most common matters pertaining to household hygiene in Vera Cruz which are perfectly revolting and give one impressions of its filth which almost blot out its attractions.

As soon as we had landed, we went at once to the Hotel de las Diligencias. It had evidently been built long before the railroad found its way to Mexico, in connection, as its name indicated, with the diligence lines. We entered a court, passed up a flight of broad steps to a corridor brilliant with tropical plants, and thence into a lofty parlor floored with marble. The massive doors were half glazed which led from this into the room allowed to Cora and myself, and the ancient woodwork of these doors wore generations of green paint. Being a corner room it was delightfully situated with two balconied windows overhanging two of the principal streets. The furniture with the exception of the beds had evidently been brought from the States. Once, perhaps, it had been among the Lares and Penates of some disappointed American who found his "things" put up at auction, and shook the dust of the City of the True Cross forever from his feet. It was extraordinary as to fragility, and commanded respect only on account of its age. The mirror was about twelve inches square with no frame to speak of. The bureau drawers were obstinate and disinclined to open and when once opened were disinclined to close. The table was recklessly uncertain, with no two legs of the same length. A bottle of cologne we placed upon it, as if shocked to find itself in such unreliable company, threw itself headlong to the marble floor and was no more. The little wooden washstands, were, however, quite steady affairs and well supplied with soap, water and fresh towels in abundance. Two single beds occupied the eastern side of the room. Over the frame of each was tightly stretched a dressed bull's hide for mattress. Above, a wooden frame covered with a thin white cloth formed a canopy. From this depended curtains of clean, white figured muslin, now drawn back and looped by cords. At night these loops could be loosened and the thin curtains made to serve as very poor substitutes for mosquito bars. Cora insisted upon my having the "best bed" which was in no way distinguished from the other save by a very pallid pink satin bow pinned against the muslin ruffle which edged the canopy!

An intelligent looking young Indian boy, dressed in white pantaloons and a shirt of spotless neatness, entered our room to arrange it for occupation. In my choicest Spanish I asked him to send me the chamber maid. He pointed to himself with much evident pride at his command of the English language and replied, "Me, her." He then deftly made up the beds, by spreading on each two sheets and a thin cotton counterpane. It looked to us like rather inadequate covering for winter time with a norther blowing, but we entered no protest. He then shook the hard little pillows into clean little cases, hung out brown linen awnings over the two quaint balconies, gave the monkey jugs on the bureau a supply of fresh water, and with another look of intense satisfaction for his lingual accomplishments, he uttered that comprehensive American ejaculation "all right," and disappeared.

We attempted at this juncture to lock our door but, as there was no key, we placed a chair against it, and looked about for our trunks. To our dismay they were not there. We were informed that the norther had increased so rapidly after our departure from the ship, that it had been impossible to land any luggage. As we were dripping wet, this left us in a sorry plight. There was nothing to do but station ourselves in the balcony and be blown dry. At eleven o'clock we were presentable for our first breakfast in Vera Cruz.

The dishes served at this repast were all strictly Mexican, and many of them were very hot with a sauce of red peppers, which, though burning to the mouth, is said to be very cooling in the effects upon the blood. The ice we used had been brought from the peak of Orizaba which from the earliest government of the country has been one of its sources of revenue, being regularly rented out as a snow farm. This estate in the clouds furnishes unfailing crops and a tax is levied upon every load that enters a town. It is packed on the backs of donkeys which are driven in by Indians. It seemed rather comical to sit down among the Vera Cruz sand banks taking saucy little bites of a stupendous ice peak eighty miles away. They have now an ice manufactory also in Vera Cruz but, in spite of this formidable rival, Orizaba will no doubt hold his own. During the repast, a tawny skinned lottery vendor would occasionally slip in and display his tickets. Sometimes he came in the shape of an old, decrepit man, sometimes as a bright eyed youth, sometimes as a little child. As he was never importunate, nor impertinent, and as he served for a target at which someone of our party could now and then fire a shot of rusty Spanish, he added considerably to the pleasure of our meal. In return several of us invested a few dimes in tickets "sure to draw," which ultimately did draw—a blank. Throughout Mexico the lottery is sanctioned by the Catholic Church while the State Government receives a certain percentage of all tickets sold.

"Oysters on the half shell" were among the delicacies provided for that breakfast. They appeared like "blue points," seen through the wrong end of a lorgnette. They were not fat, and they were not salty; but they were the very best Vera Cruz afforded. Oyster beds could easily be established in the neighboring waters and the bivalves be grown there as well as anywhere in the world. Of fruits, we had a great variety—oranges, sweet lemons, chirimoyas, which so resemble in taste and consistency a preparation of eggs, milk and sugar, that it is called by Americans "vegetable custard," mama and papaw apples, and grenadittas. In flavor these last are like the fruit of our passion vine which children call *May pops*. Like them they are seedy and pulpy, but unlike them they have a tough yellow rind somewhat like a species of gourd. One can hold this by the stem, slice off the top and within this natural cup lies the fragrant cool refreshing mass which is either eaten with a spoon or fork. Beneath this, in the bottom of the cup, remain a few drops of juice— nectar fit for the gods! Be it said in this connection, of knives, forks and other table implements, together with tablecloths and napkins, there is no dearth in Vera Cruz nor in other parts of the Republic where white people live. As for the Indian, his repast, his knife, fork and spoon are all one. When he has finished scooping up with it whatever else he may have besides his tortilla, he eats his tortilla and so has no trouble to count his silver.

Breakfast being over, it was proposed we should go to the shore to see the Gulf under the influences of a norther. What a wind! Nothing save a Minnesota blizzard could be compared to it. It came filled with fine particles of sand, and so strong that to keep on *terra firma* seemed almost impossible. We were borne along as if we had been thistle down. It threatened to blow the very buttons off our boots and the hats off our heads. The appalling zopilotes sat all about us on housetops and window ledges with their feathers also in a flutter, while they looked contemplatively down at us as if considering whether, if we blew about much more, one should be good to eat or not.

We reached the Customhouse quite out of breath and were introduced to the officers of the port who showed us some handsomely printed and illustrated works published in Mexico and other interesting objects peculiar to the country, among the latter a framed copy of the ancient Mexican coat of arms made entirely of feathers. All conversation was carried on by pantomime, so deafening was the roar of the sea. Through the sand stained windows we looked out upon the Gulf. What a change since two hours before. The norther, in whose frolicsome arms we had been borne ashore, was like some gay young god with beryl hued eyes full of mirth and his sunny locks streaming over shoulders full of strength and joy. Now it was a gray haired giant, while with wrath, dealing blow after blow upon the shuddering reefs, his lips foaming with savage fury, his voice like the roar of cataracts, his presence terrible to behold. As far as the eye could reach the whole surface of the sea was one boiling, seething, sheet of foam. It was a wild scene. Not a human being was in sight along the shore, not a small boat that was not drawn high and dry beyond the reach of the most ambitious wave. The water broke clear over the mole and the gloom of a dark leaden sky hung above all. Between the ships at anchor beside the island of San Juan and the beach whence we beheld them rolled a roaring, terrific, impassable expanse. All communication between ship and shore was as utterly cut off as if between them rolled the gulf which divided Lazarus and Dives. What a grand sight such storm water is when one is safely off of it!

As the gale seemed increasing, we deemed it prudent to lose no time in retracing our steps whilst any possibility remained of taking steps. The officers of the port bowed us through the door and the moment we were outside, the wind smuggled us through the Customhouse without any regard to "duties." We caught a glimpse as we swept through of many men opening with great caution, lest the contents should blow out, boxes and bales of merchandise. Sombreros were flapping, shirtsleeves fluttering, and nether garments seemed struggling to make their escape. We took refuge very soon in the old church of San Francisco, the door of which stood hospitably open and level with the street. This building had once been a large and handsome structure and is one of the oldest here having been built in 1568. It now stands partly in ruins, having suffered from bombardment. It is occupied as a State Library and contains upwards of ten thousand volumes, representing nearly every department of literature. Its tower is used as a light house and burns a revolving light.

We found the librarian a very clever and accomplished gentleman and after spending a delightful hour in the spacious library, we resumed our windy walk.

Vera Cruz has, since the demolition of its walls which until recently surrounded it, greatly increased in population and, it is said, in health. Its principal public edifices are the Governor's Palace, the Parochial Church, several large and airy hospitals, and the Poor House erected under Governor Zamora. Architecturally, Vera Cruz is a one-story town—that is, one story above the ground floor. Very few houses exceed this height, although occasionally one sees an "addition" shooting up in the shape of a little square tower from some flat roof. Most of the building material has been taken from the coral reefs in the bay, there being no stone quarry nearer than twelve miles to the city. The shape of the town is a half oval with the straight edge on the sea. The principal street is not more than a mile in length and from the Gulf to the western limit it cannot be more than three quarters of a mile. The place is supplied with water which is brought by an aqueduct from the Xamapa River a distance of about fourteen miles. The expense of this work was enormous and only finished after prolonged and vexatious delays. But, it was deemed of the first importance to the health of the inhabitants to secure this river water, as otherwise they were dependent upon cisterns or such water as could be obtained by digging a few feet in the sandy soil and so securing a marshy and poisonous well water. There are several large public fountains—one in the Plaza and two in the main street.

The city is well paved with small, waterworn, cobble stones brought here from the dry beds of mountain streams. They are so uniform in size and so smooth they look like multitudes of small skulls protruding from the ground, as if the earth had suddenly opened and swallowed up an army of infants all except the tops of their heads. There is a considerable depression from the sidewalk to the center of the street and there a gutter runs for the purpose of drainage. It is apt to kiss the hem of one's garment in a sly and underhanded manner and after one has been subjected to this in various crossings and recrossings, she becomes painfully conscious that the penetrating eye of the zopilote is upon her and she nervously remembers it is his business to rid the thoroughfares of everything unclean! At the street corners were hitching posts made of old cannon planted muzzle upward and most of them with a ball in the mouth. What tales we might hear if those mouths could but speak. Rust and time have so scarred their forms that at a short distance their exterior is mistaken for the rough bark of a tree.

There are no banks of issue in Vera Cruz. The currency is specie and every man is his own banker. If Mr. A. receives twenty thousand dollars in cash which after business hours he would deposit, he has it carried to his own house. The dwellings are all about as strongly built as a bank vault, and large sums in silver are more embarrassing to burglars than would be nice little fortunes in banknotes which could be more conveniently carried off. We were assured a robbery of money was a most unusual thing. Many of the merchants ship large amounts of specie and do a heavy business in exchange.

The people represent many different nationalities, the largest proportion being Mexicans, the next Spaniards. A strong German element has of late years been infused into the business portion of the community, increasing its strength and vitality. Socially, the people are refined, high toned and cultivated, and the leading families are possessed of wealth and influence. Vera Cruz being the chief sea-port of the country, and the principal entrepôt for American and European trade and travel, it is a city of great commercial importance. Some of the houses here do a business which annually amounts to two million of dollars and more than one half of the National Revenue derived from the receipt of Customs is furnished by this port. The general character of the people is marked with candor and a disposition for fair dealing. They are generous, brave and open hearted, and inclined to advance everything pertaining to art, literature or science. In politics they are liberal, and its political strength is such that other governments have no disposition to offer open opposition to the State of Vera Cruz. It treasures the names of those of its men who have attained literary eminence, among them Xavier Clavijero who died in 1787, a noted and able writer of Mexican history, Fray Xavier Alegre, Eduardo de Garastiza, the writer of several fine dramas, Miguel Santa María and Sebastián Camacho. All of these men of accredited genius have passed away. Among its living writers of talent are Joaquín Castilla y Lanzas, José Estena, José and Manuel Díaz Mirón, and the younger race of graceful and ready writers like Aguinere, Yazas, and others. The well known works of Don Rafael Zayas Enríquez have about them the charm of true poetic genius combined with strength, taste and dramatic power.

We found the Plaza a very pretty spot. The fountain in the center threw its bright drops among the dense foliage of tropical trees which surrounded it. The hibiscus and other flowers were in bloom, and the almond, the cocoa palm and other trees adorned the grounds. In the branches of these, tame monkeys and pet squirrels gambolled and chattered and birds sang in spite of the norther. We met no ladies upon the streets and were assured that they kept themselves much secluded going out only for an evening stroll in the plaza or to attend church on Sundays and fête days and for early mass.

Finding there was no hope of our trunks reaching shore that day, our toilette for dinner consisted of a vigorous use of the clothes brush. While we were at table martial music attracted us to the windows. A regiment was passing which had just returned from Yucatan. The men were well armed and equipped. The officers were white, the ranks composed of Indians. The

music was excellent; the marching, to eyes accustomed to the precision of the
American drill, seemed careless and slovenly. A large number of women followed these soldiers. They trudged along wearing immense straw hats, the
short skirt and rebozo peculiar to their class, and walked under burdens
which would have been heavy for donkeys. Every imaginable superfluous
weight which a soldier could get rid of, together with camp furniture and
cooking utensils, was heaped upon these patient women who seemed to constitute the baggage train of the army.

That night chanced to be a fête night. The churches were open, the bells
rung. The pulquerías were adorned and illuminated and knots of tawny natives gathered in and about them. Bright eyed señoritas attended by grim
duennas, peasants in their picturesque costumes, here a soldier, there a priest,
here a child and there a leper went to swell the crowd. Songs, jests, laughter
rang upon the air and, now and then, a horseman gaily apparelled with his
lasso at his saddle bow rode clattering down the stony street. Upon the dome
of La Parroquia and away upon its tower and on the cross that surmounted
the tower sat the zopilotes into the clear light of the moon. They sat upon
the top and on the arms of the cross, making those portions of the white
stone emblem black. Now and then, they would change positions, moving
awkwardly and solemnly about. One cannot help watching them. They are
at once repulsive and fascinating. They seem especially devoted to the sacred
edifices as if born of the overthrow of the church, and doomed to cling to the
crumbling domes, the shattered walls, the tottering towers of temples which
once rose as evidences of the wealth and empire of an all powerful religion
against which the hand of fate is now turned, and which the voice of civil
power has doomed to restrictions and limitations. They look like hideous
goblins and only long association with them could make their ugly presence
tolerated. For my own part, I do not believe they are as beneficial to the city
as is supposed. They must produce quite as much filth as they consume. They
are carrion eaters. Their appearance is uncanny and their presence repulsive.
These facts alone are sufficient to make them deleterious to human health
but who knows what "germs" they may propagate and disseminate? Vera
Cruz has spent immense sums for sanitation. She has attributed yellow fever
to the sun's rays upon her sand banks, to her stone walls which prevented the
free sweep of the sea winds and to the miasma of neighboring swamps. Un-
suspected of being connected with the evil, the hideous zopilotes sit calmly

above all counsels and unmolested have seen the terrible *vomito* scourge the city year after year for centuries. I saw them nowhere else in Mexico, but wherever yellow fever exists in the coast towns there they are sure to be. They lend to the town the appearance of a great rookery and the sight of them is enough to give a stranger a fit of sickness. They are universally acknowledged to be birds of uncleanly habits, and they are unpleasantly suggestive of un-buried things. As an experiment the health commissioners of Vera Cruz might for one season banish the funereal zopilotes and note the effect of their absence upon the general health in "the great mart of European and Oriental trade, the Commercial Capital of New Spain."

7

❇

A Trip to Jalapa

Costumes and customs. A trip to Jalapa. What may be seen along the road. Scene of the battle of Cerro Gordo. Pasture lands of General Santa Anna. "Bridge of the King" or national bridge. General Guadalupe Victoria. Jalapa and las Jalapeñas. Buildings. Business climate. Antiquity of the town. What Jalapa is to dwellers in Vera Cruz. Its attractiveness as a summer resort for people of the United States. A trip to the village of Medellín. Scenes in la tierra caliente. Jamapa River and Sarsaparilla groves. Compound architecture. The Street of Delight. A fiesta. A Mexican dancing girl. Pledged hats and how they are redeemed. The jungle. Moonlight and no marauders. The Plaza once more.

The next morning no norther was blowing. The day was like one in June in Louisiana. Bright awnings over all the balconies gave the streets a gay appearance. Indians were moving about never seeming in a hurry nor appearing to have any object in life except to do exactly as they chose, and to take their own time about doing that. They wore white shirts and trousers, the bright colored *faja*, or sash, about the waist, immense hats, and no shoes. Until about ten in the morning business houses are not very generally opened. The fast is broken upon rising in the morning with coffee, bread, and a sort of sweet rusk. The offices are then opened and the businessman is at his post until noon, when he goes home to take his breakfast. After breakfast he reads, smokes, perhaps takes a siesta, then returns to his office where he remains until it is time for dinner, a meal taken between six and seven o'clock. After this hour no business is transacted.

For amusement Vera Cruz has a pretty theater and every evening a fine band plays in the Plaza until ten o'clock. To an American with his active stirring habits it seems very odd to see transactions representing millions of dollars carried on in this apparently quiet and nonchalant manner within the limits of a small portion of the day. The custom is well known and conformed to by outside representatives of trade, without grumbling or opposition. Men who can be thoroughly businesslike in business hours, yet who know so well how *not* to allow their business to absorb their entire daily life ought to be the most cultured and accomplished men in the world. They certainly do not lack time for social intercourse nor for the highest cultivation of themselves mentally and physically.

Some Mexican friends called to urge us not to leave this portion of this country without visiting Jalapa (or Xalapa), a city lying northwest of Vera Cruz about eighty miles. We were offered a choice of conveyances: private coach, the diligence or horseback. Even the *Litera* was suggested that we might have the novel experience of one of the early modes of travel in Mexico and one which is still in existence in some parts of the country. A horse cart road extends the whole distance, and that is the surest and most comfortable mode of travel to be chosen for the trip.

The first part of the road as one moves along is anything but enticing. Sand and hillocks of sand with an occasional shrub protruding, as if to make more marked the surrounding desolation, alone meet the eye. But gradually the verdure increases and the scenery, though wild, is novel and interesting. One is surprised when at last he plunges into a wilderness of the most prodigal vegetation. Flowers of rare hues scent the forests, there are masses of marvelous moss, and festoons of vines which clamber, fall and climb again then run hither and yon as if gone mad with their own luxuriance. The palm rises like a prince and rears his feathery crest aloft while the pure, white faced water lilies rest their calm faces on the breast of the brown brook at the roadside. Occasionally, through the thickets, one espies a bridle path which leads the fancy away into unknown depths of tropical forest. Here and there we pass Indian huts made of upright pieces of bamboo and quite open to the weather. Their low steep roofs are thatched with palm or dried banana leaves. No windows are necessary, for the light entereth where it listeth. They look like rude bird cages which someone has forgotten among the bushes. About the doors of these huts dusky little children play. A small sample of cotton cloth fastened about the hips constitutes their costume. In one instance a bracelet of wild red berries wound around a fat, little brown wrist was the entire extent of the toilet! Still, it is not so shocking as one might suppose to see so near an approach to the garb of Adam and Eve in an Eden such as their Indian villages are now seen. The land about them is rich, and produces bananas, corn, sugar, tobacco and cotton. Again encountering the wild lands, myriads of butterflies are seen of the most beautiful colors, and brilliant humming birds. Mexican pheasants flutter into view and by the still pools the musing crane stands silently. The convolvulus opens its many hued blossoms and stretches, like a string of jewels along the ground or hangs from the treetops swaying in the fragrant breeze a rope of bloom and color. The luxuriance of vegetation increases until the highway is like a path leading through a garden.

Every rod of it is fraught with historical interest as well as beauty. It was constructed by the early conquerors of the country and is the road by which Cortez and his army made their way to the city of Mexico. It is the highway by which the Kingdom of New Spain sent out its gold and treasures to the Old World and by which its traffic was carried on with her Eastern Colonies. Along this road were fought bitter frays in the struggle for Mexican independence and in its neighboring heights took place the battle of Cerro Gordo between the Mexican and United States troops in 1847, General Scott leading his men by this road to the Capital. It extended from Vera Cruz to Puebla, thence to Mexico, and thence to Acapulco on the Pacific Coast. To what romances and adventures had [it] been the aider and abettor! Santa Anna once lived at Mango de Clavo on this road in the midst of grounds of great beauty and extent which bordered the highway on both sides for more than thirty miles. He was the owner of immense herds of cattle himself and absorbed into his estates so much valuable pasture that his rancheros were permitted to rent out grazing lands to others at the rate of forty dollars a year per hundred head, a rate still maintained in many portions of the country for pasturage.

The villages of Santa Fé and Zopilote and Tolume are passed. They are of bamboo or adobe with thatched roofs, miserable enough as habitations but wonderfully picturesque. At last *El Puente del Rey* is reached, now called

Puente Nacional, celebrated as the scene connected with sharp contests when Mexico revolted against Spain and where Guadalupe Victoria, a very distinguished Mexican General and afterward her first President, held the bridge against the passage of Spanish troops and treasure to the sea in 1815, and from which point he was driven by the Royalists in the following year and took up that romantic and solitary existence which forms one of the most interesting phases connected with lines of Mexican heroes.[1] The bridge is of stone with beautiful arches and spans the wild and rapid torrent which leaps along over its rocky bed among scenes of grand and romantic beauty.

One constantly but gradually ascends and the vegetation changes as he proceeds. He reaches *El Plan del Riva,* [a] bowl-like valley, surrounded by forests of great value and beauty and, when he has reached *Las dos Rivas,* [is] led by groves of palm and orange and lemon and fig trees to the picturesque city of Jalapa, which lies upon a beautiful plateau, the red roofs of the tiled houses rising among groups of banana and lime trees, while its more imposing edifices stand out against a background of hills covered with magnificent forests. The town lies at an elevation of 4,264 feet above the level of the sea. It is beautifully located among the foot hills of the Macultepec mountain, and contains 13,000 inhabitants. It has several cotton factories and is a very thriving town, with a climate which, for the greater part of the year, knows no extremes of heat or cold, is soft, bright and indescribably delightful. It is quite noted for the beauty of its women, the two types, blonde and brunette, each asserting its distinct attractions here with a perfection not known elsewhere in the Republic. To be as fair as a Jalapeña is considered a compliment to receive and many residents of the town boast of carrying the blue blood of old Spain unadulterated in their veins as it has come down to them from ancestors of the Conquerors.

Flowers in abundance adorn the courts and gardens of Jalapa, and not only are the fruits of the torrid zone to be obtained here, but those also of the temperate regions such as apples, pears, cherries and peaches. It seems to be a spot where everything can be found which grows everywhere else, and when one reaches Jalapa his inclinations are to go no further for he feels that

1. Guadalupe Victoria, President of Mexico from 1824 to 1828, was one of the last surviving guerrilla leaders of the independence movement begun by Father Miguel Hidalgo in 1810. His original name was Félix Fernández, but he changed it during the revolution to Guadalupe Victoria.

he has found all that the human heart can desire in the way of an abiding place. Cortez founded on the heights of Jalapa the great church and convent of San Francisco and, though it has suffered the fate which institutions have met with in recent years, it still commands the magnificent view of lake and forest, field and far off ocean, which induced its founder to select its site. There is also a fine hospital, the church of St. Joseph and other substantial and handsome public edifices. Yellow fever never visits it, it being situated at a height which the *vomito* never reaches. Where the oak grows this deadly disease gains no footing in Mexico. The streets of Jalapa are somewhat hilly; its dwellings are built in the style of architecture peculiar to the country, and its whole aspect is quaint and pleasing. In summer its climate is simply perfect. In fact, for nine months in the year it is all that could be desired, cool and dry with an average temperature of 65° F. The *convolvulus Jalapae*, growing in vast quantities in and about the town, furnishes the valuable medicinal root "*Jalap*" which takes its name from this ancient city of Xalapán founded and laid out by the Aztecs. "Jalap" is well known to generations of physic-taking mortals who have become acquainted with its peculiar properties, and it is the only disagreeable association one is likely to connect with Jalapa. Ferns of the most remarkable variety grow here, among them tree ferns of exceeding beauty, whilst besides all the fruits produced in abundance are found all the products of the soil known both to temperate and tropical regions.

From December until February, however, during the season when *el norte* prevails, the blue, beautiful skies of Jalapa become cold and grey, and she enwraps herself in mists and vapors from which a chill, light, penetrating rain descends, which the natives very graphically call *chipi a chipi*. These are the dense sea fogs that rising from the Gulf touch the mountains here and descending assist in developing the opulent verdure which beautifies this lovely region. During the prevalence of these chilly fogs the mercury frequently falls five or six degrees and this temperature with a thick fog prevailing does not tend to make Jalapa enticing during the three winter months. But during the summer it is unexceptionably beautiful and delightful with the bluest of skies prevailing and a clearness of atmosphere that renders visible and seems to make near far distant objects and landscapes. All Mexicans love Jalapa and regard it as a second Eden. The wealthy merchants of Vera Cruz fly thither in summer from the intolerable heat, the mosquitoes and the deadly vomito.

Many of them have elegant homes kept in constant readiness for occupation at this point; so that in a few hours they can reach the salubrious hills and delightful temperature. A magnificent view of the snow peak of Orizaba is obtained from there and also of the *Cofre de Perote*. This is an extinct volcano something more than thirteen thousand feet high rising to the northwest of Jalapa from a plateau of much greater elevation. It derives its name from a coffin shaped rock of porphyry[2] of immense size which stretches itself along its summit with a shaft of similar stone rearing itself like a monument at one end. Near its base lies the town and castle of San Carlos del Perote, a long day's climb of thirty miles from Jalapa. This celebrated castle was built by the Spaniards to serve both the purposes of a fortress and a deposit for treasure taken from Mexican mines. It is said at one time to have contained forty millions of silver dollars! It was also used as a military prison in which more than one ambitious head found unwilling shelter. But Perote as a town is dull and uninteresting, having none of the natural beauties which render Jalapa charming.

It was by way of Jalapa that Cortez, after leaving Vera Cruz on the sixteenth of August 1519, made his way toward the palaces of Montezuma. The historian in speaking of the Conqueror and his force at this place says, "From this delicious spot, the Spaniards enjoyed one of the grandest prospects in nature. Before them was the steep ascent—much steeper after this point—which they were to climb. On the right rose the Sierra Madre, girt with its dark belt of pines, and its long lines of shadowy hills stretching away in the distance. To the south, in brilliant contrast, stood the mighty Orizaba, with his white robe of snow descending far down his sides, towering in solitary grandeur, the giant specter of the Andes. Behind them, they beheld, unrolled at their feet the magnificent *tierra caliente*, with its gay confusion of meadows, streams, and flowering forests, sprinkled over with shining Indian villages, while a faint line of light on the edge of the horizon told them that there was the ocean, beyond which were the kindred and country they were many of them never more to see."[3]

This picture is as fair today as then, and the landscape wears for a traveler

2. Porphyry is a fine-grained igneous rock containing large, conspicuous crystals, especially feldspar.

3. William H. Prescott, *History of the Conquest of Mexico*, 3 vols., 3d ed., edited by John Foster Kirk (Philadelphia: J. B. Lippincott, 1873), 1:389.

in the nineteenth century an aspect but little changed from that presented to the adventurous Spaniards three hundred years ago. It seems very probable that Jalapa will someday, and at no very distant period, become a summer resort for health and pleasure seekers from all parts of the United States and, especially, from the southern states of the Union. To these it lies so near, only a short sea trip now dividing them, while it is possessed of every advantage which their usual summer resorts can claim, besides many delightful and novel elements to them totally unknown. As railroad enterprise continues to penetrate into Mexico, a railway must in time touch Jalapa from the west or northwest. This will make it easy to access at any time of the year without the necessity of passing through Vera Cruz during its sickly season, while in point of time it would be as convenient and accessible as summer haunts of our own country.

Retracing his way from beautiful Jalapa the traveler visits four leagues south of Vera Cruz (a Mexican league is two and a half miles) the village of Medellín. The town was founded by Hernán Cortez who bestowed upon it the name of his birthplace in Spain. It is now a favorite resort for pleasure parties from Vera Cruz during the winter, and in summer many families take up their abode there. It is accessible by rail; a steam train running to and from daily over a very smooth and level road.

We took the cars near the Alameda, a pretty promenade filled with tropic trees and flowers, and soon passed the Barracks which are located in one of the massive old stone edifices once sacred to religious rites. We swept away across the level country in a special car handsomely fitted up, and the sun, beginning to drop westward, cast lengthening shadows which relieved the glare. For some distance our way lay through [a] wonderful forest of cocoa; then emerging upon cleared lands we came upon a rancho, the buildings which were remarkable neat and orderly and surrounded with flowers. The *administrador* sat reading on his gallery and in the field the sugar cane stood in full blossom. Crossing a bridge which spanned a pretty river we saw a superb grove of mango trees. With that picturesque country, some Indians had selected the spot as a site for a village and erected there a group of bamboo huts. Inside of them we could see suspended from the roofs strings of red peppers and sometimes festoons of corn in the ear, made by turning back the dry husks and braiding them together just as one can see it in the Teepees of the Sioux in Minnesota. Occasionally, we could see a little tobacco hanging up to dry beneath the ridge poles of the roof, and always every living occupant of the miniature houses came out to see the train pass. The journey being a short one we soon halted at Medellín. As we left the cars, we saw quantities of Fustic, the yellow dyewood so abundant in the State of Vera Cruz, lying beside the track ready for shipment.

It is a remarkably heavy wood and weighs like iron. We had seen some sticks of it fall overboard at Tuxpán, and they went to the bottom like so much lead. As one walked into the little town we were struck with the intense quiet that everywhere prevailed. Now and then, an Indian child would stop its quiet play in some open doorway and turn to gaze at us with wondering eyes, or some heavy-haired Mexican girl would walk to a window, lean her elbows on the sill and look out at us, but no pedestrians were in the streets, no sound of horses' hoofs was to be heard, no human voices came to us upon the air so fragrant with tropical odors. It seemed as if with the last puff of our engine the place had breathed its last.

We passed on into the center of the town walking on sidewalks, very narrow and elevated about two feet above the level of the streets. Closed doors looked forbidding at us from under the thatched roofs of unpeopled cottages, and all the dwellings confronted us with signs of the fact that "*the season*" was over. There was one handsome building with tiled floor and attractive appointments, evidently the principal fashionable resort of the little place and kept open to the public. It was scrupulously clean and handsomely decorated. Here and there family groups were to be seen seated at neatly laid boards partaking of refreshment; beautiful birds were hanging about in cages and there was a profusion of flowers distributed about the spacious apartment. Some gentlemen, gathered in knots, were smoking cigarettes and talking in quiet tones, while sundry tables covered with green baize and with packs of cards lying on them gave silent evidence of one of the chief attractions of the place. What game was played here I did not learn, but on one of the tables a heap of silver was lying apparently uncounted and certainly not guarded. We enquired of the Mexican friend who accompanied us if this was not a dangerous way to leave money about, and he replied, "Oh, no. Gentlemen, of course, would not steal, and as for the servants about the place, that class never appropriates money or anything else *entrusted to their charge.*"

Medellín is situated upon the Jamapa River which flows down through sarsaparilla groves to the Gulf and gives to Vera Cruz its precious water supplies. Here at Medellín, the water is supposed to possess medicinal qualities of very superior nature both for drinking and bathing purposes. Strange to say, the original buildings have all disappeared in this quaint and quiet little hamlet. Strange, because the solid structures of the Spaniards seem built to defy time and decay and even thunderbolts and earthquakes, and appear as stable as the hills themselves.

It is nowhere recorded that, here in the tropic forest, Cortez discovered the ruins of one of those prehistoric cities of the country which long antedated his own coming, as well as that of the Aztec whom he conquered. Yet, such might have been the case, and upon it might have reared a fragile village such as he at different times erected along the sandy coast. No such thing is supposed but, on the contrary, it is believed that here he founded and built a city of stone as regularly laid out, and constructed of materials as enduring in their nature as those used to build Jalapa or Vera Cruz itself. Yet, they have all passed away. Whether they were destroyed by fire, or flood or earthquake or war, no deponent saith now. Little, fragile cottages have taken the place of the massive stone buildings of the conqueror's time, and it is a very easy thing to find a ten dollar hut upon a thousand dollar foundation. Having given the town the name of his birthplace in Spain, one might deem that a reason why its founder should have made it especially lasting and beautiful. Beautiful it still is, but its transitory walls have vanished utterly in the grasp of time, "to endure no more forever."

We became interested in a little cane hut built upon a portion of what was once the large and massive base of some heavy structure of ancient times. Its stone foundations were almost buried in the ground and judging from the area they covered must have supported a capacious edifice. We searched in vain for any date to indicate the age of these ancient shoulders supporting with such grim humility the gay little airy cottage. The happy Indian to whom we addressed some questions concerning it, caressed the long braids of the dusky girl beside him, smiled, and only answered *no sé*,[4] as heedless of and indifferent to those, who in past ages there had lived and died, as to the strangers of today marveling and musing above the mute stones which kept their secret so securely.

We walked down a pretty lane called the Street of Delight which was

---

4. *I don't know.*

shaded by the guava, the zapote, and the mango. The latter is a superb tree with a trunk running straight up some ten or twelve feet before branching. At this height its limbs put out in all directions and the cool, dark leaves are so plentiful as to form a mass of thick verdure almost impenetrable to the sight. Its fruit is somewhat the shape of an enormous bean with a green rind mottled with brown and yellow. It is yellow inside, soft and sweetish, and contains one large, oblong, shining seed.

Orange trees with laden branches bent under the weight of their harvest and lemons in abundance contrasted their tints with the rich, green foliage of the fruity groves where they grew, while in the neglected gardens roses and other flowers bloomed in abundance. We strolled on through the enchanting "Street of Delight" to the river and stood at the head of a rude stairway cut in the bank. This stair led down to a gay little floating bath house. A large tree stood on the opposite bank which might have been a sapling years before the first Spaniard looked on Medellín. It leaned over the river and sheltered it and a brightly painted boat drawn up to the shore in its shadow. Its curiously gnarled roots had once been buried out of sight in the soil. Time and tide had resurrected them and left them, as Cardinal Wolsey[5] has it, "naked to the world." They now thrust themselves out of the earth like long, grasping fingers eternally striving to clutch the swift waters which eternally eluded their hold. On the hither side, a little further up stream, a man in a sombrero and with a sarape of bright tints thrown about his shoulders was watering a span of mustangs. The sun was slowly sinking, and a Sabbath hush was hovering over and settling down upon the quiet hamlet. We turned reluctantly away from the peaceful picture and walked back past the one-story houses through the scented, silent streets while crickets chirped drowsily in the grass and the white *flor de bondis* sent out from its carven bells waves of delicious odor. One can readily believe Medellín to be a pleasant place in summer. Gay groups on the river bank, glad voices in the houses, children playing in the green lanes, lovers strolling under the palm trees; such must be Medellín when fashion, and the "heated term" have breathed into it the breath of life.

---

5. Reference here is to English Cardinal Thomas Wolsey, Lord Chancellor to King Henry VIII, 1515–1529, immortalized in William Shakespeare's *Henry VIII,* first produced in 1612–1613. For biographies of Wolsey, see A. F. Pollard, *Wolsey* (1929; reprint, Wesport, Conn.: Greenwood Press, 1978), and Charles W. Ferguson, *Naked to Mine Enemies: The Life of Cardinal Wolsey* (Boston: Little, Brown, 1958).

Sometimes, to relieve the winter monotony, a *fiesta* is held here by the rancheros around about and the pleasant maidens. There are flowers and garlands; guitars and viols and bandalons; lights and dancing and a feast. One of the principal amusements is to have performed some of the popular dances of the country. After some preliminaries, one more accomplished in terpsichorean feats than her mates is chosen from among the rest. She advances to the middle of the floor in her short dress and *rebozo,* her pretty feet encased in neat hose and dainty slippers. The Indian band strikes up its sweet, wild music. The girl poses herself for a moment upon her toes then, sinking back, her arms are lifted in most graceful and bewitching motions above her head, as if invoking the spirit of the dance. Her scarf slips to her slender waist, where she fastens it in a loose knot, and her arms, head and shoulders are thus left bare. Then her lithe, agile body sways to the music of the instruments, her cheeks glow, her eyes brighten, as gradually the strains of the viols and guitars animate and entice her. Her feet, no longer capable of remaining idle glide into rhythmic motion. The dance is less one of "steps" than general grace of movement in which the head, arms and supple limbs, all bear their harmonious part. Applause breaks out. She advances, she recedes; she floats forward and back, her flower-like face blooming and brightening, her rich, dark eyes now melting in dreamy softness, now darting, gay, coquettish glances. And now, the dance really begins. Flowers fill the air with their subtle and delicate perfume, the lights glow, the music throbs, and the young, graceful, swaying form of the dancer fixes every eye. She performs the most intricate and difficult figures; her little feet seem to flutter like happy birds above the floor they scarcely touch, and her motions are so full of grace and beauty they seem but a visible part of the harmonies to which she moves. Murmurs of approbation fill the room, for an impressionable people are these Mexicans, keenly alive to grace and loveliness in any form, and appreciative of its highest types. The girl now seems drifting in the air, and now, to sweep with no more noise than a rustling leaf would make, down the center of the room. A young man rushes forward and with an approving and admiring gesture offers her his hat! She places it upon her head, bows, smiles and dances on. Another comes forward and offers *his* hat. The etiquette of such occasions demands that no preference shall be shown, the last hat offered must have the place of honor on her head, and the one that preceded it is removed and held in the hand; a third, fourth, fifth, hat is proffered and coquettishly received. A bright silk scarf or *faja* is now thrown before her. She flies toward it as though on winged feet and with dainty steps, while never failing to keep time to the music, she ties it with her toes into a pretty and perfect knot. In the same way she unties it, then shapes it into numerous devices of the most varied and intricate designs as she hovers like a bird about it. Then, from all sides the enthusiastic admirers rush forward praising and applauding and, with profound obeisance, handing in hat after hat until the head is sometimes crowned with four or five, all that the annoyed neck can support and the hands have all they can hold. With scarlet cheeks and panting bosom, the dancer stops. The music subsides in a slow, fainting, dreamy measure, and with beaming eyes the dancer awaits the redemption of the hats. The gallant owners advance, one at a time, each offering for his sombrero such ransom as he can afford. Sometimes it is five *pesos,* sometimes ten, sometimes fifty according to the wealth of the owner, his desire for ostentation, or the degree of admiration excited in his breast. In this way an accomplished dancer has been known to win one or two hundred *pesos* (dollars) in an evening.

It was almost dark when we again took seats in the cars for Vera Cruz. As we moved away from the hamlet the intense quiet of the place, the new houses on the old foundations, like new tombstones over old graves, the still and grass-grown streets, the thought of all those who once ate, drank and made merry on this spot and, who had now crumbled into dust their names unknown and their histories unwritten, impressed one with the feeling that he had strayed into some dim alcove in the library of the past and opened there a rare old volume in a language he could not read!

Faint lights burned under the shade of the mango grove indicating the Indian village and strange, spicy perfumes moved like fragrant, invisible banners from the thickets by the road side. Now and then a bridle path leading away into the forest called to mind those warnings we had had about bandits and blunderbusses, highwaymen and robbery before leaving home. Knowing how frequent such things are in the United States, as our daily papers make patent to the world, it would not have been very surprising to have had our railway train on its lonely road waylaid here and the passengers ordered to "hold up their hands." But, not a footpad nor a horseman emerged from the gloom, nothing more obstructive than a moonbeam was laid across the rails; no carbine's gleam glinted in the openings of the wood, not a bandit's plume revealed itself from behind the heavy curtains of vines, and scarcely a sound was heard at our few halting places save the hum of insects in the depths of the jungle.

Leaving the cars near the city limits we walked back through the Plaza which we found thronged with people, ladies and gentlemen and little children promenading and listening to the band. Evidently, as the norther goes down the people in Vera Cruz come up. We were entertained that evening at a most sumptuous banquet which would have done credit to any of the first cities in the United States for its refinement, elegance and good taste but, with the exception of a few dishes, there was nothing especially Mexican on the *menu* card.

8

⊛

Fort San Juan de Ulúa and Departure from Vera Cruz

Fort San Juan de Ulúa. Dungeons and towers. Soldiers and convicts. Some historical incidents connected with the island fortress and its coral castle. The Tabascán slave girl. Flamingoes from Yucatan. Departure from Vera Cruz. A cargador and luggage. Charges for same. The railway station. Cars. Price of railway fare. Number of pounds of luggage allowed each ticket. Old modes of travel. The Litera. Some facts connected with the building of the first railway in Mexico. El Camino de los Consulados. Soledad and its connection with important Mexican events. A costly bridge. Vegetation. Sunrise on the snow peak.

The next morning we secured a row boat of most quaint appearance but with ample room to accommodate our little party and started away over the blue waters of the harbor to visit the fortress of San Juan de Ulúa. The day was like one in late June at home. The water was so still and clear that in many places we could look straight down to its coral floors. No wind was blowing, and our Indian oarsman arrested his dripping blades now and then to wipe with the back of his dusky hand his dripping brow. The precise distance between the shore and the fortress nobody seemed to know, but all agreed it was not more than a mile and others declared it to be considerably less than that. When one crosses it during a "Norther" he will estimate the distance, probably, according to the roughness of the water and in a calm, according to the heat of the sun. As we neared it, we rowed past the dreary, grated windows of some of the cells which are so built that the greater portion of them are below high water mark. It has served as a military prison and a penitentiary, having fallen from its high estate as a defense, and during our visit seemed manned by convicts rather than by soldiers.

We were met at the landing by a native Indian in military uniform who politely conducted us about the place. The sun, blazing upon the white walls and walks, was blinding to our eyes and scorching to our feet, and it was a relief to escape from the glare and the heat to the workrooms where the prisoners were employed. In one, a carpenter was busily engaged planing mahogany boards, the bright shavings curling away from the swift sweep of his plane. In another, we found carvers of cocoa nut shells who smoothed and cut upon the exterior of the shell numerous devices. For patient and painstaking work much of this carving reminded me of that done by the Japanese. Besides these were various other fancy articles made from tiny shells picked up on the edge of the island by the prisoners at low tide, all of which could be bought by visitors. We visited the lowest dungeons and the loftiest tower, were shown the mess rooms and the "quarters" and the stone cisterns in which is gathered the pure water which supplies the fortress. Some of these are said to have the capacity to hold a thousand cubic feet of water. The Lighthouse tower is on the southwestern rampart and very solidly constructed of stone, while the famous *Caballero Alto*, or at least its ruined remains, are on the southeastern rampart. The *Caballero Alto* was the lofty watch tower where a vigilant guard kept ceaseless watch for vessels coming in from sea. Upon the bastions we heard the bugles blow their notes, floating softly off seaward, and at the same time a line of prisoners filed past below us each in his convict suit of blue and white striped cotton cloth, their heads protected by the wide brimmed straw sombrero of the country, and their implements of labor in their hands. Many of them, in passing, held out to us little parcels of shells which they mutely besought us to buy. They, of course, are not permitted to speak with visitors, and we watched the silent, dismal, dirty procession until it turned an angle of the wall and disappeared through a low arched doorway where they were to have their dinner. I asked the officer if escapes were not frequent since with the shore only a mile distant a man might manage to elude vigilance, drop into the sea and swim to land. He replied that it was well known the water about the castle was full of sharks and for a prisoner to attempt to swim was to find swift and certain death in the jaws of these voracious creatures.

The island being first visited by a Spanish navigator named Juan de Grijalva in 1518 and his landing being effected on Saint John's day, he named it San Juan. Afterwards, from a corruption of the Indian name *Acolhua,* by his interpreters, to *Ulúa* supposing the latter to be the local name of the little isle, he called it *San Juan de Ulúa.* In its center he found a temple and evidence that it was a spot devoted by the Indians to human sacrifice, as were other islands in the vicinity. The foundations of the fortress are cut into and out of the solid rock of the island. A chapel and hospital first occupied the site, and the fort was not commenced until early in sixteen hundred. Different inscriptions in the stone indicate when different portions were completed. These dates range from 1633 to 1778. It cost the Spanish government forty millions of dollars, a sum, the King of Spain declared, which must have built it so high it ought to be in sight when he looked out across the sea toward the kingdom of New Spain. The walls are built of coral drawn up from the water and again faced with heavy stone. They are in some portions twelve feet thick, and were considered at one time bomb proof and wholly invincible. The side of the fortress facing the city, we were told was three hundred and twenty five feet long, and that fronting the channel, something over two hundred. Its garrison at one time consisted of two thousand men and its armament of twenty six and thirty two pounders to the number of three hundred and fifty bristled upon the walls, so planted that any enemy's vessel approaching within range would be exposed to the fire of seventy five of these cannon. The Spaniards regarded it as impregnable and believed the walls to be so impervious that they were accustomed to boast they had only to remain in their casements and permit an enemy to fire away all his ammunition, then rush to their guns and make easy capture of his fleet. In 1839, however, it was bombarded by the French fleet commanded by Admiral Baudin to the utter discomfiture of the garrison, which carried out its pet theory of allowing the enemy to have his own way until it saw fit to demolish him. When an attempt was made to return the fire of the French, the powder was found so worthless it would not carry the balls and, at the same time, one of the magazines exploded almost destroying the famous tower of the *Caballero Alto* in the fortress, killing and wounding hundreds of men and making resistance impossible. Again, in the spring of 1847, the Great Coral Castle failed to withstand the siege of the American forces under General Scott, to whom the garrison capitulated as did the City of Vera Cruz, the troops being permitted to evacuate their position with all the honors of war.

It was beside the island of San Juan de Ulúa that Cortez anchored his little fleet on Holy Thursday, April 20, 1519, the day previous to his landing on the present City of the True Cross. Here, for the first time, were called into requisition the services of the beautiful Tabascán slave girl, Marina, one of the twenty Indian girls whom the chiefs of Tabasco had presented to Cortez at the time of their defeat scarcely a month before. To her, as much as to his own prowess and valor, the Conqueror owed his triumphs and the subjugation of the Aztecs. On the day when she was given into his hands, the people presented him with the most potent weapon he ever possessed to turn against themselves. She was a Mexican by birth and possessed of great beauty and remarkable talents. Whatever patriotism she might have originally possessed was ultimately perverted by and absorbed in her profound love and admiration for the Spaniard who had come to conquer her country and overthrow her people. Speedily converted to his religion and his ambition, she conscientiously betrayed her kindred and her native land, her altars and their worshipers into his greedy grasp. The success of Cortez was assured that Holy Thursday at the island of Ulúa when, unable to understand the Aztecs who had put out from shore to confer with him, he summoned Doña Marina as his interpreter. She subsequently learned Spanish and became as indispensable to Cortez as his shield or sword.

The fort at the time of our visit was neither effectually armed nor strongly garrisoned, and considering the power and perfection of modern munitions of war it is probably better adapted to the purposes of a prison than those of a fort. Returning to our boat we found our *botero* during our absence, wishing to kill two birds with one stone, had fished so industriously he had filled the bottom of our boat with a lot of most disgusting, slimy looking fish. We remonstrated, but he begged to be permitted to carry them on shore, and, as he managed to cover them so as to secure us from contact, we yielded and he soon pulled us and his additional freight back to the mole. Passing through the gates we amused ourselves watching a flock of tall, red flamingoes which had just arrived in a vessel from Yucatan. They went stalking about the streets driven by their proprietor much as Christmas Turkeys are driven about the streets of New Orleans. Their plumage was very bright and pretty, but their long legs, long necks and awkward gait were unlovely to the last degree. With every step the tall creatures made a profound bow and marched along in silence. They were so ridiculous; we wanted to purchase a pair to act as a sort of comic relief to some sentimental nightingales which had come into our possession but were dissuaded from doing so. Someone else did buy them, however. Upon going to our room in search of a book, what should Cora and I find, but two of the Flamingoes promenading up and down our corridor, their long legs taking high steps, and their extensive necks coiled up like a section of gutta-percha gas pipe. When they stopped marching and went to sleep they looked like exaggerated boiled lobsters on stilts. They roost by standing on one leg and folding up the other like a three feet rule. Even then, thus limbered up for repose, their height is such they looked as if they had gone to sleep up stairs. They had the freedom of the corridor until such time as their purchaser could procure a wooden cage in which to ship them to the United States, and moved around in their temporary abiding place looking in their brilliant feathers like a pair of tropical sunsets that had been lost or gone astray.

After a few days of notes and queries in Vera Cruz the hour for taking the midnight train is welcome when it arrives. This is about midnight. The distance between the hotel and the depot is so short it is easily walked. The street cars run directly there, but few travelers avail themselves of the convenience, preferring the stroll along the quaint streets among the quainter buildings.

About a quarter past eleven o'clock P.M. a *Cargador* or street porter is summoned who straightway proceeds to load himself up with luggage in a manner that would astound one of his calling in the States. On a rope which he carries, he strings three or four shawl straps and their contents and such satchels and valises as there is rope enough to contain. These are slung over his shoulders. On his head he will carry a good sized trunk, and one hand is still free for sundry other packages. If there is enough luggage for the services of an assistant, he will be called in and laden by his "boss" as if he were a pack mule, and the two then start off on a brisk trot as if entirely unencumbered. The transportation of all such luggage has no connection with the porterage which brought it ashore and placed it at the hotel. It must be paid for separately. The charges are not excessive, those for our little party of four only amounting to two dollars.

The railroad station and adjacent freight rooms are neat, substantial buildings with tiled roofs, and decidedly more modern in style of architecture than other edifices in the city. One does not find about them the crowded noise and bustle which characterize a prominent railway station in the United States at train time; but if a less numerous assemblage is a general thing, it is more novel and picturesque. The cars are all made in the English style. Those of the first class are divided into compartments for carrying eight persons who sit *viz-a-viz*. A door opens on each side. The seats upholstered in dressed leather are comfortable and capacious. As yet there are no sleeping cars but negotiations are now pending to secure such as will be of suitable weight for the steep grades.

Upon starting, the doors of the compartments are locked and, upon arrival at stations, are unlocked. A guard of thirty armed soldiers invariably accompanies every passenger train; a precaution which if adopted in the States might diminish dangers from train robbers and the risks run by Express Messengers.[1]

The passenger cars consist of a first, second and third class. The price of a first class ticket to the City of Mexico from Vera Cruz is $16, second class $12, third class $8. Each passenger is allowed sixty pounds of luggage and a trifle less than five cents is charged for every extra pound. Hence, it will be seen this is not a country for Saratoga trunks.

Soon after midnight we moved out of the depot under the light of a tropical moon which made visible the dull landscape of long, dreary, uninteresting stretches of successive sand hills which mark the Eastern terminus of the road. The trains run with delightful smoothness and at a good speed, averaging twenty-seven miles an hour. The grades are heavy and, besides, the engineers drive very carefully. One result of this caution is that accidents on this road are almost unknown.

Only two score years ago and in how different a manner did the traveler set out upon this trip from the sea to the city! Filled with dread of ambush

1. Paul Vanderwood, *Disorder and Progress: Bandits, Police and Mexican Development* (Wilmington, Delaware: Scholarly Resources, 1992), provides an excellent account of travel conditions in Mexico at the time of Townsend's visits to the country.

highwaymen who were known to be lawless, ferocious and unscrupulous, looking forward to every imaginable discomfort and not a few dangers, he started at about this same hour in the morning in a great, lumbering dili- gence drawn by six, eight and, sometimes when the roads were heavy, ten mules for a journey of four or five days, not infrequently extended to seven, over roads for the roughness of which even the beauty of the magnificent scenery could scarcely have compensated. He was exposed for continued pe- riods to excessive heat and excessive cold, as he journeyed through all the climates of the world to reach that of the city of Mexico. The distance was considerably more than two hundred miles, and the cost of the trip not less than seventy five dollars with bruises, bandits, broken bones and malediction not counted into the incidental expense account. A gentleman who had taken both trips assured me that from Vera Cruz to Europe was a mere swal- low's flight compared to a journey from Vera Cruz to Mexico in old times. There were other modes of conveyance besides the diligence; all of which still exist in unrailroaded parts of the country. Among them was the *Litera,* a sort of conveyance which was now a cot or lounge and, again, an immense basket with shafts at each end with a mule behind and a mule before, both animals, of course, "heading" the same way. The passenger occupied the stretcher or *chaise lounge* which hung between, and which was more or less luxuriously appointed. The motion was by no means disagreeable, and one could smoke, read, sleep or gaze out between the curtains at the landscape.

There was also the private coach and horseback travel with the accompa- niment of armed servants and a mounted guard, but each and all were at- tended by discomforts and delays undreamed of by the happy tourist who today enjoys the more reliable, if less romantic, mode of travel and leans back in his cushioned and curtained rail coach to speed away, unjolted and almost unwearied, toward the "Shining City" now reached in less than eighteen hours.

It was not until the close of the eighteenth century that any other road was projected between Vera Cruz and the Capital than that pursued by Cor- tez and his followers when they invaded the country. The Conquerors liter- ally "made their way" northwest to Jalapa, then a romantically located In- dian village, thence southwest to Tlaxcala and Cholula; thence, they pursued a northwesterly course and, passing between the two great snowy heights,

Popocatépetl and Ixtaccihuatl, turned southeast to enter the magnificent valley of Mexico. This line of travel excluded Córdoba but was connected with Vera Cruz and Mexico only by the footpaths of the Indian runners. Finally, after much halting of opinion, two splendid highways were built by the Spanish *Consulados*[2]; one following the old route to Mexico, the other going by Córdoba and Orizaba. The distance was just the same, ninety three and a half leagues by both roads, but the greater difficulties by the Jalapa route made a difference in time when the diligences began to run of one day. Merchandise of every description was transported by oxen or mules or by donkeys, and at the best of seasons it required from fifteen to eighteen days to convey goods from the port to the capital, and in the rainy season from twenty to thirty days were consumed in carrying stores from Vera Cruz to Mexico. In the very best of weather, if not interrupted by such little incidents as breakdowns or an interview from bandits, the diligences claimed to make the trip by the Jalapa road in four days, and by the Orizaba road in three; but, in the rainy season no definite travel could be counted upon, and running up to schedule time was, at all seasons, more easily said than done.

Many portions of *El Camino Real* still exist, together with its massive bridges with their solid arches of stone to testify to the ability of the Spaniards as road builders. Its construction could scarcely have cost less life and labor and money than the railway itself. The Royal Road is very broad, is solidly built, resembling our own Macadamized road and is bordered on each side by a low, stone wall. There are sections of it still in fine order which excite the admiration of all who understand such works. There are others again which leading over loose or marshy soil were not easily kept in repair, and where the bottom at times seemed to fall out. Upon these, at certain parts of the year, travel became, not only hazardous, but absolutely unsafe. It is not much to the credit of the Mexicans that they allowed these portions of this magnificent highway, through carelessness and neglect on their part, to go to utter ruin. Forests have grown up and are permitted to flourish in the

---

2. The *consulados* were merchant guilds, or chambers of commerce, representing the mercantile elite, especially of Mexico City, where the first was chartered in 1592, but also found at the close of the colonial period in Veracruz and Guadalajara. The Mexican consulados came to have broad authority over commercial litigation and public works, including the supervision of the construction of roads, bridges, and ports.

very line of what was once this priceless path of national travel and commerce; and in their tangled and shadowy maze every vestige of the road is lost and has as completely disappeared as if swallowed up by an earthquake.

When the railway was projected, both routes, the one by Jalapa and the one by Orizaba, were considered. The distance, as I have said, was the same; Orizaba lying as far to the southwest of Vera Cruz as Jalapa lies to the northwest, and the two routes, from the starting point at Vera Cruz to their juncture in the state of Puebla, form in their general course an almost perfect ellipse. Both surveys were undertaken in 1857: that by Jalapa by the prominent Mexican Engineer Señor Almazán, that by Orizaba by Mr. Andrew H. Talcott, an eminent American engineer, with his corps of able assistants. When the two surveys were compared, that by Orizaba was chosen as offering fewer difficulties and easier grading, besides touching the two beautiful towns of Córdoba and Orizaba. The troublous times which agitated the country in 1857 prevented the commencement of any railway work; though Mr. Talcott successfully carried out his survey and completed it in the fall of 1858. When the country had again become settled, Mr. Antonio Escandón, one of the most public spirited and enterprising men Mexico then possessed and whose memory she honors and reveres today, was granted the exclusive right to construct a railway from Vera Cruz to the Pacific with a branch road to Puebla. He was a man of immense wealth and influence, distinguished for patriotism and philanthropy; and, clearly seeing the value of the railway to his country and her people, he threw himself heartily into the enterprise, determined that nothing should defeat its completion. "But wars and rumors of wars" with their usual paling effects, again put a stop to public works, and, in 1864 there was only a beginning of a road at the two extremes, Mexico and Vera Cruz. Mr. Escandón now transferred his privilege to a company of English capitalists, who still retained him at their head; the line of original survey was somewhat changed and the stupendous undertaking was energetically proceeded with. It was found expedient to follow in some sections the course of the old highway, and some of its massive stone bridges were utilized for the passage of that iron horse which had not been conceived in the mind of man at the time of their construction. Nearly twenty years elapsed from the time the railroad was projected until its completion, which was effected in 1873 and celebrated with all due ceremonies. Its cost was 30,000,000 of dollars, some ten millions less than it cost the Spanish government to build the Fort of San Juan de Ulúa in the Vera Cruz harbor. What an incalculable difference between the value of the two works to Mexico! It was the first railroad founded in the country and was constructed in the face of obstacles, which to any but [those with] the most audacious and dauntless courage united with the most consummate skill, must have bid defiance. With its curves and cuts, and tunnels and bridges in its two hundred and sixty-nine miles of railway, it may be said to be like man himself most "fearfully and wonderfully made"; and it comprises some of the most remarkable triumphs ever compassed by science. Its grades vary from one to four meters per cent, and the scenery for beauty and grandeur are unsurpassed, while some of its features are unequaled in the world. This wonderful road climbs through a climate three stories high: the hot, the temperate and the cold; while a corresponding scale of vegetation meets the eye of the traveler from the feathery palm tree of the tropics to the stiff pulque plant of the central table lands.

The names of the men prominently connected with this inaugural Mexican Railway deserve to be known and held in grateful remembrance by every tourist whilst making the delightful transit from Vera Cruz to Mexico. Among the projectors and engineers were Antonio Escandón, William Barrón, Manuel Escandón, E[ustaquio] Barrón, Guillermo Ortuño, George B. Crawley, S. Samuel, Andrew W. C. Buchannan, Thomas Braniff, Blas Balcarcel (Minister of Public Works); a list of names in which any American, Mexican, Scotchman, Englishman or German can find [one] to make him exclaim, as Thackeray puts it in quaint phrase, "You do me proud."

We found it damp and chilly enough even in *la tierra caliente,* our thick traveling suits no more than comfortable, and it was soon necessary to assume our woolen wraps. The cemeteries and the plains of *Los Cocos* were speedily left behind us, together with the marshes which are supposed to contribute so bountifully to the epidemics of Vera Cruz. We arrived at a station called *La Soledad* [de Doblado] about fifty miles from Vera Cruz where we were served with delicious coffee, and where for the first time in my life I beheld blazing in the resplendent heavens the constellation known as "The Southern Cross." It was a vivid and unmistakable sign that we were in a strange land and under foreign skies. There is a fine bridge at this place thrown across the Jamapa River by the *Consulado* in the construction of their highway. It cost them about three hundred and thirty thousand dollars and was utilized by the railroad company who built an iron one above it. Excepting this, there is nothing especially interesting at Soledad, save for the historical fame attached to it from having been the spot where, in 1862, the French, Spanish and English Commissioners met and signed a treaty of peace between the allied powers and General [Manuel] Doblado. This solemn agreement the French saw fit to violate with results that were written in blood and dire disaster along the loveliest hills and valleys of the lands. There is a portion of the road in this locality which was built by the French under harassing difficulties, workmen being scarce, and attacks from guerrillas often interrupting all construction work.

The negotiation now constantly became more luxuriant. We caught a glimpse of the Chiquihuits Falls singing to themselves among the rocks and ravines and exuberant undergrowth. The glimpses of steely water were like dagger gleams among the tangled thickets in the moonlight.

Whilst to us in the valley it was yet gray dawn, looking up we suddenly beheld the rising sun's rays smite the lofty snow summit of Orizaba! Seen under any light this stupendous sentry of the Land wearing his helmet, visor down always, it is one of the most sublime and imposing objects in nature. Its grand splendor and its awful silence form a combination ever impressive and exalting; but at the sunrise when, as it has done for ages, the first light of morning greets and receives its greeting, showing hues of gold and bronze, and rose and purple, and white, like swift signals being interchanged between distant ships at sea, there is something inexpressibly solemn and beautiful and magnificent in the dumb glory of this height which one is not likely to forget in a lifetime and which only to see once is worth a journey of thousands of miles. Memnon[3] can have no music to equal the color gamut which this solitary peak displays.

3. In Greek mythology, the statue of Memnon at Thebes was said to make a musical sound at daybreak, as Memnon greeted his mother, the goddess of the dawn.

9

❁

Córdoba

Arrival at Córdoba. Everything edible reserved for the Governor. The founding of the town by the Spaniards. Climate and public buildings. The Plaza. The sword of Acuña. Number of inhabitants. Gardens. Medicinal plants. The Chinchona tree. Soil products. Price of lands. A visit to a coffee plantation. Description of the coffee tree. Its cultivation. Mode of gathering. What a coffee orchard will produce. Córdoba oranges and other fruits. A village fair. The fair grounds at night. The gambling booths. Traditions connected with the Casa de Cevallos. Mexican ghosts. Indian tribes. The village of Amatlán de los Reyes. Indian braves and maidens after the close of market day. Leaving Córdoba. The donkey and its importance to Mexican commerce. Roadway scenes. The palm tree and its associations. A representative of the palm family. The great viaduct of Metlac. La tierra templada. The Pass of the Bull.

We arrived at Córdoba early in the morning. The station is some distance to the south of town, in a valley from which one sees of the little city only its domes and towers rising above tropical thickets of verdure. In the distance, dense forests are seen clothing the hills, and palm trees and cedars unite their grace and fragrance. We drove over to the hotel where, to our infinite amusement and no little annoyance, we found landlord, servants, and hotel itself absorbed in the fact that *"the Governor was expected."* Ours was a hungry party, and when we sat down to the most meager breakfast ever spread before famished mortals, we called the attention of the landlord to the fact that there was scarcely enough provided for *one* person, and how to divide it satisfactorily amongst *four* was a problem for him to solve. He only shrugged his shoulders, threw up his hands palms outward, and assured us with great volubility that it could not be helped; *el Gobernador* was coming. Everything was being reserved for *el Gobernador*. When we meekly asked for clean napkins, those provided having apparently absorbed the eggs and coffee of a generation of day boarders, the answer was still the same; no new linen could be brought out before the arrival of *el Gobernador*. We even had great difficulty in securing apartments for the same reason and had to content ourselves with the worst in the building, because "*el Gobernador* must have the best." The servants skipped about with anxious countenances and no ostensible purpose in life, oblivious even of a proffered "tip" and animated apparently only by the overwhelming consciousness that "the Governor was coming." It soon became evident that nobody need expect to have anything in the shape of creature comforts until the Governor had come and gone. We, ourselves, became infected with the prevailing excitement and grew anxious to behold this Great Mogul and found ourselves paying with much calmness for dinners and suppers which we never did have, because "the Governor was coming." We never laid our eyes upon him, however, and we think now he was a myth, a delusion which served mine host as a standing apology for sundry shortcomings which possibly he could not help.

Córdoba is a very interesting place, lying 2,500 feet above the sea level on the eastern slope of the peak of Orizaba. It has a delightful climate and is situated in the midst of a rich agricultural district. The early Spaniards speedily learned that the existence of an Indian town or temple was indubitable evidence of a choice locality, and, without taking trouble to look up valuable sites for themselves, they secured the ready made ones by driving out or slaughtering the original inhabitants. The site of Córdoba, hidden away amongst its flowery valleys and wooded hills and lying away from any direct line of travel, for some time escaped the grasp of the conquerors. In 1618, however, the Spaniards descended upon it, made war upon and overthrew its Indian occupants, took armed possession, and founded a town which they named in honor of the reigning Viceroy, Don Diego Hernández de Córdoba, Marqués de Guadalcazar. It was one of the earliest stations upon the old

Royal Road, but it was not until 1830 that it assumed the rank and title of a city.

Architecturally, it resembles Jalapa. It has the same style of dwellings, streets similarly laid out, and undulating and crossing each other at right angles. Similar turrets and domes rise from among clumps of orange, lemon, mango and banana trees or thick groves of dark leaved coffee.

It has two hospitals, one for men and one for women, and a theater which was built out of the fines imposed for drunkenness. There is also a Preparatory College established here, besides other schools, and we were assured that two-thirds of the inhabitants knew how to read and write. The girl's college is presided over by ladies, with gentleman professors who teach different branches. We heard the name of Señorita Jacinta Jarillo mentioned with pride, she being the first lady in the District of Córdoba who had won the title of "Professor."

The Parochial Church is a handsome building and one of the oldest in the city. Besides this, there are four others, the tower of one of which shows signs of having been injured by an earthquake which occurred, I have quite forgotten when, but which shook the bells from their swivels and cracked them and made other wrecks which the repair has not yet effaced. The old Convent of San Antonio is also in ruins. The Plaza is very pretty, and its center is adorned with a monument erected to the memory of heroic patriots of Córdoba who lost their lives in the War of Independence. In the Municipal Palace, which like the Parochial Church faces the Plaza, is preserved, amongst other cherished relics, the sword of *Acuña,* a hero of Córdoba who was killed in the defense of Puebla in 1867. I have seen the works of a young Mexican poet named Acuña whose fate was a most melancholy one, but I do not know that the soldier and the poet were connected by the ties of blood.

Córdoba contains between five and six thousand inhabitants, and numbers among them many men distinguished for their attainments in science and literature, and many refined and cultivated women; so that "Society" is composed of elements which render it attractive and delightful. The site of the quaint little city is on elevated ground which is dignified by being called a hill, and the hill rejoices in the name of "*Hilango.*" The town and its environs possess much that is attractive for the tourist, the student and the antiquarian. It is historically noted for having been the scene of events known as the *Tratados de Córdoba*, one of which was the treaty which gave it birth and name. The other treaty of Independence [was the one] signed by Augustín de Iturbide and the Spaniards and sanctioned by the Spanish Viceroy who bore the very un-Spanish name of *O'Donojú*.[1] He was the last of sixty-four viceroys who had represented the Kings of Spain and, with him, closed her long line of royal representatives in Mexico. Among her relics Córdoba can show the table and the room in which, and upon which, was drawn up and signed the treaty of *La Independencia*. Both the room and the table are in the *Casa de Cevallos*, now a hotel, and the very one where, at the time of our visit, the Governor was expected. Iturbide, Juárez and Maximilian, each in turn, have had their royal quarters there, and the old hotel is one of the most interesting buildings in the town. It is told of the proprietor of a hotel located near some noted sulphur springs among the Virginia mountains in the United States that upon being expostulated with an account of his preposterous charges for board and lodging, he drew himself proudly up and with a grand air replied, "Board and lodging, Sir! I never charged anything for board and lodging in my life, Sir! What I charge for," with a comprehensive glance and majestic sweep of his hand, "what I charge for is this air, Sir, this *magnificent* air!" So perhaps the Córdoba landlord charges for nothing save the historical associations connected with his hotel.

One of the finest horticultural gardens in the Republic flourishes at Córdoba. It may be called a garden within a garden; for in the town and in its suburbs, a bewildering profusion of plants and flowers is seen on all sides. The roads are bordered by blooming hedges, a wealth of *orchidae* in endless variety lends unexpected grace and brilliancy to the somber places; other parasites drop from the lofty trees and swing their verdant ropes in the perfumed breeze, whilst the fern, that Adam of the vegetable creation, grows so abundantly and in such infinite variety as to perplex the eye it charms. A remarkable indigenous growth of medicinal plants abounds, to which was introduced about twenty years ago, through Commodore [Matthew] Maury of the United States Navy, the invaluable Chinchona tree. Commodore Maury obtained the seeds; and from them the Córdoba naturalists Mr. J. A. Nitto and Mr. H. Finch, both distinguished scientists, succeeded in propa-

1. Juan de O'Donojú, New Spain's last viceroy, was representative of the significant emigration of Irish to Spain, escaping British oppression in Ireland.

gating plants and in making the foreign tree so at home in the generous Córdoba clime that it grows there like a native. The soil in this district is remarkably fertile, and produces corn, rice, coffee, tobacco and sugar; while the oranges, mangoes, lemons, pineapples and other tropical fruits are abundant and delicious. The surrounding heights are rich in precious woods. Mahogany, magnificent oaks, cedars, rosewood and many other valuable timber trees form a treasury from which the hand of industry shall draw stores of future wealth. Lands can be obtained in the neighborhood of Córdoba at very reasonable rates; labor is cheap, and living inexpensive.

We were invited to the plantation home of Señor O., a coffee plantation on the outskirts of the town. We were proffered horses, but preferred to walk. It was a stroll never to be forgotten. How sweet the flowers were in the long uneven lanes! The azaleas in the hedges, how fair and delicate; the great scarlet blossoms of the Tulipán, how brilliant, while the air was laden with the rare fragrance of the tropics! Birds of the most beautiful plumage greeted our ears with strange notes, and we lifted our eyes from palm trees and banana groves to the solitary peak of ice glittering above them all. We rested awhile under a tall mahogany tree, then proceeded to our destination, where we were received by *La Señora* with all that charm of manner which is characteristic of the Mexican hostess. Accompanied by herself, her children and her husband, we went soon to the garden where Indian servants placed chairs under the thick boughs of a spreading mango tree. Here we were served with iced drinks, cake and delicious fruits. Among the latter were several varieties of luscious orange. After an hour in the garden, we were taken out among the coffee orchards. The tree under cultivation is only allowed to grow from eight to ten feet high, being topped that it may spread rather than grow tall. Left to itself it will attain the height of fifteen and twenty feet. It is an evergreen, with rich, dark, serrated leaves, and long pliant branches which tend downward from the main trunk, and curve slightly upward at the outer end. The leaves grow opposite each other along the branches. Just at the base of the leaf and close to the limb are bunched the dark, crimson beans, the cluster containing from three and four to ten and twelve. The tree laden with fruit is an object of great beauty, as it also is when in blossom. The flower is white, and its perfume delightful. In few instances does nature condescend to so combine great commercial value and exceeding beauty as she does in the coffee groves. The trees from the young plant bear after the third year. If raised from the seed, four and five years are required to bring it to perfection. Each tree produced on an average from sixteen to twenty ounces of husked coffee. The berry, or bean as it is called, somewhat resembles the cranberry both in size and color. The red fruit of the coffee, however, has a sweet flavor and is very pleasant to the taste. In each bean lies enclosed the precious seeds, two grains of coffee. From their juxtaposition in close bunches on the branch the berries cannot redden uniformly save in cases where there are but few in a cluster. When they are perfectly ripe their color is a very dark red; but this evidence of perfection is not waited for by the harvesters. So soon as the fruit begins to show a general tinge of red indicating that its full growth has been obtained, the time to gather it is deemed at hand.

In some plantations the coffee is gathered by lightly shaking the tree so that only the ripest beans may fall, and they are then gathered from the ground. If the really green berries chance to be gathered with the ripe, assorting is rendered necessary, as the green bean, lacking in quality and flavor, injures the marketable value of the ripe. In Córdoba the coffee is generally *picked* from the tree. The coffee gatherer needs to understand his business thoroughly. Otherwise, he will gather green and ripe alike, tear the leaves from the branch with the fruit and make a sad harvest. The expert with quick eye and dexterous fingers strips a tree very rapidly. Children also are especially useful as coffee pickers, being quiet and careful.

Sometimes, to avoid the heat of the sun, the Córdoba coffee gatherers work in the orchards under the light of their brilliant moon. These people work silently at all times. Silence is one of the striking characteristics of the laboring classes; so that nothing of the fun and jollity of a harvest frolic in the States, or a husking or a paring bee, nor the simple festivities of the grinding season in our sugar lands pertain to coffee picking. I have never heard the Mexican laborer whistling, singing nor talking while at work. The man is silent at his plow, or in the mine; the woman silent in her kitchen, but none the less they make a pretty picture in the coffee groves; the men, the busy children and the bare armed women under the light of a tropic moon.

From the coffee fields we were taken to see large, shallow, cemented basins called "*secadores,*" where the gathered coffee is raked through and through, and turned in the hot sun and so dried. It is then rolled and husked, and winnowed and made ready for market. The Indians, who raise coffee for their own use in the immediate vicinity of their hut, dry it in the sun on a large straw mat called a *petate* which, though more picturesque, is a much slower process.

Mexico produces all the coffee necessary for home consumption, and, with proper exporting facilities, could readily supply the United States with an article in no way inferior to the product of Arabia or Brazil. Its exportation to the States is not at present increasing although its excellence is being extensively acknowledged and appreciated. The coffee of Córdoba is especially rich in oil and flavor, and experienced coffee tasters who have studied the bean in all quarters of the globe where it is grown, and who, like wine tasters, pride themselves upon their judgement of quality, have assured me that the coffee of Mexico cannot be surpassed in any part of the world.

Selected coffee from Urupam and from Colima on the western slope of Mexico is worth one dollar a pound where it grows and is very rarely exported. We had the pleasure to drink of these celebrated coffees, and, although the flavor was very delicious, it was by no means sufficiently superior to the Córdoba coffee to warrant the difference in price.

As each coffee tree here yields on an average a few ounces more than a pound of husked coffee, it is estimated, by those familiar with the cultivation of the bean, that a coffee farm of one hundred thousand trees will have cost at the end of the fifth year from planting, from the seed, twelve thousand dollars. A full crop the fifth year will reimburse the outlay. This estimate includes the ordinary price of coffee lands which here range from five to twenty five dollars per acre, our measure. A coffee farm, if judiciously cared for and cultivated, will yield abundantly for fifty or sixty years. It must be spared either excessive heat or excessive cold. In localities where the rays of the sun are too intense for it the coffee plants are set under lofty trees which soften without excluding the light and heat. Some planters set the banana among their coffee for the purpose of obtaining the requisite shade, but many of them consider its use injurious rather than beneficial to the growing plants. A special time of year is chosen for transplanting the young coffee which has been started in nurseries. After the vernal equinox is considered the best period. The coffee when ready for market is worth about thirteen cents a pound. In New Orleans, the Córdoba coffee grades above that of Brazil, yet the importation of the latter far exceeds that of the Mexican bean in our southern ports.

The coffee plant is productive throughout the tropic coast lands of Mexico at an altitude of from 3,000 to 4,000 feet above the level of the sea. It always requires a mean temperature of from 64 to 70 degrees Fahrenheit.

From the coffee fields we visited other points of interest upon the plantation. Among these were the mango groves, the dense foliage of which creates perpetual twilight below them. We also saw the *Chinchona* tree which produces here from its bitter bark as good a quality of quinine as can be found in the market, and to our unaccustomed eyes the sight of the allspice growing, the pepper and the Chirimoya was equally novel and interesting. The fruit of the Chirimoya is a dull green in color, and its size is about that of a fine apple. Its rind is full of little lumpy prominences but inside is found a whitish, most delicious pulp, so mellow it can be eaten with a spoon and of a rich, delicious flavor which seems a combination of that belonging to several other luscious fruits. It contains one round, smooth seed about the size of an English walnut. Here again we enjoyed the delicious grenaditta and also the zapote which is the fruit of a species of mimosa, the wood of which is very valuable for building purposes being hard and extremely durable. Besides these we tasted the sweet limes and the sweetest oranges. Upon leaving we were accompanied some distance on our way back by our host, hostess and their young, attractive daughters.

It seems strange that the oranges of Córdoba, as well as her coffee, do not find their way to the United States. They are not surpassed by any in the market, are delicious in flavor, firm and large and juicy, are hanging ripe upon the trees in December and are but little more than three days direct from New Orleans fruit stalls by steamship. If proper facilities for speedy transportation were afforded, the products of this favorable spot would furnish a large trade with the most luscious and abundant and varied supply of fruits including the banana and pineapple.

It so happened that we reached this place upon its weekly market day or fair. The scene in the streets at night was very novel and picturesque. The great plaza and the market building itself were thronged with Indian men and women who had arrived at night in order to be ready for business early the next day. They encamped in the open square, each one beside his little stock of this world's goods. They cooked their simple suppers, hushed their children to sleep, and then setting up a lamp which burned with a dull, red glow, each spread a mat of straw upon the ground and went to sleep beneath the stars. They seemed to have no dread of murder or robbery, and rested out in the open air with no especial guard. The gathering partakes of the nature of the fair to which each has brought the best he has to sell, and perhaps a little money with which to get the best that he can buy. Accompanied by friends, we ventured to enter and perambulate the unprotected camp. No one disputed our right to do so, and we strolled where we liked. Here lay one sleeper beside a little crop of black beans brought an incredible distance, which at the utmost, would only bring a few *real.*[2] Beyond, another who had three chickens and a fist of *chile,* the Mexican pepper. Then, an Indian woman sleeping with a baby at her breast, a chicken under each arm, and a pig with its legs tied and lying at her feet. There were pottery vendors from Guadalajara, away in the West, who had traveled scores of miles on foot to bring to market a few handsful of native pottery of the coarsest finish and design, the whole stock worth perhaps a dollar or two. Near these lay a more wealthy merchant, who slept beside some sacks of wheat, and so on through all the crowd. The small portion which each one possessed, when weighed against the distance he had brought it, made the prospective profit seem ridiculously small. But the Indians appear to consider that "it pays," and trudge to market from immense distance to dispose of a little corn or other merchandise, the whole amount of which would not amount to the price of a clean shirt. They pay out nothing to live, each having brought to town the charcoal and the furnace and the corn for their own *tortillas,* the corn cake which is the staple article of food with these Indians year in and year out. As we walked among them the stolid sleepers never stirred, although I half suspect that many of them slept with one eye open and, had the slightest necessity arisen, both would have been found wide awake and vigilant.

The shops and eating houses were doing a brisk business, many people having been attracted to the place from the adjacent neighborhoods, and all things wore a gay and festive aspect. In some of the shops and saloons all the crockery of the establishment which was not in immediate use was hung up against the wall, often covering it from top to bottom. The articles were suspended by means of a hole in the rim, and arranged in most fantastic groups, which often presented a bewildering combination of hues. Booths had been erected on one side of the square, and here a busy scene presented itself.

2. The *real* was a principal coin of the Spanish empire and was equal to one-eighth (hence, "piece of eight") of a peso or U.S. dollar. Its use continued well into the nineteenth century in independent Mexico and other Latin American countries.

Motley clusters of people were gathered about under the long, low roofs, and every imaginable species of gambling went on there. Dealers and players were alike curious in aspect, and the rattle of dice and dominoes, the slapping of packs of cards, the cries of the Monte banks calling out numbers and the constant repetition of a word which sounded like "loto" came with the regularity of continuous hammer strokes to our ears. Everybody played, the little children as well as those "of a larger growth," and it was pitiable to see the small, eager faces watch with almost haggard interest the turn of a card or the fall of a die. Late into the night, long after we had returned to our hotel, Cora and I could hear the cries from the booths, where no doubt the games went on until morning.

Tradition states that the hotel in which we are quartered was once the family palace of the Count Cevallo. The spacious court, the long corridors, suite after suite of rooms, the mighty old doors, the strong casements are none of them the architecture of today, and are "grand, gloomy and peculiar" enough to satisfy the most ardent lover of the romantic, the mysterious and the antique. Under the grand staircase we were shown the treasure vault, a sort of oven with an iron door, in which the Cevallos stored their wealth, "and took it out," our informant said, "uncounted, by the shovelsful; the identical shovel which they used being still in existence." Of course, we peered into the empty ovens with eyes interested enough to satisfy the most exacting story teller. After all, there was something impressive in the sight of the grim, empty vault, with its ponderous iron door. What measures of joy and desolation, of misery and pride and ambition, of guilt, perhaps, and crime, have come out of that frowning portal which ever now shuts in histories without end, which will be known only in that day "when the secrets of all hearts shall be opened." It was not with unstrung nerves that we went to bed; yet if ever ghosts perambulated any house, they did this ancient stronghold while we lay prone and tried to sleep. Our beds shook, our doors swung open untouched by visible hands (to be sure they had no fastenings and a high wind was blowing), our windows quaked, and strange sounds filled the air. Still, the honor of all Mexican ghosts be it spoken, nobody was hurt, and notwithstanding the throng of strangers in the house, and the crowd of idlers, gamblers, waifs and strays in the city, no one was robbed or molested in any way.

The town in the morning presented a most animated appearance. The marketers were all astir, and buyers and vendors were driving a big business.

Wheat, corn, beans, pottery, dry goods, *dulces*,[3] beads, birds, flowers, vegetables, baskets, poultry, coffee, calico, cookery, cooks, fruits, seeds and ribbons occupied the scene of the campfires of the night previous. It was amusing to note the morning arrivals of marketers, as from all directions they came pouring into the little town. Here would come a stalwart Indian trudging manfully over hill and dale, as he had trudged for many a mile, with a handful of tobacco! Behind him would come a donkey; on the donkey's back a woman; on the woman's back a baby; and the goods which this group brought to market consisted of a single chicken! Immediately in the rear of these would trot a barelegged Indian beside a bare-bosomed wife, both with loads strapped to their foreheads, which would have sufficed to burden any descendants of the beast which spoke to Balaam. In the multitude of marketers many different tribes of Indians were represented, some of them as distinct types of race and condition as in the days when their ancestors first beheld the great *Conquistador*. These still appear in precisely the same style of costume which was that of their tribe in the days of Cortez.

Just under our window a corn buyer established himself. Seated on an immense straw mat he awaited those who had corn to sell. They soon came in numbers, some bringing but one small measure full, others, perhaps, with a couple of sacks, the contents of which went swishing down upon the bargaining merchant's mat, where he sat like a great spider in the midst of its web. In every instance the man who received his pay rung and tasted, and bit each coin to make sure that it was silver before, with an air of supreme satisfaction, he put it in his purse. There were women of a certain tribe, the name of which I could not learn, who appeared upon the scene in a long, white gown, made something like a minister's robe, with immense hanging sleeves, the whole robe embroidered around its hems in bright colored thread of different tints. Sparkling beads or gay ribbons were worn about their dusky throats, and the head dress was a piece of white cloth folded flat, with a curtain hanging down over the back of the head, precisely like the head dress of the Italian peasant. There were also representatives of a tribe of independent Indians who have a village about a league from Córdoba. Their bamboo town is exceedingly pretty, they call it *Amatlán de los Reyes* and cling to and sustain the traditions and customs of their ancient race. They are a self

---

3. Sweets, or candies.

supporting community, and are reported to be immensely rich, with hoards of treasure securely concealed among the mountains! They have a chosen chief to whom they look up, and whose counsels they obey. They are a serious faced, good looking people, very honest and very industrious. They have their coffee lands and their vegetable gardens, and come regularly to market, where their "Truck" finds ready sale. They have never been known to come to town "to trade," to gamble, or in any way to dispose of their earnings. They have the respect of all the better class in the town and country round about, while the humbler portions regard them with admiration not unmixed with awe. Their chief's daughter was a very pretty maiden, and like all these Indian girls, possessed of beautiful hair and a remarkably fine figure. We saw her going home laden with baskets, and bundles, and cages which had been brought to market. She trudged bravely along on foot with her bundles, while a young man who might have been her brother or her lover, serenely bestrode a splendid horse and, wrapped in a fine sarape, rode a length in advance of her, himself carrying nothing, unless it were a very exalted opinion of his own merits and good looks.

Such fairs date from a period probably long antecedent to the Spanish invasion. Cortez, in his letters to his King, in describing the *Tlaxcalans,* alludes to their "market day, which drew together thirty thousand souls." Prescott states "these meetings were a sort of fair, held as usual in all the great towns every fifth day and attended by the inhabitants of the adjacent country, who brought there for sale every description of domestic produce and manufacture with which they were acquainted." Early morning found us wending our way toward the station. About the doors and windows of the depot, in bamboo cages hung a variety of native birds, many of them with brilliant plumage, all of them sweet of song. Men and women moved about offering cakes and fruit for sale, or stood in groups gazing down the track, while an old man, one of the most picturesque of figures, offered coffee sticks for sale. These sticks, stripped of their bark and scraped, are ready to be polished and converted into walking canes. The wood, when varnished, resembles a rich mahogany anywhere, is strong and lithe, and one of these sticks is considered a valuable addition to the stock of a cane collector. To make one, a young tree is sacrificed, as it is the trunk, not the branch which is needed for the purpose.

Mules and horses attached to vehicles of the quaintest description were gathered about the depot, and donkeys, of course, without number. The donkey is always an object of interest in this country. His heels may have bad habits, and his voice may not have sweetness in its upper register, but nevertheless, he deserves and commands respect. He may be imposed upon, but his forbearance is exemplary. He finds out his lot in life and endures it without useless complaint. He takes up his burden, be it a hat or a haystack, and bears it without rebellion. He has discovered that he is weaker than his master, and never wastes time in fruitless attempts to assume rights that do not belong to him. When smitten on one cheek, he turns the other also. If he has nothing to eat, he chews "the cud of sweet and bitter fancy" without a protest. If he can establish himself on the south side of a sapling he deems himself well stalled. His back may get sore, but his temper never sours. He has a position and maintains it with a quiet self assertion that nothing disconcerts. Steam has not exterminated nor progress undermined him, and if, as asserted, he is stubborn, it is only because he is endowed with resolution and a just consciousness of his own importance. If ever a cranium had a right to a big lump of self esteem it is that of a donkey. It is the lump that carries many a man along and over the rough roads of life, and the burro needs it for the same purpose. He is to be seen everywhere in this country, his panniers now filled with ice, now with charcoal, now with glass, and now with iron. Thus, the extremes of commerce meet over his much enduring backbone, while he plods on, always wearing the same aspect of serene dignity and heavenly patience.

We noticed about the station many beggars. They were horrible deformities, cramped, withered and distorted. Some could not stand up, and some could not sit down; and all took great pains to display their malformations and crawled about appealing to every stranger for charity. Their wretchedness was apparent enough to soften a heart of stone, and their needs sufficiently evident to loosen the purse strings of the meanest of misers, but so shocking is the appearance of these unhappy beings, and so revolting are some of their deformities, that as a mere measure of prudence, they should be kept away from so public a place as a railway station.

As Córdoba passes from view, we gaze out at the luxuriance of verdure which clothes the hills on either hand. There is the greatest vagabondage among the vines which climb and twist in every direction, always full of blossoms. There is the liquid-amber, the tree to which the vanilla loves to cling, the castor bean, the sarsaparilla, the beech and the mimosa. Odors, balsamic and aromatic, fill the air, which is delightfully cool and fresh. Here and there above all the wealth of shrubbery a tall palm tree lifts itself, arousing in him who gazes at its feathery crown sentiments of admiration, almost of veneration. One feels his heart grow reverential in the presence of this superb and graceful tree. It glorifies the spot where it grows not only by its own classic beauty, but by the sacred associations which are connected with it. It grew beside the River Jordan; it reared itself in Jericho, and gave to that ancient city the name of "The City of Palms." It is promised to the righteous that they "shall flourish like the palm tree," and when the children of Israel murmured against Moses because they "could not drink of the waters of the Marah, because they were bitter," "The Lord showed him a tree which, when he had cast [it] into the waters, the waters were made sweet." This, historians assert to have been a palm tree. When the chosen children had journeyed further and "came to him, there were twelve wells of water and threescore and ten palm trees, and they encamped there by the waters." To the Jews it was the symbol of joy. Its graceful boughs were borne in their festal gatherings, and it was an emblem chosen for their choicest sculptures. When our Savior entered Jerusalem, the people went forth to greet him "with palms in their hands." It symbolizes patience, constancy and fortitude. With martial heroes of all ancient history it was the emblem of triumph, the symbol of victory. In chapter after chapter of Holy Writ it is named; and though time has sadly diminished its number on the plains of Palestine, it is a tree which must ever be associated with the pages of Holy Writ even as is the olive branch and the Cedar of Lebanon.

We spin along over culverts and gorges, through cuts and along curves, through hills and dales and flowers and forests; the many medicinal roots and shrubs which add a dispensary to this conservatory of nature, and occasionally the landscape has been varied by plains covered with the sparse vegetation peculiar to the dry season. The grade, meanwhile, has varied from 260 to 280 per cent [Townsend undoubtedly means 2.6 to 2.8 percent here, ed. note], and we reach Fortín, a little station where in former times a fort existed to protect Spanish treasure and troops passing to and fro upon the old road. It is of no especial interest today, and our engine halts here only long enough to take a long breath before moving on to the famous *Barranca* or ravine of Metlac which lies less than a quarter of a mile beyond. We round a curve and find ourselves turned away from our course and traveling almost in an opposite direction. We are upon a path with a four per cent grade terraced into the almost perpendicular walls of the Barranca with a precipice towering above us and profound abyss below. There is a sheer descent of 375 feet while the width of the ravine from side to side at its widest is but little less than 1000 feet. So immense is the chasm it looks as if a mountain had been wrenched out of it by some terrible convulsion of nature. At the bottom of the ravine, lessened to a mere ribbon by distance, flows a stream like the last drop left after some midnight orgy in a Titan's punch bowl. This is the river Metlac which runs hither and thither, as if terrified at that strange monster the steam engine which has penetrated to its solitudes, and at last it darts under ground to hide itself, emerging again some distance beyond only to throw itself over the rocks in sheets of silvery foam among a multitude of admiring flowers and ferns. It is impossible for the eye to follow its course as half fascinated, appalled, creeping along the perilous path one gazes down into depths which seem every moment growing deeper and up at heights which seem every instant growing higher. A dense forest rises on one hand, the great abyss yawns below, oval in form, and along its wall like a centipede crawling around the edge of a vast cauldron creeps our train with its windows crowded with eager faces gazing up, gazing down, looking forward, looking back and expressing all the varied emotions of surprise, delight, awe, wonder and fear. The mingling of the grand and the picturesque, the sublime and the beautiful, the sense of danger as one peers down into the yawning gulf over which he seems to hang suspended, and the assurance of safety he experiences as the train sweeps steadily forward, all serve to create an impression upon the mind not soon to be forgotten. Now over a culvert and through a tunnel and we emerge by a curve upon the stupendous viaduct of Metlac which unites the two sides of the Barranca. This viaduct is 440 feet in length. Nine iron piers support it, standing at regular distances between its two staunch stone abutments. Each one of these piers is in itself a massive monument of iron, formed of upright and horizontal bars; yet at a little distance they appear as light and delicate as if made of blown glass. From the center of this bridge we can look down at the foundations of these piers, which are planted in the ravine three hundred feet below. Here too, we have a full view of the glen. The rank tropical verdure in the wildest luxuriance clothes and beautifies the steep banks from base to summit, and chiseled into the solid hills our track lies where before a mountain goat might with difficulty have climbed. Trees grow below us, their tallest branches not level with our wheels and parasites of every hue cling to and adorn the branches. Six tunnels, roofed and faced with stone, and several of these built upon curves are on the section of the road which traverses this Barranca. We leave the viaduct as we came upon it by a curve, and doubling on our track, go back on the hither side with the road opposite in full view. Glancing back, we see the mighty bridge which is at once a model and a marvel of engineering skill. Now we traverse down grades and up grades, and dart in and out of tunnels as if our dignified engine had condescended to play a game of peek-a-boo with the rugged old hills. Finally, we turn sharply westward again upon our direct course, and emerge upon a plateau where the eye takes in a landscape of a somewhat different character. The *tierra caliente* lies behind us now, and the palm tree of the tropics has long ceased to greet our eyes. We find ourselves in the *tierra templada*. Though the vegetation is less rank, it is no less beautiful. Flowers still are abundant. The woods are green, the rivers bright. Nature is still the artist and the poet, reveling in light and shade, in form and color, and every beauty of expression. We cross several bridges, over beautiful and romantically situated streams with such names as "The eye of the water," "The Pass of the Bull," etc., and our next halt is at Orizaba which is distant from Córdoba about fifteen miles.

10

Orizaba

Arrival at Orizaba. Its appearance. Hotels and price of board. Height of the town above sea level. Its origin. Ahamaializapán, village of merry waters. Conquest by the Spaniards. Factories and other public buildings. The climate. The town considered as a health resort. The environs. The famous Cerro de Borrego. Sights and sounds. The ensign Nun. Birds. Peasantry. Whistling to pigs. Baby cages. Mode of advertising. Indians and Indian lanes. Sandals. Sarapes and rebozos. Fiesta. Decorated streets. Outdoor cookery. Mexican coins and their value. Maximilian's clock. Another fiesta. "Religion, Union and Independence." Novel decorations. Prayers and pyrotechnics. Economical fun. Tallow and tissue paper.

The first view one obtains of Orizaba in the early part of the day is, if the weather be fair, one of great beauty and attractiveness. He sees the grey churches, old convents, great domes covered with flat, variegated tiles, one-storied red and brown roofed houses, here and there an ancient ruin nestled amidst a vegetation which, if not of the *tierra caliente* is a blood relation to it, all peacefully nesting at the base of its surrounding heights and watched over by the glittering summit of the snow peak which stands out sharp and clear against a sky of the most beautiful blue imaginable. The brown hill of the Borrego is in plain sight, with the famed military road made by the French stretching up its eastern slope and, at its foot, winding off westward between other hill slopes, goes the old road of *los Consulados*.

A street railway is in operation between the depot and the town, but the distance is such as can be easily walked. We made our way to the Hotel de las Diligencias situated on the principal street. Like all hotels of its kind in this country it was built of stone with walls of great thickness. The entrance was through a doorway swung in a stone arch. This admitted one to a large, square patio or court open to the sky. A tiled colonnade surrounded it, upon which the dining room, the kitchen and the various offices opened. Parlor, or reception room, there was none. Opposite the entrance a broad stone stair-case leads to the corridor above, upon which the sleeping apartments, all with thick wooden doors, open. Each room fronting the street has its stone bal-cony with iron railing below its broad window. The windows are simply glazed doors within two outer doors, and all divided in the middle length-wise. The floors are brick tiles. Some of the rooms are slightly frescoed, oth-ers have only the side walls plastered, with the boards and heavy rafters painted overhead, and so high the American housewife falls to wondering if any cobweb broom could ever reach them. Single bedsteads of iron, generally two in each room with muslin mosquito bars, to remind the Southern trav-eler he is not out of the reach of the pestiferous insect, a chest of drawers, a wooden washstand, a little table, some chairs and two or three straw mats upon the floor comprise the furniture of the *apartamientos;* unless the sun has free access to them they are pervaded with a disagreeable chilliness during the winter months. From two to two and a half [pesos] according to the room occupied is the charge for each person for board and lodging. A room without board can be obtained for much less and there are a number of places where excellent meals can be had at very reasonable rates. The usual meals consist of *desayuno* which is taken upon rising and consists of coffee, bread and light cakes. It is a *go as you please* meal, served without formality in one's room or at the dining table, and one takes it when or where he chooses. Breakfast is from twelve until two. Dinner at six. Our first breakfast over, we went out to walk about the pretty town and its environs.

It is one of the oldest in the country, is in the rich state of Vera Cruz and lies in *la tierra templada* four thousand, two hundred and seventy eight feet above the level of the sea. It has its poetic legends connecting it with the ancient god Quetzalcoatl and historical traditions dating back to its occupa-tion by the *Chichimecas* in 1300. It lies beneath the sparkling peak of Orizaba, which the ancient tribes called *Chitlaltepetl* (the star mountain), which stands

17,375 feet above sea level. The town is situated at one-third of the distance between Vera Cruz and Mexico, being ninety miles from the former city and [one hundred and] eighty from the latter. The old highway, whose importance is not usurped by the great railroad, passes directly through the city. In the early days of the diligences this was their day's run from Vera Cruz; that is, passengers by the diligence left Vera Cruz at two o'clock in the morning and arrived here to sup and sleep at nine in the evening. The cars now make the same distance in five hours including the numerous stops at stations on the way. As I have said, local history places the founding of the town at a very remote period. In the lovely valley which lies on the slopes of these grand old mountains once existed the Aztec villages of Izhautlán, Tequila, Tesmaloca, and others. These comprised the province to which the natives gave the musical name of Ahamaializapán, which means merriment of the waters, or playful waters. These independent tribes were subjected to Mexico by Montezuma in 1457, just when they had attained the most flourishing period in their history.

Upon the arrival of the Spaniards, this was one of the first points of which they took possession, believing that here they would find abundance of riches. The name of Ahamaializapán they contracted to Aulicaba, and this was gradually corrupted into Orizaba, by which the town and the snow peak have ever since been known. In 1520, the Indians revolted; but in the following year Gonzalo de Sandoval reconquered the province and brought it again under Spanish rule. This was a bloodless conquest, it is said; but, after the succeeding victories of Cortez, this kingly but conquered race suffered hardships and misfortunes which reduced them to the most abject condition.

The descendants of these ancient tribes are numerous here and still remain a distinct race. With the instinct of the Indian to hold himself aloof from the white, they dwell in villages of their own and form a part of the population of Orizaba which to the stranger is one of its most interesting features.

The first Spanish colonists who assembled here established themselves near the ancient village of Exhautlán. They were chiefly muleteers and were soon followed by merchants. Thus was founded the venerable town, and the descendants of the aboriginal founders exist here in numbers, maintaining unmolested their traditional habits. The city is irregularly laid out and contains something more than 20,000 inhabitants. It is situated in a beautiful and fertile valley, well watered and encircled by wooded mountains. It has numerous churches, two theaters, two hospitals, a public library, several schools, a preparatory college, three large flour mills and three cotton factories, besides four or five hotels. Three rivers are near, the Río Orizaba within the city limits, the Río Ingenio and the Río Blanco. The Governor's Palace and the *Lonja Mercantil* are the finest buildings, on the main street. The shops are small, goods dear, and the choice very limited.

The climate is variable but delightful. In winter, the highest temperature averages 72 degrees F. In the early morning and the evening it is as low as 65 degrees, and blankets are always required upon the beds at night. The same clothing that one wears in the States in Spring and early Autumn is the kind one needs in Orizaba. It is a limestone region, and without medicinal waters, so far as I have been able to learn, but it is considered a most healthful locality, beyond the reach of yellow fever and is resorted to by those in delicate health, and by pleasure seekers who find the city of Mexico too cool, and the lower coast too hot.

The chief drawback to the perfection of the climate in winter is the "norther." With this wind comes fog, rain and chilly weather, and during its prevalence the glittering crown of Chitlaltepetl is obscured for days together. As the people are essentially a people of the sun, with no fireplaces or chimneys in their houses, it is easy to understand how much to them must be the veiling of the genial orb in whose light and warmth they so revel. Frost is almost unknown here, and, notwithstanding the "northers," flowers bloom always in the open air; oranges and bananas hang upon their boughs; the coffee tree brings its clustered berries to perfection, and the cane stands uninjured in the fields until cut for the crusher.

A beautiful river in a deep ravine, its sides bordered with nodding banana trees, ferns, vines and other ever verdant vegetation, goes laughing and sparkling and winding through the town, turning the several mills upon its way. It is crossed by three or four massive stone bridges, one of which has a stone tablet surmounted by a carved skull and crossbones. The skull wears a crown, and the whole is surmounted by a cross about two feet high. The tablet, which is set in the solid masonry that walls the sides of the bridge, bears a Spanish inscription stating that it was built in 1776 and paid for by the people in the vicinity. To stand upon any of these bridges and look down into the ravine, where the bright and joyful water runs clear as crystal over its pebbly bottom, where one sees it here breaking into foamy rapids, there stretching like a smooth ribbon between its banks, always shining and always singing and always playing among the rocks which would impede its course, one recognizes the keen sympathy with nature which they possessed who named the vale that the stream enriches *Ahamaializapán*. It is not a navigable river, but at any time of day it is picturesque and beautiful. Indian women are there seen washing clothes in wooden troughs which are drawn up under the shadow of banana boughs, or moving about to bleach or dry the linen on sunny stones, while Indian children sit around in pretty groups or paddle half naked in the shallow water, laughing as its silvery tide rushes over their dusty feet.

Just beyond the bridge with the inscription, which the old diligence road crosses, stands the ancient church and the ruined convent of San José de Gracia. The former is a large and massive pile, and its interior bears many traces of the wealth which once characterized all church property in this country. The convent is no longer used for the purposes to which it was originally devoted. Its dome and tower are gray and stained with time; it is partly ruined and in the lofty halls where once the nuns sang their vespers or chanted their matins, in the corridors through which they passed to prayer or meditation with softened footsteps and telling their beads, now sweep the wide winds and birds take shelter, or the Indian woman, surrounded with her pottery pans, deals out to occasional customers *enchiladas,* served hot from her charcoal fire. Passing on a little way, one turns to the north, and soon finds himself at the Alameda, the principal public square of the city. It is prettily laid out, and has three fountains with such enormous stone basins they seem like lakes. There are benches of earth covered with turf upon which people sit, even on damp days, with no apparent thought of pneumonia or bronchitis. Ferns grow in profusion, and the hibiscus mingles its scarlet blossoms with the gay green of banana leaves and the lower branches of lofty trees. A carriage road winds about within the inclosure, and here, on Sundays and Thursdays when the band plays, the beauty and fashion of Orizaba, the dignified citizen and the gay caballero, walk, ride and drive, or sit about upon the turfy seats unless the norther blows.

Near the Alameda we pause to look up at the historic height which towers near it. It is a lofty and precipitous hill which barely escaped being a mountain. Its slopes are rugged and rocky, and on the eastern side which faces the town a road is seen clearly cut, extending up along its face until it reaches the very summit. This is the *Cerro de Borrego* or hill of the sheep—so called probably because no sign of a sheep is ever seen there. Its arid sides do not show enough grass to feed a goat and scarcely a bush is visible upon it.

After the defeat of the French by General [Ignacio] Zaragoza in Puebla on the famous 5th of May 1862, they fell back upon the city of Orizaba. Zaragoza having died of fever, General [Jesús] González Ortega took command of the Mexican army. Knowing the position of the French he attempted to effect a "surprise," which, had it succeeded, must, it is believed, have resulted in the utter overthrow of the French. A forced march of more than thirty miles over rough and toilsome and steep mountain paths brought [González] Ortega and his soldiers at nightfall to the summit of the *Cerro de Borrego,* their presence undreamed of and undiscovered by their foes below. Issuing strict orders that no one should leave the camp, but failing to guard it as they should have done, the Mexicans in fancied security, officers and men worn out by their fearful march, lay down to rest and slumber.

A woman—"who was she?"—one of the many who make up the trail of camp followers in this country, stole away and managed to descend the rocky steep and reach the town. Her presence instantly excited among the alert French soldiery surprise. [They] questioned [her] almost within earshot of the quiet sleepers on the hilltop dreaming perhaps of the victory soon to be theirs on the morrow; a victory they had toiled for over hill and dale, rocks and thorns and precipices, making, considering the path they traversed, one of the most remarkable marches on record.

Taking immediate advantage of the unusual darkness of the night, a division of French infantry as silently as possible made their way up the steep face of the hill while cannon were dragged up the easier incline on the eastern side. Suddenly, fire was opened on the sleeping Mexicans. The tables were completely turned upon [González] Ortega. So unexpected was the attack, so wholly unprepared were the Mexicans, so profound was the darkness and so dire the confusion, it seemed to the half roused soldiers that the whole French army was upon them. Amid the shouts and shots of the invaders, the rattle of musketry, the cries of the wounding and the wounded, the slaughter was terrific; the rout complete. The day dawned upon a scene of blood, ruin and disaster, a slaughtered army and a broken hearted leader, while over all floated the French flag in triumph. Having taken possession of the height, other pieces of artillery were subsequently dragged up the hillside path and a substantial road built which exists as we see it today, not difficult of ascent, often traversed by visitors and tourists and writing as it were, in one line, the tragedy and triumph which made historic the *Cerro de Borrego*. Tradition goes on to state that the French, in digging an excavation in which to plant a cross, found a buried treasure in Spanish gold amounting to more than eighty thousand dollars. For the truth of this, ¿quién sabe? I only know that there are several crosses planted along the French road—and that upon certain feast nights the people extend their illuminations along and up this rugged hillside, often with a weird and picturesque effect. Recently a vein of marble has been discovered in this hill. When polished it much resembles the Puebla marble, and "works up" beautifully under the lathes. The vein is an extensive one and is regarded as a great "find" which is expected to prove of great value.

At the foot of this hill facing the Alameda and the west are the Exposition buildings erected in 1881. They are built of wood and lighted by numerous windows. They are rectangles, one story above the ground floor and floored with brick tiles. The cost of erection was 50,000 dollars, and every inch of timber in them was brought from the United States. With all her magnificent timber trees and her fine water power, I did not see a saw mill in Orizaba.

The beautiful scenery, the soft delicious atmosphere and the novel sights and sounds with which we found ourselves encompassed in this enchanting "valley of mirth" made out of door life fascinating and almost converted us into Gypsies. Our nearest approach to staying in the house (save when we slept) was to occupy the stone balcony which overhung the street. Cora constantly found something to allure her there which she as constantly called me to behold.

Our window faced the southeast and commanded an extended view. In the distance, lofty mountains were beautiful; their stern grandeur softened by ever changing shadows of clouds and sweep of sunshine. At their base, stretched fields of luxuriant sugar cane the vivid hue of which stood out in bright contrast to the russet rockiness of the heights. Through the plantation groves at certain hours floated a banner of blue smoke announcing that the down express train was on its rapid march to the sea. On the hither side of the cane fields came into prominent view the old church of San Juan de Dios founded in 1618, the first edifice of this kind erected here by the Spaniards. A portion of it was ruined by an earthquake in 1695, a misfortune which added

to its picturesqueness. Like everything else in town, it had been recently
freshened up and was very buff where it was not very white, and its ancient
tower and single dome looked almost as good as new. Here was buried, aged
65 years, the *Monja Alferez,* a noted nun whose history has served for drama,
song and story for many a day. She was a spirited Spanish girl, tradition
states, endowed with great beauty and remarkable talents. Her parents placed
her in a convent in Spain and announced to her their determination that she
should lead the life of a religious recluse. She rebelled against this disposition
of her youth and energies and resolved to escape the bondage which she
found unendurable. She carefully laid her plans, and they succeeded. In male
attire, after many struggles, hardships and adventures, she made her way at
last to the shores of Mexico and, at one time, owned a pack of mules near
Orizaba which she worked and managed as well as any muleteer in the country could have done. Her adventures and escapades were manifold. She was
at times a nun, at times none at all. She acted in the capacity of servant and
master, fought as a soldier, bore hardships like a hero, struggled like a man
and suffered like a woman. She was known as Doña Catalina de Eranzo and
was born in the province of Guipúzcoa, Spain in 1585. The historian in closing an account of her strange and romantic existence states that finally "at a
poor inn near Orizaba she died an exemplary death to the general grief of all
the persons present." Why an exemplary death should have caused "general
grief of all the persons present," he does not explain. She was buried with
great pomp in the cemetery of the Church of San Juan de Dios in 1650, but
time has obliterated every trace of that resting place to which she was con-
signed more than two hundred and thirty years ago. That her memory has
survived so many years and is still being handed down from generation to
generation is a fact more astonishing than anything connected with her career remarkable as that was. What hosts of pure and saintly nuns have gone
to their eternal sleep in the graveyards of Orizaba of whom not a name nor
a memory survives while the Ensign Nun with all her wickedness and un-
womanliness the world will not let die.

Looking westward beyond the church the eye passes from glimpses of
alluring gardens to thickets of verdure on the river bank, to the low reddish
brown tiles of house roofs and then the street immediately below our balcony
on the opposite side of which a flight of stone steps leading down toward the
river seemed to bid us descend and explore what lay below them.

Now, an Indian woman stands at the head of these stairs with a parrot on her hand which she offers for sale. Another Indian hangs beside a doorway a bamboo cage in which a *Clarín* (to my fancy the sweetest singing bird in Mexico) is pouring out his exquisite song. Donkeys, laden with every imaginable shape, size and color and quality of burden, go trooping along driven by men wearing a most incongruous garb consisting of an immense hat, sandals on their unstockinged feet, a heavy, woolen sarape about the shoulders and short white cotton trousers on their legs. A woman passes leading her laden donkey. In the rebozo in which she is half wrapped, a baby rides securely at her back while an elder child, barefooted and almost naked, trots patiently along at her side carrying a bundle on his shoulders almost as large as himself. Now, comes a man with a great drove of fat, stout legged hogs. Some of them are black, some are rust color, and many of them cannot walk without sitting down to rest. By a peculiar whistle of two or three staccato notes, which the unwieldy beasts understand and obey, the man in front lures such as can move to follow him. Assistants are in the rear who punch the loitering porkers forward.

At the same time one hears the *arrieros* hissing continually at the donkeys. This seems to animate them much more than the lash. It is a sharp, rasping hiss, almost like the *fizz* of a rocket, and the poor little burros wince under it as if they had *amour propre* to be insulted. Here is one with his back roofed by two boards about ten feet in length, extending far beyond his head and far beyond his tail, so nearly concealing the little animal that the boards seem to be moving along on four hairy legs of their own. On top of the boards rides a complacent turkey, lashed on and going to market, wholly unconscious that he is doomed to the sacrifice. He is followed by another burro bearing huge mats in which vegetables are bound up, and between the packs ride two fine little pigs, one on either side of the patient burro. They are tied; one is black, and the other has bristles of the fashionable Titan red, and they sleep as they journey to their death.

We desert the balcony, put on our hats and go out. There are multitudes of long, narrow, crooked streets, each one bounded on either side by a row of low, one-story, stone houses. The sidewalks are narrow, and often the inner half is of brick and the outer, of stone. The heavy eaves of the houses are wide enough to extend over these pavements which frequently are worn hollow by the generations who have trodden them. The streets are all clean. As in Vera

Cruz, they are paved with small cobble stones, the grade towards the center, where a shallow depression receives the drainage, and running water constantly passes, making it clear and clean as a country brook. Sometimes we find in a side street a woman on her knees beside her wooden trough doing her "week's wash" in these limpid little gutters.

Small as the greater number of houses are, they are ponderous in appearance. Massive doors of wood, often heavily studded with immense brass or iron spikes, and equally large windows form the entrance and furnish light. The window is a curiosity! Sometimes its base is level with the inner floor, and sometimes it is slightly raised above it. Its width from side to side in many instances is nearly six feet, and it projects beyond the face of the house about eight inches. It is not much more than a foot above the pavement, and the window seat thus formed, the width of the house wall included, is a trifle more than two feet wide. It is often seen paved with antique porcelain tiles and always enclosed on the outside with upright iron bars, each one an inch in diameter and set three inches apart. These perpendicular rods extend the whole height of the window from the base of the projecting seat to the cornice above which is nearly up to the eaves. There, they are finished with some slight, ornamental work of iron, and frequently surmounted with a cross. There are glazed doors set upon the inner edge of this window ledge which can be closed at will, and these are sometimes curtained; but, as a general thing, they are open and the passerby can look through the bars into the rooms, and very pretty rooms they often are, suggestive of sweet home life and house happiness among the Orizabians. Occasionally one sees several children seated in these windows gazing out or playing with their toys, and the effect is that of a great cage full of babies, hung upon the outer wall. The dwellings were built thus in the old Spanish days. Perhaps the strict lines then drawn around a young girl's social life may have had something to do with it. If a duenna locked the massive door and took the key, she certainly held prisoner whoever was within; and no ardent Romeo could possibly approach nearer than the frowning bars beyond which smiled his bewitching Juliet. What is built of stone and iron is built to endure, and however social customs may have changed, or burglarious dangers have passed away, the old houses with their massive *ventanas*[1] will probably last yet for centuries. Nu-

---

1. Windows.

merous are the tints employed in coloring the houses and public buildings. Fortunately, they are all delicate hues. Robins' egg blue, pale green, pink, gray, yellow, lavender and faint purple are all employed. Signs are never seen swinging in the street, but are painted on the outside of shops and stores, and if a house is for rent or for sale the fact is painted in very large letters on the front with accompanying directions as to where inquiries may be made concerning price, etc.

The freshening up of the old churches reminds one of the well-known habits of the ostrich. They conceal the rusty front with its prominent tower and the dome under a coat of fresh paint. The rear is left uncovered; its decay in strong contrast to the rejuvenated facade. Passing on through the town and down a side street we suddenly find ourselves among a succession of the most beautiful lanes stretching in every direction; unpaved and bordered on either side with lofty, verdant walls of foliage, the topmost branches of which meet overhead, arching the cool path underneath. These hedges are of orange, banana, azaleas, a species of palm and the rich, dark foliage of the full-fruited coffee tree, all knit together by luxuriant vines which swing their festoons and tendrils in the gentle breezes. Behind these beautiful barriers nestle the bamboo huts of the Indians. Here and there an opening among the leaves reveals the hut, with Indian children playing in the enclosure, mats on the ground upon which gathered coffee is spread to dry, bunches of bananas suspended from the humble roof for daily food and Indian women seated on the ground busy with needlework, or weaving *petates,* or preparing the dishes and *dulces* they will sell at evening in the Plaza. Meanwhile, the only sound is the rustle of the leaves, or the rattle of the drying coffee as the children stir it in some sunny place, or the twitter of a bird and perhaps the cry of a parrot. Enough sunshine filters through the arching trees which roof the lanes to call the grass into life, and through the middle of this verdant carpet runs a narrow brown path worn by the bare feet of the dusky dwellers in the village as they pass to and fro with their simple wares to town.

To emerge from the stone built city with its lofty domes and turrets, its rough streets, uneven pavements and hum of business into these peaceful lanes with their huts and flowers and fruits; their depths of tropic verdure and cool shadows and birds and primitive life in all its unaffected simplicity, is like turning from a stately page of Milton to one fervid with the glowing color and languorous dreams of some Eastern poet. These Indian villages are the great charm of the suburbs of Orizaba. They are enchanting. At the same time a pathetic interest attaches to them when one remembers that their inhabitants are of those tribes who were originally lords of the land, kings of the valley.

The Indian women all have luxuriant black hair coarse in quality of which they take great care. We often saw them in our walks seated before their doors combing it with large yellow combs made of orange wood. They part the hair in the middle and wear it in one or two plaits hanging down the back. Sometimes they braid with it strips of scarlet cloth which a little way off has the effect of strings of coral beads. Both men and women have remarkably small hands and feet. The women and children go barefooted. The men wear what seems to be precisely such a sandal as was worn by the ancient Greeks and Romans. It is made of ox hide, home tanned with leather strings to fasten it upon the foot. Cora and I purchased a pair of new ones with a view to bringing them home, but even after many days of exposure to sun and wind on the balcony they were so odoriferous, they never became sufficiently "aired" to be packed up.

The grace with which the men wear the sarape and the women the rebozo is something which at once strikes the lover of the picturesque. This ease is the natural outcome of that uniformity in dress which pertains to a simple and poor people. There is but one fashion. It does not change and long, long continued conformity to it has brought the way to wear it to perfection.

The rebozo is simply a long shawl about one yard and a quarter wide and from two and a half to three yards long. The ends are finished by a deep, handmade, netted fringe. It is usually of cotton although some are made of silk. One made of fine cotton is as costly as that made from the cocoon, and the price ranges from $1.50 to $25.00. The usual style of wearing it is to lay one edge upon the head just back of the forehead, leaving the width to drop below the waist behind. Both ends are now hanging in front. The left-hand end is left to fall straight down upon the skirt displaying the elegant fringe to the best advantage. The right-hand end is then carried under the chin and tossed over the left shoulder where it falls in graceful folds, partly over the left arm, partly down the back.

There are many other ways of wearing this garment, and it is made to serve purposes the variety of which amaze a stranger. Without it the Indian woman's costume is simply a chemise with a drawing string at the top which makes it high in the neck or partly so. With this she wears a skirt made of printed cotton reaching to her ankles. Sometimes the skirt consists of a woolen blanket pulled straight around her, lapping over at the sides. In her long trots to and from market she can be seen any day with a heavily laden basket at her back swung from a strip of braided straw passed across her forehead. Her rebozo, now dropped to her neck, has a baby swathed and tied in its ends in front where it serenely rides, its little head sticking out at one side, its two little feet sticking out at the other. Both head and feet go jig, jig, jig, keeping time to the mother's almost unbroken trot, but the placid infant turns its dusky little head all about, and its shining black eyes peer here and there taking keen observations of things in general and of many things in particular. Then one sees this arrangement reversed. A woman carries in each hand horizontally a light pole. On each pole hang two laden baskets. The ends of her rebozo tie up other commodities, while in it at her back sits a child, its little feet dangling below, its head appearing above, sometimes dropped in sound, sweet slumber against the mother's shoulder. Not seldom the rebozo carries two babies and the two ride contentedly in their cotton carriage apparently forgotten by the mother, who pays them not the slightest attention, nor seems in the least degree inconvenienced by them. It need not be supposed the Indian girl does not know how to flirt. Her rebozo is there her chief auxiliary. What the fan is to her more fashionable sister, the rebozo is to the Indian girl. It shows or shields her smile, betrays or hides her blush as she may choose. Sometimes it is drawn across the face so as to conceal all the features save the eyes, sometimes thrown back, so as to display the shining hair with its plaits coquettishly braided with scarlet strings. Now it is a signal; now it is a mask. It may conceal among the mysterious packages it covers the laundry basket or a love letter, a lottery ticket or a votive offering, a bunch of onions or a cluster of flowers. It no doubt mantles a multitude of excellences but, also like charity, it doubtless covers a multitude of sins.

The sarape is much the same style of wrap but is made of wool and usually has a combination of gay tints and a brightly colored border. It looks exceedingly well worn with the large picturesque sombrero. What the effect would be if worn with a silk "stove pipe" hat one can fancy. It is of all qualities and costs from six to thirty dollars, and extra fine ones are a much higher price. Carlota was so well pleased with this garment that several were manufactured at her order of exquisite color and quality at a cost of five hundred dollars each. These are still in the City of Mexico and can be seen there. No man is so poor as to be without one. The master, the servant, the Indian all regard it as a "necessity." On bright days it is seen folded across the shoulder if walking or strapped behind the saddle if riding, ready for any change in the weather. On cold days one sees bare feet, half naked legs and miserable cotton trousers below the warm sarape in which shoulders, arms and chest are closely snuggled up. It is said that nowhere in the world can a man don this simple garment with the picturesque grace of a Mexican. Once in a while on a dark, misty night a tall figure, half hiding under a crumbling arch or deep doorway with his sombrero drawn low over his eyes and his sarape thrown high over his shoulder nearly concealing all the lower part of the face, is a sight to make one feel startled and inclined to walk fast, albeit the lurker has nothing about him more dangerous than a few tortillas or dulces which he is sheltering from the rain.

We were surprised one morning as we walked out to find every house displaying draperies of white muslin or of lace. These were hung on the *outside* of the great barred windows, and falling half way down from the top, were caught up with blue and white ribbon, or with strips of blue and white tissue paper. On a few houses upper story balconies were draped in the same manner. As the sun was shining and the sky cloudless, the ancient town wore a gay and festive appearance. It was a great feast day in the Catholic Church to be observed with those contrasts of gaiety and solemnity which mark such occasions. The streets were thronged with donkeys of every imaginable age and color, laden with all sorts of merchandise for the market of the day. Loads of brick, loads of wood, loads of hay, of bedding, or corn, coal, vegetable, dry goods, crockery, bird cages, baskets and poultry went walking through the town, [the donkeys] completely concealed under their enormous burdens. Then women and children, equally laden, hastened along the highway, and meanwhile all the bells in all the churches rang clamorously making anything but a concord of sweet sounds. Even the dome of one of the principal churches had been painted blue and white, and from its tallest tower a blue and white banner streamed. Everyone was dressed in his or her best. The newest rebozo, the gayest sarape, the broadest and most silvered sombrero were out, and throngs poured into the sacred edifices (the interior of which wore the prevailing blue and white) to admire the lights and the flowers and the festoons, to listen to the music and to pray. Nowhere can be found a more devoted people than the Mexican Indians. How much they understand of the moral grandeur of the teachings of Christ, *¿quién sabe?* but the graven images, the splendid ceremonials with their accompaniments of lights and decoration and music wield a beneficial influence which could not perhaps be exerted over them by less imposing means. The mysteries, the magnificence and the poetry of the Catholic religion gratify and appeal to an aesthetic element inherent in these children of nature as is shown in their love of flowers, their appreciation of beautiful scenery, their delight in music and the picturesqueness of their villages. There is something very impressive in the sight of a congregation of them, the women wrapped in their uniform draperies kneeling on the floor and lifting up adoring faces and soft worshiping eyes; the men as they cross the consecrated threshold removing their hats and going forward to kneel down with an air of deep respect and most humble reverence. There are no pews, only a few scattered benches which are seldom occupied. In the street the priests wear a long, full black mantle, not unlike the Spanish cloak, and a tall silk hat, a garb which is strikingly distinct from the general costumes of the country. It is the secular dress adopted by them when the power of the church was overthrown in Mexico, but it indicates the sacred calling of the wearer quite as plainly as could gown and cross.

In the evening the whole town was a mass of blue and white illumination. The houses, the mills, the factories, the bridges, and even the tall church tower displaying the colors of the day. When a gun fired, we almost expected to see a blue and white flash precede the report. The balconies of the hotels and the cage-like windows of the dwellings were all gay with soft brilliancy of blue and white lanterns. It was the Feast of the Assumption observed everywhere in Mexico with great ceremony, and in some parts of the country with most remarkable demonstrations, such as peculiar dances which attract multitudes and are kept up with an absence of fatigue attributable entirely to the strength-giving powers of the Virgin, in whose honor the rejoicings are held. In Orizaba, besides the church festivities there were many delightful private entertainments, though when one walked the streets and saw the dense crowds it did not seem as if enough of the population were absent to make up a dinner party.

The scene in the Plaza was one of peculiar interest. Torches and flambeaux were flaring there, lighting up the dusky groups seated beside them on the ground. Brands were burning on tripods, sending up a lurid glare among the tropical foliage and lending a weird aspect to the scene. Indian children in long cotton skirts reaching to the ground, a bit of blue and white tissue paper pinned upon the rebozo or hat, ran joyously about. Men were quietly gay, women were smiling, and around the charcoal furnaces gathered an eager crowd of customers ready with *tlacos and cuartillos*. A *real* is a Spanish coin of silver worth twelve and a half cents. A *medio* is half a real, a *cuartillo* is the fourth part of a real and is a copper coin as is also the *tlaco* which is the eighth part of a *real* and is used to purchase the frying cakes hot from the fire. The *tamale* maker, the *dulce* vendor and the *enchilada* seller all were there busy with their cooking and their selling. Booths were bright with foods and wares, small tables were crowded with tempting viands and made gay with cheap decorations while up and down forward and back moved the quietly joyous and interested crowd. The loops and festoons of colored lanterns, the red gleam of the glowing furnaces, the yellow flames of the flambeaux and torches, the moving multitude of human beings in their picturesque garb moving about the narrow street and among quaint stone houses formed a novel scene of light and life and enjoyment.

We stood for some time before an Indian woman who was seated on the ground before a large pottery griddle placed over a bed of glowing charcoal. Her rebozo had fallen back leaving her neck and hair uncovered. Her arms and hands and shoulders were beautiful, and a flower of bright scarlet burned in one of her shining braids as she made a dough of wheaten flour and water. This she patted in her pretty hands, looking up at us meanwhile with a beaming smile that displayed her white and perfect teeth and lent her face an expression of sweetness well calculated to convert admiration into money. When she had patted the lump of dough for several minutes, she flattened it in her hands then proceeded to spread it over her knees which were covered with a clean white napkin. There she stretched and pulled it into a cake of extreme thinness. It seemed to be as cohesive as gum elastic, and when she had given it the shape and size of an immense pancake she baked it on the pottery griddle in a little grease. She laid it on a pile of similar cakes at her side. There was a great demand for these, and each one sold was spread with a sweet syrup when handed to the purchaser. These cakes were called *buñuelos*. The process of kneading and baking and handling them was no doubt as cleanly as that of making any kind of bread, but we did not feel tempted to taste one.

A wind sprang up, and the lanterns began to sway in the breeze and to blow out and to burn up. The flambeaux began to smoke, the streets began to thin, and the clock in the tall tower of La Parroquia was striking a very late hour as we turned away from the Plaza. This clock in the Parochial Church was presented to the city by the Emperor Maximilian. It strikes the hours and the divisions. After the lapse of half a minute it repeats the hour. Its dial is illuminated at night, and the timepiece in its lofty turret serves as a constant reminder of its illustrious but unfortunate donor for whom time is no more.

Another *fiesta* which we witnessed in Orizaba was an affair of the State rather than of the church, and called together many of the most prominent men in Mexico. A holiday of any nature, a celebration of any kind, is a matter of absorbing interest to the Indians who always expect to have their full share of pleasure in it and look forward to it with childish eagerness and delight. The day chosen this time was Sunday, and the drizzling rain called here *chipi a chipi* filled the skies with gloom and the atmosphere with dampness to the great disappointment of those who had looked forward to the coming of the day with so much gentle patience. Still the weatherwise looked at the mountains and declared they saw signs that the day would prove clear, and workmen planted tall poles on each side of the main street's sand, swathed them from top to bottom in stalks of fresh sugar cane or wound them with wreaths of evergreen. As if in response to the longing of the people the rain ceased. Then to the tops of the poles were fastened slender staffs from which floated the bright national colors—green, white and red—the three colors chosen to represent the principles "Religion, Union and Independence" which formed the basis of the political platform upon which Mexico established herself when separating in 1821 from Old Spain. When we went to desayuno in the morning there was a sound of clattering hoofs in the street, rumors going about to the effect that the President had arrived, occasional *vivas* ringing from zealous throats and a man was beginning to hang colored lanterns on the wall of the opposite building. All this was very encouraging and more banners of red, white and green appeared in different parts of the town, and finally the national colors were flung from the Governor's palace and also draped its balconies. From our own little balcony we hung the American and Mexican flags entering cordially into the spirit of the hour. Soon the street became animated by the presence of soldiers wearing white linen suits with black glazed caps. They were accompanied by a guard of twenty-five mounted men, all on white horses, caparisoned in the Mexican style. The men wore uniforms consisting of trousers and jacket of buckskin with a large grey felt hat. Each was armed with carbine, sword and pistol. A band of forty musicians played, and the concourse halted in front of the Governor's palace for the band to greet him with some of its choicest *morceaux* after which he rode out, accompanied by his staff, and took his place at the head of the column of marching men. More poles were now erected and tied with wreaths of flowers while each bore a long streamer of a solid color so arranged that the first bore a green streamer, the next a white one, and the next a red one thus repeating the colors of the country in regular order.

Every house displayed some decorations, indications of the general delight, and so various were these and composed of such materials that "still the wonder grew" where was to end the ingenuity in devices and appliances which the Orizabians displayed. Flowers and vines and boughs were abundantly used, and many of the ornamentations were made from the colored shining portions of a plant belonging to the agave family. The sections used were much like exaggerated sections of the pine cone. These, formed into every imaginable design, were placed on doors and windows and, sometimes, mingled with the petals of the scarlet orchid. They covered the facade of a church or the entire front of some dwelling. Yellow, red and blue in color they resemble mosaic work at a short distance or brilliantly painted tiles. The Mexicans call them *cucharillas*—little spoons. In the trees and upon every available place colored lanterns were hung, the gay paper of which they were made serving to adorn the city by day as well as by night. On all such occasions the Mexicans are rich in expedients and make a beautiful and tasteful display out of the most simple and inexpensive materials. Such a celebration in the United States with the usual gas illuminations and display of bunting must have cost thousands of dollars. I doubt if more than a hundred on this occasion was expended for banners and lights, and yet the effect was surprisingly beautiful.

The streets rapidly filled with delighted faces as the clouds began to disappear, and all the bells in all the steeples rang and rang and rang as if they never meant to stop; while *vivas* rent the air, and speeches were made, and soldiers marched and bands played. When, however, the hour came for church it was wonderful what a change took place and how quiet all things became. How deserted the streets, how silent, how vacant the public places, how full the sacred buildings. We went from one church to another finding a large attendance everywhere. The populace which a short time before had rent the air with shouts now knelt upon the stone floors and bowed their heads apparently oblivious to the fact that the outside world held anything besides their aves and paternosters.

When the sun went down and darkness came, however, all the rejoicing was renewed. The whole town burst into a blaze of artificial light with not a gas jet amongst it all. One could scarcely be made to believe, without seeing it, how much brilliancy and beauty this people can get out of a piece of tissue paper and two or three inches of tallow candle. Little paper buckets of green, white and red faced arches of evergreens which spanned the streets. A bit of candle in each of these made a bucket full of light and countless numbers of them were everywhere. The great mills vied with each other in their display of illuminations. The entire front wall of one was covered with many hued lanterns, arranged in arabesques. The effect, when all were lighted was admirable. At another every one of the many windows on the front and two ends was surrounded with colored lanterns, and a kiosk of illumination rose from the water above the mill dam, while in front of the dam lanterns were so arranged in rows, one above another, that as the water poured down behind the transparencies it seemed almost like a cascade of rainbows. The bridges were strung with lanterns, and from poles at each side of the streets ropes were stretched, and on these colored lights were strung, until the whole avenues were one succession of illuminated festoons which, as the breeze stirred them gave the streets an appearance of being all color where they were not all light. It seemed as if no place that could hold a colored lamp was denied it. Balconies, eaves, the great cage-like windows, down in the hollows of the river, up on the sides of the *Cerro de Borrego,* in gardens, on ruined walls, on gateways, in the lanes—lights, lights, lights; streets absolutely roofed with them and the gay hues of the tossing and floating banners as distinctly visible as in the broad glare of day. I had never imagined what beauty lay in tallow and tissue paper before, and as the story books used to say, we walked, and we walked, and we walked through the streets San Rafael, Calvario, Cinco de Mayo, de la Parroquia, de las Damas, de la Beneficia, de la Alameda and las Calles del Puente de la Borda y Segundo Principal, until we could walk no more over the worn, hollow sidewalks and the rough cobblestone crossings. At about nine o'clock a large concourse filled the main street, and every man and woman and boy carried a banner of green, white and red, on a long bamboo. Presently men with torches began to appear and at last everyone had a torch in one hand and a little flag in the other. Then mammoth transparencies appeared, magnified representations of such as one sees anywhere else on similar occasions, then Roman candles began to turn and powder lights to burn. Through the throng went the dulce vendor, his tray of sweetmeats on his head and in its center a colored lantern adding one more point of light to innumerable others. Rockets were now sent up, and there were loud calls for the Governor. He seemed to enjoy unlimited popularity and had evidently studied Chesterfield's advice and learned to take the people by the heart. He appeared upon his balcony and made a speech which was received with signs of great approval. He was frequently interrupted by shouts of applause and salvos of fireworks which seemed to go off in a frenzy of approbation. In every instance as their crackling and rattling died out the echoing mountains caught up the sound repeating it near and far and calling the words of the psalm to mind—"and the hills clapped their hands."

Then came a gang of workmen who planted immense batteries of fireworks at certain distances apart along the middle of the street. There were towers and triangles and wheels and serpents and arches and above them all rose stupendous affairs which the people called "castles in the air." These were a combination of all the other devices and were quite new to my rather limited experience in pyrotechnic architecture. When one after another of these were set off it was not difficult to believe the world had exploded. Such a noise! Such whizzing, and fizzing, and shooting, and floods of fire, and avalanches of sparks and everything apparently going in an opposite direction to everything else all at the same time! In the meanwhile were sent off rockets and bombs and "bouquets" and Roman candles which roofed the town with flashes of flame their green, white and red lights braiding themselves together in the zenith to untangle, as they fell, into strands of glowing fire which melted into darkness only to be renewed again and again. It was past midnight when we closed our massive doors against the boom of the last bomb, the hiss of the last rocket, the last burst of strange music.

These two *fiestas* furnished us examples of the manner in which public festivities are conducted in the country. They also showed us what a people cut off from expensive playthings and appliances of amusement either by poverty or by living remote from centers of wealth and abundance can evolve from their own taste and simple resources to embellish and render attractive an occasion of this kind. I never realized before the possibilities which lay in tallow and tissue paper, nor how a great celebration can be conducted on the most extensive scale to the satisfaction of thousands of people with no appearance either of meanness or extravagance. The Mexican are adept in making fireworks. Their manufactures in this line are declared by judges to fully equal those of the Chinese.

II

✦

Scenes around Orizaba

The cost of hack hire in Orizaba. Our coach. Victor, the cochero. *The bird catcher. A drive to the* Rincón Grande. *Cascade of the* Barrio Nuevo. *A visit to Jalapilla and its sugar house. The apartments of Maximilian. A view of Orizaba from the housetop. The young hacendado. Public amusements. A bachelor's comments on social life in Orizaba. The* Polacos. *The games and the gamblers. The dealer. The cotton factory of Cocolapán. Calico, its price and quality. Braniff's factory at* El Ingenio. *Workmen and system of payment. The Orizabian mode of washing clothes. The ancient church of Ostotiepac. Living pictures. Roadside groups. The blind man of the orchard. His remarkable powers. The village of Zocietlán. Its inhabitants. A visit to* La Escamela. El Conde del Valle. *A ride to the sugar estate known as El Jasmín. Mexican mode of peeling an orange. Mexican children and their usefulness. Soil of Orizaba. Products and possibilities. Enterprises which suggest themselves as paying investments.*

Hack hire is seventy-five cents an hour ordinarily in Orizaba. After working hours at night, however, on feast days and on Sundays it is one dollar an hour. The hacks are none of them new or elegant but all are closed, black, funereal looking coaches save one. This one, taken for all in all, is a very remarkable carriage and its equal probably could not be found anywhere else in the world.

Its body is a dull cinnamon red, much marred by time and weather. Its lining is of so many hues one is led to fancy that Joseph's coat of old had been made to serve the purpose. It has a caleche top, covered with a very ragged and much soiled white canvas. It will accommodate six persons—two on the back seat, two facing the back seat and two on the driver's seat. The running gear of this wonderful coach looks heavy enough for a locomotive, and the vehicle is drawn by two very small mismatched mules in a curiously patched up harness of ropes and chains and leather. Because it was the lightest and the "easiest" coach in town, and not because it was the ugliest, we chose it as a regular conveyance. Its crazy old top could fold back a great *desideratum* in this land of lovely scenery. "Victor" was the name of the driver—Victor with a red *banda* around his waist, a silver cord around his broad brimmed hat and his white cotton suit always showing a marked affinity for his "native" soil. He was a good looking Indian with shining eyes and hair and very white teeth. His weak point was *dulces* of which he seemed never to have enough, and the aim of his existence appeared to be how to obtain more. He knew how to make as few miles to the hour as the shrewdest of his class, but this was counterbalanced by his love of plying the whip lash which, being dexterously and incessantly laid on, accompanied by much hissing we rattled over the ground at a rate maintained by any of the "carriage people" in Orizaba.

A favorite drive was out through the Indian villages and past the hut of the bird catcher, an Indian whose occupation was to search the mountains for the sweetest songsters and sell them to passers by. He was learned in bird lore and an interesting person to talk with. We usually found him seated in the dark doorway of his little cabin while on its outer walls and all about on neighboring trees and among the bushes hung bamboo cages made by himself and containing some fine singer or ornamental bird of gorgeous plumage. On our way we were sure to meet scores of Indians walking into town; men, women and children trotting along with their various loads of merchandise up the narrow way. Nothing delighted Victor more than to drive so near he forced them to huddle like a flock of frightened sheep up the steep bank. Then with a disastrous upward whirl of that unerring whip lash, he would cut off a flower from some one of the blossoming trees which lined the path on either side looking as unconscious of the proximity of any pedestrians as if none were in existence. We passed through *con permiso* the gate of a large sugar estate known as the San Antonio, where the mills are grinding and the tall chimneys smoking and an air of business pervaded the place. Our road thence was merely a farm track and lay through open fields until we reached an old stone gateway. There we left the carriage to proceed on foot along a narrow footpath leading along a high narrow promontory extending into the river which makes its way around it in a secession of laughing rapids. On the other side of the river and opposite the terminus of the promontory, the eye beholds another stream plunging over banks of moss and ferns and divided by rocks into seven cascades which leap down into the river below which seems trying with all its might to run away from the seven demons plunging down. This waterfall, famous for its beauty, is called the *Rincón Grande*. The wildness and solitude of the spot so near a great city lends the charm of contrast to its other attractions prominent among which is a great variety of orchids glorifying the old trees which constantly bathe in the delicate spray tossed up from the tumbling waters.

Returning to the carriage we made our way through romantic lanes and wild roads to the *Barrio Nuevo*, where another beautiful cascade came sliding down the wooded heights to join the river now making its way along the floor of a ravine with rocky and precipitous banks. The water is parted by an inclined rock before reaching the river, and a natural curiosity is this shown in an immense face quite as clearly depicted as that which gives the name to Profile Mountain in New Hampshire. This represents a full face lying up-turned to the skies somewhat distorted as would be any face in such a peril-ous position, yet full of expression and quite complete in general outline. About the mouth and chin the moss has formed a fine green beard which the spray keeps in excellent condition. The oldest inhabitant declares the face has always been there, fast asleep at the foot of the fall. Cora tossed a handful of flowers to this Rip van Winkle of the *Barrio Nuevo*, and we hastened up one hill and down another across a brook on stepping stones and thence up a steep bank to regain the coach, it being impossible to drive nearer than within a quarter of a mile of the cascade.

We found the little mules dragging the old carriage about according to their own sweet will and cropping sugar cane from the unfenced fields *ad libitum*. Victor, meanwhile, sombrero in hand was flirting desperately with a dusky maiden about starting to town with a tray of the most tempting dulces on her head. Being well acquainted with Victor's propensity for *dulces*, we had our doubts about his attentions being exclusively directed toward the vendor of them for her own sweet sake and, in fact, as we called to him to drag his team from their stolen sweets we saw the tray lowered and Victor's best bow and brightest glance given in return for a handful of the best the tray contained. We then paid a visit to *Jalapilla,* one of the finest sugar estates in this region. It lay about one league southeast of the town, and the road that led to it possessed all the features which made every road about Orizaba delightful. As we drove through the gates of the plantation we found ourselves in front of a large, stone dwelling presenting to the road a long succession of white arches sustained upon strong stone pillars. Upon the roof a "mirador," or lookout, promised a magnificent view of the surrounding country. We were met as we left the carriage by a tall, handsome, young Mexican, whose language and graceful manners were those of his country although his dress was altogether English. We were invited to enter and were served with some refreshments in the library where we saw the works of some of the best English and American authors as well as those of France and Spain. We were allowed a peep into the sumptuous home chapel and after a long stroll in a beautiful garden visited the sugar house which was directly underneath a portion of the dwelling. The machinery was run by water power, and the crusher was fed by Indians, two attending to putting in the cane brought to them by others from laden carts near at hand, while two more on the opposite side of the cylinder took out the pressed and juiceless refuse. We were shown the sap boiling, cooling, graining, until it appeared before us in a tall semi-white loaf weighing an *arroba* or twenty five pounds in which shape it was piled into ox carts that moved slowly off towards the town. These loaves, broken up into irregular lumps or rolled fine in the kitchen for daily use, are the only kind one sees and are sold in the retail groceries at twelve cents a pound. We were taken to the brandy cellars and shown the huge butts of *aguardiente* looking rotund and burly and as if they would go reeling away were they budged one inch from their places. All of this brandy was made upon the place. Multitudes of black birds, almost as tame as chickens, flew about the sugar house and stables in immense flocks often alighting on the backs of the horses and cattle which showed no aversion to their presence. They are one of the common sights of the country, being part and parcel of all plantation premises. They seem to be much like the Minnesota black birds which there infest the harvest fields in immense numbers, although I never discovered among those of Mexico the orange-throated blackbird which Minnesota claims as being peculiar to that state.

Jalapilla was at one time occupied by Maximilian, for whom the father of the present owner entertained the warmest friendship. He lived here for some months during the brief period that he held the reins of Empire in Mexico, and it was hence he went determined to relinquish his crown and abdicate the country. On his way to carry out this wise resolution he was met by those who induced him to abandon it with what fatal result he learned to his bitter cost at Querétaro.[1] We were shown the sleeping apartment he had occupied, the sitting room and library which had been his, and also a large alcove at one end of the corridor about eight feet high by six in width which he had had fitted up for his birds. It was enclosed by wire on the outer side and was communicated with from one of the Emperor's rooms by a glass door let into the wall. The bird palace was entirely empty now, and the voices of the once happy inmates as hushed as his who loved them.

We were invited to the *Mirador* on the roof whence we could see picturesque roads down which wound in slow procession the oxcarts laden with their glittering *arrobas* of sugar, the oxen staggering under their primitive and unwieldy yokes. The sun which was descending threw lengthening mountain shadows upon the valley. In these shadows we could see men ploughing and groups of peasants, women and little children among their brown huts which stood out against the green of cane fields. In the distance shone the white wall of *Calvario* in which is reverenced a Christ that was presented to the church by a renowned Bishop, and further on rose the russet roofs and lofty towers of the town.

Our young host pointed out to us a neighboring mountain on which he had recently shot and killed two wild boars. The mountains abound in an infinite variety of game. Wild turkey and birds are plentiful, while the leopard, the tiger and the mountain cat add the excitement of danger to the pleasures of the hunt. Our host spoke enthusiastically of the sport and stated that notwithstanding its abundance the Indians had never been known to sell game in the market nor do more than inadequately supply themselves with it on great feast days. This reminded us of the fact that the nearest approach to a broiled bird we had ever had in our hotel was a broiled chicken which a member of our party went in to the kitchen and taught the cook to prepare.

1. Following a military trial, Maximilian von Habsburg died before a Mexican firing squad at Querétaro on June 19, 1867.

It had been unknown in that domain before and when cooked was peeped at by landlord, waiters, scullions and all as a *rara avis* indeed. We were urged to remain and dine at Jalapilla and taste some of the mountain game, but a servant appeared in the court below leading a fine horse very handsomely caparisoned evidently ready for its owner's daily ride. We therefore declined the polite invitation and drove away accompanied some distance by the young master of Jalapilla who rode beside our carriage. His lot seemed an enviable one. He was the youngest of three brothers who jointly owned the magnificent estate. He was college bred, had traveled extensively for a year or two, had tasted the pleasures of Paris and spent nearly the same length of time in London. He was accomplished in all manly sports and exercises and fitted by birth and education for the salons of the "best society" or the more ambitious ranks of the "professions" or the preferments of the political arena. His choice was the contented and happy life afforded by this quiet country home. His gun, his horse, his books and his share of the supervision of the place supplied him with sufficient business and pleasure to agreeably balance an existence which he found congenial and which certainly possessed the charm which pertains to freedom and independence.

Orizaba did not lack public amusements. A bull ring was established there in the ruins of an old convent, a circus from the States drew crowded houses, and concerts were occasionally given by a band of Mexican musicians so that we had classical music delightfully interpreted and also the beautiful Mexican airs which seem so in accord with the skies and hills and tropic valleys of the country that they sound nowhere so well as among them. Still, with all these resorts wherein to while away time, we met one evening an English gentleman whose business made him a resident of the place who complained that there was a lack of sociability among the people, and foreigners who came to dwell among them were excluded from all home life and were unwelcome in domestic circles. "You see," he said, "the routine of the day is over; one has risen early, taken desayuno, attended to business, breakfasted at noon, probably taken a *siesta*, gone back to business, returned for dinner and then what is there for a fellow to do? I mean a fellow who is here, a single man, who has no house but who is 'well accredited,' respectable, and considers himself a gentleman? He is tired perhaps of bull fights and circus rings; he is not expected to make any social calls, it not being the custom, so what is he to do?"

As the question seemed put in all seriousness I ventured to suggest he ought to establish a home of his own.

"Ah," he replied, "that is easier said than done. Save at church, I have not seen a young Mexican lady since I have lived here. No, there is only the circus or the *Polacos* now for one's evenings. I will go to the Polacos."

The "Polacos" are duly licensed and authorized games which during certain winter months convert the part of the city where they are established, in the neighborhood of an old church, now an interesting ruin. The booths are wooden sheds. The larger and rougher ones are enclosed with straw mats, and furnished with bare, board benches ranged on each side of long, rude board tables which extend across the whole width of the apartment. Here the highest stakes are lost and won and being always in money attract the largest crowds. In these particular booths there is nothing to attract except the excitement of the game itself. The lamps burn dully; the neutral tinted petates which form the walls bulge or hollow as the night wind moves them and absorb much of the light while the room is absolutely thronged with a dark uninteresting mass of human beings: men, women and children, all Indians, who sit in impressive silence studying their cards and listening to the voice of the dealer as he calls off the numbers from his platform near the center of the floor. Uninteresting masses did I say? Not so if one will stand awhile and watch their expressive faces which, eagerly attentive to the dealer, betray the exultant hope, the bitter despair, the triumph of gain, the disappointment of loss, all the excitement and pleasure and suppressed misery which belong to every species of gambling. Many of these Indians bring the savings of a whole year to the Polacos and lose them in an hour.

The smaller booths are also rough sheds inclosed on all sides, save the front, which is entirely open to the street leaving the gay, attractive interior in full view of the public. Here are tables and chairs for the players which are being constantly vacated and constantly filled as the crowd comes and goes. Numerous lights make these places brilliant; there is a quantity of tissue paper flags, enticing music, and a general air of festivity. There are prizes also in full view consisting of cheap but showy glass and china and plated silverware; red, blue, yellow and green and white cotton handkerchiefs; shawls; cravats and socks strung on lines across the booth or hung against the rough board walls and numerous other things to attract those who move up and down in the street outside drawing nearer at every turn like moths magnetized by the glitter of the light. The game is probably keno although to the uninitiated it seems very like loto. The player pays a *medio* (about six cents) for each chart of numbers or cards which he takes. This chart he places before him on the table. Grains of corn are distributed with the charts as markers.

In the middle of the room on a raised platform stands a man who resembles an automotor more closely than I ever supposed any human being. His dress is gay and bright lights display its colors and the glitter of its silver adornments to the best advantage. He keeps his sombrero on his head and draws off his cards rapidly, one after another, as rapidly naming each one, as he turns it face outward toward the spectators with the accuracy and dexterous monotony of a machine. The players meanwhile sit wrapped in rebozos and sarapes watching their charts. The men smoke, so do some of the women incessantly, and every man keeps his sombrero on his head. They mark with a grain of corn such numbers on their charts as may correspond to the card called out by the crier. When three numbers come out in regular order the player has won and announces the fact by a loud rap on his table—sometimes by a loud ejaculation. Otherwise, all are profoundly silent save the crier. When anyone wins he can either take a prize representing the value of the sum he has gained from among the articles exhibited or he can have the money. The men as a general thing take the cash. The women, however, delight in the bright china, the rebozos or toys for the little ones and seem to think they have won much more than money when their lucky numbers entitle them to its equivalent in any of the attractive prizes.

The cards used are Spanish cards, and their appearance is so entirely different from those in common use in the States that they are regarded in the light of a curiosity. There are four suits, but only ten cards in a suit. There are four face cards in each suit, viz: "As," "Rey," "Caballo" and "Soto" (ace, king, horse and fool); *Bastos* correspond to our clubs and somewhat resemble big sticks; *espadas* answer to our spades and resemble straight swords in shape; *copas* (cups) correspond to our diamonds, and *oros* (gold pieces) correspond to our hearts, constituting the pack of forty cards. Black and yellow are the predominating colors.

There is a sort of fascination in watching the intensely absorbed faces of the players. They are chiefly composed of the working classes, and there is something pathetic in the sight of these poor people staking their toil-earned wages on the turn of a single card. The patience with which they lose, the quiet delight with which they win, the anxious interest or apathetic resignation with which they listen to the cries of "As de oros"—"Dos de espadas"—"Siete de Bastos"—"Caballo de copas," and so on while the dealer flashes the cards, one by one, adroitly before their eyes has that in it which stirs the heart with sentiments akin to profound pity.

The cotton factory of Cocolapán is situated very near Orizaba and is one of the very interesting points to visit in the environs of the quaint town. It was established in 1856 and is the oldest manufactory of the kind here. It is run by water power furnished by the *Río Blanco* and within the last two years has been making, besides its white goods, a fair quality of calico, thus supplying a need long felt. The cotton prints hitherto sold here were of French, English or American manufacture, and low grades commanded high prices, the duties being very heavy. Calico is very extensively used, and there is a growing demand for it which is not likely to decrease. The majority of the Indian women dress in these prints and display such costumes on holidays with great pride, and well they may, for they are really costly garments. I paid eighteen cents a yard for American calico at a store in Orizaba such as I can buy anywhere in the United States for five cents a yard. It will be but a short time before every Indian woman lays aside her blanket skirt for the cleaner and lighter one of calico, and men array themselves in calico shirts with a pleasure which is not likely to lessen a demand for the article. There are but three or four cotton mills in all Mexico which supply cotton prints, and it would seem that there is not only ample room but absolute need for more.

Leaving Cocolapán with its beautiful garden and lovely natural surroundings we found our comical old coach awaiting us nearby. With an abundance of wraps for the cooler temperature sure to come with the evening, we started off in the warm sunshine of the afternoon for *El Ingenio,* a hamlet something more than a league westward on the old diligence road. Our objective point was another cotton factory which had been established near there by Mr. Thomas Braniff, an enterprising and wealthy American gentleman formerly connected with the Vera Cruz and Mexican Railway. There is so much that is romantic and poetical in the dreamy, tropical valley of Orizaba that one turns from the ever present picturesque to the contemplation of the practical with something like a sense of relief. Its mills and factories are to the visitor what the introduction of the comic element is to a tragedy.

Our little mules were fresh and gay and wore their nondescript harness with an air of great pomp; while Victor, a new cracker on his whip lash and his eye keenly alert for something to use it on, hissed industriously at the tiny beasts as we clattered along. How delighted he was when he found little Indian boys and girls sitting on a bank by the roadside! Deaf to our remonstrances, he would drive so close to their toes that it seemed only by a miracle that our big wheels were kept from going over them. Everyone, however, seemed to know Victor. The toes always twitched themselves out of the way in time, and the small faces of the owners glanced smiling up at the big *Cochero* whose broad hat was constantly tipping itself to some glossy haired girl when its wearer was not giving some quick word of salutation to men or women, strong or crippled, young or old as we passed them by. Of course, every donkey had to receive a greeting from that ever busy whip; but, at the same time, Victor managed to dexterously toss an orange (stolen a moment before) to the patient child trotting barefooted behind the chastised beast.

We were cordially received at the *Ingenio* and shown over the building where the music of the busy wheels was most pleasant to the ear. We saw the great staple as it progressed from its bale to the woven cloth in the folding room. The factory is a handsome, substantial structure built of stone, run by water power and illuminated by electric lights. A telephone connects it with the station at Orizaba, and the modern improvement principle is applied wherever possible. The "hands" are all native, many of them women and some of them children. These people work very deftly and intelligently and are paid according to what they accomplish by the so many pounds, then so many pieces and so on. This system of placing a premium on skill and industry appeared to meet the approval of all. They seemed cheerful and content and adroit at their work. There were in the factory six thousand three hundred and twelve spindles and forty looms. From twelve to fifteen hundred pieces of cotton are manufactured every week, besides the calico prints which is a branch of the business only established within the last few years at Orizaba. Each piece of cotton contains thirty-two yards—the Mexican yard is about 32 inches—and sells for four dollars a piece. The fall of water at this mill is some sixty feet, and the mill lands comprise the highest rise and lowest fall of the river commanding for the factory almost unlimited "power." American cotton is chiefly used, the staple of the country being too short though it is often mixed with that imported. The quality of cotton cloth made is what we know as unbleached factory goods. It is strong and warm and cheap, three great requisites where the purchasers wear it in cold weather as well as hot, wash it as if it were made of metal, and are obliged to buy it with very little money.[2]

No cotton cloth, nor any other washable material can last long here on account of the way in which it is laundered. As it must wear out rapidly its constant destruction insures constant demand. The Orizabian laundress usually takes the soiled clothes to the river. By the water edge a nice large stone is selected and after the garments have been sozzled awhile in a wooden trough with a little soap, they are placed upon the stone and paddled out of all consistency. They are then taken off and soaked again, then dragged about in the river awhile, then beaten again. They are then spread in the sun until their colors, if they have any, grow so weak they faint quite away, then they are rubbed a little more and paddled until the fabric has lost most of its strength. They then are hung up on bushes to dry and are rent by winds and pierced by thorns. Then they are dragged off the briery bushes with no consideration for their tender places, and afterwards are pulled and stretched by merciless hands until all such vanities as trimmings go utterly distracted and fall into shreds of despair. They are then scourged and scorched and pressed under the relentless flatiron and at last sent home with the assurance, which one glance substantiates, that they are very well "done up." For this process one must pay at the rate of one dollar and a half per dozen, and I don't know that he could get his garments worn out any cheaper elsewhere.

The scenery at *El Ingenio* is very beautiful and the tower of an old church rises from a neighboring hill side to contrast its grey walls with the ever blooming verdure. Of course, the church is very old, and of course it was built by Cortez! The edifice belongs to the ancient village of Ostotiepac. *El Ingenio* is upon the Río Blanco and a little country hotel with delicious baths occupies the former site of a sugar mill. It is quite a resort in summer for the neighboring townspeople who appreciate its shady nooks and cool, sweet waters, and the delightful quiet of its hills and glens.

We stepped again into our queer old wagon, and as the gray stone walls and glittering windows of the factory were lost to sight, our attention was

2. For an overview of the cotton textile industry from this point in Mexican history, see Stephen Haber, *Industry and Underdevelopment: The Industrialization of Mexico, 1890–1940* (Stanford, California: Stanford University Press, 1989).

called to the road over which we were passing, one of the oldest, as well as one of the most beautiful in the valley. Great mountains, rising on either hand, their towering slopes sometimes shaggy with pines and oaks, sometimes broken into gray, precipitous cliffs and occasionally beautified almost to their summits by the growing crops of the husbandman, shut us into a broad, level line of land through the middle of which ran the old Spanish road we were traversing. This was lined on each side with a luxuriant growth of trees and shrubs including a species of tall palm, which with its stiff, spike like leaves grouped in bunches, formed a marked feature in the thick verdure. Frequent bursts of roses brightened all this greenery, as they thrust their glowing faces through the hedge as if to see what was going on in the world or clambered to the tree tops as though to obtain a more extended view. The great white blossoms of the *Flor del bondés* drooped like sculptured bells among its branches waiting for the night wind to carry their fragrance out through all the valley. Of course, there was a living picture at every turn. Tobacco grew green and thrifty in the fields close by the highway, and tobacco in all stages of drying was hanging under the broad low eaves of the dusky little huts set here and there in the hedge. In the cabins or about them groups were seen so made up of youth and childhood, extreme old age, grace of attitude and novelty of surroundings that, familiar though they grew, we never ceased to see them with pleasure. Here perhaps is a bright eyed Indian woman, her sleeping child slung in a rebozo at her back. She has flowers for sale. We buy of her irresistible wares, and her serious face lights up with pleasure. There in a doorway, low and dark, is an octogenarian leaning on a stout staff with Indian children grouped about him of all ages and sizes. A little apart from all stands a crone so bent, so grizzly haired, so shriveled, and with such piercing black eyes she seems like some old Aztec witch who has been handed down from generation to generation. She leans upon a long, jagged stick. She wears no rebozo. Her white head, her skinny arms and neck are bare, as are her feet; and her thin cotton skirt and loose, low necked chemise constitute her only attire. She looks old enough to be the grandmother of the octogenarian in the door! She is ugly but invaluable in the picture. Back of all these is the hut; its roof thatched or covered with old russet tiles exactly the color needed here among the palms and vines, and over all and beyond all rise the mountains, blue and fainter blue, as they recede into the far distance. Further on we make our way past the droves of inevitable donkeys and their equally inevitable *arrieros* and the merchandise of the country which seems to be perpetually on the road, always going from somewhere to somewhere else. We come upon a group by no means uncommon in town. It consists of a party of Indians seated on the ground at the roadside taking their morning meal. They look up as we pass to utter the usual greeting, "adios señores" then turn again to their pulque and tortillas, as Victor cracks his whip with a loud report which sets our infantile mules in their heterogeneous harness off on a lively scamper.

Strolling one day through the narrow and crooked streets of the town waiting for horses to be saddled and brought around, we found ourselves before the bulging window of a neat little house in a street which an immense church and dismantled convent quite overshadowed. The window was inclosed by upright bars of wood instead of iron and the inner casement being open the interior of the house was in full view. It was lined, ceiled, furnished, almost floored, with pictures. It was an artist's studio, and the artist was at his easel making more pictures. Catching sight of us he politely invited us to enter, and once within the number of pictures we had seen from without was tripled. Among them were excellent copies of excellent old pictures and some admirable original sketches. We could not learn whether the artist painted merely for his pleasure or not, but from the appearance of his studio it did not seem likely he had ever parted with anything he had ever painted.

Among the portraits was one of a blind man, now dead, who had been blind almost from his birth, three weeks only of eyesight having been allowed him. He had been a remarkable man in some respects; the artist, as he had the painting in his hand, proceeded to give us some bits of his biography. The original of the picture was born in Orizaba, received a good education, studied medicine, and before his death came to be regarded as a very good physician. He was known as *el ciego del huerto*—the blind man of the orchard, and his peculiarity consisted in detecting and diagnosing a disease by the patient's voice. His sense of hearing was rendered doubly acute by the loss of sight, and he regarded the voice as the sensitive indicator of "all the ills that the flesh is heir to." He claimed that as it was capable of expressing all emotion, so could its tones and inflections unconsciously betray disease of any nature. A patient who came to him from Cuba wrote his life from accounts she had taken from his own lips and published it. Whatever foundation there was for his theory, he at all events performed wonderful cures. With a certain class of people, however, to believe in a physician is to be healed unless the disease is beyond all relief.

We wished to purchase a picture of the snow peak which struck our fancy, and we were immediately proffered it as a gift! This we courteously declined only to have it proffered again and again on our part politely declined, and in this way we made our way out through the multitude of stretchers leaving the devotee to art bowing in the door with the snow peak in his arms. We then put ourselves into habits and saddles and cantered away to Zocietlán, one of the largest Indian villages in the environs of Orizaba. It lay about four or five miles away to the southeast, a very old town whose inhabitants were said to be exceedingly rich. We arrived by fences of trees, shrubs and flowers shutting each house into a little park of its own. The shady lanes, for they cannot be called streets, are beaten smooth and had and have no stones, and there one can ride for hours in a solitude that is most impressive and a silence broken only by the tramp of the horses' feet or the sudden barking of a dog which has been left at home "to keep the house." The flame of a scarlet orchid will flash a bit of bright color before the eyes; ferns will swing in great clusters in the notches of aged and moss grown trees; some vivid vine will wed the palm tree to the orange; bits of venerable stone peep out looking soft as velvet in their coat of lichens, and overhead boughs intertwine roofing the lonely road. So dense are the thickets between which the pathways lie, one is obliged to be very watchful to get a glimpse of the thatched cabins shut in by all this shade and fragrance and beauty. The people are away at market or at their daily work on farms, and save in the early morning or at evening any one of these Indian towns recalls the image of Goldsmith's "Deserted Village."[3] No smoke curls up above the quiet homes; there is no sound of voices, and the "honest watch dog's bark" only adds to the strange yet pleasant loneliness. The inhabitants are of that class who "earn their bread by the sweat of the brow," beasts of burden in human form, but the love of the beautiful is ever present with them sure to manifest itself in one way or another, shining out from the hardships of their rude and rough existence like the vein of gold glittering in the rugged quartz. No hut [was] so poor it did not have its little

---

3. Oliver Goldsmith (1728–1774), *The Deserted Village, A Poem* (London: W. Griffin, 1770).

treasury of birds and flowers. Not seldom we caught glimpses of little household altars—a picture of the Virgin duly adorned and a cross below it, and the unfailing bunch of blossoms close by. To move along these floral and fragrant places, then to allow the gaze to go across it all on and up to the eternal snows on the summit of the mountain was to greet beauty on the threshold of sublimity.

We rode on to the little stone church, the facade of which was covered with *cucharillas*. Near the top was the national coat of arms and above that a picture of the Virgin. At a little distance the cucharillas looked like mosaic work, and the designs and coloring were highly creditable to the simple folk who out of their crude knowledge and material produced so good an effect.

From Zocietlán we rode back to the old camino real, passed through an ancient gateway of arched stone surmounted by the coat of arms of Spain, all of the time of Cortez, and drew rein again at the portals of *La Escamela*, a fine sugar estate belonging to Señor Don A. Arnaud. Refreshments were served, among them a drink made of the juice of oranges. Then came a brief visit to the sugar house where grinding was going on after which Señor Arnaud and his son, after seeing us mounted, had their own horses brought around. A friend of Señor Arnaud's also joined us, and, followed by two mounted servants, we all rode off to the cane fields. We met on the way processions of carts drawn by heavily yoked oxen by which means the cane was carried to the crusher. The plantation train-way had not found its way there yet though the immense crops and this slow method of transportation suggests its necessity to the American visitor. Grass roads divided the unfenced fields, and as we rode along on horseback the tall stalks were high above our heads and of remarkable luxuriance. Eighteen months are required for the first planting of cane to mature, but replanting is only necessary in from three to five years. The cane is considered at its best when it does not exceed eight feet in height, as beyond that the stalk becomes slenderer and the yield of juice is no better. Even the horses in Mexico are fond of *dulces,* and as we moved along our gentle nags managed every now and then to get their noses among the cane blades and seize a luscious mouthful.

The King of Spain bestowed upon Cortez the whole valley of Orizaba with the title of "the Count of the Valley." A large portion of these lands and the title still belong to a direct descendant of the great Conquistador and adjoin the hacienda of Señor Arnaud. *El Conde del Valle* resides abroad and lets out at a merely nominal rent the Orizabian lands which no money can buy.

From La Escamela we rode by a road somewhat rough but exceedingly pleasant toward *El Jasmín,* a magnificent sugar estate which belonged to Señor Don Amor Escandón. We were accompanied for a considerable distance by the courteous master of La Escamela, together with his son and servants. We had hitherto been prevented from accepting the cordial invitation to El Jasmín by northers which seemed to know just when we intended going there and always arrived in time to prevent our doing so. The "lay of the land" of this place is beautiful, being chiefly upon a plateau which makes the farm, with its green fields and gray stone buildings, an elevated landmark from many distant points. Our visit there was thoroughly delightful, and we especially enjoyed the extensive and beautiful garden kept more carefully than any we had seen. Pansies, violets, roses and other flowers were blooming in abundance, and orchids, rare and curious, were putting out their splendid blossoms from among pretty rockeries. There were groves of coffee, banana and orange trees, and we were served with fruit seated under the branches where it grew. Our host peeled my orange in the manner usual here. A fork thrust firmly into the stem held the orange on the plate. A keen knife cut off the rind from top to bottom, and one more thrust severed it entirely from the juicy mass leaving it to be lifted on the fork and there eaten. Only the luscious parts are thus obtained, the pithy portions being left upon the fork. I must say it did not strike me as a very elegant way of eating it as I looked around at our party each holding his fork and fruit and making rather sad work with the "new process."

This sugar farm comprised about three thousand acres and produced yearly forty thousand arrobas of sugar and great quantities of brandy. We witnessed the process of manufacturing the latter and visited the sugar houses where once more we saw the saccharine commodity in all its phases from the living, juicy stalk to its arrival at the gates of Commerce in its different shapes and qualities. I have often been impressed with the usefulness of Mexican children, and I was again struck with it here. A gang of twelve little boys from six to eight years old, I judged, all dressed alike in cotton pants and shirt and a woolen poncho over their shoulders and big straw hats on their heads were busily carrying off refuse from the sugar house across the yard. A large piece of sacking fastened to two long poles formed the receptacle into which they industriously heaped the pressed cane. Then one boy placed himself between the two poles like a little pony in shafts and took the ends in his hands. A boy at the other extremity did the same and so they marched away, forming quite a line as the sacks succeeded each other, and in this fashion carried off the loads of bagasse which were by no means light being quite as much as they could lift. They worked quietly and attentively without fun or play or mischief of any kind interrupting their business and with no one watching or directing them; I stood for some time watching the funny little procession going and coming as busy and as silent as ants and all looking contented and happy as if they felt themselves of considerable importance in this great world. I thought of sundry little African, Irish and American boys in and about great cities in the States whose mothers and fathers toil and suffer while their children loaf about the streets and drown kittens or place obstructions on car tracks or put themselves under locomotions or into calabooses and get themselves disliked in various ways, and I wondered what industry could be devised to use them up in a more remunerative manner.

As the skies began to look threatening we made our adieus and rode away from *El Jasmín,* its hospitable host in his high boots of undressed leather, his spotless suit of white duck and his broad brimmed hat walking beside us as far as the gates. No matter how unexpectedly one arrives at these haciendas in Mexico he finds the proprietor or the *administrator* not only always the gentleman in speech and manner but also the gentleman in dress. We never found "slouchiness" of any kind. No old boots, no battered, rusty hat carelessly worn, no shabby coat and untidy trousers considered "good enough for the country." The *hacendado* is always neat, even to elegance, and his hospitality is only surpassed by his courtesy. Before going very far the rain descended in torrents. It seemed as if the mountains had liquified and were pouring themselves down into the valleys. To eyes accustomed to seeing the floral treasury of the tropics guarded in conservatories, it seemed all wrong that they were permitted to be out in such a storm. The priceless orchids braved the tempest with the coffee and lemon trees and rested upon the boughs where they had enthroned themselves fearless and serene. The roads passed from moisture to mud, and from mud to mire, and we reached our hotel as thoroughly drenched and besplashed as an hour of such weather could make us. One of the boarders who could speak but little English met us in our wet habits as we hurried to our room and throwing up her hands exclaimed, "I think you *Americans* be made of gum arabic to go out such times as dis." We presumed she meant to say she believed us made of *India rubber.*

Should one go to Orizaba during the winter season with only a few days to spend, and those few days as might be the case should all prove cloudy and damp, he would receive and bear away not only a very disagreeable but also a very false impression of the climate and general attractiveness of the locality. Notwithstanding the "Northers" and the accompanying *chipi a chipi* and occasional violent rain, one does not suffer from the change of temperature which they cause. One day of sunshine is glorious compensation for many cloudy ones, and I have observed that invalids improve there in spite of fireless houses, in spite of bad weather, in spite of themselves.

It is an enchanting valley and being well watered and admirably located must, it would seem, attract capital and enterprise to profit by its advantages. Many "openings" suggest themselves and the situation of Orizaba upon the railroad makes the home market, as well as exporting facilities, accessible. Besides sugar and tobacco, corn, barley and beans are grown here. Oats, I never saw and I do not remember any fields of clover. Vegetables of every kind thrive well and are easily raised, and for live stock there is abundance of food, with a most favoring climate. I heard of no regularly established dairy—although we always obtained plenty of pure, rich milk. Butter there was no lack of, but it was pallid and unsalted always, and more like stiff and savorless cream than the rich, fragrant, golden product so familiar to American palates. No public laundry exists although the need of one is greatly felt, and if established, it would no doubt be well supported.

Lesser avocations of various kinds would readily take root here and expand themselves ultimately. This might equal the valley of the Var in the production of essential oils. Roses bloom in all seasons, also violets, and heliotrope, and fragrant orchidaceous plants; while the orange blossoms drop their luscious petals to the ground their commercial value not even suspected. The intelligent flower farmer has but to wind his way hither to recognize the fact that here is a rich, rewarding field for his delightful calling. Here can be produced attars and essences, oils and cosmetics, sweet scented sachets, and precious perfumes and flavoring extracts as successfully as anywhere in the world. The precious incense of the East and the odoriferous fields of France will find powerful rivals, someday, in the exquisite and exhaustless perfumes of the hills and valleys of Mexico.

The canning of fruits and vegetables ought also to be successful enterprise here. Fruits and vegetables are abundant, and very cheap. So is labor. The high duties on tin oppose themselves in some measure to the canning business, but this might be circumvented by using glass. Confections and preserves could be produced in infinite variety. The natives already excel in the manufacture of dulces, or sweetmeats, and understand how to work economically and neatly. They "work up" in this way many things which would be wasted. For instance, they use melon and pumpkin seeds in making certain drinks and cakes, and for candies resembling New Orleans *pralines* and also common "peanut candy"; they also use melon seeds in place of nuts. They prepare delicate and delicious sweet syrups, sweet pastry, candied fruits, *meringues,* and dried bananas. Coconuts, oranges, apples, melons, sweet potatoes and even pumpkins are used for *dulces.* There is no great establishment for these things, they being the home products of the people. They seem able to convert everything that grows into some sort of delicious preserve for which they have only local street sales; a tray on the head or a little temporary booth in the plaza furnishes them with a satisfactory market. Were their industry and experience in this line systematized and enlarged as they easily might be, the famous "Shakers" and the manufactures of favorite canned goods would have to look to their laurels. No country has a bigger "sweet tooth" of its own than Mexico, and it would prove a sufficient market for such products independent of exportation.

The mulberry tree grows well in Orizaba and the silk worm thrives. Experiment has proved that an excellent quality of silk can be produced there, and every element for the establishment of a silk business lies right at hand in the beautiful valley waiting only for capital and enterprise to combine with them for success.

12

✸

Puebla and Cholula

The Fairlie engine. Parting glimpses of Orizaba. The Meadows of Maltrata. The ascent of Las Cumbres. Wonderful scenery. Orchids. Apizaco. A branch road to Puebla. Arrival at Puebla. Its situation and appearance. Its cleanliness. Healthfulness of this locality. Price of living in this beautiful city. The marble works and quarries of Totamehuacán. The State Library. Famous tile kilns. The San Pedro Hospital. The St. Xavier Convent. The Laundry. Public baths. Public squares. The Cathedral and the tradition connected with it. Magnificence of the interior. The gold and silver chandelier and General Miramón's use of it. The highway of Cortez. Battle hills. Military chieftains. Porfirio Díaz. The mill of San Domingo and Don Esteban de Antuñano. Tlaxcala as Cortez saw it. The first Christian church. The banner of the Great Captain. Portraits of Aztec rulers. The old city of Cholula and the road leading thereto. The Toltec god Quetzalcoatl. The pyramid of Cholula. Its appearance. Obsidian relics. A pulque gatherer. The nopal and its uses. The Bishop's palace. Lampreys from the Volga. Again en route for Mexico City. Snow peaks and their heights. Stations. Pulque carts, arrieros. Approach to Anahuac. Arrival in Mexico City.

The Fairlie engine is a conception of inventive genius which has resulted in the birth of twin locomotives. A sort of double headed steam giant, the motors, in every respect the duplicate of each other, stand back to back, more perfectly blended into one than were those human doubles the famous

Siamese brothers. The Fairlie is mounted on two separate trucks, and the mechanism is such that one can be worked independently of the other where it is not necessary to utilize the power of both. It weighs about 20 tons, and is wonderfully powerful. At Orizaba it is substituted for the engine which comes out of Vera Cruz, and its utmost strength is needed to carry the train up the ascents it encounters between this point and *Boca del Monte.*

When the time came for us to depart from the enchanting valley of merry waters, our train was drawn away by one of these mammoth engines; its size and strength rather appallingly suggestive of difficulties to be surmounted. We moved out on a steep grade, which grew steeper after passing one or two small villages and crossing the Ingenio River. Looking back, as we wound on and up, the whole beautiful plain we were leaving smiled below us, and on a grade varying from 4 to 5 ½ per cent our track curved until the part just traversed lay in full view below. Up, still up. It seemed very much like being translated! If only some mantle had gone fluttering down to the plain below, we might have felt sure some modern Elijah was "aboard." The scenery was magnificent. Rocks, cliffs, gorges met the eye. The hills closed in upon us until they came and stood on tiptoe on the very verge of the track, waiting for the courageous monster dragging the train up the steeps to dash itself to pieces against their flinty faces. Through such rugged scenes we approached the grand, precipitous gorges called *infiernillo* or little hell. Emerging from it upon the beautiful vale of *La Joya,* before we could congratulate ourselves upon the change, we suddenly swept upon the second *infiernillo,* hell number two, I suppose it would be politely named—and again found ourselves shut in by mountains, mountain cliffs and gorges, and vast chasms whose depth the eye could not penetrate. Heights, barren and stony, divested of every vestige of verdure rose hundreds of feet above our heads and descended hundreds of feet below our wheels. We sailed around rocky promontories; we doubled awful capes; we tacked; we skimmed the edge of fearful ledges and swept across yawning gulfs. Here, the hills seemed to stand with their brows touching and there, knee to knee, like combatants suddenly parted. At last, a sunbeam dropped its ray like an arrow against a mountain's rocky shield, and we passed out of all this gloom and grandeur upon the pretty meadows of Maltrata. This is a thriving little town of several thousand inhabitants. Originally, it was an obscure Indian village, consisting of a few fragile huts hidden away among the hills, and known only to the hunter and the trader. It is now an agricultural town of considerable importance, and its huts have given place to neat and comfortable houses. The railroad found it out, touched its face with the magic signet of enterprise, and the first locomotive did the rest. Looking out upon this valley, the traveler marvels how he is to escape from it. There lies the path by which he came, but where is one by which he may depart? He looks to each point of the compass, but among all the defiant hills of stone he sees no way of exit. Westward he espies a path in the distance, a mere wrinkle on the face of one of the heights. Can that be his way? No. It is an old road known as the "Zig-zags," and looks as much like a crooked line drawn by a child on a black board as it does like the great thoroughfare where the diligences once ran. Suddenly, the engine gives a preparatory snort, and a whoop like the concentrated yells of all the Indians who ever lived in those parts, and away it goes curving this way and that and, having skirted the little valley of *La Bota,* begins the ascent of *Las Cumbres* up a steep path it has found for itself. Far, far above, like a fragile gallery projecting from the mountain's side, hangs a slender bridge. Oh, so high! And oh, so slender! Will that apparently frail structure sustain the weight of our ponderous engine? Dare we to venture on its iron stanchions which look, in comparison with the stony hills, like mere supports of straw? The heart beats with a mingled sense of terror and of triumph as we grope our way through cuts and tunnels, and surge around curves, all the time mounting, mounting steadily, surely, till at last we reach the bridge where we seem to hang over the village of Maltrata lying more than a thousand feet below. Looking down the sheer descent, the pretty town, with its rectangular streets, looked like a toy village set out on a chess board. One is reminded here of the famous old lady who in crossing [the] suspension bridge at Niagara said she felt all the time "like holding in and bearing up in order to make herself as light as possible." Should she ever cross the lofty viaduct of Maltrata she would probably make an "airy nothing" of herself at once. The bridge passed, still we go climbing on up, up, as steadily as ever went Jack up his beanstalk. We are five thousand, six thousand feet above Maltrata's meadows, so high that one begins to think he is making a balloon ascension. But, the grim monster guiding us boldly overcomes all obstacles, and leads us safely "over the hills and far away." Nothing can oppose his progress; not crags, nor cliffs, nor rocks. Here, aiming at the left of one, he suddenly turns and passes on its right. This one, he crumples under his feet and crawls over; that one, he rushes at, head on, strikes it "below the belt," and runs under it with the ease of an athlete. Precipices strut out and seem to stand directly across our track. He cautiously feels his way around them. While our train creeps along the narrow ledge vouchsafed it is like a procession of ants on a telegraph wire. Just as one begins to feel familiarized with the stupendous climbing and the immense cuts whose walls crowd so close one grows saucy and inclined to jog the elbows and poke the ribs of these old fogy upheavals called hills, the train sweeps out upon the edge of *Las Barrancas Gemelas* (the twin ravines). We lean from the car windows to gaze down upon venerable trees and the greatest profusion of orchids. All down the banks they shoot up in blood red cones, or hang in variegated fringes, or droop in pendulous, grass-like groups sensitive to every motion of the air. Gnarled knot and crooked branch are covered by them, and even the arid and deformed rock lies under a carpet of lichen so intricately woven, so rich, yet, so subdued in hue, it might serve as a model for the looms of Persia. Here, too, was a plant like a thistle though its blossom was the most vivid red and its stalk and leaves of an equally gory tint. One of the orchids had a scarlet cone shooting up about twelve inches from the center of its spiked, stiff green leaves. This the Mexicans call *el corazón de Jesús* (the heart of Jesus), why, this deponent knoweth not. When fully grown, tiny blossoms of purple and gold put out all over the surface of the red cone. It is much sought after as a decoration plant for hanging baskets and for pots to adorn the corridors of Mexican houses. All the way from Maltrata, the grade has been from four to four and a half per cent, but the long ascent is almost ended now. At every portion of the long climb one is impressed with the conviction that there is no audacity of nature which the audacity of man will not attempt to overcome. The greater her opposition, the more ingenious are his devices to master her. He storms her strongholds, captures her secrets, conquers her conquests. Science transmutes his dreams into realities, his ambitions into successes. If today the world holds its breath in awe at his boldness, it is only to shout the louder tomorrow at what his courage has achieved.

At *Boca del Monte* the ascent ended. The wild grandeur of the Cumbres was exchanged for pastoral scenes among the broad fields of the central table lands. We were now on the last of the steps that lead up from the coast to the Metropolis of Mexico and in the third climate—that of the *Tierra Fria*. The crops had been gathered, and here and there we saw threshers treading the grain and winnowing it by tossing it in the air for the wind to blow away the chaff! Occasionally, a plowman could be seen patiently following a wooden plough of the most primitive construction—antique enough in appearance to have turned the furrows of Pharaoh. Our road now lay through farms, and the dust from which we had not suffered at all in climbing the mountains became almost intolerable. The stations of Rinconada, San Marcos, and Huyamantla followed each other in quick succession, possessing little of interest excepting their foreign sounding names. Great stacks of grain and fields of corn stubble spoke well for the lands agriculturally, but the great drawback to the farmer here is the long dry season and lack of proper means for irrigation. It has been suggested that if a system of artesian well sinking were adopted, the productiveness of these plains could be doubled. The haciendas form a striking feature in the landscape, and most of them indicate wealth and prosperity.

At Apizaco, which is eighty-seven miles from the City of Mexico, a branch road forty miles in length leads to Puebla. As we wished to visit the latter city, we left the upward bound train to await the one which would leave for Puebla some time between midnight and morning. The sleepless ride was a very cold one and made our fur wraps an absolute necessity.

We were met at the depot by the Governor's aide looking very chilly, despite his long cloak of fawn colored cloth with ample cape and hood; the latter drawn over his head. As additional equipment he wore a pistol strapped about his waist outside of his cloak. The Governor had sent his own carriages to convey the party to the best Hotel. Here to Cora and me was assigned a vast sleeping apartment with two single beds situated in corners diagonally opposite, and at such remote distances apart the occupants could scarcely be in speaking distance of each other. The delightful baths which are a prominent feature in every Mexican city were not lacking in Puebla, and we were soon refreshed and ready for breakfast. Whilst partaking of this meal callers arrived and came at once to the table which seems to be a social Mexican custom, one certainly pertaining to hotel life. Declining to share the repast, but politely begging us not to interrupt our own, they chatted until we were ready to go out for a walk. The temperature in the middle of the day is of a charming Indian summer mildness, and the wraps required for early morning and for evening are then unnecessary.

Puebla is situated upon a beautiful plain which the Indians, long before the coming of the Conquerors, called *Acajete*. It is the capital of the state of the same name, and the seat of a Bishopric. It is one of the very few notable towns in Mexico which was not founded upon the site of some aboriginal village wrested by conquest and slaughter from its primal possessors. The Spaniards found here a rich agricultural district, the lovely river Atoyac flowing near at hand, and here and there a few straggling huts pertaining to neighboring Indians in Cholula. A little colony, consisting of 33 men and one widow, accompanied by a priest named Julián Garcés, first chose the spot as a dwelling place for the whites. The city was founded September 28, 1521. The first houses were made of mud and thatched with straw, but straightway a substantial church was built. That the city flourished cannot be doubted; inasmuch as within forty years a decree of Madrid established the Inquisition there, whose Inquisitor General, Don Pedro de Contreras, was the first to carry out the terrible decree of the *auto de fé*. And still it flourished; for in 1736, the fearful epidemic which overran the country carried off 54,000 victims in Puebla. But still it flourished, and continues so to do for, although it has passed through waves of bitter fortune and known the horrors of battle and of siege, at this present writing it has a population of seventy-five thousand, and no city in the Republic excels it in beauty of architecture, regularity of plan, cheerfulness and cleanliness. Its streets are wide and run at right angles, its parks are spacious, and a fine aqueduct conveys water to more than forty fountains in different parts of the city. It contains numerous benevolent and educational institutions, and, besides its marble works, it has manufactories of glass, china, pottery, tiles, soap, tobacco, cutlery, cotton and woolen goods. It has been asserted that its cutlery fully equaled that of Toledo. The town lies about seventy-five miles southeast of the city of Mexico, although the distance between the two places by rail is a trifle more than 133 miles. The inhabitants feel a very natural and commendable pride in the prosperity of their beautiful city which holds such high commercial rank in the Republic. Rent is much less and living cheaper in every way in Puebla than in Mexico [City], and the general health is quite as good, if not better. The very sight of neatness is conducive to health, and it is constantly in sight in Puebla.

Accompanied by Professor —— we went to visit the college, which is a building originally erected by the Spanish Jesuits, and used by them as a theological seminary. When church power ceased in Mexico, the building passed into the possession of the government and was converted into a State educational institute. A very thorough system of instruction is provided for one thousand students, and it has been the *alma mater* of many of Mexico's most brilliant men. The rooms are pleasant and well lighted, and the religion of cleanliness is everywhere apparent. It contains a large and very valuable library, including many rare and ancient, vellum bound books. The department devoted to chemistry is very interesting, as well as those pertaining to geology, entomology and ornithology. The Professor is an ardent scientist himself, and the earnest aim of his existence is to promote similar taste in others. The feathered tribe was represented in a remarkably fine collection. Many of the native birds were exceedingly curious and had lost not the least of their marvelous hues in the hands of the taxidermist. Humming birds in great numbers and of infinite variety were suspended on delicate wires in most natural attitude, their brilliant throats looking as if they had been fed on tidbits of splendid sunsets all their little lives. They could have easily been mistaken for brilliant jewels fashioned in the form of this winged darling of the Aztecs.

We found the famous marble works located in one of the old convents, the ruined walls of which attest to the iconoclasm of Progress. The song of the busy machinery today goes up where formerly priests chanted and nuns knelt. Which truly serves God, the convent or the workshop? The hum of the engine, the rasp of the saw, the whirl of the great polishing wheel are the hymns which intelligent labor now sings upon the very spot where ignorance and superstition once blocked the wheel of advancement. We were shown many specimens of the Puebla marble or Mexican onyx, and all were beautiful. This marble is brought from the quarries of Totamehuacán, two leagues from the city, and from Tecali [teocalli] which is seven leagues away. The Pueblans deem the quarries inexhaustible; one of the workmen quite seriously said to us he believed they contained "enough to pave the world." For mantles, columns, tiles, tables, etc. it is admirably suited. Its tints are rich, and their variety unlimited. It is translucent, takes a beautiful polish, and in some pieces the veining makes such distinct outlines and the hues are so admirably dispersed that figures and landscapes are clearly seen, as if sketched there by an artist. These they designate as picture marbles. The quarries provide one of the chief adornments of old Mexican churches, where the marble is seen wrought into pillars as smooth as crystal and as delicately tinted as the choicest china of Sevres. The churches also use it for panels and tiles, and in some

of them thin slabs of it serve for windows and admit a light as soft and
subdued as stained glass. Some of the baptismal fonts made of it are marvels
in size and magnificence. It has not the whiteness and consistency necessary
for statuary; but for decorative and many other purposes it is unequaled. The
Emperor of Brazil is said to have made lavish use of it in the adornment of
his palace but, very little of it, strange to say, finds a market out of its own
country, and to be seen at its best it should be seen in Mexico.

We visited the state library where, in addition to thousands of rare and
valuable books, some exceedingly choice collections of engravings are preserved. The floor of this library is of square, red brick tiles intersected with
small ones of glazed blue china. The effect is pretty though extremely quaint.
Puebla has numerous tile kilns the products of which are acknowledged to
be the best made in the Republic, and she is their own best advertisement.
They are profusely used for many of her beautiful churches both upon the
outside walls and upon the interiors. In the old convents the display of them
proclaims that the austere nuns were not entirely dead to "the pomps and
vanities of this wicked world," and it is a common sight to see them set into
the fronts of shops and houses against a ground work of rich red, and arranged in divers patterns. Sometimes they are managed well and have the
appearance of mosaic work and again are so introduced upon the building
that the whole fronts look as if covered with gay oilcloth. But, even when
inartistically arranged, they are suggestive of great cleanliness and have a
bright, cheery aspect; besides relieving the city from that prevailing stone
gray tint which pertains to nearly all the other towns of note in Mexico. The
San Pedro Hospital, located in a large building which was once a convent, is
a notable institution admirably conducted and sustained by the State. The
different schools of medicine are provided with ample accommodation there,
so that a patient can be conducted back to life, or out of it, by any path he
prefers. The grounds about the building are very pretty and well kept up.
There are two lunatic asylums, one for women, the other for men. They are
both state institutions. That for men is in a convent from which, by the overthrow of papal power, the nuns of Santa Rosa were driven. Whoever desireth
to feast his eyes upon tiles let him go there. Tiles are everywhere, above,
below, beyond. The whole interior is tiles, and someone dared to say it was
the most *tilish* place we had seen. They had been left off of no place that
could hold them, and one is apt to remember there that he is in a glass house

and mustn't throw stones. We drove to the battle hills and the Alameda and enjoyed the lovely walks in the promenades where the Pueblans congregate in their fashionable outings. We saw the sulphur baths and had a look at the convent of St. Xavier, the battered walls of which give bruised and broken evidence of the terrors of the long French siege. We visited several churches, in some of which the carved ceilings and graven stone were very beautiful and the next step, naturally, as "cleanliness is akin to godliness," was to the laundry.

In this establishment we found nearly a hundred Indian women employed. They were kneeling before stone troughs which were supplied with water from a running stream admitted to the building. They soaped and rubbed and dipped and dawdled and rinsed and wrung their washing with pertinacious patience, grave inspection of garments submitted to their cleansing care, and great expenditure of strength which might be saved in some measure by the introduction of a few patent wringers and washing machines and other modern improvements. After the laundry we were shown more baths where for a few sous a pauper may wash himself as clean as any prince. When Cortez entered the ancient city of Tlaxcala he remarked the existence of baths "both of vapor and hot water" and alludes to the fact in his letters "as evidence of the refinement of the people." That evidence of refinement has been scrupulously preserved by succeeding generations. All over the country baths abound, many of them luxurious, all of them delightful and [they] form a prominent feature in the general provisions for public comfort. They are either of marble or porcelain with a supply of hot and cold water and are particularly inviting when lined with bright, gaily tinted tiles which always shine with cleanness.

Puebla boasts of more than a score of public squares. All are pretty, flowery, enticing looking places, but the grand plaza in the center of the town presents the most interesting features. A street surrounds it. On the east and west sides arcades face it. Here vendors of an infinite variety of small wares are established, and there are throngs of passers by. On the north side is the Governor's palace and on the south side raised in majesty is its famed and beautiful Cathedral which, tradition states, the angels helped to build. The material used in its construction seems rather heavy to have been put in place by immaterial hands, but anyone will tell you, and hosts of persons devoutly do believe, that when the Cathedral was in course of erection, two angels

nightly did descend and add to the walls the same amount of work the builders had put upon them during the day. Thus, when the masons returned in
the morning to their labor, they found it mysteriously advanced, and by this
divine assistance the sacred edifice was completed in a miraculously short
space of time! The legend has been repeated in the household and taught in
the convents, and handed down from generation to generation, until the
beautiful story is likely to be always connected with the beautiful church.
From this tradition the city came to be called *La Puebla de los Angeles*. The
town of the angels.

The Cathedral stands upon an extensive platform raised several feet above
the level of the street. We ascend the eight or ten steps leading to this elevation and find ourselves upon an extensive plane entirely paved with foreign
marble and kept scrupulously clean. From the middle of this shining floor,
placed apart and above its more worldly surroundings, rises the majestic
church, grand in general outline, beautiful in detail. The effect is noble and
imposing. It is built of dark, grey stone known, I believe, as blue basalt. It has
two lofty towers and two domes: the large one in the center, the smaller one
at the back. Between the turrets and facing the north is the main entrance
with sculptured saints and martyrs in niches on the outer walls, and above
the great portals are bas reliefs and other sculptures representing scriptural
scenes. There is another entrance on the western side also adorned with
chiselings, and a date in carven stone records the completion of the edifice in
1664. On the face of the western tower is set an ancient clock sent from
Madrid two hundred years ago to mark the fleeting hours in the marvelous
kingdom of New Spain. The marbled space in front of the main entrance is
divided from the street by an ornamental iron fence, its sections supported
by posts of staunch grey stone. Each post has a bronze bas relief set upon its
outer face, and its top is adorned by a bronze or iron angel with outstretched
wings. The architecture of the building is generally conceded to be of the
most superior character and surpassed by few if any of the ecclesiastical
edifices noted for their beauty.

The effect of the interior is splendid and solemn. Everywhere is felt the
"glory and the majesty." Stone pillars ninety feet in height sustain the lofty
ceiling which is most elaborately and beautifully carved. These massive columns divide the vast space into three parts, the main body and the side aisles.
Beyond the side aisles are the smaller chapels all elegantly fitted up and par-

titioned from the main floor by tall, light open railings of iron. The principal altar was erected by a noted Bishop of Puebla in 1812. Marble steps and massive railing, taken from Pueblan quarries, lead up to a circular floor elevated about ten feet above the floor of the church. The sixteen fluted pillars which support the roof of the altar, the edge of each groove inlaid with gold, display twenty-eight different varieties of Mexican onyx varying in hue from the purest alabastrine whiteness to the richest and most exquisite tints. The whole is surmounted by a golden image of the Virgin. Beneath this altar is the sepulcher of the Bishops, to which we descended. The most precious materials and careful workmanship have been lavished upon this crypt. Around its interior are built the horizontal niches, each sealed with its sculptured panel, where lie the dead ecclesiastics. The floor is marble, and the vault is covered by a richly ornate depressed dome of marble from the center of which is suspended a beautiful silver lamp kept perpetually burning. This magnificent mausoleum, despite its pomp and splendor, has something repelling in its emblazoned grandeur which does not pertain to tombs domed by the sky and played upon by sunshine. Facing the front of the altar is the choir rich in antique carvings and mosaics. The chairs of massive cedar, almost black with age, are inlaid with ivory, and the carvings on the woodwork are elaborate. Above the seat of the Bishop hangs a picture of one of the saints. The flesh, the drapery, the expression, all are so skillfully wrought that one can scarcely realize it is a wood mosaic. The inlaying has been so artistically managed that the different woods produce the effect of an oil painting.

In one of the side chapels a picture was shown us of a kneeling saint which has long been in possession of the church. It is admirably executed and in an excellent state of preservation. Ten thousand dollars had been refused for it, yet no one seemed to be able to tell us the name of the artist. We were taken to the sacristy which we found hung with needlework tapestry, not unlike the Gobelin,[1] said to be the work of the Ladies belonging to one of the ancient courts of Spain. It represented landscapes and life size figures depicting some legend perhaps. Maximilian hoped to purchase three portions of the tapestry for his palace in Mexico. He offered twenty thousand dollars for it, which offer was declined. Above the hangings the walls were adorned with the por-

---

1. Reference here is to the Manufacture Nationale des Gobelins, a tapestry works in Paris founded in the mid-fifteenth century by Jean Gobelin.

traits of the twenty-eight Bishops. The antique chairs, the table and other opulences of the sacristy were very curious and costly.

Time was when to enter this church must have been like entering one of the fabulous caves described in Eastern tales. Around the base of the principal altar stood massive candlesticks of solid gold and silver so heavy one man's strength was not sufficient to move even the least of them. Near the principal altar the life size image of the Virgin wore a crown of pure gold studded with priceless emeralds. Her gem embroidered satin robes were girdled at the waist by a zone of diamonds. Every portion of her person where a jewel could be displayed possessed one of great price while from her neck descended ropes of pearls of incomputable value. Under the vast, central dome at one time was suspended the stupendous gold and silver chandelier of almost fabulous price. The worth of workmanship upon it far exceeded the immense cost of precious metals of which it was made. It is known that four thousand dollars was paid at one time to have it cleaned and reburnished. Revolution and decrease of church power have done away with something of all this. There are still massive candelabra in profusion. The Virgin is still there, life size and magnificently attired, though far less sumptuously than once upon a time, but as for the great chandelier, General [Miguel] Miramón, in order to meet exacting necessities of the army in 1862, caused it to be taken down and melted to cancel his urgent requirements. The church denounced this act as an outrage and a sacrilege but Miramón, like Dionysus in the temples of old deemed it his right to "make use of the bounty of the gods." He made out of the great luminary between forty and fifty thousand dollars with which he paid his troops and relieved other pressing military necessities. One can scarcely realize that the splendid interior has been despoiled of any of its treasures. There seems no room for more. The quarries and the mines have yielded up their most precious stones for the adornment of the edifice, and the most cunning artificers have wrought them into things of beauty. Gold and silver, gems, marble, mosaics, carvings, hangings, illuminated missals, pictures and statues yet remain. Yet also remain the three wonderful sets of jewels consecrated to the Bishop's use, and costly antique altar services and lesser costly things innumerable; so that although much has been taken away its absence is not even suspected by those previously ignorant of its existence. Though on a lesser scale of grandeur, the earliest Spanish churches in the country were built with the same view to imposing effect.

All the magnificence possible to command was lavished upon them. The oldest edifices of this kind throughout Mexico show gilding without stint, and frescoes, images and carving. Could it have been difficult for Cortez to win over with all his pomp and splendor so impressionable a people as he found here? What were their brick and lava pyramids to the resplendent temples which he reared? What their grave images to his bedecked with marvelous stuffs and gold and gems? What their rude drums and ruder pipes to his grand and pealing organs and his reverberating bells? The frescoes of his lofty roofs, the mosaics of his floors, the sheen of his altars, his resounding towers, the swinging of his scented censers, the pomp of his bloodless ceremonies must have found in the susceptible nature of the Indians speedy recognition and acknowledgment. But, not content to sign the entire nation with the sign of the cross, his spirit demanded that the sign should be made always in human gore.

There are no pews in the Cathedral of Puebla, no seats of any kind provided for the congregation. The broad floors of the vast building are free to all, and the lowliest Indian has as much right to choose her place and kneel there as the proudest lady of the land. It may strongly test the spirit of true, Christ-like humility sometimes to worship in this way where one must find it difficult to "love one's neighbor as one's self," especially if the "neighbor" be a blanketed Indian in a condition of supreme unwashedness and uncombedness, but where should the law of equality be fully recognized and carried out if not in the Christian Church?

We ascended the winding stone stairway to the towers in each of which a keeper lives with his family. Everything was beautifully clean. In the western tower hang nineteen bells in the composition of which a generous proportion of silver was used. There is a ponderous central bell and eighteen of smaller size. The largest one bears [the] date 1729, and the dates upon the others come well down into the present century. We heard them ring. It was a case where distance would have lent enchantment. They were no doubt "sweet," but one doesn't find it out with his ears too close to the clappers! An indentation was pointed out to us in the stone on the inside of the tower where a chance ball from the hill of Guadalupe came crashing in during the French siege. A carved inscription records that the towers were finished in the year of our Lord 1678 at a cost of 100,000 dollars. We felt personally grateful for the expenditure of so much money when we beheld the extended and varied

view commanded by the costly turret in which we stood! The beautiful city
with its broad streets, its curious, tiled facades, its arcades, fountains, plazas,
palaces and picturesque ruins lay spread out below us, bounded there by
brown hills and here by fertile fields devoted to the raising of corn, wheat,
tobacco, barley and the maguey plant. Eastward shone the silvery sign of
Orizaba, its western face toward the great plateau of *La Tierra Fria*. Westward towered the snow capped heights of Popocatépetl and Ixtaccihuatl,
their crowns carved in eternal ice against the deep, blue sky as they stood out,
kings of the kingdom of hills over which they reign. Between these last two
mountains is discernible the rough and precipitous road by which Cortez and
his soldiers wended their way to the valley of Anahuac and the "Shining
City." It is rapidly falling into disuse and will soon be one of the forgotten
paths of the people. Here too is obtained a fine view of the mountain aborigi-
nally named Matlalcueyetl. It is in the state of Tlaxcala and is now called
Malinche, a name bestowed upon it by the native allies of Cortez in honor
of the conqueror and Doña Marina both of whom they called Maliutzin or
Malinche. It is an extinct volcano and does not soar into the regions of snow.
At certain times of the day seen from the church tower it assumes an especially interesting aspect, as near its summit lies a gigantic face with a strange
fascination in its wonderfully distinct outlines. All the features are there—
nose, mouth, eyes, even the eyebrow. Upon close inspection, no doubt, the
nose would be found to be a butting crag, the brow an overhanging cliff, the
eye a gorge and the mouth a broad ravine. When nature condescends to
carve "heads" she does not stint herself for material.

Near the edge of the town lay the vast pile once the convent of San Francisco, and in the distance rose countless domes and towers consecrating the
slopes and crowning the hills giving mute testimony of former church power
in and about Puebla. Historic sites are also plainly discernible here, from the
ancient town and pyramid of Cholula, linked with the memory of the Aztecs
and their conquerors, to the hills of San Nicolas and San Juan associated with
the fame of [Carlos María] Bustamante and [Antonio López de] Santa
Anna in 1832. Plainly in view also are the famous hills and fortresses of
"Guadalupe" and "Loreto" where the Mexicans under General [Ignacio]
Zaragoza gained a signal victory over the French. The anniversary of this
event is celebrated annually with just pride and patriotism all over the country. The battle was fought on the 5th of May 1862, and the day of the month

has become a title of honor bestowed upon everything from a plaza to a pulque shop. Everywhere in Mexico one runs against *el cinco de Mayo* on sign posts and shoe shops or indicating some grand building or handsome street. Zaragoza, the hero of the battle, sleeps in *el cementerio de San Fernando* in the city of Mexico where also slumber President [Benito] Juárez, [José María] Arteaga, [Carlos] Salazar, [Tomás] Mejía and Miramón; all names which call up memories of Maximilian and his times. Other interesting points are seen from this lofty outlook associated with the Mexican army under General [Jesús] Gonzáles Ortega. This military chief, for a period of 83 days in 1863, held the city with his troops against the besieging French until to hold out longer was impossible, and the Mexicans surrendered with their banners in ashes and their arms rendered worthless. One listens here in the towers to anecdotes told with pride and affection by Mexicans of the gallant and heroic soldier—President General Porfirio Díaz. Of his capture by [Field Marshal Francisco Aquiles] Bazaine, and his imprisonment in the fortress of Loreto, whence he was removed for surer keeping to the church of *La Concepción* and thence again to the tower of *La Compañía.* How he made a daring escape from the latter place, swinging himself down by an improvised rope to the ground. How he evaded the sentinels and made his way safely out of town. Then, after a series of brilliant military exploits, how he returned at the head of his army in the spring of 1867 and took Puebla by assault, thus linking his honored name with the city's history and renown forever.

From warlike scenes our attention was called to the numerous haciendas in view with their grazing herds and broad acres and taken to the site of the first cotton factory ever founded in the Republic. There originally stood a little outside of the city the mill of San Domingo. This was purchased for one hundred and eighty thousand dollars by Señor Don Estebán de Antuñano for the purpose of erecting a manufactory on the spot. He was obliged to employ foreign workmen at great expense and soon sunk so much money that his scheme became the subject of jokes and jeers and was generally regarded as a most fool hardy experiment. He was, however, a man of remarkable enterprise and tenacity of purpose, and having undertaken the project he allowed nothing to deter him from carrying it forward. From 1831 to 1833, he and his family were subjected to economies which amounted to absolute want but still he persevered. He met loss of fortune, debt and a thousand other obstacles which would have defeated a less courageous man with renewed effort and unflinching determination. Three times the machinery ordered from the United States was utterly lost by shipwreck, but, at last, after he had served his grand project for as long a term as Jacob of old served for Rachel, the unconquered and unconquerable persistency of Señor Antuñano was rewarded with complete success. In 1837 his palatial manufactory with its beautiful grounds was the pride of all the country round about, and the name of *La Constancia Mejicana* was bestowed upon it in consideration of the unswerving fidelity of purpose to which was due such a vastly beneficial result. The influence of this enterprise upon home industry was felt at once. It gave employment to hundreds of people, and numerous *fábricas* which soon afterward sprang up in Puebla owed much to the impetus given to local trade by Don Estebán. The Mexican steamer at present plying between New Orleans and Vera Cruz is named *Estebán de Antuñano* in honor of the founder of *La Constancia.*

We were invited to see some fine pictures in private collections. Mexico claims to possess sundry original Murillos, and Puebla asserts that she has her full share besides genuine work of other celebrated artists. In the throwing open of convent doors and the spoliation of richly adorned churches, works of art long in the custody of the priesthood found their way to the public. Many of them have suffered injury in the vicissitudes through which they have passed, and all betray the influence of the church in their choice of subject, but the touch of the Master and the fervor of genius is unmistakably apparent in some of them, the mutation of centuries having failed to put out the spark divine which first illuminated their canvas.

We were urged to attend the theater in the evening. There are several in the city; the largest and most fashionable is called De Guerrero. The interior is spacious and handsome. We left before the performance was over, being too tired to enjoy it, and returned to our hotel which had once been a lordly palace and still retained evidences enough of princely grandeur to render it interesting beyond the mere fact that it was a pleasant place for food and shelter.

In this land, among dusky descendants of the conquered, and the white-faced people of the conqueror, where so many natural features of the country remain exactly as the Spaniards first beheld them, one becomes imbued with a desire to visit every scene connected with the march of Cortez. Especially, every one associated with his days of trial and uncertainty; when the weight of power trembled in the balance, and he was as yet only the adventurous invader not the triumphant conqueror. True, his path amongst a people who fought to defend their altars and their homes was stained with such deeds as most often cause the cheek of History to flush with shame, but the virtue of valor must be accorded him, as well as the honest zeal which in many instances amounted to heroism. *Tlaxcala,* signifying "The Land of bread," the smallest state in the Republic with its once famous and prosperous capital lies directly north of Puebla within two or three hours by rail and stage. One does not feel like quitting the locality without seeing the ancient province, the subjugation of which was of such vital importance to the fortunes of the Spaniards. The valiant and independent little state walled in on three sides by mountains had barricaded its eastern frontier before the time of the Spaniards with a vast defense of rock which Cortez himself describes in his second letter as "a large wall of dry stone about nine feet in height, extending across the valley from one mountain to another. It was twenty feet in thickness and surmounted throughout its whole extent by a breast-work a foot and a half thick." Bernal Diaz says, "It was six miles long, and its stones were united by a cement so strong as almost to defy the blows of the pickaxes."[2] Everyone remembers how, passing beyond this wall, Cortez fought his way forward, met at the outset by determined opposition, and destroyed in two days, according to his own account, more than sixteen villages one of which contained more than three thousand houses. How, because he bore "the banner of the cross," his small force was always successful, taking a town containing twenty thousand houses, and again in four hours routing the enemy to the number of *one hundred and forty-nine thousand men,* always without loss to the Spaniards. How on the third day, when fifty Indians came among them as messengers from the leading men, bringing presents and courteous messages, he became convinced they were spies and sent the whole half hundred back with their hands cut off to carry their king a defiant message; now at last the Tlaxcalans surrendered and flocked to the Spanish standard from that hour remaining the faithful and powerful allies of the Crown. When they invited him to their Capital, Cortez expressed his astonishment to Carlos V at finding it "larger than Granada and much stronger, with as many

2. Bernal Díaz del Castillo, *True History of the Conquest of New Spain,* trans. by Maurice Keatings (London: for J. Wright by J. Dean, 1800), was an eyewitness account of the conquest of Mexico, written in 1568 and first published in Spain in 1601.

fine houses and a much larger population than that city contained at the time of its capture." His letter goes on to say that, "besides many other places for the sale of merchandise in and about the town" there is in this city a market in which everyday thirty thousand people are engaged in buying and selling an immense variety of goods, including all kinds of shoes, ornaments of gold, silver and precious stones, together with curious featherwork and earthenware of every style, and a quality equal to the best Spanish manufacture. He proceeds to speak of barber and bathing establishments, of the admirable police arrangements and declares the people greatly superior to the most civilized Moorish nation, enjoying an admirable government and a well regulated police system. He asserts that "the valleys are fertile and tilled in every portion, no part lying unimproved" and that "the population of the province is five hundred thousand inhabitants." Alas! as one looks upon Tlaxcala now he can with difficulty recognize the portrait and involuntarily exclaims, "how are the mighty fallen." The foot of the Spaniard seems to have touched with ineradicable blight the peaceful and prosperous state. The principal points of interest about the city now are of Spanish, not Aztec origin, and one looks in vain for remnants of the grandeur and glory which belonged to it under ancient Tlaxcalan rule. Then through the town on the 23rd of September, 1519, from days and nights of anxiety in their camp on the hill of idols called Tzompach, the conquerors rode; the vast populace thronging to meet them to the number according to one historian of 100,000! Then Tlaxcalan maidens decked men and horses with wreaths and roses, and carpeted the way they trod with flowers or roofed it with verdant arches and swung festoons of the most fragrant blossoms across from one house to another; while *azoteas*[3] and thoroughfares were thronged with people who cheered them forward to the sumptuous banquets spread for them in the dwelling of the intrepid Xicontecatl. All this has passed away. Scarcely a ghost of its former greatness remains of Tlaxcala. Modern authorities do not even class it amongst cities containing six thousand inhabitants. Still, it is a place which must always be interesting for its historical association if nothing more. Its valleys are just as fair and fertile now as then, and the same beneficent Zatuapán River winds near. The scenes from its hill slopes are just as pleasing and are enriched by memories of the past, while in the old church of

3. Roofs.

San Francisco built in 1529 is the first pulpit from which Christianity was preached on this hemisphere and the stone font which held the first Christian baptismal water in America.[4] Here was baptized Xicontecatl and the other three chieftains who ruled the four quarters into which the city was partitioned at the time of the invasion. At the same font the Holy Water sanctified the brows of the daughters of nobles who were bestowed as brides upon the Conquerors. The ancient chapel still retains some relics of valuable ornaments presented to it by the Crown at the time of its completion, and its cedar paneled ceiling is an interesting type of the work of the period. The edifice, however, has been partly dismantled; its convent has been taken for military purposes and the whole pile is touched with that mildew of retrogression the conquest left upon it.

In the Governor's palace is shown a faded and tattered but veritable banner carried in the army of Cortez and presented by the "great Captain" to the town. At the same place are some interesting ancient documents relating to the early government of the city and the portraits of the four Aztec rulers of the town who were its civil and military chieftains at the time the Spaniards crossed the eastern frontier of the sturdy little province. There are also a few relics of Aztec worship in the shape of stone and pottery idols, and on the wall of one of the oldest houses in town is a fresco painting or picture writing supposed by some to represent that fatal tradition so long current among the early races of the country that white rulers would ultimately come to dwell in their land. The painting represents white men leveling Mexican forests to build ships, and in all probability it was painted after the fall of Tlaxcala, and perhaps illustrates the building of the brigantines which Cortez had ordered to be constructed in that Republic after his entrance into the Aztec Capital, the timber for which was cut from the vast forests of Tlaxcalan hill slopes.

From Tlaxcala Cortez journeyed to Cholula, an ancient city lying six leagues southwest of the province of his allies. No Puebla visited then, but it is now the starting point whence the traveler follows the path of the most remarkable and romantic conquest the world has ever known. So, one bright, beautiful morning we drove out to visit the famous pyramid of Cholula or "Churultecatl" as Cortez in his dispatches to his king designates it. The Gov-

---

4. The author here apparently does not include the Caribbean islands of Hispaniola, Cuba, and Puerto Rico, where the Spaniards established Christianity well before the conquest of Mexico, as part of the "hemisphere." She has also overlooked Panama.

ernor's own carriage, with most kindly courtesy, was placed "at the disposition of the ladies." Another vehicle which accommodated the other members
of our party was drawn by six frisky, sturdy little mules who knew how to trot
and raise a dust. The air was bracing; the sky without a cloud. Just outside of
the city an armed escort of thirteen mounted men sent by his Excellency the
Governor joined us. They carried sabers, carbines and pistols and all rode
admirably. They were led by a very handsome, young Mexican Captain who
was mounted on a superb white horse of remarkable beauty and symmetry.
Time was when all the roads in the neighborhood of the Town of the Angles
were infested by robbers and the boldest atrocities were committed within
sight of the very towers of the church which heavenly hands helped to build.
The Piñal, the pine forest through which the highway led, was a noted resort
for bandits who awaited the passing stages or chance traveler with irresistible
persuasions, so that to start out with money or valuables was equivalent to
donating them to the inexorable knights of the road. Such events are now no
more common to Mexico than to other peaceful countries and, although a
highway robbery may occur occasionally, an adventure of this kind is not
more characteristic of Mexico than of the United States.

Cholula lies three leagues west of Puebla. A railway is in operation between the two places. The wagon road is good and leads across a pleasant
stretch of country with magnificent mountain views and remnants of old
Spanish architecture and groups of Pueblan peasantry to gratify the eye. On
all sides the century plant—the argus eyed maguey—ran its tall stalks up to
their extremest height, sentineling the way. The organ cactus grew wild,
astonishing us by its exuberant growth. Its green palisades rose from ten to
twenty feet, and of proportionate thickness, its green pipes so close together
they formed a natural and almost impassable barrier wherever planted about
house or field for that purpose. In some parts of the country it attains the
height of 30 and 40 feet. In contrast to the stiff cactus and aloe the beautiful
Arbol de Peru (Peruvian pepper tree) was seen, graceful as an elf, and reminding one, with its bunches of crimson berries, of the mountain ash. One would
suppose Cholula to be the kitchen garden of Puebla to judge by the loads of
"garden truck" met running to town on the backs of men, women and children. Many of them carried a long balance pole and ran with it in hand much
as do rope walkers. We encountered none who walked, all kept up a monotonous jig-jog trot. The mounted guard kept now upon our left, now upon our

right within easy hailing distance riding always in Indian file and forming a gay and glittering line with their beautiful horses and military equipments, making a novel and attractive feature in the landscape. Beyond making this line of beauty there was nothing for them to do, as we met no objects more formidable than pigs, poultry and papooses jogging town-ward on Indians' backs.

The town of Cholula has dwindled to a mere hamlet in comparison with its size and splendor when Cortez first beheld it and described it thus to the Emperor Charles V: "The city of Churultecatl is situated on a plain, and contains about twenty thousand houses within the body of the town and as many more in the suburbs. It is independent, with boundaries well defined and yields obedience to no sovereign, being governed in the same way as Tascaltecal. The fields are all under cultivation and are exceedingly fertile, and much land which is well watered pertains to the town. The aspect of the city is more beautiful than any in Spain, as it contains many towers, all of which were towers of temples within this city." Bernal Diaz also speaks of it as "a city surrounded by cities and villages," five of which he names and says "the others are so numerous I will not attempt to mention them." He speaks of the fertile corn lands which supplied the people with bread and with wine; of an abundance of red pepper, and classes all other products of the soil under the general term of "other vegetables." He speaks of a "very fine kind of earthenware made there, red and black and white, adorned with various designs, and for its crockery the town," he says, "was famous and furnished supplies of it to all the neighboring provinces, even as did Talavera and Palencia in Castile. At that time, the town had more than a hundred very lofty towers which were *Cues* where idolatrous worship was held. One, especially the largest *Cu,* was even higher than the one in the city of Mexico, lofty and sumptuous as that was. For every tower there was a spacious court, devoted to the ceremonies of the Cues, and we were told there was to be seen one very large idol, the name of which I do not remember; but the people paid to it their most earnest devotions, coming from distant places to offer sacrifice and to lay before it presents of such as they possessed. I remember," he concludes, "that when we entered that city, and when we saw so many tall and shining towers, it seemed like Valladolid itself."

Cholula was already an ancient town when it fell into the hands of the Spaniards, having been founded by the Toltecs long before the Aztec empire.

Tradition teaches that its great pyramid was reared by the Toltecs in honor of the benign god Quetzalcoatl, the *"god of the air."* During the wonderful reign of this deity, cotton grew of all tints in the bolls, corn stalks were like trees, and a single ear of corn was as much as a man could carry; while fruits and other products of the earth were in proportion to the extraordinary size of the corn! Great wealth and profound wisdom were his, and under his laws the nation flourished and knew such happiness as made his sway the golden age of Mexico. He discountenanced human sacrifices and taught the people to keep their altars bloodless and lay upon them only fruits and flowers. Extraordinary festivals were held at certain seasons in his honor, marked by innocent rejoicings. The Chichimecas having, it is said, destroyed Tula in the year 1064 and driven out the inhabitants, Quetzalcoatl led his people from the ancient Toltec seat of empire, where he had long been High Priest and, influenced by some mysterious agency, brought them to this plain where they built a city and called it Cholulan (the City of Exiles). Here a mighty pyramid was reared to him by men's hands on which was erected a temple. Thence his worship spread all over the land and even nations at war with one another bowed down in peace together before the altars of Quetzalcoatl. After a glorious reign of twenty years duration in Cholulan (or Churultecatl) he departed toward the sea in search, as he declared, of another kingdom; but promising that he would surely return some future day to abide among them. He was said to be [a] fair skinned, blue eyed god wearing a robe embroidered *with red crosses.* To him the Mexicans ascribed their calendar, he being the god of the seasons, and to him also they owed the noblest rites of their religion and their knowledge of the use of metals. Probably much of the success of Cortez was due to the fact that the white conqueror carrying the banner of the cross was connected in the minds of the Mexicans with the cherished promise of Quetzalcoatl to someday return to them again. The great Tecali was found here upon the plain of Cholula by the Aztecs, and it was converted by them into a temple for human sacrifice. Everyone is familiar with the divided opinions concerning this pyramid, opinions which are not likely to be definitely settled until the immense mound is taken down for the purpose of ascertaining how it was put up. There are indications that this outrage is not far distant for the hand of Iconoclasm is already upon the wonderful hill. Many assert that it was a natural eminence which the Toltecs terraced and merely faced with adobe to preserve it from the washings of rains. Others believe it to have been erected for a tomb and to be entirely constructed of earth and sun dried brick wholly the labor of human hands. The theory that it is all built by human labor is sustained by appearances where a road has been cut through a portion of the Tecali. What a stupendous undertaking it was may be realized by the following description of it as given by Prescott. "The perpendicular height of the pyramid is one hundred and seventy seven feet. Its base is one thousand four hundred and twenty three feet long, twice as long as that of the great pyramid of Cheops. It may give some idea of its dimensions to state, that its base, which is square, covers about forty four acres, and the platform on its truncated summit embraces more than one."

Leaving our carriage we ascended the cone by a broad pathway, a sort of staircase about twenty feet wide. Wild flowers grew in the interstices, and the defiant cactus flourished by the way. Soon, we stood upon the apex of the colossal mound which lifts itself, the wordless monument of those who built it, the mute sign of a lost race, of which scarcely more is known than of that gentle but mysterious god to whom it was first consecrated. The mutability of all human effort and design impresses one as his feet press this ancient summit, and he looks down upon Cholula, once the renowned religious center of the nations. From this mystic monument was cast down the image dedicated to the "god of the air," to give place to the sumptuous temple of the Aztecs, upon the altars of which were lighted the undying fires, and from the lofty turrets of which the priests proclaimed at night the passing hours, while the jasper block and the obsidian knife lay always ready for the living victim. The soil of this spot, as well as that of many other places of worship in the city, has drunk deep of human gore. An ancient historian asserts that no less than six thousand human beings were immolated every year in Cholula! All this is changed. The temple of Toltec and Aztec and even that of the conquering Spaniard has passed away. A modern Catholic Chapel dedicated to the Virgin of Remedios crowns the hoary site. It contains an organ and a pretty altar and some simple decorations. Rosaries, crosses and medals are offered there for sale as talismans and souvenirs. About the little chapel are several graves. They were level with the ground and covered by a full length stone slab bearing a heavy inscription. A little distance off, at what was once the edge of the temple terrace, stands a carved cross dated 1666. Time has softened and altered the early outlines of the pyramid, and modern enterprise has hewed its way across its base to make paths for railroad and highway. Still, its primal dimensions are easily traced, with its four sides set to the four cardinal points and its four terraces, gradually narrowing from its broad base, to the pinnacle where sat the stone image of its god with gems in his ears, plumes of fire in his crown, a jewel scepter in one hand and a gorgeous shield in the other. Great trees have grown upon the terraces where once the victims and priests ascended to the scene of sacrifice, and the rose and cactus quarrel for supremacy in the soil. The view from it, however, is but little changed and still remains one of the most beautiful in the world. True, the four hundred shining pinnacles visible from this spot when "the Cholulan capital was the great commercial emporium of the plateau" are no longer to be seen. But here is the same teeming plain with its fertile wheat and corn-fields, its peaceful streams and level lands stretching away to the foot of the great heights. Westward marches the mountain wall which nature built about the valley of Anahuac, and everywhere the horizon meets the pale blue of far distant hills. All the snow peaks are visible from this point. With their feet in the realm of eternal flowers and their brows in the realm of eternal ice they look down unchanged, as they have looked for ages, on all the changes of kings and kingdoms, of gods and men. Churches are on all sides, near and far. From every heathen temple was apparently a seed from which sprung a Christian church. We can count from the great pyramid from twenty to twenty five villages smiling on the plain, each with one or more churches. In the distance Puebla lives and flourishes. At our feet Cholula lies and languishes. Just there, where we might toss a pebble, is the great square where Cortez, warned by Marina of the hostile intentions of the Cholulans, assembled the caciques, captains, and other prominent men and soldiers and turned upon them the heart sickening massacre they had intended for his army. Marina sat by the conqueror's side when the signal was given which slew three thousand of her countrymen and paved with the dead bodies of her people the conqueror's way to Mexico. One cannot realize such a scene of horrible slaughter was ever enacted in the immense area of the grass grown plaza and the heart of a town which now wears such an inactive air and seems so entirely run to church. That day, as we looked down upon the plain, how peaceful were all things. Gardens glowed with flowers, villages rose among quiet groves, pastures were green, sheep bleated among the maguey fields. Arches and domes of convents and monasteries made pictures on the pages of the meadows. Now and then a cock crowed and occasionally was heard the distant report of guns proclaiming that a fête was being held in some one of the neighboring haciendas.

We found several fine bits of obsidian in the loose earth of the old teocalli, which a skeptical member of our party declared to be nothing but wrecks of shivered champagne bottles which former travelers had emptied on this height. We, however, were not to be ridiculed out of our treasures and were rewarded later by learning that they were veritable pieces of that natural glass which the primitive races put to so many uses, of which the Aztec priest made the knife with which he cut out his victim's heart, of which the Indians made their arrow heads and with which ye ancient barber in the neighborhood of the Grand Plaza in Mexico made the sharp and serviceable razor which shaved his ancient customers.

The moment we descended from the mound we were surrounded by Indians who wished to sell us fruit or flowers. Others brought bits of pottery and others masks and idols, the latter they averred having been dug out of the ancient mound. The fruit was very stale, and the idols were very fresh; but we bought some of all things offered, with a view to "encouraging trade." We had no difficulty in immediately discovering that our idols were not only common clay but had eyes and eyebrows made with an excellent quality of lead pencil!

As we drove homeward we saw a pulque gatherer with his calabash and pig skin wandering after his noonday yield. He good naturedly allowed us to inspect the apparatus, and even put his gourd to its full powers for our benefit. Here and there great clumps of the nopal grew; its thorned and fleshly sections seeming to warn away assailants with the reminder that it was the chosen cactus of the Aztecs and is even today a proud emblem in the escutcheon of the Nation. It is this plant which nourishes the cochineal insect, the value of which as a dye was known to and utilized by the native Mexicans long before the Spanish invasion. It was unknown in Europe before the conquest of Mexico but was among the first tributes sent by Cortez to his king and subsequently became a source of large revenue to the Spanish crown. This cactus grows high and scraggy. Although the commercial value of cochineal has greatly diminished, substitutes having been found for its dye, the plant is held in high estimation for other purposes. Its macerated leaves are used for their curative properties, and it produces a crimson fruit, the "Tuna," in abundance which is used as a conserve and a pickle, and the juice of it when ripe makes a pretty coloring fluid used in many ways. The plant and fruit closely resemble our prickly pear. We had all heard of the great *Ahuehuete* or cypress which grew in one of the villages of Puebla, the circumference of the hollow trunk of which is said to be seventy-six feet. This "ancient monument of vegetation" seemed to have outlived its fame, however, for the most careful inquiry failed to elicit any knowledge of it; not even its stump or roots ever having been heard of by anyone we questioned concerning it in Puebla. A Holy Father whom we met said that far to the northeast, in the old city of Tlatanquitepec, an ancient cypress once stood and might be standing yet, since these trees attain great age, under which tradition claimed the horse of Cortez was tied when he and his followers stopped in that town on their march to Mexico. Beyond this he knew of no remarkable *Ahuehuete* nearer than the garden of Chapultepec in Mexico; although in times past the Spaniards had found great numbers of these trees in the vicinity, which they had felled to build the numerous edifices which rose under Spanish sway. Then asked if from its ancient forest of cypress the original name of the Pueblan plain might not have been *Ahuehuete* instead of *Acajete* the answer was that comprehensive one which is met everywhere in Mexico, *¿Quién sabe?*

It was our good fortune to be honored with an invitation to visit the Bishop's Palace. We found it a spacious, handsome building situated very near the Cathedral. We were immediately ushered into the presence of the learned and venerable Bishop, a man of most benevolent aspect and noble bearing who at once called to mind Hugo's Bishop in *Les Miserables*. After giving us a most cordial reception, he led us in person through all the immense building. The walls of some of its apartments are adorned with frescoes of remarkable merit, painted by two Mexican artists. Certain peculiarities of these paintings the Bishop pointed out with manifest enjoyment which he was eager to share with others. Many very fine paintings, both copies and originals, graced the rooms of the Palace, especially one fine copy of a Guido which the Bishop had had copied for himself in Rome. In one of the chambers were old and very valuable needlework hangings beautifully wrought and somewhat similar to those in the chapel of the cathedral. When the tour of the very interesting building had been made, the good Bishop pressed us to remain and take chocolate with him, but the hours were flying, and we were forced to say adieu. As we descended the stairs we turned half way down for the usual last salute. The tall, noble figure of the Bishop stood framed in the ancient doorway where he had paused to see us descend. His face was lighted with an expression of the loftiest serenity and kindliness. One hand was resting on his breast, the other was lifted with a farewell gesture which seemed almost like a blessing for us. It was a picture of blended dignity, grace and gentleness never to be forgotten, to remain with us long after we may have ceased to remember all else that adorn the Bishop's palace.

When at the close of this our last, busy and happy day in Puebla we all gathered at the hotel, it was late in the evening, and we only managed to seek our rooms and lie down a short while before it was time to arise. The huge apartment assigned to Cora and myself was not lighted with gas, and the sickly flame of one tallow candle only increased the gloom. We soon fell asleep, and the candle burnt out. We were awakened at midnight and told to make ready for the train. Springing up in the darkness, we groped for the table where the light had been. We had known the room was large when we went to bed, but it was amazing how much larger it seemed to have grown whilst we slept. There was no bell, no servant within call; about the longest walk we took in Mexico was around and around that immense apartment in the dark, trying to find the matches we had left on the table in its center. Once in a while we encountered each other, shook hands, parted and continued our ramble.

It was a relief when through the huge key hole of the door shot a ray of light which guided us to the portal. Upon opening it we found a servant with a tray of chocolate and a light. As we had lain down to our brief slumber dressed, we had risen in ready-made toilets. Hats and wraps were quickly donned, and going to the corridor we found some of our party making merry over the magnificent dinner we had had that day, as set forth in the appetizing items of the bill of mine host. According to that list, the most remarkable fowls of the air and the beasts of the field had been served up to us in flocks and herds, whilst untold number of "Lampreys from the Volga" had been consumed by our apparently ravenous party. It was by far the most sumptuous banquet we ever had in Mexico—on paper. A little investigation brought to light that the "Lampreys from the Volga" were the boxes of sardines!

At two o'clock in the morning we descended the broad staircase and passed the stone lions that crouched upon the lower pillars of the balustrade. Servants carrying lanterns threw shifting gleams of light about the patio, in

the middle of which stood a diligence with six mules attached ready to convey us to the depot. How we all ever got into that coach, and how we all ever
stayed in after we were there will ever remain a mystery. Cora and I had
wished for a diligence drive from the time we first entered the country. As an
experience this was useful to us. Nearly every passenger had some curiosity
he had purchased in Puebla. There was enough marble to make everyone a
tombstone and enough parrots to talk us all to death, and we were half buried
under bird cages, wax figures, etc., etc. Our driver talked Spanish volubly to
his half dozen mules, interspersing his oration with much hissing and many
lashes. Finally, after a great expenditure of persuasion on his part, there was
a long pull, a strong pull, and a pull altogether on the part of our mules, and
suddenly we were rushed off with astounding alacrity and rattled over the
stone with a jolting and clattering that promised permanent deafness and
dislocation of all joints. Even a Joint Stock Company would have been broken up on that drive. Fortunately, the distance to be traversed was short;
therefore, no one had to be taken from the vehicle in pieces.

Having retraced our way to Apizaco, we found ourselves once more on the
direct road to the city of Mexico, crossing the farms and dusty plains of the
great central table lands. Our first station was Guadalupe, a name venerated
throughout Mexico as pertaining to the miraculous Virgin of the Catholic
Church of Mexico. From this point the three great snow peaks, the marvelous Pyramids of Mexico were distinctly visible. Interest is apt to center on
Ixtaccihuatl, "The White Lady." It is less lofty than its snowy sisters, its
height being 14,705 feet. Upon its summit is seen the prone shape of a
woman lying rigidly stretched face upward with arms folded on her breast.
The snow that covers it is like the white sheet over a corpse, beneath which
the outlines of the stiffened form are plainly discernable. She seems to have
been borne like some dead Parsee to the top of this lofty monument, whence
her mourning and lamenting friends have turned away leaving her to the
cold, the silence, the days of tempest, and the nights of desolation. There is
a fascination in the white, motionless shape which from some points assumes
a startlingly real and human aspect.

Popocatépetl, "the mountain that smokes," although he did not indulge in
any such propensities during our sojourn in the country, is the highest of the
three glacial peaks, rearing its icy apex 17,884 feet in air. Its ascent has been
several times effected. Its interior is described as dismal in the extreme. In-

side of the crater is a stone hut occupied by the sulphur miners. Visitors say this hut is the best hotel in the place and has two decidedly attractive features, one being its novel site, the other the fact that it keeps no brass band.

The stations were none of them interesting. A small number of one story houses and shops snuggling up to a railroad in the midst of a dusty plain was the character of all. Here and there the rural guard, amounting to fifteen or twenty men on spirited little mustangs, stood well armed and equipped ready for police duty. The arrival of the train gave them opportunity to display some splendid horsemanship, an accomplishment which is second nature with all Mexican men. The stiff lines of the century plant became more and more frequent until whole farms were given up to its cultivation. This plant, supposed in the United States to bloom but once in a hundred years and the flowering of which attracts crowds to witness the unusual sight, here grew on every hand as plentiful as palmetto in the south or Canada thistles in the north. We saw it serving as fences to wheat fields and sturdily bordering lanes that led down to the most unpretentious houses. It stood in full blossom along boundary lines as numerous as telegraph poles and resembling them not a little. Its stalks are tall, stately and an interesting feature in the landscape. The walls of hacienda or rancho rising at the termination of long avenues of the agave; the broad, neutral tinted plains from which the mountains stood afar; the low cabins of the peasant built close beside the road, their primitive roof of boards held in place by the weight of heavy stones, formed a striking contrast to the rich soil, exuberant vegetation and laughing rivers of the *tierra templada*.

Whilst our train halted at Apam, other trains were moving off with pigskins of pulque and casks and barrels of the liquid as freight, while carts were moving to and fro laden with the same sort of merchandise. Men and women in rebozos and sarapes crowded about the cars with pulque in jars, pulque in bottles and pulque in mugs urging the passengers in the sweet, mellifluous accents of the land, and the few words of English they could command, to "take pulque," "buy pulque," "drink pulque?" Only one or two of our party acquiesced, and they made such wry faces over the beverage as deterred the others from making the experiment. The Indian peasants who thronged the station, like all those we had seen, were a distinct race from the Spaniards of the country, as much so as the Negroes in Louisiana are distinct from the whites. The children who played about the doorways were odd little creatures, apparently not much given to laughter and still less to tears. Those able to walk were always mounted children; riding on fierce and high mettled steeds of bamboo, and throwing imaginary lassoes and imaginary lances with great skill at imaginary bulls. They were comically earnest in their play, while the babies, too small to amuse themselves, blinked their shining, black eyes and seemed solemnly awaiting the time when they too could enter the imaginary arena.

Moving out of Apam, stations became more frequent and at most of them the Diligence, with its team of many mules, was drawn up awaiting passengers for "across country." Once more our iron path began to lie parallel with the old stage road, and again we came in sight of donkey droves followed by the dusky arrieros slowly and patiently passing on their long and devious way. Byron's lines rose to mind:

"How carols now the lust muleteer?
Of Love, romance, devotion is his lay,
As whilom he was wont the leagues to sheer
His quick bells wildly jingling on their way."

No song parted the lips of any muleteer we met that day, nor did any "quick bells" jingle from any donkey's neck. A silence almost pathetic, a subdued and placid air of patience characterized the man and the beast wherever we encountered them. Both turned to gaze at the locomotive as it swept past and seemed to say with their wistful eyes, "It is an interloper, an iconoclast. It may outspeed us, but it cannot depose, and it shall part us never!"

Gradually the broad acres that spread out on either hand, the green fields of maguey, the distant snow peaks and the nearer hills put on the cap of invisibility. The rumbling train rushed on across the shadowed meadows, and we swiftly approached the historic vale of Anahuac. What magic was in that name, Anahuac! It seemed to swing open the centuries like ponderous gates, revealing vivid pictures which lay beyond them. There was Cortez marching down with his mailed and mounted men upon the doomed city of the plain. There was the Aztec monarch coming forth in all his regal pomp from that "fair city of Mexico which rose from the midst of its surroundings like some Indian Empress with her coronal of pearls." There was the royal palanquin glittering with gold and gems borne by dusky nobles with downcast eyes and bared feet. The gleam of gold and sheen of silver glitter in the sunlight. Magnificent canopies and gorgeous plumes add pomp or color to the royal retinue as it moves along the ancient causeway to greet the Spaniard, in whom the Aztec Emperor believes he sees the strange being predicted of his oracles whose achievements proclaim him something more than human. Montezuma meets him with kingly courtesies, loads him with rare and costly gifts, offers him sumptuous hospitality and distinguished consideration. In return he receives treason, insult, butchery and spoliation. Belief battles with belief; superstition grapples with superstition. The conflict is to the strong. Amid the bewildering roar of artillery, the ringing of terrifying hoofs, the glitter of steel armor, the wary manipulation of skilled forces, the crown drops, the throne totters, the Indian vale and the beautiful city are the spoil of the invader. The idolaters fall and die among their shattered and overthrown idols. The victor casts down the sacrificial stone to plant the Inquisition in its place. Meanwhile Spanish blades and Spanish bullets have made all the plain one vast altar of sacrifice, whereon the blood had not time to dry and the bodies of the victims no chance of burial. In the midst of wrong, ruin, death and desolation the king and his kingdom passed away forever, and the haughty voice of Spain announces to all the world the conquest of Mexico. Oh, cross of Christ, how many atrocities have been committed in thy name!

The halt of the train, and the announcement that we had reached our destination woke us all from our reveries. The atmosphere was very clear, and it seemed to us we had never been so near the skies. They were so wonderfully blue and brilliant. Friends were at the station to meet us, and in the midst of cordial welcomes, much English and more Spanish, we entered a carriage and were whirled away, around sharp corners and through broad streets to our hotel, enjoying the opportunity to see Mexico in all its stately, stony grandeur.

13

✳

Mexico City

First night in Mexico City. Mysterious signals. The belfry music. The Cathedral turrets. Legend of the bells. "Who's dat knocking at de do?" Mexican flowers. Dimensions of nosegays. A floral welcome. Hand clapping for servants. On a house top. Appearance of the town. No chimneys, no window shutters. Light and sunshine in houses. The patio. Matutinal pictures. Two climates in one street. La Profesa. *Its dignified beggar. The lowly man with a holy name. A Mexican broom. Servant wages. Signals explained. Los Serenos. Table visitors. Peddlers of queer poultry. Remnant of Aztec feather work. The School of Mines. The National Library. The Museum Santa Rosa. The cell of expiation. Gods on the ground floor. A* tableau vivant. Huitzilopochtli. *The sacrificial stone. Antiquities in the Museum. Its library. Maximiliano's dinner service. Hidalgo's chair. Portraits of noted men. The Museum as an educator. The mysterious mummies. Church and convent of San Domingo. The Inquisition. The Academy of Fine Arts. Outdoor pictures. Encouragement of native talent. Old churches. Church and Hospital of Jesus of Nazareth. The associations it has with the Conqueror. The several tombs of Cortez. His last known resting place. Valuable ancient documents. Autograph of Cortez.* Yo El Rey. Yo La Reina. *A house of cedar and stone put together without a nail.*

Our first night in Mexico found our slumbers much disturbed by shrill, peculiar, shreek-y sounds which seemed like mysterious signals given and answered from all quarters of the town. They were frequently heard just under our balcony, but they also proceeded from the near and far distance with most surprising clearness and regularity. In our sleeping apartment, the lofty ceiling of which the rays of our candle scarcely reached and the dim and shadowy corners of which they did not pretend to penetrate, we lay listening and dreading "treason stratagem and spoils" and fancying a revolution must certainly be brewing. The sounds were long, piercing, mournful notes like the cries of a strange bird in distress. Now they would break out loud and clear, then sink into a prolonged wail to be caught and repeated in the distance again and again and again. We could not by the greatest possible stretch of the imagination construe these sounds which "made night hideous" into any serenadel intent on the part of gallant Mexicans, and at last despite our anxiety the very monotony of the notes lulled us into a prolonged slumber from which we did not waken until the sun was stretching his early rays across the crimson carpet on our floor.

Then the bells began to ring, the near bells and the far bells in many towered Mexico. From the great Cathedral just at hand swung out the inaugural signal to be answered from a hundred belfries and repeated again from the responding domes of distant Guadalupe. It was as if the ceremonies of the ancient sun worshipers had been transmuted into sound, and instead of fleet footed messengers receiving fresh-lighted fires from the lofty altars to distribute over the land, the brazen bells from their tall turrets announced the first glow of the sun in the east and so kindled the fire of devotion in every heart and home. The bells of the Cathedral boom rather than ring and with intervals between each stroke of the clappers upon the deep, base-toned bell metal. They shock the air with one tremendous stroke, then leave it to quiver under the blow for some thrilling seconds while all the surging tones palpitate past and roll away into illimitable space. Then, the stroke is repeated. What volumes of sound! What vibrations! They thrill the stones beneath one's feet, the bed upon which one listens appalled and impressed. In their solemn roll seems to swing the voices of vanished races, the death of ages; as if the bells had gathered to themselves up there in their lovely turrets the secrets of all time, the unwritten histories of lost nations, the sweetness of life, the bitterness of death, the darkness of burial and the glory of resurrection as these have pertained to generation after generation. What must have been the effect upon the native Indian when he first listened to those sounds? To him, they must have seemed like the tones of Jehovah himself summoning him to renounce his idols and to deny his gods.

Tradition tells us that when these bells were cast, proud Spanish dames contributed their ornaments of gold and vessels of silver to be melted with the metal, and the youth and the maiden cast in their trinkets and their love tokens. Tradition further states that with these gifts, both great and simple, were connected sacred associations; so that many a touching sacrifice and noble instance of self abnegation and pious devotion was connected with the fusing of the metal and lent to the voices of the Cathedral bells a profound tenderness and solemn pathos such as belongs to no other bells of all the many in New Spain!

Whilst listening in awed silence to the surging of the sound waves, as stroke after stroke set them in motion, a continued tapping at the entrance to our room caused me to hurriedly don a wrapper and respond to the summons. I turned a queer knob of our queer little door. It swung slowly outward into the narrow entry. In the aperture confronting me were two immense bouquets. No doubt there was an Indian servant on the other side of the flowers for I caught sight of a dusky hand and one black eye, but the hallway was so very narrow, and the bouquets were so very big that no more of the bearer's individuality was discernible. There was scarcely time to close the door and read the names on these when there was another knock, another glimpse of an Aztec descendant and two more nosegays handed in of such vast dimensions we began to wonder what idea our Mexican friends had of the proportions of our American noses. More knocks, more flowers, more cards, and the cards and the knocks and the flowers continued to come until our apartment was a bower of fragrance and bloom. There were pansies, carnations, pinks, violets, roses, heliotrope, geranium, orchids, orange blossoms, camellias, and foreign flowers whose names were quite unknown to us; and the least of these bouquets was eighteen inches in diameter! Each was so constructed, upon long stems evened off, that it had a pedestal of its own and could stand alone wherever placed. I arranged them about the floor, and the room soon had a complete set of most novel floral furniture. Four or five bouquets in a row formed a couch fit for a god; a group in the center of the floor made a gorgeous divan, and single ones placed here and there gave hassocks and ottomans of the richest color and beauty, with plenty left over to serve as sofa pillows and decorate tables and brackets. They were fragrant, but on account of the lightness of the atmosphere all flowers seem less rich in perfume in Mexico than in moister climates. A handful of violets in New Orleans will pour out more sweetness than was given from any one of these immense clusters although the latter were composed of the most generous odored blossoms. This floral welcome to a strange land was as charming as it was graceful, and the courtesy was continued day after day so long as we remained in the City of Mexico.

We had been told to clap our hands when ready for *desayuno*. We did so. Two Indian servants instantly appeared with such startling promptitude they seemed to have sprung out of the ground. It was so like an Arabian Nights!—proceeding that for a few seconds both Cora and I quite forgot what we had clapped for.

Immediately after partaking of our coffee, we made our way up a long, stone staircase leading from our floor to the *azotea* or flat roof of the hotel. Here we stood side by side to take a bird's eye view of the oldest city in America. What a valley for such a city, and what a city for such a valley! How delightful the air we breathed, and how matchless the skies that hung above us! Such brightness and softness of atmosphere, such clearness, such depth of ethereal blue-ness had nowhere save in Mexico ever bent over our uplifted brows. Afar off, the summits of Ixtaccihuatl and Popocatépetl in glacial grandeur lifted their gelid crowns against the marvelous azure of the sky and, turn whichever way we would, we beheld the mountains girdling the almost level valley with its gleam of distant waters and its verdant plains. All about us rose the strong buildings, with their terraced roofs, giving evidence of the Moorish influence in architecture which dominated Spanish taste and through the Spaniards built Mexico as it is. On all sides rose the massive domes and towering turrets with their holy symbol indicating the house of God. The war against Catholicism, whatever else it overthrew, never struck down the cross.

The city is squarely laid out and, although the Aztec town was, with the exception of its towered temples, architecturally inferior to the City which occupies its site today, the Spaniards found its plan so excellent they merely in rebuilding expanded the original Mexico. They found the streets wide and straight and crossing each other at right angles. Those of today are merely extensions of the ones which then existed. The buildings are of stone—handsome and stately in style. The effect of all is solidity, strength and durability. It is essentially a stone city. Stone stores, stone dwellings, stone roofs, stone arches—soaring stone towers and hemispheric domes meet the eye everywhere. The prevailing hue is a neutral tint of grayish granite. Such a thing as a window shutter is unknown on the outside of the houses; the nearest approach to it being an awning projecting over windows where shade is required. The Mexicans love light and get as much of it into their houses as they possibly can. Across the acres of roofs one looks in vain for a chimney. Not one is visible. Dwellings have no chimneys because such a thing as a fire place is unknown in Mexican houses. Beyond the limits of the kitchen, a fire can never be found. In the latter domain great brick tables, with openings at the sides and top, furnish charcoal furnaces which serve for all culinary purposes and accommodate the many servants necessary for each well appointed Mexican household. A fireplace in a room and the mantel, such important features in United States houses, are never seen. Although they are among the first appointments an American woman misses, they are also among the very first she learns to do without. Gazing out upon the city in the quiet of early morning, one is struck with the air of age distinct from decay which rests upon all things. The new buildings which go up are of the same material and style of the old, and as the old undergoes but little apparent change everything wears the same venerable and substantial aspect as though all had been constructed at the same period. It is not a city of front yards or side lawns. The walls of the dwellings rise sheer from the sidewalk with one, wide front entrance even with the street and balconies at the upper windows. Each is built around a square court, upon which the windows and doors of the inner wall open, and over which hangs a balcony or corridor usually extending along all sides of the building. In that court or *patio* every Mexican household has a dear little isle of its own, a region of delight where flowers grow, birds sing and fountain plays; while the seclusion and privacy are as perfect as though it were fifty miles in the country instead of in the bosom of a big and busy town. We obtained glimpses of these from our lofty perch as we stood watching the great city wake from its slumber and cast off the covers of repose under which it had passed the night. A gate here and there would swing open and the still drowsy porter come out to the milkman for the morning's milk or a supply of vegetables, leaving the open portal revealing to us fuchsias of immense size tossing their jewel-like blossoms, geraniums tall as trees, in full flower, and gorgeous lilies looking at themselves in the fountain's basin. A general stir began in the great thoroughfares with all that individuality and characteristic quaintness which as yet pertains to Mexico. Pictures began to form themselves in alcoves and doorways as vendors of small ware arranged themselves and their belongings for the business of the day. A group of newsboys already imbued with love of calico and an American style of dress amused themselves playing marbles whilst waiting for their patrons to awaken. A pillar of smoke shot up from one factory to be followed by another and another and another, showing that soap and glass and porcelain and matches and tiles and dozens of the necessities of life were getting themselves made as fast as possible. There was heard the shriek of the locomotive, the rumble of wheels as hacks moved to their stands or rolled away with early passengers; street cries increased every moment; stores were opened and markets; work and business were at their height and the life of the great town at its fullest.

How we enjoyed that morning on the house top I shall always remember! Neither of us were invalids, and we thought if that morning were a sample of the climate it was perfect! The air was bracing without being too cool, the sunshine genial without being too warm. We reveled in the cool comfort and enlivening glow of temperature 7500 feet above sea-level and felt as if we had been carried above all "the ills that flesh is heir to." One can "get along" on less breath in Mexico than in lower localities; one finds that a very little goes a long way unless he is thoughtless enough to run up a flight of stairs or make any other ascent too rapidly and then—well then one may "look out for breakers" in the way of blood vessels, be he weak or strong! Violent bleeding at the nose is one of the most harmless results of forgetting the good old admonition *festa lente*. No matter how lovely the day, winter covering is necessary every night upon the beds. The early mornings and evening are cool enough for light wraps which are not needed during the day. The temperature, as I have elsewhere stated is equable; never higher than 70 degrees, never lower than 62 degrees. Every day, however, two climates lie within a few feet of each other, represented by the shady side and the sunny side of the street. The difference is so marked that house rent is influenced by it; dwellings on the sunny side being more eagerly sought for, and commanding much the higher price.

Walking about there on our *azotea* we found our hotel was literally under the very drippings of the sanctuary, of which, in fact, it once formed a part, having originally been the convent attached to the church of *La Profesa*. The roof of that edifice rose, with its dome and bell tower so close beside ours that we could easily pass from one to the other as though all covered one building. *La Profesa* we found to be a handsome structure standing upon the corner of San José and San Francisco streets. It has a very elaborately sculptured facade in the niches of which stand marble saints, about whose folded arms and holy heads and far above them in the deep chiselings doves fly in and out, and nest and coo, and dress their shining feathers all day long. In front of its portals in the shadow of one of its massive buttresses a beggar stood that early in the day. We afterwards found he always stood there. He seems to have a preemption claim to the place. He was an old, blind beggar, so old he looked as if he had been founded when the church was and so had become part and parcel of it. Other beggars come to the locality, but they always kept at a very respectful distance from him, and lottery vendors liked the vicinity, but they never encroached upon his rights. He was always neatly dressed, carried a handsome walking stick and wore a Spanish cloak with one end thrown gracefully over the left shoulder. His black hat was a cross between "the slouch" and "the sombrero," and he wore it constantly. His sightless eyes were his only appeal to passers by. The hat was never held out, the hand never extended, and he never spoke either to ask alms or give thanks. Whatsoever he received was literally pressed upon him as donors were obliged to press into his hand such coins as the pathetic sight of his blind, speechless face induced them to bestow.

La Profesa was originally founded in 1592. The first structure was pulled down to give place to the one now existing, which was built about a century and a half ago. During the long period in which the Catholic Church maintained its supremacy in Mexico, La Profesa held rank among the wealthiest and most aristocratic edifices of its kind. Its foundress was the wife of Don Juan Luis de Rivera, and her statue stands in the main chapel. The matins and vesper bells and the clock strokes in the old towers we considered with a personal interest for they bade fair to make things lively for us, just down below, morning, noon and night.

Descending again to our room we clapped our hands to summon the chambermaid. A tall, lank, cinnamon-hued Indian who answered to the name of *Jesús* sprang into sight. His hair was long, his clothing nothing to speak of and he proceeded to make our beds and "clean up"; which service he performed as dexterously as any woman possibly could have done. He then prepared to use his broom, and such a broom! It was merely a handful of coarse, stiff hay or "brush" which grows in the mountains, about twenty inches long, and tied tightly about at top with maguey fiber. There was no handle attached, and to use it the servant must go half bent, literally stooping to conquer wielding his awkward implement with both hands. It raises plenty of dust, and drags quantities of wool from a carpet, but it is the Mexican broom in common use. Such as are known in our United States houses are imported goods in Mexico and quite costly. The scrubbing brush which our solemn servant took up when he laid down his broom was of the same primitive make and material, but it was well adapted to withstand the wear and tear induced by constant contact with rough stonework and brick floors. Housework made easy by the thousand and one patented house-hold utensils known in the States is as yet undreamed of in Mexico. The wages of servants range from eight to ten dollars per month for housework and for the cook and the coachman they are but little more.

We went to breakfast about half past twelve with appetites which had not been lessened by our housetop promenade. The first questions we asked were regarding the cries we had heard during the night. They were simply police whistles! Instead of carrying clubs and rapping on curbstones, all signals are produced by the whistle. Calls—answers—a summons—announcements of danger—assurances that all is right—everything is whistled with every imaginable degree of sound that can be wrested from the small instrument. It is a very simple, wooden affair on the same principle as the ordinary willow whistle with which every school boy is familiar, but the police friend of Mexico manages to extract from it such shrieks and cries and wailing sounds as would put any Irish Banshee to the blush. The uniform of the policeman is a close fitting, dark blue suit and a white cap. A pistol is strapped conspicuously about his waist; and at night a glass lantern with a lighted candle in it is added to his accouterments. It is his custom to then place his lantern in the middle of the street crossing. Then doth the guardian of the peace betake himself to a comfortable doorway, or the shelter of some overhanging balcony and pipe away. In the States, it is hinted that the policeman is given to "wetting his whistle," but in Mexico he conscientiously blows it night in, night out. A Mexican gentleman assured us "they do this to advertise to the robbers where the watchmen are, so that thieves and burglars may avoid be-

ing caught." He added that "it is believed the Mexican policeman has attained such perfection in his calling that, after this lantern is duly placed, he
rolls himself in his sarape, puts himself into some cozy corner, goes sound
asleep and blows his whistle from mere force of habit, and with as much ease
as some people snore." As each one at stated intervals is expected to use his
whistle diligently, a concert of the most astounding nature is the result, and
sad is the stranger who listens if he has not previously been informed what
it is all about.

While we leisurely breakfasted, we received many visits. The visitors came
in the most social manner, sipped coffee or chocolate whilst proffering us all
sorts of civilities and making themselves delightfully agreeable. Upon the
presentation of each card we signified our readiness to see the caller, having
learned by experience that such is the practice in Mexico. It struck us as a
much franker, pleasanter and more hospitable custom than that which makes
the fact that "the family are at breakfast" or dinner sufficient excuse for repelling a friendly caller. It certainly is more courteous than to allow a servant
to hold a door half shut in one's face while he makes the announcement that
"the family being at table, beg to be excused." Eating one's meals is not an
occupation to be ashamed of, nor yet one that need be indulged in secrecy
and seclusion, provided the china be neat and the table linen clean. A family
"at prayers" has a right to repel intrusion, but being "at table" scarcely seems
a sufficient reason for banishing friends.

The windows at one side of our breakfast room opened to the ground
facing the great court where there were plants and flowers and where orni-
thological families in huge, wire homes sung and made merry. Through these
open windows ventured, every now and then, vendors of curiosities and
pretty trifles peculiar to the country. Among these articles were colored birds
wrought in natural feathers upon cards of different sizes. These last are the
remnants of the exquisite art of featherwork in which the early Aztecs so
excelled. The work offered us was executed with extreme neatness and delicacy, the body being made of natural feathers arranged so as to preserve perfect shading while the feet, bills and legs were painted in watercolors. Pulling
one we had purchased to pieces, we found this branch of the art consisted in
drawing an accurate outline on the card, filling it in with a thin coat of white
wax and upon these carefully adjusting the plumage. We bought ducks, turkeys, parrots, hummingbirds, flamingoes, fighting cocks, demure hens and

whole broods of chickens at the rate of one dollar per dozen and thought them by far the cheapest lot of poultry that had ever come in our way.

We went early in the day to visit some of the principal buildings. The Minería, or School of Mines, is one of the finest of the edifices and would be an architectural ornament to the best built city in the world. It is of solid stone from foundation to Azotea, is four stories high and has spacious rooms, courts, corridors and a fountain. The original plan of the building was made by the Mexican architect and sculptor Don Manuel Tolsa and the structure, which covers an immense area, was completed about seventy years ago at a cost of nearly two millions of dollars. Its front entrance looked rusty and ill kept, and the edifice also shows indications of having "settled" about midway on the walls so that regret and apprehension mingle with the admiration one bestows upon a structure of such majestic proportions. A thorough knowledge of metallurgy and of all matters pertaining to mines, mining and engineering can be acquired there. The College is ably conducted; the collection of minerals is very fine, and all the scientific apparatus is complete and kept up to the standard of the age. The building and its contents suffered from despoilers during the latest revolutions, but so much remains a stranger does not miss what is gone.

Through streets filled with living pictures, and where we not infrequently met those children of nature, the Indians, carrying on their courtships as simply as the birds and walking with their arms about each other as their errands permitted opportunity for such demonstrations, we reached the National Library. We were surprised at the beauty of the building. Its sculptured exterior is a study, its proportions grand. It was fashioned from the old convent of San Augustín, but the ancient building has been so remodeled that it may be said to have undergone transformation, though the ancient walls were not pulled down. It is a magnificent structure of carved stone; well worthy the pride felt in it by the people. The progress of the work was slow, years having been consumed in its rebuilding, but the time spent upon it shows rich results. Carefully selected additions are being made constantly to the already large collections of books, and this edifice and its contents rank among the very first of its kind in America. There is a sort of poetical justice in having these walls, which once regarded the exclusion of knowledge as the fundamental principle of their existence, now devoted to the dissemination of learning. Even to the most prejudiced it cannot but be more agreeable to have the emptied convents devoted to such uses rather than degraded to stables for donkeys or dedicated to the mad gymnastics of infuriated bulls as so many are throughout the country.

From the San Augustín we went to the Museum which stands in the street called *la calle de la Moneda*. The Museum forms a part of the National Palace, but is so extensive that, with its own vestibule and court, it seems an edifice apart and independent from the spacious ground entrance; broad staircases lead up on the right-hand and the left to the several departments above. Beyond them the lower entrance leads on to the gardens in the Patio. Indians were dragging in that morning on wooden rollers an immense mass of sculptured stone found a short time before by workmen digging on the east side of the Cathedral. It represented a ferocious looking god in *bas relief,* an image of great size originally, but the stone had been found broken in two lengthwise, and the other half had not been discovered. Hereafter, like the moon, this deity can only show one side of himself to the world. Whilst his godship's carriage blocked the way we looked about us. Near the Museum rises the dome of Santa Teresa's church. This dome was thrown down by an earthquake about half a century ago and was rebuilt only to witness a still more serious downfall of the entire church power. When the convent system was broken up by the government and the nuns driven from this sanctuary, the cell of expiation was found bearing upon its bespattered walls bountiful evidences of the self-imposed scourging these devoted women had undergone. Here it was their habit to smite themselves with thorny rods or steel chains spiked with sharp nails until the blood leaped from their lacerated arms and shoulders. By this sanguinary torture, they had thought to atone for sins real or imaginary, and striven, by reducing their physical powers, to increase their spiritual strength. The heavy sculpture having been placed at one side, we passed into the courtyard and paused a moment to contemplate a picture which was not wholly of the dead past. At the base of the great stone of sacrifice two Indian soldiers in full uniform were seated smoking. They were young and handsome fellows to whom the military dress was very becoming. To their left, under an arcade where were heaps of idols and other Aztec relics awaiting a place in the Museum, stood a beautiful white horse stripped to his bright hued halter, the end of which was fastened to a hook above him on the sill of an old, dust begrimed, unused arched window. On this great hook sat a brilliantly tinted macaw looking down and pluming its many hued feathers. On the floor of a small, sunny balcony adjoining, nearly fronting the soldiers, sat an extremely pretty Indian girl with her rebozo thrown off leaving her rounded arms and brown neck bare. In her black hair, which was braided neatly, a scarlet flower was placed. In her ears were large, gold hoops; about her throat, thick strings of coral beads. From a quaintly shaped, shining cage which stood in front of her she had taken a parrot which she held upon her right hand, while she leaned upon her left and turned her face up toward the bird as she sang a gay little song beginning *"Lorita, Lorita, si tu me quieres bien,"* then she cast coy glances down toward the soldiers and changed the parrot to her left hand, and allowed it to run up and down the pretty arm and across her shoulders pausing in her song, now and then, to caress the bird as it chattered to her some unintelligible answer. At this the Macaw ruffled its feathers and cried out jealously; at which the girl laughed, displaying her white and even teeth. When the soldiers looked up at her, she immediately became coquettishly unconscious of their existence, and toyed with and sang to her parrot as if that and that only were the object of her thoughts. When they did not look up at her, her bright glances were upon them; she varied her graceful poses and sang her ditty more gaily and more clearly, absorbed in the one thought to win their gaze again. Upon this scene gazed with stony eyes the Aztec god of gods Huitzilopochtli, the deity of war. Also Quetzalcoatl, the gentle god, also a gentleman in stone from Yucatan who, in half sitting posture, leaned back upon his elbows as he has doubtless been doing a thousand years or so, and turned toward the girl a very Greekish cast of countenance. There also were other gods, big and little, frogs in stone, and serpents in stone, and greatest among them all the sacrificial stone, that "mighty block of jasper" from whose surface hundreds of thousands of tortured victims passed down into "the Valley of the Shadow." In shape, it is like an immense millstone, its sides covered with sculpture. It is three feet high and nearly ten feet in diameter. The surface is slightly convex, that the martyr laid upon it should present his chest in the best possible position for the priest to tear from it his living heart. Beneath where the victim's bosom was opened a hollow basin is scooped in the stone to receive the blood, and from it a narrow gutter to the edge of the stone is cut to lead the gore away. There are those who contend that the stone is dyed through and through with the torrents of human blood shed upon it. Possibly this is true. It is of porous basalt, and there are indelible stains distinctly to be traced among the sculptures at the sides which the rain and winds of centuries have not washed away. The rooms upstairs contain an immense collection of curios, instructive and valuable objects. The room devoted to natural history is exceedingly interesting, as well as the departments for minerals and geology. The emeralds, opals, and amethysts native to the country are very fine. The opal is abundant in Mexico, but it is claimed that it fades quickly and loses its original fire and brilliancy. Two of the largest aerolites[1] in the world are in this Museum, and the room devoted to Mexican Antiquities contains a magnificent collection of Aztec relics: idols, vases, jars, pottery of all descriptions, weapons of warfare, fully jeweled gods, musical instruments, personal adornments, temple ornaments, feather work, picture writing, torture collars, sculptures, remnants of the army equipment of Cortez—even the portions of the armor worn by him at the time of the conquest—marvelous Spanish stirrups, horrible spurs, and the tiny mirror of polished metal in which the Toltec maiden surveyed her charms. The room is well lighted, tastefully arranged, and one of the most interesting places in the world to visit. Mexico has suffered in all directions from numerous revolutionary struggles and bitter wars which not only have arrested the progress of culture from time to time but have depleted her treasuries of literature, of art, and of antiquities. After each blow her *savants* have gone courageously to work to restore, as far as possible, her severe losses and have succeeded so well that only those who knew of former treasures miss anything from the splendid collections remaining. Notwithstanding all she has been robbed of, Mexico has never failed in a noble generosity to other cities. With an unselfishness which appears like indifference to one not familiar with the character of her people, Mexico has allowed libraries, manuscripts, pictures, sculptures and collections of Indian antiquities of immense value to pass from her keeping. London and Paris, New York and Philadelphia and Washington all have enriched their museums with priceless collections from these regions, but it is evident Mexico has thus enriched others without impoverishing herself.

One room in the Museum contains a remarkably interesting Library; a smaller apartment adjoining contains the curious relics of its dead Emperors and Chieftains. There is the table service used by Maximilian. It is bountiful

1. Stony meteorites.

and of good design, but none of it is solid silver. Plated ware sufficed him. Let those who are not kings and queens make a note of it. Here are many souvenirs of Iturbide, and the chair in which Hidalgo[2] used to sit. There is a portrait of the last viceroy, O'Donojú,[3] and a fine one of the great Conquistador.[4]

On certain days the Museum is thrown open to the school children and the masses generally. Great numbers of the very poor take advantage of the opportunity thus afforded to see the collections and to instruct themselves in many ways. No matter how poorly one is clad, or how lowly his position, any questions asked regarding the objects in any of the departments, are cheerfully answered and explanations clearly given by the attendants in charge. The crowd upon these Open Days is always as interesting as the collections of curiosities. It is pleasant to note the quiet intelligence and eager desire to learn manifested by many in the very humblest walks of life. The progress they make in this sort of education is often surprising. One man, woman or child thus interested brings others and rejoices to see them introduced to paths of knowledge they themselves have found so enticing. I heard a young Indian lad, who had only made his first visit to the Museum three months before, describing to a group of companions the specimens of ore exhibited in one of the cases, telling how they were obtained, where they were found, and to what uses they were put. He gave in a clear, concise manner the information he had received and remembered, passing his learning along the line in a manner evidently pleasing to, and appreciated by, his listeners.

In one of the large, well lighted rooms are two tall, narrow glass cases. One contains the upright figure of a woman with her child at her feet; the other, the figure of a man alone. These mummies have long been noted among the possessions of the Mexican Museum. Whether this man and this woman, who lived three hundred years ago, were in their lives distinguished in any way, ¿*quién sabe?* When they became mummies, and were discovered, they at

2. Father Miguel de Hidalgo, leader of the Mexican revolution of 1810.
3. General Juan de O'Donojú (of Irish descent) arrived in Mexico in July 1821, as *Jefe Político Superior,* the office that replaced the viceroy under the restored Spanish Constitution in 1820. In this capacity he worked out the details of Mexican independence with Augustín de Iturbide, and he continued to serve on the governing junta of the independent Mexican empire until his death in October 1821.
4. Hernán Cortez.

once became distinguished—as mummies—and will no doubt continue so to be until they crumble back to dust and that leveler of all distinctions the grave. They tell at least that they lived, loved, suffered, were human and were martyrs. The bodies are in hue like leather. The attitude of the woman is natural and reposeful. It is a small woman, and her hands and feet retain evidences of remarkable beauty. The hair had been jet black and braided as the women now braid the hair. The slightly drawn lips reveal the teeth of a woman in her youth. The face is bowed and wears an expression of supreme resignation. From the position of her arms she must have been holding the infant now lying at her feet and looking at it when she died. Her right hand and arm, which evidently stiffened in death while she clasped the babe, are round and full having escaped the shrinking which has made unsightly the rest of the body. In sharp and terrible contrast is the attitude of the man. As he died, so he stands. He had drawn himself up on the very points of his toes—his hands clutched at awful nothingness. His shoulders are lifted, and express dire agony. His neck is stretched, and his head thrown back and eyelids strained up as if like one struggling for one's last glimpse of light, one last breath of air. One can fancy the open eyes gazing out of some fast closing orifice into life and the world for the last time, forever! So manifest is the suffering depicted, one seems to see that "dying groan" which the Greek artist so lamented he could not paint. These mummies—man, woman and child—were found between two walls in the old convent of San Domingo where they had been immured alive and suffocated long after the overthrow of the heathen Aztecs. The three figures in their grim, eternal silence tell fearful tidings as their dead, distorted faces look out at us stamped with the piteous anguish that thrilled their blood in the terrible hour of their doom. The mystery of their history is sealed forever from the world to be revealed only in that promised hour "when the secrets of all hearts are opened."

The ruins of the church and convent of San Domingo are among the most interesting in the city. When the property passed into the keeping of the Government with other church wealth, the buildings were partially destroyed by the authorities. Streets were cut through it and other changes made. The edifices were dedicated in 1575 and were magnificently endowed and adorned. They adjoined and partly occupied the site of the first Inquisition building which was established in Mexico in 1571. In 1813 the Inquisition was suppressed, but only to be re-established with all its cruel powers a year afterwards. Not until 1820 was it finally abolished. From its ancient and ruined precincts leaped into light the terrible testimony of the torture chamber, testimony which one reads today in those agonized faces in the halls of the great Museum. Between the altar of martyrdom, the sacrificial stone and the secret cell of the Inquisition which rose beside it, is there not something like a distinction without a difference? The School of Medicine occupies the edifice in which was established the last Tribunal of the Holy Inquisition. Thus, everywhere in Mexico one finds Progress placing her shiny light in the dark socket of the Past.

In the beautiful galleries of the Academy of Fine Arts one finds a display of pictures which, if he be a lover of art, tempts him to return again, and again to the contemplation of the works upon those walls. It is true that art has a formidable rival in this region of country in nature herself. Nowhere could be found such a beautiful sky, such hills and plains, such effects of light and shade, such contrasts of foliage, such stupendous heights, vast rocks and lake and stream combined in so limited an area. Then, on every hand the beggar is a picture in his rags, the humblest artisan, the simplest peasant, a "figure piece" ready made. The flowing rebozo, the Spanish mantle, the thick sarape which they wear afford constant studies in drapery and pose, and where all out door is so replete with picture one is led to wonder what art halls can have to delight so truly. But, he will find in the Academy an answer to such a query in a great display of paintings, many among them being of remarkable excellence. Old and new Mexican art is amply represented, the Church School predominating in both. There is a foreign as well as a national gallery, and in the former we noted an Albrecht Dürer, a Teniers, a Murillo, a Rembrandt, a Leonardo da Vinci and a Rubens, besides other works of famous masters. In the Mexican department several Cabreras were pointed out to us with great pride. Miguel Cabrera [1695–1768] was a Mexican artist who died about one hundred years ago after having won extensive fame. His works display imagination and a certain distinctive delicacy of coloring. Modern Mexican painters were represented by some exquisite landscapes, beautifully reproducing the picturesqueness of Nature in that favored region. A very impressive figure piece was a striking picture by Luis Monrey entitled the Death of Atala. The artist has so ably caught the writer's thought that the figures seemed like a materialization of the spirits Chateaubriand had evolved from his fancy. The picture had won the highest praise and a

prize, I was told, at a National Exhibition. A very grand and effective painting by Don Félix Parra was a large canvas representing Las Casas[5] protecting
the Indian slaves from the cruelty of their Spanish masters. It is a picture
teeming with force, sentiment and great beauty of execution. There were
numbers of other excellent works well warranting the pride the Mexicans
feel in this Institution. Mexico is not blind to the merits of genius, but en-
courages its efforts even though just now her treasury is much depleted. Several artists have been sent abroad to study at the expense of the government,
and private citizens of wealth are liberal patrons of native art. Drawing,
painting, engraving and sculpture are taught in the Academy, and in the last
named branch there were pieces of work on exhibition executed by the pupils
which would do credit to any school of art in any part of the world. Groups
of modelings were shown us and portfolios of drawings executed by the pupils which were in the highest degree excellent. In the same building is a
large collection of casts, coins, ancient medals, a number of very choice old
engravings, and wax work portrait medallions; the latter is very curious and
interesting. All the departments are well arranged and admirably managed,
and if there is a place in the country to make one oblivious of the good, old
warning *Tempus fugit,* it is within the walls of the Academy of Fine Arts in
Mexico.

A visit to the numerous old churches we found to be decidedly worth our
while. There are scarcely any pictures of real value left upon their walls, wars
having despoiled them of these and many other treasures. But, as evidences
of the Spanish domination and the taste of that period, as well as of the
wealth lavished upon the construction and ornamentation of these buildings,
which are monuments of a power that for so long ruled the very rulers of
Mexico, they are exceedingly interesting. They are marvels of carving, and
crosses, and sculptures and lavish gilding, and often we were favored by being
shown the silver plate and jewels yet remaining to them, and which are usually kept in undiscoverable hiding places of undoubted safety. The massive
buildings were some intact and some in ruins. There are about fifty Catholic churches, theirs being still the prevailing religion. There are but five well-

---

5. Bartolomé de las Casas, the sixteenth-century Dominican who worked tirelessly on
behalf of better treatment of the Indians.

established Protestant places of worship. The general plan of all the Catholic edifices is very similar. In the decorations and arrangement of each interior, however, was always to be found some one distinguishing feature. Every structure of the kind has suffered spoliation and disaster to a greater or less degree, while convents have been either torn down and their walls obliterated, or they have been left half ruined to serve as barracks and bull arenas and stables and storehouses, or any use to which they can be put. The first circus I've attended in Mexico was within the walls of an old convent which, when the arena's company left it, was used next day for a bull fight!

At the Hospital [*sic., Church*] of Jesus, in the street of Jesus, and adjoining the hospital of the same name we spent an hour or two delightfully. The building is spacious and rich in adornment and possessions of value. In the sacristy of the church is a work of art in the shape of a cedar ceiling carved in the most elaborate manner, its sculptures divided into sections by richly gilded wood. It is a work of incomputable labor and intricate design. In this room, also, besides some curiously carved antique chairs was a huge, circular table, its round top eight feet in diameter of one, unpieced plank of native mahogany. Vast sums have been offered for this table which the church is rich enough to refuse. We were shown into the church which has a richly columned altar, much gilding, a vaulted ceiling and the usual images and pictures. This structure, with its annexed hospital, is closely associated with the memory of Cortez. He founded and endowed the building four years after the Conquest. It originally bore the name of "Our Lady of the Conception" which was subsequently changed to that of the Hospital and Church of Jesus of Nazareth. The laws by which the Institution was to be conducted were noble and charitable and are carried out to the letter even to this day. In 1562, when he had been dead fifteen years, the remains of Cortez through means of his son were brought from Seville to New Spain and placed in the Chapel of the Monastery of St. Francis in Tezcuco. In 1629, after more than sixty years of quiet rest the bones were removed with great pomp and ceremony and borne along in a coffin covered by a sweeping pall of black velvet, embroidered in silver, accompanied by a cortege comprised of immense numbers of people in splendid mourning trappings, bearing banners and marching to the beat of muffled drums, and deposited, with every token of honor and respect, in the vaults of the Church of St. Francis within the city gates. Here, the ashes of this illustrious warrior were left in peace for nearly two hundred years. Then, for reasons not set forth, the bones of the first Marquis of the Valley were by special permission of the Archbishop on the 2nd of July, 1794, at 8 o'clock in the evening removed in secret from the church of St. Francis in the carriage of the Marquis de Sierra Nevada, then Governor of New Spain. The remains were placed in a shroud of cambric, embroidered in gold, with a fringe of black lace four inches deep. They were then placed in a wooden coffin, which was enclosed in one of lead; the latter being the identical one in which the body had journeyed from *Castilleja de la Cuesta*, near Seville in Spain, to Mexico. This leaden coffin, in its turn, was placed in a casket of crystal which had plates and crossbars of silver. Then, the oft disturbed dust of the Conqueror was laid away in the sanctuary of the Church of Jesus, which he had founded, and the gifted Mexican sculptor, Manuel Tolsa, erected over it a bronze monument bearing the arms of the warrior's family and surmounted by his bust. Once more he was left to repose quietly, his tomb a shrine visited by thousands for a term of twenty nine years when, the impulsive Spaniards in their zeal at the establishment of a national independence, threatened destruction to everything connected with Old Spain. Strange to say, the grave of him who had given them the country narrowly escaped desecration at their hands. They were bent, in their patriotism, upon tearing open the tomb and flinging the dust of Cortez to the four winds of heaven. This was prevented by the prompt action of one high in authority who saved the remains by entering the Chapel at night and with trusted assistants bearing them out of reach of the sacrilegious despoilers to a secret place of safety.

While we stood beside the spot where he had lain, away up among the carved capitals of the altar a little bird was flying and singing. His note began high and came trickling down the scale for six or eight tones, beautifully loud and clear and sweet. The sacristan said the little creature had found a hole broken in a pane of glass away up at the top of one of the lofty windows. There it made its exits and its entrances, brought its mate to do the same, built its nest among the capitals of the columns and made the church its home, often mingling its notes with the music at High Mass. We had been assured there were no cloistered nuns in Mexico, but we certainly came upon one, or the ghost of one, kneeling in her sable serges, on the floor in a portion of the building absorbed in silent prayer. Above her, clear and fresh, rang out at intervals the song of praise of the little *Salto Pered,* as the bird is called. It almost seemed as if from his exalted perch he were singing responses to the nun's unuttered petitions.

From the church we went up stairs to the Hospital, a delightfully clean, sweet-looking place with delightful baths both hot and cold. We were shown all over the building, out upon the cheerful and clean corridors, up to the Azotea, into the wards and into the living apartments of the superintendents. The ward devoted to the women boasts of having in its chapel an image of The Mother Mary brought by Cortez from Spain and given to this altar. Mass is said there for the benefit of the invalids. In the wards we found a scrupulously clean, well-lighted hall with the doors of the bedrooms opening upon it from either side. Between every cot was a wooden partition extending up some six or seven feet, so that each patient was spared the sight of any other patient's misery. Every place was ventilated well, and the people in the wards were all in clean beds and in clean clothes. A careful record was kept showing when each patient entered, with what disease he was suffering, his name, age and nationality, the name of the physician who attended him, when he was cured, when discharged or when he died. We were shown the enclosed space on the house top used for dissecting purposes. There, too, mattresses are taken upon which any patient chances to die; the contents are shaken out, thoroughly aired and cleaned, and the sacking washed before being used again. The godliness of the cleanliness pervaded every part and portion of the building. We were permitted to inspect among the treasures pertaining to the house old documents pertaining to it and its famous founder. There we saw the original paper furnished by a member of the Cortez family, descriptive of the funeral obsequies of Hernán Cortez and his descendant Don Pedro Cortez as the double ceremony was observed when the Conqueror's bones were removed from the monastery to the Church of St. Francis. We also saw, bound in vellum and yellow with time, papers concerning the hospital signed by Hernán Cortez himself. There were others bearing the signature of *Yo El Rey* and *Yo La Reina* as they had been signed by the long since quiet hands of Felipe el Segundo and the Queen of Spain. There were other objects of the kind over which we lingered, and we were especially interested in two portraits of Cortez, one representing him erect and in full armor, the other in a kneeling posture with the face half averted. I failed to find in the pictures indication of those qualities which made him so remarkable a man. He was by no means tall and was slenderly built.

In passing out of the building we were shown that it was entirely built of cedar and of stone and put together without the aid of a nail in any portion.

14

❋

Bull Fight

Inducements to attend a bull fight. Don Manuel's turnout. People who attend such amusements, people who do not. Our party. The Street of San Francisco. Mexican mansions. A sumptuous ball. Former Palace of Iturbide. The Alameda. Statue of Charles the Fourth. What a great man said of it. The Paseo de Bucareli. *The Empress' drive. The statue of Columbus. Dust or robbers? The Indian and his sprinkling pot. Approach to Chapultepec. The indifference manifested to highwaymen. The glimpse of gardens beyond the gates. "The run" to the Arena. Old Juan's excitement. Las Mulas. Shady side and sunny side. A cockpit at a church door. The amphitheater. The spectators. Sombreros. Dress distinctions. The arena. The opening of the gates. The grand entry of the troop. The combatants, the game, the bull. Gaviño, the famous Matador. His mode of slaying the beast. Other games. More bulls. The* Morale *of bull fights. A grand dinner. El Teatro Nacional. The President's box. Miramón's daughter. A peculiar statement regarding the corpse of Sontag.*

Of course we attended a bull fight. Many Mexicans remain away from the bull ring. Many Americans do not. Our friend Don Manuel E[scandón]. proposed we should go, and Don Manuel was used to carrying his point. Our scruples were merrily, yet earnestly borne down. We were assured that this was to be *"una gran función extraordinaria"* gotten up expressly for *los Americanos en la ciudad.* We were shown splendid illuminated posters, setting forth this fact in vast letters of red and gold, and we were, moreover, confronted with the enticing statement that "the greatest living *Matador,* Gaviño," was to be in at the death on this occasion, while the bulls engaged were from a certain famous "bull-raising farm and all A–No. 1." Who could withstand so seductive a proclamation? A party was made up. Two Mexican ladies, who had never in their lives attended such an exhibition, accompanied by their husbands, who never in their lives had remained away from one, joined us. Never mind what day of the week it was. Suffice it to say it was not Sunday—in Paris! Don Manuel ordered his mail-coach brought to the door. To it were attached eight perfectly matched little black mules, dressed in yellow leather harness ornamented with scarlet tufts and plumes. Each mule wore a string of eighteen, joyous-toned, tiny bells. Don Manuel was a splendid whip, and it was his delight to take a party of eight or ten of his friends on top of his coach where there was ample room for them all, place his grooms and footmen in the capacious interior, and drive off to Tacubaya or some one of the Mexican gardens where a little feast, a little dance, plenty of music and flowers, and a charming drive back to town would round with pleasure a delightful day. Cora and I had many happy little trips of that kind, where a graceful host and his agreeable and cultivated friends, added to the beautiful spots we visited charms never to be forgotten. Don Manuel was a young man of the frankest and most winning manners, totally unspoiled by his vast wealth, and enjoying a well deserved popularity. He could get up a party on the shortest possible notice, even his sisters would break through the Mexican rule of female seclusion for him. Indeed, no one said him "nay" when he proposed an excursion. With perfect manners and a thoroughly kind heart, speaking with fluency three or four languages, this young Mexican knew how to ensure for every guest of his a delightful time and any social affair in which he engaged was sure to be a success.

That day of the bull fight the weather was perfect, as winter weather usually is in Mexico. Our party had soon all reported at the hotel, and it was, as usual, decided that Don Manuel himself should drive, and that we should occupy the top of the coach. In all drives about Mexico one desires an open carriage or an outside seat for, no matter how familiar the beautiful scenery may become, it never loses its fascination nor leaves one less eager than at first to enjoy its loveliness. I know a Mexican whose life has been chiefly spent within the shadow of his glorious mountains who never forgets to wave adieu to Orizaba as the snow peak fades from sight when he journeys from it nor to take off his hat in reverential greeting to it as he returns. So, the servants were all allowed to ride in state inside and our party, ten in number, clambered to our places on top. Don Manuel drew his silvered sombrero firmly over his brows, grasped his long whip, gathered up the reins, and we were off; our mules making music wherever we went. The bull ring is no longer allowed to exist within the city limits, and we were to drive four leagues to a place called Tlanapantla to reach the *Plaza de Toros* of the day. A railway extends to this locality and has an immense deal of patronage on bull fight days, chiefly Indians.

We made an early start in order to linger by the way if we liked and drove out through the street of San Francisco, one of the finest in the city. There is the church and remains of the convent from which the street derives its name, and on this avenue are located the town residences of the Escandón and Barrón families, names associated with the foremost social, benevolent and commercial enterprises which have benefitted the country in the last thirty years. There is also a very peculiar house occupied at one time by an eminent lawyer, now dead, Martínez de La Torre of Mexico. It is a spacious edifice, its exterior entirely covered with dark blue and white porcelain tiles. The Escandón mansion is magnificent, very large, adorned on the outside with carved columns, statues and bronzes and well deserves to be called a palace. As we drove by it Don Manuel's young sisters waved a greeting from the balcony.

The Barrón residence is smaller, and outwardly plainer, but with a grand court and beautiful interior and in both dwellings are the embellishments of culture, refinement and taste, while a frank hospitality ennobles the sumptuous halls. I remember a ball which was given at Mr. Barrón's residence in honor of a foreign Prince which had some novel features that recalled descriptions of Eastern magnificence. The entire house was thrown open. Every apartment was a *boudoir* or a *salón* beautifully fitted up and lighted by wax candles in sconces and candelabra of solid silver. Vines and tropical flowers abounded of the rarest and most delicate nature. The entrance to the court below was an arch of living blossoms, and the great court itself was domed by an artificial firmament of dark blue velvet in which multitudes of gas jets were so arranged as to represent stars. The floor of the *patio* was laid out as a *portiere* with walks lined with tropical trees in which living birds flitted and sang. Below them blossomed the rarest exotics in beds of earth bordered with violets in bloom. At the foot of the grand marble staircase an immense mirror was laid representing a lake which was bordered with the rarest ferns and luxuriant lilies. A graceful bridge thrown over this to connect the terminus of the main walk with the stairs made the illusion complete. On the floors above everything was on a corresponding scale of magnificence. Three rooms were devoted to refreshments. That in which punch and ices were served had its tables laid entirely in the richest cut crystal. The supper room laid for the ladies had an entire table service of solid gold, that for the gentlemen was correspondingly laid in silver. Exquisite music from musicians so placed as to be invisible lent its harmonies to the enchanting surroundings, where all that luxury could devise had been arranged with the most cultivated taste. They get up such things in Mexico with wonderful ease. What wonder? There is great wealth, much love of the beautiful, taste and a poetical bias. Even among the ranks of the working classes one finds artistic instincts and excellent judgement combined, while the love of flowers is national, and their grace, color and beauty in all decorations is fully understood.

The former palace of the Emperor Iturbide[1] now converted into a fashionable hotel is also on this street and other fine buildings. We passed the Alameda, a beautiful, flowery, public park or garden some 1600 feet long by nearly 700 feet in width. It contains a variety of large, handsome trees, several fountains, quantities of flowers, leafy thickets and romantic nooks. Its very prettily designed drives, bridle paths and walks lead among the scented shrubberies and splashing waters. The street of San Francisco leads past it on its southern side, that of Tacuba on its northern, and handsome residences are all about. It is a rare thing to find, so near the center of a great town, so large a plot of valuable ground thus devoted to a magnificent garden and the pleasure of the people. Nowhere could it be more appreciated than in Mexico, where a love of trees and flowers is part and parcel of a Mexican's nature. The Alameda derived its name from the great number of *Alamo*— quivering aspens—originally planted in this delightful spot. It is the oldest park in the city, having been planned by the Viceroy Don Luis Velasco in 1592. More than a century elapsed before it assumed its present proportions,

---

1. Augustín de Iturbide ruled the Mexican Empire as Augustín I from 1821 to 1823 following independence from Spain.

but since the time of the Marquis de Croix,[2] its thirty acres have been kept up to the existing grade of elegance and beauty.

At the terminus of the street at the western end of the Alameda in an open space stands an imposing equestrian statue of Charles the IV. It rests upon a substantial pedestal of native stone and was modeled, founded and placed by the Mexican sculptor Manuel Tolsa [1757–1816]. It was executed at the order and expense of the Viceroy Marquis de Branciforte,[3] who little dreamed the royal statue would ever adorn republican walks. The artist took seven years in which to complete it. In 1803, Baron von Humboldt assisted at its unveiling and declared it to be second to none in the world excepting perhaps that of Marcus Aurelius at Rome. It is one sole piece of casting, contains six hundred weight of metal, and was the first work of the kind ever executed in America. It adorned the center of the grand plaza until the declaration of Mexican independence in 1821 when, the country having shaken off the thrall of foreign kings, the statue of *Carlos Cuarto* was ordered out of public view. It disappeared, and for years remained in some one of the many secure hiding places which the strong old city affords. Not until 1852 was it once more brought to light and placed upon the site it now occupies. It is colossal, and when first brought to its present locality lent its bronzed dignity and kingly sanction to a bull arena close at hand. Of late years the *Plaza de Toros* has been abolished, and its space devoted to lovelier uses.

From the statue two broad drives lead to the Garita de Belén at Chapultepec. One of these is the old and now almost unused Paseo de Bucareli, a grand old avenue which for many years held dominion over all other popular Mexican drives. It leads almost directly south from the Carlos. We drove a little way upon it. Evidences of its former beauty were still apparent. There are beautiful trees, remains of fine fountains, and the way is broad, but there is no denying the fact that the road would be materially improved if some of its stones were put in some of its holes. When Maximilian came into power in Mexico, Carlota laid out a new paseo which for some time after she left the country was called the "mad woman's drive." It starts from the same point, but lies further north than the old road and leads in a perfectly straight, southwesterly line from the King's statue to the ancient King's pal-

2. Carlos Francisco, Marqués de Croix, was Viceroy of New Spain from 1766 to 1771.
3. Miguel del a Grúa Talamanca y Branciforte was Viceroy of New Spain from 1794 to 1798.

ace. It has continued to be embellished since Carlota's time and is now called
the Paseo de la Reforma and is the most fashionable promenade about
Mexico. It is a beautiful avenue, very broad, its center adorned at regular
intervals with circular parterres where in time statues will be placed. One of
Cortez certainly should be there, one of Doña Marina, and one of that Aztec
hero and martyr, Guatimotzín. The road for some distance on the hither side
of Chapultepec is thus adorned down the middle, so that carriages can pass
down on one side and up the other. There are beautiful trees, ornamental
platforms for musicians, stone benches and, also, walks on each side for
pedestrians.

Mr. Antonio Escandón before his death ordered from the sculptor [Char-
les] Cordier a statue of Christopher Columbus to adorn this beautiful promenade and presented it to the City of Mexico. Mr. Escandón did not live to
see it placed, but it is erected there, an enduring proof of his public spirit, his
encouragement of talent and his great liberality. The monument occupies the
center of a circular parterre of flowers with stone posts and chains separating
it from the public path. The pedestal nests on a granite base and supports
four bronze figures besides the colossal center one of the daring navigator
himself. The Colón monument is about midway of the drive; the whole
length of which is one Mexican league. Clusters of lamps at each point of the
octagonal base illuminate the spot at night, and many terminate their outward drive at this place, sweeping around it to go down the opposite side, or
they draw out of line and wait to see the moving throng pass by. As far as
this monument, and a short distance beyond, the dust is kept down by the
indefatigable Indian and his sprinkling pot. Few, during the hours for fashion
to be on wheels in this league-long avenue, go beyond the moistened limits.
The reason is not, as an American writer recently said, "because beyond the
Monument everyone is afraid of robbers," but because the whole drive is not
kept watered, and the dust, therefore, is intolerable. The same writer declared
that the Alameda, in open day, was also "a resort for highwaymen, and the
passerby might expect at any moment to be halted by the presented pistols
of these road agents." A greater absurdity was never penned, and the passerby
is just as likely to be halted by highwaymen in Central Park New York as in
the public drives and promenades of Mexico. Our experiences proved this to
our own personal satisfaction, and we did not presume that our experiences
were exceptional in this respect. We went time and again after that day on

excursions to Tacubaya, Tacuba, Chapultepec, San Angel and other points without accident nor dread of danger. Before leaving home we had been told by American tourists that the owners of homes in these suburban places derived neither pleasure nor comfort from their possessions, as they dared not reside there nor to go to and from there for fear of robbers. We never heard anything of this kind from the owners themselves. We visited these places with the proprietors and their families, and they certainly evinced neither alarm nor hesitation at any time, although the drive back was often after dark and along a lonely road. No guard ever accompanied the carriages. We were assured the owners spent several months of every year with their families in their country homes, and the son of one of the richest men in Mexico married while we were there and took his bride to his palatial country seat in Tacubaya going to and from the city every day by himself, and he, especially just at that time, would have brought an immense ransom to his captors!

As we drove on, the grand old castle of Chapultepec rose in plain view crowning its magnificent height. We caught glimpses beyond its gates of historic trees and rare flowers. The old aqueduct leading from the castle to the town extended its picturesque arches on our right, forming itself a theme for many thoughts and frames for many landscapes.

As we turned sharply to the right and drove under the aqueduct out into the open country, we were soon a part of a great crowd all bent upon reaching the same destination in the shortest possible time. There were horsemen of all ages, sizes and condition, vehicles of every describable and indescribable make. Indians trotting on foot, and even dogs running along with an eager air as if they already sniffed fresh meat in the distance. The dust was very deep upon the roads, and we were speedily enveloped in its suffocating clouds. There was only one way to escape it and that was to pass everything upon the road. Don Manuel cracked his whip and uttered an encouraging ejaculation. The little mules set their thirty-two little hoofs into a faster trot which speedily broke into a gallop. The servants inside the coach began to put their sombreroed heads out of the window. Old Juan, who had been coachman in Don Manuel's family ever since the latter was a little boy, looked out with a face beaming with pride to see how his young master managed his octuple team. The delight manifested in his countenance as we sped past carriage after carriage was a study; his head protruded further and further through the window, and at last his excitement became so great he opened the coach door and stood upon the step, and when we all thought the mules were running away and we were holding ourselves atop of the coach with a vise like grip, old Juan, from the step, was swinging his great hat wildly in air hissing and shouting to the team at the top of his voice to "go faster"—"faster"—"faster"—to "pull"—to "gallop"—to "run" and *las mulas* did "run" at such a rate we began to doubt if anything would be left of us for the bull fight, when a man approaching us on horseback at full gallop shouted, "*un caballo muerte!*," pointing back in the direction we were going. Don Manuel immediately pulled his team down to a trot and held them steadily, as they sped with pricked up ears past the defunct horse, which had fallen under its rider stone dead and been drawn to one side of the highway, the first victim of the fete we were hastening to see, and a terror to every other quadruped going that way.

As we had distanced everything on the road, we now drove soberly along and speedily arrived at Tlanapantla where the crowd, having secured places, rushed shouting and gesticulating toward the ring evidently eager for the fray. The "crowd" was made up chiefly of Indian men and boys, with rebozoed women adding to the number. They all pushed for the cheap side for which their ticket had been taken, and ticket vendors were offering for sale "seats on the shady side" and "seats in the sun" the latter being very cheap and rapidly bought up by the poorer classes. The scene in many respects was like that in the neighborhood of a circus in some large town in the States. Every sort of vehicle that ever went on wheels was represented there from the glittering, crested family coach and fancy turnout, to the humblest wagons and carts; while every rideable animal from the thoroughbred of the man of fashion, to the sore backed, half starved, shaggy little donkey was to be seen tethered by rope halters or held by liveried grooms. Everything in the world seemed to be for sale there, and everybody seemed to be selling it. There were all kinds of dulces and drinks, paper plumes and banners to be carried into the arena, and all sorts of tempting small wares to be carried away from the arena as souvenirs. Leaving our carriage, we walked toward the amphitheater, passing on our way an old stone church under the very eyes of which the scene of the bull fight lay. At the church gates a row of game cocks was tied. They were to be pitted against each other as soon as the larger game was killed. The birds were restless and tugged at their fetters and, now and then, sent out loud, exasperated crowings, which roused the echoes over the numerous graves where the dead slept about the church, and soon jubilant answers from cocks on neighboring farms.

I have forgotten what was paid for our seats on the shady side, which is the "swell" side at a bull fight, but it was not a very large sum though more than double that asked for the sunny side. The arena was large with several gates, and rude staircases, steep and narrow, led to the tiers of seats above. We found places in a roomy wooden box which had been especially reserved for our party. The wooden chairs were on a bare wooden floor and all covered by a wooden roof. The seats had been temporarily cushioned and some gay hangings suspended from the front of our box. The seating capacity of the amphitheater was sufficient, I think, for at least twenty-five hundred persons. On this occasion its double tiers of boxes were packed on the side of the sun and very well filled on the side of the shade, though the spectators even there were chiefly men. All the women belonging to a French opera troop then in town were conspicuously present, and also all those connected with a circus company then stationed in the city. These, with two or three other scattered Americans, were the only representatives of our sex besides our own party. Not a Mexican lady, save those in our own box, was to be seen, and they looked ill at ease and out of place. Large numbers of the best classes of Mexican men were there, however, and every Mexican lady who stayed at home was represented by father, husband, brother or son. Everyone kept his hat on his head, and the sombreros worn on this occasion were a show in themselves. Some were gray, ornamented only with a silver side wreath on the crown enclosing the monogram of the wearer. Some were bright scarlet, embroidered in threads of yellow gold and in the most elaborate fashion. Some, again, were black, so ornamented with heavy, glittering silver trimmings the foundation could scarcely be made out. All were big enough to serve the double purpose of hat and umbrella for the owner's shoulders. Had these shining sombreros been on the sunny side of the amphitheater, the dazzling glitter must have put out all the eyesight on the shady side. The Indians opposite wore sombreros equally large but of straw, and dress distinctions never more plainly divided rich and poor than the blanket and the straw hat of the Indian that day with the sun shining full upon him and the embroidered sombrero and fine broadcloth of the wealthy Mexican puffing his cigarette held between gloved fingers in the cool protection of the shady side.

The arena was roofed only by the soft, bewitching sky which belongs to

Mexico. Its floor was hard beaten earth. At intervals within the immense arena was a barricade or enclosure of stout-wood about eight feet wide, standing at two or three feet from the lower circling wall of the amphitheater. These were to afford protection to the flying *chulos* and *toreadors* when too hard pressed by the belligerent bull.

A box gaily draped with brilliant hangings and gay flags awaited the Alcalde or mayor of the town with his officers without whose sanction the play could not begin. Around the lower tier of seats a rope was passed, and on it fluttered every imaginable fanciful device in tissue paper with attached streamers cut into minute strips to flutter in the least suspicion of a breeze. These lent a wonderfully gay if gaudy aspect to the scene. Vendors of such things also passed about among the crowd so that soon every seat displayed some gorgeous party-colored symbol while other vendors carried about trays of pulque and *limonada* and oranges and *dulces*. Oranges sold conspicuously on the sunny side, for oranges in this country are very cheap. So far all was well. There was a great deal of talk, a great deal of gesticulation, a great deal of enthusiasm on the part of the audience, and we became interested both in the novel appearance of the spectators, and in the interest they exhibited for the opening of the approaching fight. We even began to regard our own presence at such a scene with decreasing repugnance and to feel a sympathy with the impatience of the other spectators. So does the horror of a bull fight recede from one whilst waiting for it to begin. By this time nearly everyone was supplied with oranges on the sunny side, and every man on the shady side was puffing away at a cigarette replacing the last with a fresh one so soon as needed. Suddenly, amidst the striking of explosive wax matches, the peeling of fruit and the hum of general conversation there was a burst of music followed by a long relieved "ah-h-hh" from the waiting multitude. The Alcalde, surrounded by his lesser officials, had entered his box and taken his seat. Another blast from the bugles and everyone sat silent, expectant, even eager. The bugles rang out clear and sweet again, and at this third call the great gates swung wide open and through them came a gay pageant all aglow with gorgeous hues and all aglitter with shining spangles of silver and gold, shaking tassels and fluttering fringes. The goodly company was composed of those who were destined to take part in the day's sport. The splendor of their costumes, the graceful yet athletic figures of the men, the enlivening music, the thronged amphitheater formed a stirring spectacle which kindled the

blood, excited keen interest and blinded one for the nonce to the tragic possibilities involved in all this inspiriting display. The procession was made up
of *Matadors, Banderilleros, Toreros, Picadors* and *Chulos.* The *Picadors* or
Toreadors who fight the bull on horseback were mounted and carried long,
iron tipped lances. The horses themselves were poor, miserable creatures
which should long since have been in the bone yard but, under a stout leathern armor which protected chest and flank and wearing the Mexican saddle,
their deficiencies and imperfection were quite concealed. The only armor
worn by their riders was a pair of strong leather leggings. Other mounted
men wearing jaunty costumes rode much better horses and carried no
weapon, unless the lariat coiled at the saddlebow could be called one. The
business of these was simply to employ their skill with lasso if the beast
proved himself unworthy of his foemen's steel.

On foot, in silk and silver costumes came the gay, nimble footed *Toreros;*
composed of *Banderilleros* and of *Matadors* less famous than they liked to be.
Among the latter were some amateurs, who were that day to flesh their
maiden swords in hopes of winning applause from the crowd, as well as practice in an art of which they were ambitious to be masters. Two agile *chulos,* or
clowns, grotesquely attired were conspicuous figures in the *grand entree,* their
costumes in comical contrast with those of the plumed knight of the arena
beside whom they capered and leaped and grimaced. The noted *Matador,*
whose duty it was to finally dispatch the bull, the famous *Gaviño,* headed the
foot-fighters wearing a plumed, round cap from beneath which at the back
fell a short clump of false, braided black hair upon his neck. His spangled
vest was of black and gold; his pink satin jacket blazed with embroidery and
tinsel adornments, and besides a softly folded dark red *faja* or sash about his
waist he wore black satin knee breeches, silk gartered hose of deep crimson,
and slippers. He carried a sword and crimson silk *capa* or cloak. The *Toreros,*
who were to tease and torment the bull, were similarly costumed, but carried
no weapon. They wore velvet jackets either green, scarlet, blue or white,
richly ornamented, or were clad in entire suits of satin wrought profusely in
gold or silver thread, and trimmed with shimmering fringes of the same metals. All wore knee breeches, silk stockings and black slippers. In color and
material there was a wide range of fancy; the cut of the costumes alone being
uniform. All carried bright mantles of silk or light wool thrown gracefully
over one arm.

The *banderilleros* wore a similar dress and marched also on foot. They carried in their hands the *banderilla,* an innocent-looking cluster of artificial flowers and gay streamers, affixed to a steel stem which terminated in [a] sharp prong or barb. The device, which takes many forms, being sometimes a group of gay little flags, sometimes paper rosettes concealing fire-works, and sometimes gorgeous, tissue paper bannerets, hiding fire crackers, and tied by satin and silver ribbons, is intended to be thrust into the bull's neck by a skillful maneuver on the part of the *banderillero.* If well placed it cannot be shaken out, and the greater the struggle of the animal to relieve himself of it, the more firmly the barb imbeds itself in his flesh; whilst the fireworks concealed in it begin to explode and by their heat and noise goad him to fury. The thronged arena, the flags, the music, the gay mantles made the scene one of great animation, grace and color and brought to mind something of the olympic games of old. The procession advanced to the front of the Alcalde's box where all saluted. They then proceeded to make the circuit of the arena. At sight of the famous *Matador* Gaviño, the multitude shouted and vociferously called him by name and cried, "*bravo, bravo,* Gaviño," and waved their hats in air. When the round of the amphitheater had been completed, the group departed. The *Picadors,* lances in hand, drew out to their places; also the mounted men with lassoes. The *Chulos* with nimble pranks took stations, the amateur *Matadors* looked to their swords and the toreros adjusted their mantles. One clown swung himself up to a perch above the great gate which led to the *toril* or pen of the bulls. That gate was exactly opposite our box, and as it opened we looked into a dark, narrow aperture illuminated for a second by two flaming eyes. The next instant a young, handsome bull leaped into the arena, receiving as he passed a stroke from an iron goad bestowed by the clown. With that goad quivering in his hide the bull trotted straight across the ring, stopped immediately below our box and looked up in our faces with a mute, appealing gaze in his great eyes sad enough to touch a heart of stone. He moved his great head from side to side, scrutinized the faces, uttered a low excited moo which seemed to say, "this may be all fun for you, but it is death to me. Can you be happy in seeing me tortured? Be merciful! Let me escape!" At this juncture the *Toreros* came. They swept across the arena light and graceful as so many Mercuries. Their gay mantles fluttered in the air. They shook the silken folds before the poor creature's eyes. It ran a little distance this way, a little distance that but offered no more resistance than if it had been a frightened young heifer. Loud groans and hisses issued from the spectators. The *Picadors* advanced and poked and pierced the animal with their spears. It merely moved clumsily out of their way, while the multitude assailed it with abusive epithets and whatever tangible things they chanced to have at hand. Finally, when it was evident there was no fight in the bull, two horsemen rode toward [it] and as the animal ran bewildered hither and thither, two lassoes were lifted and went circling gracefully through the air. This, caught the undemonstrative bovine by one of its hind legs, and that, by one of its horns. In an instant the beast was down and being dragged out as an ignominious failure, a mean, spiritless thing amid contemptuous showers of orange peel, cigarette stumps, hisses and loud anathemas of the multitude. Its peaceful nature had saved the creature's life for this time at least.

There was another flourish of trumpets. This time a great black bull came bounding into the arena and paused midway with a defiant glare at the people, while he pawed the earth with nervous hoofs and uttered a fierce, belligerent bellow. There was a sprinkling of yellow hair along its tawny spine, as if its back had received a share of the gold that fell to Danae's tower. Its eye "in fine frenzy rolling," and its excited demeanor were warlike demonstrations, which were received with cheers and shouts by the sunny side, and clapping of hands and other unmistakable evidences of delight by the shady side. The *Toreros* skipped lightly across the ring fluttering their scarfs—which are by no means always red, but of orange, green, blue, chrome—any vivid hue. For a moment, it seemed as if it were only some picturesque dance—some new figure in a german.[4] But as the maddening mantles came closer, the bull dashed first at one, then another, putting them to hasty flight and often chasing the *Torero* to the shelter of the wooden screens, against which the heavy thud of the bull's horns gave evidence how close had been the race and how hard would have been the blow upon the body of the fleeing fighter. It was now merely an exciting play, a sort of "puss in the corner" game—the movements of the excited but clumsy bull were in striking contrast to the graceful celerity of his agile opponent. Now a *Torero* less skillful than the last flaunts his bright *Capa* and comes rushing down

4. Townsend here undoubtedly refers to the German cotillion, popular in the nineteenth century.

toward the bull. He has miscalculated his chances and is caught on the lowered horns and tossed in air like a rag doll, but falls to earth unhurt and, gathering himself up, beats a hasty retreat for the nearest barrier crest fallen and discomfited.

This bit of self assertion on the bull's part drew renewed cheers from the spectators who shouted, swung their hats in air, laughed and clapped their hands and moved their rainbow-hued banners excitedly. The bull was now wrought up to a pitch of fury. His small success had rendered him triumphant, and this taurine Alexander waited new worlds to conquer. He tossed his horns, pawed the ground, moved his tasseled tail and sniffed the air. A *Picador* now rode at him, his spear in hand. The bull charged at the horse but was held off by main strength by the *Picador* who pressed his lance into the thick hide while a *Torero* flung down his gorgeous cloak to divert the animal's attention. No sooner were the contestants separated than the bull shook his horns and repeated the assault. This time he struck the horse full in the chest, which was protected by the leathern armor, and although the *Picador* with all his might pressed his spear against the bull's back, so powerful was the animal he lifted horse and rider and overthrew both. They fell with a dull, sickening thud just in front of our box and at this point Cora turned her back, hid her eyes, and by no argument could be induced to face the arena again.

The *Picador* nimbly extricated himself and before the bull could follow up his advantage his eyes were dazzled by half a dozen *Capas* or mantles flaunted in his face and, as he turned upon his new tormentors, the tumbled horse and rider were helped up. We were told that worrying dogs were sometimes let into the ring to add to the bull's excitement, but nothing of the kind was done at this *gran función*. The next rush of the bull was at a horse and rider stationed nearly opposite. This time the animal got its horns under the stiff leather mail and, although the spear was made to do savage service in its back, so that it bled freely, the bull gored the poor horse badly, and he fell stone dead to the ground. Even as in the arena of human strife there was at once another waiting and ready to fill the vacant place. The saddle and trappings were dexterously stripped from the prostrate animal. The stiffening body was dragged out, and almost immediately another horse was led in arrayed in the very armor and saddle, yet warm with life, of the fallen equine whose same rider mounted the fresh beast. Meanwhile the play had gone on. A *Banderillero* came flying across the ring, a *banderilla* in each hand. A *chulo* with his antics and a waving mantle kept the bull's ferocity up to the required standard, horsemen darted hither and thither and, as the bull charged full upon his antagonist, the latter, poised like a bird to flee from harm's way, planted a gorgeous *banderilla* in each shoulder of the bull. The maneuver is a very dangerous one and was beautifully executed. The grateful crowd manifested its appreciation by prolonged applause. The poor brute's headlong course had been arrested by the planting of the barbs and, with this new torment in his flesh, he shook his head, pawed the ground, and gave a low bellow. Then he rushed furiously at an approaching *Picador* who with an exercise of prodigious strength resisted the bull's attempts to overthrow him but could not prevent the goring of his horse which, in a shockingly disemboweled condition tottered out of the ring to give place to another. Meanwhile, the bull's attention was diverted by the distracting play of the mantles in which the *Toreros* were wonderfully expert. Here one ran beside the bull flirting the silky folds in its eyes; there one approached full in the face of the animal almost spreading the scarf over its nose. Now one, by a graceful fling, swung it over the beast's horns, and as quickly withdrew it, or left it where it was clinging, and darted deftly away while the bull plunged here and yon, forward, sideways and often made a most unexpected turn which put all his tormentors to flight. But now, a signal from the bugles called for the *Matador*. He bowed to the Alcalde's box, turned his attention for a moment to the tiers of spectators, then advanced along toward the bull. The conflict was not a long one. Possibly the young *Matador* trembled in the presence of the great master Gaviño. At all events, his thrust, though bravely made, was a bad one and the beast plunged off with the sword quivering in his flesh and his blood pouring on the ground. A murmur ran through the crowd. The *Matador* recovered his sword and made another unsuccessful lunge. Still the bull was not killed but, rushed away a few steps only to fall to the ground weakened by the loss of blood. The crowd so lately watching the battle with wild eagerness, was now moved by a great pity and seeing the poor animal *hors du combat* and suffering, they shouted as with one voice for the "blow of mercy" which was immediately granted. One, well directed thrust from a sword and the bull's business in this or any other bull-ring was ended forever. The *Matador* turned away dejected at his ill success. At a signal from the bugles gates were thrown open, and four black mules gaily harnessed and decorated were driven in to drag away the dead body. Many ineffectual attempts were made to bring the mules near enough to the dead bull to fasten the whiffletrees to the band which had been securely fastened about the toro's horns. They shied, leaped, and several times ran away manifesting their terror and disgust in the most unmistakable way, but were finally made fast and to the sound of music, and the cheers of the crowd, dragged off the great unwieldy carcass, the *chulo* riding the corpse as it passed from the arena.

We now thought the gory game was over, but it was not. The trumpets were blown again, and another bull so like the last in appearance it seemed like a resurrection, leaped into the ring. Its hide was glossy as silk, and its condition told of the rich pastures of the famous bull farm where it was raised. It greeted the spectators with a furious roar, and began to dash about the ring. *Toreadors* rode about casting the lasso and catching the bull in the most adroit manner, now by one of the horns, now by both, now by the neck, now by the leg. The circling ropes swung and fell with such exactness it was evident the animal was totally at the mercy of the flying lariats and we should scarcely have been astonished to see him caught by his tongue or his front tooth. So soon as this play was over, a horseman dashed forward, chased the bull around the ring, overtook it, seized its tail in his hand, then quickly, while holding it in a firm grasp, threw one leg also over it and wheeling his horse, by a sudden jerk brought the ponderous beast flat upon the ground. This is a favorite bull game in Mexico and is called *colear.* To overthrow a bull in this way is considered a great feat. To accomplish it requires courage, splendid horsemanship, dexterity and great muscular power. After this performance, which was more than once repeated and greeted with ringing applause, all the previous enactments of the ring were reproduced. The *Toreros* showed no fatigue, and skipped about the arena, their gay mantles always managed with exquisite grace. Their part of the performance is always a beautiful sight. It combines with the grace of the ballet the excitement and interest of a tourney and is one [of] the most agreeable features of the entertainment. This time when the barbed *banderillas* were affixed in the bull's shoulders, the fireworks they concealed exploded. Startled by the noise, out of two other *banderillas* which had been fastened in the creature's flanks, flew up two beautiful, pure white doves. They circled about in a bewildered fashion once or twice, then were caught and brought to us as a souvenir of the occasion, together with a very pretty covered basket of Indian workmanship in which to carry them away.

When the signal was given for the *Matador* all fell back. It is Gaviño himself who with a scarlet *Capa* over his arm, and sword in hand now advances alone to the center of the ring. He faces the Alcalde's box, bows low and turns for the final conflict. All eyes are upon him, the hero of a thousand bull fights, the conqueror of scores of horrible toros. He is an old man, past seventy, but his eye is keen and bright, his form is erect, his movements light and agile, his face firm, his hand steady. A smile plays about his lips, and he glances toward the bull. A great hush falls upon the people. Everyone is silent; everyone is motionless. There is scarcely anyone who has not bought one or more of the gay *banderillas* hawked about by the numerous vendors. All around the amphitheater these gay bits of color are stirring and waving their kaleidoscopic hues. The boxes are full of them; the air seems full of them; a fringe of them hangs all around the ring. The chulos cease their antics; the vendors of dulces and drinks and flowers stop wherever they are. For a moment the *Matador* surveys the tiers with their throng of faces. He bows slightly. All the time his eye watches the bull which paws and bellows not far off. The trumpets suddenly sound. In an instant the *Matador* with his scarlet mantle draws the bull's attention to himself. Down toward him plunges the ponderous brute. The *Matador* in his gay dress, his *Capa* a graceful drapery floating about him, leaps aside from what seemed certain death, and the beast goes lunging by. Again the tantalizing mantle waves. Again the bull rushes with head-long force and blind fury at his opponent. He seems to embrace with his terrible horns the gay form of his adversary. It is only seeming. Gaviño has evaded them. Then the bull turns, and the man turns. They gaze into each others' eyes. They approach each other slowly, more slowly. Gaviño could kill him now with an easy blow. He withholds the stroke. The bull still gazing at him stops then. Can it be possible? Yes; he actually backs away, recedes as Gaviño advances. The man and the bull in this way go half way across the arena, their gaze fixed upon each other. Is it the magnetism of Gaviño's keen eye which holds the brute's gaze so fixedly upon him, or does the bull see in the famous Matador, the unconquerable conqueror against whom it is idle to contend, the unerring aim he knows he never can avoid, the calm power, agile grace against which his brute force and his belligerent horns are as naught? Whatever new instincts are awakened in him are past finding out, but certain it is when Gaviño, with his sword concealed under his *Capa,* halts, the bull halts; when Gaviño walks forward, the bull walks backward. After continuing his retreat for some minutes the great beast so recently tossing men and goring horses, the ferocious master of the field, fixes one long look upon Gaviño's face then suddenly turns short about and trots quietly away! Nobody laughs, nor hisses, nor speaks. A breathless attention is fixed upon the two animals in the ring, the man and the bull. Gaviño is already again confronting the beast, and again the beast begins to back. The *Matador* now runs at him, shakes the *Capa* in his very eyes, even slaps him with the flat of the sword. There is something fascinating in the cool daring of the man in thus trying to awaken the mad fury of an animal whose prodigious body holds enough blood to drown him and whose great strength in one unguarded instant could crush every bone in his body. At last the bull begins to paw the ground, to wave his tail. The maddening mantle waves before his eyes. How slight a thing to him must seem his adversary's form. At last he roars, leaps, plunges, chases his alert foe this way and that and is incited once more to the wildest ferocity. Gaviño stops. The monster with lowered horns rushes down upon him with a fury from which escape seems impossible. There is a flash of sudden steel; a silent blow so swiftly given one cannot say where it fell. The bull halts in its mad career. The *Matador* holds up his dripping sword. The ponderous body of the great beast pitches forward, sinks upon its knees. The bossy forehead smites the blood stained ground then. The massive shape rolls over sideways utterly lifeless. Cheers, huzzas and shouts rend the air. Handkerchiefs and rebozos are excitedly waved, and sombreros by dozens go swirling into the arena, and the chulos gather them up and whirl them back to their owners till the air seems all hats. The great *Matador* bows low. An attendant takes his sword to cleanse its blade of blood. In front of the Alcalde's box, where enthusiastic clapping of hands greets him as he passes, he bows low again, puts on his cap, for he fought bareheaded, adjusts his mantle and modestly steps aside.

The blow had been given by him in the most masterly manner. The sword had pierced the bull just at the back of the neck, severing the spinal cord and, of course, producing instant death. It is the most skillful but also the most dangerous method of giving the final stroke, as it exposes the person of the *Matador* more fully than any other way to the onslaught of the bull and requires the greatest courage as well as the truest aim.

Then, at the call of the bugles came in again the four black mules, restive, as before, at beholding the bloody bull and the ghastly work they had to perform. They were finally made fast. Both chulos this time bestrode the carcass, and amid the acclamations of the multitude and demands that the dead bull should be presented to the *Matador*, the lash was applied to the funeral team, and they scurried away dragging the slaughtered beast beyond the gates.

Three more bulls making six in all were the victims of that day's sport. Then an immense old bull, too fat for fun and too tame for temper, was admitted to the ring. His horns were made harmless by a light, wooden ball affixed to the tip of each. Boys and new aspirants for bull ring honors are permitted to play at bull fighting with this creature who, in return for such thrusts as he receives, can at most only knock his assailants down. Barbas and spears are not allowed in this sort of play, and the bull is simply dared with *sarapes* of every grade of dinginess and run at and run away from with great industry by the rabble that torments him.

The amphitheater was soon emptied. Everyone was good natured. Everyone had been pleased; the bulls had been "splendid," the *Matador* "excellent," the *función* one of the very best they had had in years. Since we had no desire ever to witness another, we were glad the one we had seen was so exceptionally fine.

Do I then approve of bull fights? It is a question everyone is apt to ask himself as he leaves the bull ring behind him. He is at first inclined to answer that "it is barbarous, cruel and brutalizing." Then he fails to satisfy himself that the Mexicans who see a bull fight every Sunday and every *Fiesta* are any more brutal and cruel than nations who do not. It cannot be shown that butchers as a class in any country are more brutal or less tender hearted than men of other classes who do not dispatch so many "head of cattle" every day. It is true, the bull is harassed and is doomed to death, but so is the one poor fox who is chased up hill and down dale by a pack of whooping hounds and forty men or more on horseback, giving Reynard about as much chance for his life as a shrimp has among a school of redfish. Viewed in the light of progress the bull fight is an advance upon the ancient Mexican practice of tearing warm hearts from the bosoms of living victims and reddening altars with streams of human gore. It is even an improvement upon the Inquisition which was introduced to heathen Mexico by its first Christians, and, no doubt, as the country makes further strides in the path of Progress, the tragedies of the bull ring will be known no more. There are reasons why a consistent American cannot make much "hue and cry" about a bull fight. When his own country no longer maintains trainers for pugilists, and rings for men-fights. When reporters are no longer sent to such combats to carefully record every "round," that the whole scene may be graphically printed next morning in the foremost papers of the land, ready for the eyes of all readers. When boxing matches are against the law, and illustrated papers are forbidden to depict such scenes for all who run to see; when all this comes about, as it is sure to do, then the American will talk about the brutality and demoralizing effects of bull fights in Mexico. As it is, the poor horses are the only actors in the fray for whom one feels any pangs of pity. The men are rarely hurt. They are wise enough and agile enough to keep out of harm's way and sometimes display a most admirable courage. The bull has freedom to fight, and finally gets killed, when in such a rage its wrath makes it insensible to pain and danger, while the death blow is usually dealt with a skill that robs it of all agony. Then, if it chances to fail, there is the blow of mercy. A Mexican bull crowd does not care to fight tame bulls and drives them off with shouts of derision; while the wounded bull they clamor to have given the *coup de grace* at once, if an unskillful thrust has failed to end the fight. But the poor horses! Without any of the excitement or fun of the thing they are reined up to the contest and held to it. It is not possible that they can find it at all pleasant to be helped half way around the arena on the tips of two goring, lacerating horns, nor to have their hearts and their entrails torn out as if they were sacrifices to the Aztec religion, nor finally to be rolled in the dust by his bull-ship to die where they drop or, what is still worse, to be perhaps dragged out and splinted up to heal for future combats as inglorious as this. Only condemned horses such as one utterly broken down and incapacitated by age or disease for other uses, are sacrificed to these sports; still, one cannot but feel a keen sense of pity at seeing them brought helpless and almost defenseless to such a fate. The Mexican thinks it a more brilliant ending for a worthless, old horse to die bravely opposing a horned foe in the bull ring, than to be ignominiously knocked in the head and carted off to the offal heap. If the choice were given to the horse he might make a different decision. With the horses left out entirely, the bull fight would lose one very repugnant feature. The bulls when killed are generally given to be distributed among the poor when the meat is considered perfectly wholesome, and a grand barbecue, attended by a most motley assemblage, is frequently the result of *"una gran función extraordinaria!"*

While we had been absent at the *Plaza de Toros* some American friends of ours had been entertained at an elegant banquet given annually by one of the first clubs in Mexico at the garden known as the Tivoli de San Cosme. The President of the Republic was present and many of Mexico's most distinguished men. Speeches had been made and toasts given expressive of the utmost good will and cordial feeling toward the United States. The President himself had made a few happy remarks, which had been expressive of the kindest feeling toward and respect for Mexico's elder sister Republic. These had been received with great applause. The dinner itself had been the perfection of French cooking and the decorations indescribably beautiful. One feature had been ropes of violets hung from wall to wall and pyramids of pansies on pedestals of camellias.

In the evening we attended *El Teatro National.* This theater is a fine, large building with five great tiers of seats forming "the glittering horseshoe." It is capable of holding 3000 persons. A few of the private boxes are sumptuously fitted up. The one formerly occupied by the Emperor Maximilian is directly in front of the stage in the dress circle and is now occupied by the President. The dressing and jewels displayed in the body of the house that night were superb, and many of the women were wonderfully pretty. We saw [Miguel] Miramón's daughter in one of the boxes. She is handsome with fine eyes. She was taken, a little infant in her mother's arms, to receive her father's dying kiss in prison in Querétaro the day before he was led out to execution with the Emperor he would not desert. It was in this theater [Henriette] Sontag was playing an engagement years ago when she was overtaken by sudden death. Her biographer makes the peculiar statement that "her afflicted husband immediately returned home leaving her body to be sent on *with other parcels.*"

15

⊛

Scenes around Mexico City

Facilities for getting about the city of Mexico. A funeral cortege to el Panteón de Dolores. *How one can belong to carriage folk in the land of the Aztecs. On the road to La Viga. Protestant and Catholic churches. The grand canal. Our boatmen. Wayside washerwomen. Statue of Guatimotzín. The village of Santa Anita. The floating gardens. Poppies from* las chinampas. *Back to Anita. The* tortillera. *The old church and its Christ. The Indian burial place. Flying skulls town. Water pictures. To the Paseo and costume of a Mexican* Caballero. *Family carriages. Mode of salutation. How man meets man. The* Jacalons. *Old Spain and New Spain.* Los Serenos. *A morning start. Off to a pulque farm. The cars for Xalapa. The Count de Regla. The old Franciscan buildings. How pulque is gathered. How it is prepared for market. Skins of pulque. The plant a source of public and private revenue. Its medicinal effects. What it tastes like. Its duties. Its value to the government. Antiquity of drink. Value of the leaves of the plant. Cattle and grain. A curious corn shelter. Hints of danger. The story of an abduction. Probabilities of such disasters now. Among the bird sellers. Their tricks of trade. At the market. In the Convent of Mercy. Street Gypsies at breakfast. An out of door kitchen. The Mexican baby. Peasant women. Doorpost literature. The street of shoes. The filigree forges.* Pulquerías. *Wax matches. Petty pawn shops. Image makers. Public scribes. Frightened friends.*

Facilities for getting about the city and to its suburbs are excellent and adequate. The tramway is ubiquitous and extends in all directions. These have first and second class cars; the number of the second class being double that of the first and the fare just half. The starting point for all lines is near the Plaza, and the central station is a handsome and substantial building. The price anywhere within the city limits is a *medio* or six cents; to Guadalupe, Tacubaya, Chapultepec, Tacuba and other adjacent places a *real* or twelve cents and greater distances in proportion. Funeral processions go to the cemetery called *El Panteón de Dolores* by the street railway, special cars being provided for the purpose. Of these funeral cars also there are different classes. The first class has a most imposing funeral car or catafalque painted black and beautifully draped with hangings of black cloth. A rest raised above the floor of the car which is open on all sides supports the coffin. A driver, handsomely dressed in black with a crepe band on his tall silk hat, and black gloves upon his hands, stands as he manages the sable steeds which slowly draw the solemn looking coach. It is a more impressive sight than that of the usual stiff and box-like hearse with its glass gilding and glittering wheels, a line of hacks following with drivers who look more like tramps than anything else in their slouchy attitude, slouchy hats, and all sorts of clothes. The coffin car, low, spacious, and softly though somberly curtained, moves on without jolting and almost without noise. A line of cars for mourners, friends, or other followers succeed this hearse also with curtained windows and closed doors. As the solemn train passes so steadily and so silently, all hats are removed by passers by in token of respect. The cemetery of Dolores is very beautiful and contains some strikingly handsome monuments. The trees and the statuary take away in a great measure that aspect of sadness and gloom which pertains too often to the abode of death. It is one of the customs of the country to carefully remember a loved one's grave, and flowers everywhere attest to that affection that survives the tombs, while they lend an air of life and cheerfulness to the spot.

Carriage hire being exceedingly low provides a ready means of outdoor pleasure and comfort. The prices range from fifty cents to a dollar an hour. The half dollar hack is not bad. It is old but roomy, has thin horses and a ragged driver probably, but the nags go at a good gait, and the coach very rarely breaks down. The seventy-five cent hack is better. It has a carpet on its floor, and all the springs are not out of the seats; but the dollar hack is a "swell" affair with five horses, a well dressed driver, and a style which induces its occupant to assume quite an *"I'm in my own private carriage"* air. All these hacks whilst on the stand have a small, stiff flag stuck up on the left side of the driver's seat to indicate they are for hire. The cheapest shows a white flag, the seventy-five cent hack a red flag and the dollar one a blue flag. From this display of the red white and blue you take your choice. The moment he is hired, the driver takes down his flag and tucks it under his cushion. This shows his coach is *ocupado*. He then carefully notes down the time on a bit of paper. You look at your watch, and off you go at a fifty cent, a seventy-five cent or a dollar rate according as you have chosen. At such fares there is, of course, a great deal of carriage use, many preferring to take a hack at these cheap rates and "gang their ain gait" than to go in the street car with its mortal miscellany, "first class" though it be, and subject to its monotonous punctuation which is always a "full stop." There are no cabs and no herdic coaches.

One day of "outing" we passed in divers places a hack was called early in the forenoon. An Indian driver wrapped in a gay sarape and wearing on his head the broad brimmed straw sombrero of his class was seated on the box holding the reins which guided two skinny and sentimental looking horses which once had been a noted American team but now concealment—"like a worm in the bud"—had preyed on all their fine points. We drove out over wide, broad streets which, no doubt, at some remote period were in a very fine condition. Just then they were awaiting the sanction of the city authorities to some repairs, so that those streets, like those of another noted place, were really paved with good intentions. We drove past the low adobe dwelling where the unhappy Señor Cervantes was imprisoned and against the walls of which his abductors were shot to death. The usual street scenes always picturesque and always interesting were on every hand, and we passed numerous churches and groups of *léperos*—crippled and wretchedly deformed beggars—who furnish a too familiar and always piteous sight about churches and in bye streets of Mexico. After a few turns about town we drove south toward the *Paseo de la Viga,* a fashionable drive that borders one side of the famous canal which leads out to the still more famous floating gardens, or *chinampas.* The canal is about six leagues in length and connects lakes Xochimilco and Tezcoco. Chalco and Xochimilco, if not artificially divided by the great stone dyke which excited the surprise of Hernán Cortez and his men some cycles since, would be virtually one water. They are the most southern of the chain of lakes in the valley, and Chalco gives its name to the canal though it is sometimes called the Ixtapalapam and, again, the *Canal de la Viga.*

Alighting from our carriage we found ourselves at the canal in the midst of scenes probably as peculiar in aspect as in Aztec days. The same sort of boats propelled by the same sort of people moved upon the water, and the door of our carriage seemed to have admitted us into a place and among the avocations belonging to three centuries ago. We secured a boat for ourselves, a long, rather broad affair with a sunken cabin in the center, with benches for our accommodation and a white awning for a roof. The deck of the boat extended beyond the sides of this, giving ample passage room, and each end of the deck had an upward slope. Two barefooted Indian *boteros* in broad hats, white cotton shirts, and cotton trousers rolled high, presented themselves as propellers of our queer craft. They were agile and carried long poles in their hands. We were soon out in the stream and breasting a current that comes down from Xochimilco at the rate of four miles an hour. There is a toll system established where, just before reaching town with his produce, the Indian is obliged to pay a certain tax on whatever he may bring to market. A bridge of a single arch thrown across the canal near the point where we embarked forms this *Garita de la Viga* where a collector is always on duty to receive the revenues levied upon everything that is brought by this way to the city. Sums large in the aggregate thus find their way to the city treasury. The bridge is Spanish, but the tax system existed in Montezuma's time at this very point on this very stream. Down the canal swept the rude boats and scows. There were loads of corn, of hay, of great red jars and of bright Indian basketry. All were propelled by poles, sometimes managed by one person, sometimes by three or four. Often a man and a woman in company worked the boat, or a woman alone while her children smiled or slept among the vegetables and flowers which formed her cargo. Frequently collisions between boats seemed inevitable yet were invariably avoided, the poles being handled with great dexterity. Some of the vegetables were giants in size. There were bright crisp radishes at the very least half a yard long and large in proportion and so fresh they might have tempted the veriest dyspeptic in the world to take a bite. The beets and turnips were also marvels in size. We thought what ponderous watermelons such soil would produce, then remembered we had never seen a watermelon in Mexico. The women carve flowers out of the different vegetables with that imitative skill which marks the race. Intermixed with a little evergreen or any bits of graceful foliage, at a little distance they can scarcely be distinguished from natural flowers and sell very well, having perhaps this advantage that after having served as a floral decoration they can be boiled for dinner! To produce a red flower they dye the carved turnip with the juice of the tuna which gives a brilliant, crimson tint. After passing *La Garita* our barefooted *boteros* ran, so it seemed, about three times faster than the four mile current. They were on a constant trot along the sides of the deck from one end to the other, lifting and dipping their long poles with singularly graceful motions and splendid posturing. Their charge for the trip was a dollar! It was bread earned well and, as was constantly evident, literally earned "by the sweat of the brow." The Paseo de la Viga lies on the one hand under its rows of trees and on the other the bank is dotted with Indian homes or enlivened here and there with picturesque groups of women washing clothes in the water of the stream and rubbing them on a flat stone at the water's edge. This convenient sort of laundry is established anywhere about the country where a steam of water amounts to enough to warrant it.

We passed a monument erected to the memory of Guatimotzín,[1] the last of the Montezumas. It stands upon the spot where the brave young hero made his last stand against Cortez. It is simply a bust in marble raised upon a handsome pedestal and bearing a carved inscription.

We met many boats coming to the city, some with merchandise, some with passengers, and now and then the single figure of a tall, graceful Indian woman standing in a canoe laden with flowers, and managing her little bark with great skill so that it shot through the water with a silent velocity that seemed like the darting motions of a swift bird. All sorts of farm products, besides adobe bricks, charcoal, etc., etc. find their way to market, principally by this canal. On feast days and Sundays this locality is one of the most interesting about Mexico. For hundreds of years its scenes have been the same. Let him who loves quaint and novel pictures go and gaze on those which move upon that ancient river. They will meet him, pass him, linger by him and revisit him in dreams. He will fancy himself among the dusky daughters of the Nile, or upon a stream which waters the land of the Moors, or in the distant vales of India—anywhere but in a spot lying so close to the busy, bustling, practical United States of America.

At the quaint little village of Santa Anita we moored our boat and

1. *Guatimotzín* was Ancieto Ortega del Villar's popular opera that appeared about 1872 commemorating the last ruler of the Aztecs, Cuauhtemoc (1494–1525), a nephew of Montezuma II. For many Mexicans this became the preferred spelling of his name.

"tipped" our boatmen who rushed eagerly ashore to regale themselves with pulque and to buy *tortillas*. The ever present, patient *tortillera*, though not one of the loveliest and neatest of her kind, was easily found, working away at the never ending task of grinding corn and cooking *tortillas*. It has been asserted that all flesh is grass; but, in Mexico I fancy, all flesh is corn.

We found the little town interesting and wandered about its streets where the people gave us pleasant greeting, and many of them offered us flowers. We paused at a great stone fountain to watch groups of Indian children at their noiseless play, and finally entered an ancient church, the oldest we had seen to judge by appearances. The heavy plank floor was scoured to a marvelous state of cleanliness, but it was so worn by the feet of generations of congregations it was difficult to walk upon it. A little dusky maiden in a red skirt and blue rebozo guided us through the building. Among the many was one fine picture—and in a glass case, like someone asleep on a couch, lay a life-size figure of the dead Christ in wax. The face was very youthful, the flesh tints natural and the hair and beard were black as jet. Out in the very old Indian churchyard one found few monuments but many graves. The burial place was so old the memory of no man living ran back to the time of its consecration. The ground was crowded by the prostrate forms of those who once had been. In making some repairs near the wall of the church some bones had been unearthed and some skulls had been carefully placed on such tombstones as stood about so to await reburial. These had grown very light and porous, and even by short exposure to wind and weather were bleached to snowy whiteness. As I looked at them a sudden blast came around the corner of the church, caught two or three of the grinning skulls which flew straight to me and dropped at my startled feet. I felt surprised, to say the least, to see such light-headedness among the representatives of the oldest inhabitants, and I picked one reverently up to replace it on the tombstone. It crumbled to dust in my hands!

Returning to our boat, we went out among the *chinampas* or floating gardens, so called. Standing up and looking about, the scene presented is not unlike any ordinary vegetable garden on a large scale with strips of water dividing the beds instead of the usual paths. Level beds of earth from a foot and a half or two feet in height and perhaps twenty feet in width and forty or fifty in length lay in every direction upon the surface of the lake. Vegetables, flowers and small shrubs grew upon them and occasionally, on some of the larger ones a primitive looking bamboo hut was built. These gardens were originally formed by weaving flags and lily pads and roots and twigs together until a sufficiently strong foundation was formed to support earth enough, drawn from the lake's bottom, to raise such marketable products as would grow in the light soil. In those days the scene must have somewhat resembled that presented by "The Thousand Isles" in the river St. Lawrence. The islands were numerous and bright with verdure. Besides their market fruits, these aquatic gardeners raised the flowers and herbs which were sacred to their gods. In those days the Indian could attach his garden to his canoe and pole his whole estate to market. This is no longer the case. The gardens are not portable. They do not float. They have all anchored and grown bulky and staid with years, and the proprietors are content to carry what they produce to town and leave their small plantations at home. Still, these gardens are very interesting. Planting and gathering is always going on, as the climate has no autumn frosts nor winter blights. As we made our way in and out among the garden patches often at some sharp corner it seemed impossible for our clumsy boat to turn in the narrow avenues of water. But the gardens still float sufficiently to be made to yield the right of way, and a push from our boatmen moved them enough to give us passage way. Sometimes our gondoliers sprang out upon the spongy shores and gathered handsful and hats full of flowers, among them glorious clusters of scarlet poppies which they scattered into our little cabin sometimes filling Cora's cap. Often I recall her as I saw her that day seated in the stern of our quaint bark weaving the poppies in the thick braids of her long, yellow hair.

Emerging once more into the canal we went with the current back to the town. It was a perfect day. The skies were soft, and the wind was laden with the breath of flowers, and the water rippling under the prow had in it a voice of other days. Boat after boat met us; great, flat-bottomed barges such as the kings and princes of the long ago no doubt made their journey in along the waters of this same Ixtapalapam River. We did not talk as we sailed on; we dreamed our waking dreams on this stream and by its borders which remain just as Cortez found them. It is the one feature in the environs of Mexico which has undergone no change. Just as of old the Indian lover seeks his maid upon the quiet stream, just as of old the sun shines down upon the boats and boatmen and their motley merchandise, and the moon gleams upon the sweet romances of the dusky descendants of a bygone race. Often we met canoes or dugouts made of a single mahogany log called a *chalupa* and again others of ampler dimensions with gay parties of pleasure always Indians with merry viols, with garlands, with guitars and the steel strung Bandalon. The shadows on the Viga began to lengthen, the rows of poplars grew golden with mellow light, the sun was lowering as we reached the bridge and moored our boat, and closed the page of one more Mexican Idyll. But the sunny waters, the verdant banks, the poppy garlands and the cane huts, the pretty gardens with their floral freight parting like fragrant gates for the passage of our boat and silently swinging together again as if moved by invisible hands, these, like lines of some exquisite poem must haunt our memory always.

There was still time to go to the *Paseo de la Reforma,* a little while before sunset being the fashionable hour for this fashionable drive. The scene presented is gay, animated, novel and picturesque. Long lines of carriages are moving, the equipages equal to anything seen in our best parks in the States. Through the plate glass windows or curtained openings one catches glimpses of sweet youthful faces, marvelous eyes and tiny hands. The toilettes are handsome, in good taste and bear the stamp of European style. Many of the ladies drive bareheaded. We saw but few mantillas and one of these was worn by a beautiful American girl. The pride the Mexican takes in the possession of fine horses is a marked trait. The Mexican horse is much smaller than the American one and for driving the latter is preferred. The danger of the sea trip for these animals, and the landing at Vera Cruz, or even the long overland journey by rail renders them a costly luxury. We had dismissed our hack at the hotel door and the American team which carried us along the Paseo have been paid for with twenty-two hundred dollars. They seem to understand their own value when they get here and hold their heads considerably above the native breed. They thrive well in the climate and always command a high price. Eccentricities in taste were seen in calico horses with bobbed tails, in spans of snow white mules and of black mules perfectly matched and handsomely equipped and in horses again evidently chosen for their unique color. Occasionally the style strikingly apparent in horses, harness and vehicle stops short when it reaches the servant—who dressed badly, sitting badly and displaying in every way lack of training seems to have been altogether overlooked in the general arrangement for fashion and elegance. The effect was comical when one beheld a spruce "turnout"—a high stepping horse, a young gentleman gotten up in the extreme of style sitting in front as properly as the best trained coachman in the world holding himself perfectly trim and his whip exactly at the right angle, while behind sat the servant whose shoulders were humped for ease, whose dress was careless to say the least of it, who used his hands and his sombrero to waft greeting to other servants and whose legs seemed to lie around loose in the back part of the wagon. It is scarcely fair to mention these things which were not the rule but the exception and perhaps lend a needed comic relief to the stately dignity which marks the grand procession. No excuse, however, can be made for the mounted soldiers who are stationed at intervals down the middle of the way to preserve order and aid in case of any accident. Their shabby appearance and slouchy attitudes are habitual and sadly out of keeping with the profession they represent and the scene to which they are assigned. Their horses look as sleepy and slovenly as their riders, and in this feature of the Paseo there is much need of and much room for improvement.

Curvetting and cantering gaily along upon fiery little mustangs or spirited American steeds, horsemen pass and repass. Some of them are mounted and appareled in the quiet manner familiar to our own parks and highways, others again in the fanciful but picturesque costume of the Mexican *caballero*. Here the latter is seen in all his glory. His horse is groomed to perfection. Its coat shines like satin; its mane and tail are so glossy and beautiful they remind one of the rich, wavy locks of a woman. The animal has been trained to the highest degree and while deprived of none of its spirit is made perfectly obedient to the gentle managed rein. He perhaps wears a cruel bit but never suffers from it while he behaves himself. The Mexican saddle which Bret Harte says, "levels all equine distinction" is upon his back, but it cannot conceal his grace of movement, his abundance of life and thoroughbred air. The saddle is beautifully embroidered in *pita,* the thread made from the agave fiber, and it is also adorned with silver ornaments. The stirrups, which are boxed in ornamented leather, are also of silver, and the pommel is silver mounted. Five and even eight hundred dollar saddles are not uncommon among the wealthy Mexican "swells." At the back of the saddle as part of the accoutrements hangs the *baquerillo,* a strip of leather heavily embroidered on the edges with gold or silver, and in the center is affixed the skin of the long haired, mountain goat, and this adornment hangs down below the boot heel of the rider. Some of these skins are black, some brown and some as tawny as the mane of a lion. Being dressed with great care, they are very pliant and the long silky locks glisten in the sun with each motion of the horse, forming a graceful addition to the equestrian appendages. I saw one baquerillo which had cost 170 dollars. The goat skin alone ready for the baquerillo is worth $30.00, the ordinary price of a goat skin being one dollar. Sometimes a gay sarape is folded and strapped at the back of the saddle just at the front of the *baquerillo*. And in this saddle the horseman is seen sitting easily and gracefully and so perfectly "at home" he seems to be part and portion of his horse. He wears a huge sombrero rich with silver braid on brim and a silver cord and tassel around the crown or else a silver coil called the *toaquilla*. At the side of the crown is also a small ornament in silver, a monogram, maybe, or some other embroidered adornment. A *chaqueta,* or round riding jacket, also trimmed with silver, and trousers, adorned with a double row of silver buttons of a fancy design extending from hip to ankle up the outer side of the leg, with silver spurs, complete the costly costume. Convenient to his right hand, toward the back, an elegantly mounted pistol is in its holster, and a handsome sword with ornamented hilt is part of the saddle trappings. Upon the pommel invariably hangs a coil of slender rope—the lasso. This rope, in the hands of a Mexican, is a weapon or a plaything according as he wields it in sport or in earnest. His skill and precision with it are remarkable, and there are few things, from a bull to a butterfly, which he cannot bring down with this implement.

The modern man of fashion, with a dignified, European air will point out to the guest at his side many varieties of the portrait I have drawn and will indicate how in many instances the costume of the *caballero* has been toned down and that so much silver and ornament is no longer *la moda* among the really *elite*. But one listens and looks after the glittering figure so picturesque, so gay, so distinctly a representative of the Mexican horseman, and utters a devout wish that it may be long before it shall be altogether "toned" out of existence in the paths of the Paseo, or Empress' Drive.

Around and around under the trees and past the Columbus statue winds the slowly moving procession of flickering wheels and polished panels and handsome horses. There are lustrous eyes and crimson lips, the glance of hope, the blush of love, neighbor greeting neighbor, the meeting and passing of grand old families' escutcheons, the pride of pedigree, the dash and fashion of the nouveau riche, in short, life in its sunniest aspect. Now and then a carriage draws out of line and stops that its inmates may chat with the occupants of some other that has also halted, or receive the salutations of some rider. When a knot of vehicles has thus gathered, men with trays neatly arranged go about offering dulces for sale, saying "buy" with their eyes rather than their lips, passing in and out among the crowd of wheels agile, alert and silent.

The mode of salutation as friend passes friend upon this promenade is peculiar, I think, to the country; though it may have had its origin in Spain. The lady does not bow nor does the gentleman touch his hat. The hand of either is lifted nearly to the level with the eyes, the palm toward the face and the salute given by a quick half beckoning motion of the fingers while a bright glance of recognition shoots through them. Very pretty and coquettish on the part of the lady, very graceful and gallant on the part of the cavalier.

When two men who are friends meet on foot their greeting consists of an embrace. Their arms are thrown about each others' shoulders, and a succession of quick little affectionate pats is administered upon one another's back. Accompanied as this mode of salutation is with an expression of true pleasure upon the face and with the eyes lighted by the warmth of cordial friendship, it strikes the stranger only as a novel, not an undignified mode of manly greeting.

I think it was the same evening that we made up a large party to go to the *Jacoloni*. This was a small theater which reared its rough temporary walls not a thousand squares away from the *Plaza Mayor*. Some performances called "Society Plays" were going on there just then, and it was said to be essentially the playhouse of the people. The admission was a real—12 ½ cents. The place as to finish and decoration was rude enough and the orchestra consisted of a very few musicians and even less music. The audience, however, was large, the house being crowded. The first performance was a bull fight by the *Títeres* or puppets. Even the ancient custom of the fighters all going to church to receive the blessing of the priest before going to the Plaza de Toros was represented, and subsequently every phase of a genuine bull fight was such perfection of action it was almost impossible to believe it was done by little figures four or five inches high. The wires were worked by skilled fingers. The amphitheater was a very good illusion, and altogether it was an admirable way of seeing men and beast "butchered to make a Roman holiday." This was followed by a play entitled "Old Spain and New Spain." The first part represented the characters, conversation, dresses and dances of old times as seen at an evening reception. The stately minuet was danced with great dignity and grace and all the respectful decorum of the period, while the manners of the dame and cavalier were given with all the courtesy and lofty breeding pertaining to the times of the old Spanish Grandees. The dresses in this play were magnificent and made one wonder how they were ever secured for such a place of amusement. The curtain fell upon this part and rose on a house scene prior to the arrival of guests invited to a modern party. Much of the family treasure had been sent to the Monte de Piedad[2] to be pawned for money to give the entertainment. The host and hostess were already quarreling over the expenses incurred. The daughter of the house, elegantly dressed in white satin and rich old Spanish lace, was flouncing about the room pouting because [she was] not pleased with her costume, and the son, a reckless spendthrift, rushed in demanding money from his already enraged sire just as the servant announces the arrival of the first guests. Instantly, every member of the family subsides into society ways, bland and smiling to the last degree. After many amusing *contre temps* the *danza* is proposed. The music strikes up, the partners take places as in the waltz. The slow steps are languidly taken; nobody talks; nobody laughs; the music grows slower and slower; the dancers move in time and finally the music dies out and the dancers all stop sound asleep in their places. It was a very good burlesque given in excellent Spanish and elicited great applause. The audience was attentive, orderly and quiet, although the men all kept their hats on and not a few smoked their cigarettes. It revealed a sense of humor in the Mexican character I had thought it did not possess. We walked home that evening amid the wildest chorus of whistles from *los Serenos* that can be imagined. These watchmen wear at night a long, blue overcoat over their day uniform of dark blue, wear a round cap of white duck and are equipped with pistol, lantern and whistle. The police regulations seem to be excellent, and a policeman is always within a call or reach when needed. The absence of liquor saloons in Mexico without doubt contributes largely to the efficiency of the police force.

At an elegant dinner we attended one evening at the palace-home of

2. National Bank of Loans and Pledges, known more popularly as the National Pawn Shop, was founded on February 25, 1775, as the Sacro y Real Monte de Piedad de Animas and is discussed at greater length below in chapter 16.

Señor and Señora [Romero de] T[erreros]., it was arranged that we should rise betimes next morning and accompany them on a visit to their hacienda at Xalpa. Señor A. R[omero]. de T[erreros]., now enjoying the simple title of "Mr.," is the grandson of the wealthy and charitable founder of that noble institution the *Monte de Piedad* and legitimate possessor of the honorable titles of "*Caballero de la Orden de Calatrava y de Conde de Regla*" bestowed upon his grandsire by the King of Spain "in consideration of his many virtues and services rendered to the Crown."[3] In his own country Señor T., of course, lays aside with true republican taste and spirit all claim to nobility save that bountifully bestowed upon him by nature. When abroad, however, his title is recognized and all the consideration which it and the cherished memory of the first distinguished Conde de Regla entitles him to is his. Señora T. we found a most lovely and winsome person; *muy simpática* as they say in Mexico and as unaffected and charming as she was graceful and hospitable.

We took the [railway] cars with them early in the day and had a most delightful little trip with the usual interesting landscape which always awaits one in that favored valley which for beauty surely is not surpassed in all the world. Carriages met us at the station and upon approaching the hacienda numbers of people from the place came out upon the road to greet and welcome the Señor and Señora. It was beautiful to see the interest this young Lady of the Manor took in them all, halting her carriage to make inquires of the health of this one's Mother, or the well being of that one's child, and brightening with affectionate delight every dusky face her kind glance fell upon. We found the hacienda a grand old place upon the grounds of which was turned the first spadeful of earth which began the famous "cut of Nochistango." The buildings were edifices formerly owned and occupied as church and monastery by the Franciscan Brotherhood. There were walls of wonderful thickness, vaulted ceilings, numerous unexpected turns and passages and vast rambling apartments which lent to it an air of romance such

3. Pedro Romero de Terreros, Conde de Regla, founded the Monte de Piedad in Mexico in 1775. A descendant, Manuel Romero de Terreros, Marques de San Francisco (1880–1968), wrote a brief biographical sketch of his great-grandfather, *Nacional Monte de Piedad: Pedro Romero de Terreros, noticia biográfica de su fundador* (Mexico, n.p., n.d.). More detailed histories of the National Pawn Shop include Antonio Villamil, *Memoria histórica del Nacional Monte de Piedad* (Mexico: I. Escalante, 1877), and Esperanza Cabrera Siles and Patricia Escandón, *Historia del Nacional Monte de Piedad, 1775–1993* (Mexico: Nacional Monte de Piedad, 1993).

as attaches to some ancient castle of medieval times. It had its family chapel where we were taken by la Señora, who stood among her dead there buried with that air of remembrance and tender regret which in the Mexican heart time never obliterates. There was the usual walk upon the house top, a tour of the rooms where, in some of them, the engravings and hunting accoutrements evinced the country tastes of the owner, and then dinner in the spacious dining room among quaint and curious reminders of times gone by. After the usual siesta we were taken about the lands and inducted into the mysteries of pulque making. This liquor is produced from the Maguey or Century plant, a variety of the *Agave Americana.* To secure the liquid the plant is never allowed to flower. When it shows a disposition to do so which is sometimes at five but oftener at eight years of age, it is carefully watched, and the two folded leaves shooting up from the center are torn out. This makes a cavity of about a foot in diameter and from eighteen to twenty inches deep. In this natural receptacle the juice collects and is gathered two or three times a day. The continuance of the flow is from four to six and sometimes, but rarely, seven months. The pulque gatherer, who, by the bye, equipped with his peculiar implements is always a singular and remarkable object, goes to the plants, as the sap gatherers of Maine and of Michigan go to their maple trees, and collects his treasure. In the morning and the evening he obtains the most bountiful yield, at mid-day something like a third less. A yield of six or eight quarts per day from each plant is considered very rich; the average quantity being about four quarts.[4]

As the tall, stiff, thorny leaves of the Maguey form a formidable fence about the precious deposit, the collector introduces between the spiny barriers an implement made of a calabash or long necked gourd with a hole at either end. One end of this he lowers into the well of the plant, to the other end he applies his lips, and by suction he draws the liquid into this receptacle. He then, by dexterous management, transfers it to a pigskin, which carefully scraped of its bristles and otherwise well prepared, he carries over his left shoulder. When filled this skin is a pig in effigy minus his snout, his hair, his tail, and his toes. When not quite filled, the motion of the fluid inside the mutilated form, as it is borne along, lends a seriocomic aspect to the body of

---

4. For comparable accounts of pulque and pulquerías in the 1920s, see Ernest Gruening, *Mexico and Its Heritage* (New York: Century Co., 1928), 537–41; and Anita Brenner, *Idols Behind Altars* (New York: Payson & Clarke, 1929), 171–75.

the defunct grunter and makes it seem to wallow in its own helpless drunkenness.

The liquid when gathered is taken home and poured into open vats. Those which I saw were bull's hide stretched between four stakes. Here a little old pulque is added to it, and it is allowed to ferment, a process which is complete in four or five days. It is then sent in pigskins to market. I have seen a carload of these skins distended to the uttermost with pulque, and, I assure you, it is a rarely ridiculous sight. A man in our party, animated probably by the same spirit which prompted one of the Georges to inquire how the apple got into the dumplings, asked with an innocent air, how the pulque got into the pigskin. Our English friend, who had been persuaded to try some of the national beverage and who had found it very distasteful replied, "Why they just hold a glass of pulque to the pig's nose, and he instantly backs out of his skin leaving it entirely at the service of the fellow who offered the treat."

"Oh, no!" said Don Pepe, "we keep the pig on short rations until he is nearly starved, then we hold an ear of corn toward him, and he immediately walks out of his skin to secure the corn, and we have no further trouble about it."

To be the proprietor of a pulque farm near Mexico is to secure to oneself a very handsome annual income without a very great outlay of labor. I know of a very small farm which yields its owner one hundred and fifty dollars a week. I know of others which yield twenty-five thousand dollars a year and am assured that some yield as much as forty thousand *per annum*, and happy is he who is inheritor of such a property. It requires seven, nine, and in very barren soil sometimes fifteen years before the plants yield, but when the flow begins, the crop is sure and the market certain. When the four or six months' "run" is over, the plant supplies no more. Its mission as a sap yielder is over forever, and its leaves can go for the many purposes they are useful for. The numerous young plants which shoot up from its root are transplanted, and the pulque farmer plants every year so that one crop of maguey may be always coming forward to fill the place of that which has been exhausted.

The generous plant grows on soil which would raise nothing else, is easily cultivated, is uninjured by sunshine or shower or cold or heat, is indifferent to tempests and is maintained with little labor and with light cost.

As for the devotees to pulque their name is legion. If pulque were a church and had the same number of communicants that it now has of imbibers, it would rule the Mexican world. Everybody drinks it more or less. Rich and poor, high and low, men, women and children. It is considered very wholesome. Its stomachic effects are said to be efficacious and beneficial. It is a corrective, a tonic, a stimulative, an appetizer, anything one desires to have it, and nutritive always. With the natives, a taste for it seems natural, but with foreigners it must be acquired. Its odor is abominable, and to a novice its taste is disgustingly obnoxious. A friend, who on this occasion indulged in a cup of it, told me that it tasted like a soup made of spoiled meat enriched with rancid butter and boiled with gutter water. I felt a delicacy about enquiring what opportunities he had enjoyed of tasting such soup, and set his remarks down to a propensity for pleasant exaggeration. Still, the oxhide vats and the pig skin bottles may impart to it a meaty flavor of questionable or perhaps unquestionable antiquity, for the taste of the liquid when first taken from the plant is by no means disagreeable.

Pulque compuesto, served in cut glass decanters and silver flagons on the tables of the rich, is simply pulque so disguised with strong flavors of pineapple or lemon or other pleasant juices that its native smell and taste are lost, and the beverage goes down one's throat in masquerade. When not artificially colored it is a white liquid of about the consistency of thin buttermilk. It is very cheap and sufficiently intoxicating to make any poor fellow as drunk as a lord for a few cents. A pulqued Indian asleep on the ground, his horse patiently awaiting him at the roadside, is no uncommon sight in Mexico, the happy sleeper being as oblivious to all things in this mundane sphere under the spell of the Maguey, as his princely master might be on his brandies and wines of the oldest and costliest vintages.

The pulque is sold at retail in glasses which remind one of our *"schooners."* At wholesale it is sold by *cargas* that weigh twenty-one arrobas.[5] Five skins make a carga, and now it is frequently shipped in barrels which originally contained about the same quantity as the five pigskins, but which have mysteriously increased in size of late years though still shipped as barrels and so paid for. The weight of a skin is from one hundred to one hundred and twenty pounds, and each skin contains from sixty-five to seventy bottles.

The manufacture of the drink is of importance to the government, which

5. An *arroba* equals 25 pounds.

derives from it annually a large revenue. The duties collected from it at the city gates of Mexico per day are between seven and eight hundred dollars. The city contains two hundred and fifty thousand inhabitants, and it is estimated that a pound of pulque *per diem* for each inhabitant is the average consumption of this drink, which is supposed both to cheer and to inebriate. It is believed that one hundred and ninety thousand pounds pay duty daily, and sixty thousand pounds are smuggled into town. Long ago it was surmised that the tax imposed, a real (12 ½ cents) on each arroba, was so heavy that it would check the cultivation of the Maguey. No signs of a decline are apparent. On the contrary, the demand for the juice is imperative and on the increase, and I was told today that from certain plantations it was even bringing an increased price. It is one of the most ancient and lucrative branches of agriculture in Mexico and will probably continue to maintain its hold upon the people and the soil. The receipt of the Company from the pulque trains pays one half the running expenses of the Vera Cruz road, and there are many avenues besides this by which the beverage enters the city. All this is for home consumption, for as yet none is exported on account of its tendency to spoil. I am told it would make excellent vinegar, but the demand for it as a drink admits of no projects for vinegar factories. Some enterprising spirit in time will, no doubt, discover some mode for preserving the liquor in all its native nauseousness, and we shall find it bottled in our markets, elbowing its way into general use alongside of English Ale and Bremer Beer. In fact, it was exhibited at the Orizaba Exposition, bottled and fitted for exportation. If the Aztec mythology be ever fairly understood we shall doubtless find the Maguey holding high rank among the gods. To the ancients it was a plant of infinite uses and still continues to be such to those who have taken their places. The leaves were used to make the paper on which the picture writing of the Aztecs was painted, and that it was durable cannot be doubted as specimens with the work upon it still exist in Mexico. It causes one to wonder that it is now used for qualities of paper which might make many utensils to supply the place of tin, upon which the duties are so high that it is not used here to any great extent, pottery taking the place of the common tinware so much in use with us. I have heard this lack of tin, and the high duties imposed upon it, given as reasons for not canning and preserving the fruits of the country for exportation. Besides papers, the Maguey furnished a thread which for many purposes had no equal; its juice, at certain stages of the plant, was excellent for healing wounds and its thorns were admirable for making them. The Indian priests used these thorns to pierce and tear the flesh in acts of penance as expiation. They also served as pins to fasten garments, to make needles to carry the thread the plant supplied, and also as nails. Thus it was dry goods, hardware and apothecary's shop to the Aztecs, and to this day *pita*, the thread made from the plant, has not its equal for many purposes, especially for embroidering saddles and other articles in leather. Of its fiber a great variety of things are made—sacks, ropes, bags, purses and many other articles "too numerous to mention." Tradition states that a young Toltec maiden of noble birth was the first to discover the means of extracting the precious juices of the maguey and imparted her discovery to the then ruling monarch of her land. The last Toltec king was the son of this young maiden.

That all these years the gourd and the collector's lips should have formed the machine for drawing up the pulque from the plant, speaks volumes for the contented conservatism which in many ways stamps this people. The instrument is quite in keeping with the wooden plough which is often seen in use throughout the country and the habit of fanning the chaff from grain by tossing it in the air, etc., etc. Someday a smart Yankee will come along and invent a pulque pump which will make the gourd explode with envy.

After due inspection of the pulque vats and plants, we visited the stables where splendid animals were trotted out for our inspection. Thence we went to the granaries containing the garnered harvests of wheat and corn in countless bushels lying "in bulk." In an inner apartment I found a little old man, so little and so old and so wizard-like in his appearance I paused, half doubting whether he were, or were not, human. His hair and a very scanty beard, which did not seem to know whether to assert itself or not, were white. His skin was almost black, and his face looked much as if made out of wrinkled old leather boots. A number of corn cobs set on end and firmly tied together with Maguey fiber stood before him on the ground, and across this curious machine the old man was dragging ear after ear of corn and thus with great facility shelling the grain. When persons pass the utmost possibilities of youth, they grow proud of their age and like to tell how long they have cumbered the ground. I watched this being awhile. He was as busy as a bee and as active as a western grasshopper, and I ventured to ask him how old he was. He looked so very aged, so very withered, so very odd altogether. I did not suppose he either saw or heard me, but at my question he rolled up at me a pair of keen black eyes, nodded his little white head briskly and out of some chuckling and some chattering and a good deal of corn shelling, I gathered the one Spanish word equivalent to our "guess." "Eighty?" I said. "No, Señora." "Ninety?" "No, Señora," with more chuckling and renewed attacks upon his funny Mexican corn sheller. "Ninety-five? Ninety-six?" "No, Señora, no, no—one hundred and nine. That is my age." He looked it. He could have passed for a Mexican Centurion or a galvanized Egyptian mummy whichever he had chosen. I scarcely knew which to consider the greater curiosity, himself or his corn sheller.

We reached the city again about dark and spent the evening at the Conservatory of Music, where we heard some excellent singing and some admirable instrumental pieces by a young Mexican composer.

We were always running across some anxious American somewhere ready to give an ominous shake of the head at our daring to ride, drive and go about as we did and eager to give us warnings about the dangers from robbers, abductors, etc., etc. We observed that the hints of danger were always from foreigners, never from Mexicans. It was in company with the latter that we visited farms, country seats, haciendas, and went about the city and its suburbs. Everybody goes out wearing his pistol, if he so chooses, and everybody seems to entertain a great respect for the pistol of everybody else. No law exists concerning the carrying of concealed weapons, and, in fact, they are seldom concealed but, if worn, are carried in plain sight on the saddle or in the belt, this being especially a common practice with mounted servants. I came to the conclusion that it was a fashion rather than a necessity. It originated in those troublous times when, distracted by struggles for freedom and torn by internecine quarrels, the usual evils, that flourish like fungi in such soil, sprang into existence. Every man was prepared to meet foes on his paths of danger, and freebooters on his path of peace. It was then that stages became arsenals on wheels, and the only railroad in the country sent a guard of thirty soldiers out with every train that moved away over the lonely and dangerous mountain defiles, and every citizen became his own policeman. The need for such precautions no longer exists, but the habit survives. There is a universal love of firearms united to a general distaste for using them. Shooting affrays, so common with us, where the carrying of pistols are "the means to do ill deeds that make ill deeds done" are infrequent, and an abduction is as uncommon there as in the United States, and is a memory rather than a menace. The fear which some visitors entertain regarding such affairs no doubt arises from the widely circulated, oft repeated, and well known adventure of Señor Cervantes, which occurred about fifteen years ago. Mr. Cervantes was a prominent and very wealthy citizen, who, one evening when about to enter his own dwelling in one of the most frequented streets of Mexico, was seized, muffled, his cries smothered, and he was thus thrust into a carriage that stood in readiness. He was taken to a miserable tenement in the outskirts of the city and half buried in a hole under the floor which had previously been prepared for him. Here he was subjected to all sorts of suffering, mental and physical, while his abductors awaited proffers of the large ransom, which they managed to make known would liberate him and restore him safely to his friends. They were only successful in their well-laid plans for his abduction. Search was instituted by the government and the most unceasing vigilance brought to bear upon all portions of the city and its suburbs. After the lapse of two weeks the wretched place of the unhappy gentleman's imprisonment was discovered. A raid as vigorous as unexpected was made upon the house, and Señor Cervantes was rescued. A brief trial resulted in the condemnation of his captured abductors. They were led out and shot to death against and in front of the very house in which they had secreted their victim. The perforated walls upon which the bullets struck in the hour of their execution can be seen by anyone who cares to look at them today, for in this climate such marks do not yield to the weather. Mr. Cervantes lives to enjoy the honor and respect which have ever been his and also to regret that his unfortunate adventure has given to the city of his birth a reputation for kidnaping and robbery which it is far from deserving.

When one calls to mind the abduction and undiscovered fate of poor little Charley Ross; the Nathan Murder in New York from which the veil of mystery never has been lifted, and many other crimes of like nature which have gone unpunished, one fails to see in the Cervantes matter, shocking and horrible as it was, a state of morals more peculiar to Mexico than to any great city of our own, where villainy sometimes gets the upper hand of law and order. The Mexican abductors within two weeks after the perpetration of their crime were discovered, tried and promptly executed. According to a woman's judgement this makes a balance in favor of Mexico in the way, at least, of prompt justice. Mr. Cervantes was a man of great wealth, and this led to the hope, on the part of the kidnapers, of securing a large ransom. It does not follow that every American commercial traveler or unpretentious tourist who visits Mexico is to be gagged and bound and run away with!

Possibly dread of disaster like fear of certain diseases brings about the very calamities from which one desires to escape. Again there can be no doubt that a good deal of the hue and cry which is raised about highway robbery in Mexico originates with persons who have no way to trumpet their courage save by fighting imaginary bandits with imaginary bullets, quite willing to cast a stigma upon a country provided they can, at so little cost to themselves, make a background dark enough upon which to make their own fancied deeds of valor shine. Morally considered I am convinced Mexico is no worse if no better than other countries boasting of a more generally advanced civilization. I have seen a printed record in the works of a foreign writer of every knife thrust and every pistol shot occurring in Mexico in a twelvemonth and published as evidence of the general depravity of Mexican character. If as conscientious a record were kept of train robbing, murders, cruelties and other atrocities committed in the United States in the space of a year, Mexico's slate would not show the longest nor the blackest list.

I remember a delightful day which Cora and I spent in wandering off to the market and other places. The streets were an unusually interesting aspect because so many Mexican ladies were abroad walking to church and wearing the becoming and bewitching mantilla which, as yet, is the headdress always worn to early mass. On our way we stopped awhile among the bird-sellers near the Plaza. Their stock in trade consisted of birds in infinite variety, the plumage alone of some of them being marvels of exquisite color and gradation of tint. The prices asked were not exorbitant. We bought for a few dimes a pretty fellow for his feathers and his tameness. He had not a note of any account in his throat, but his plumage seemed made of rainbows and tropical sunsets, while he was as tame as if he had been all his little life accustomed to perch on "my lady's finger." A Mexican friend who met us feared we had been sadly cheated in our purchase, as the cunning vendors in order to make a bird attractive by his tameness have a trick of feeding it particles of lead mixed with its food. This has the effect of making them seem tame, while only stupid from the effects of the lead which causes them to die in a short time. Another practice is to take a very plain bird and paint him with such artistic skill as to make him appear like one of the most brilliant habitants of the tropical forests. He is sold at a good price to some unsuspecting stranger who ultimately beholds with dismay all the fine colors vanish with the first bath his plumaged property obtains. Oh, land of wooden nutmegs, look to thy laurels for verily thy Indian brother bids fair to out-Herod Herod! Fortunately, our little bird proved to be neither painted nor leaded, and in this transaction as in all others in Mexico, we were dealt by honestly. We found the marketplace situated upon the former site of the Convent of Mercy. I once heard an artist who had been in Egypt in a similar place declare that when he prepared to sketch and held the diversity of costume, color, and characteristic which everywhere presented itself, he threw down his brushes in despair, absolutely unable to choose a point at which to begin. One experiences much the same feeling as he stands in the market-place at Mexico. The coloring, the grouping, the attitudes, the surrounding ruins, the existing freshness dazzle and confuse and throw the thoughts into a strange tangle from which it is difficult to weave the pattern of a distinct idea; even while the eye delights in the pictures it beholds. They are everywhere these pictures. Each group, each figure, each pose, even the drapery offers a subject for a sketch. Here bare armed women knelt beside the half ruined decorations of a fountain. From the mouth of a marble lion a stream of water poured into a hewn stone trough where these women washed clothes and look up smiling and chatting as we stopped to talk with them, while they never ceased to pat and pound and wring the much belabored linen. Further on, mats stretched upon bamboo poles shielded masses of brilliant color in fruits and flowers, the latter adorning every place, while Indian girls in gracefully worn rebozos offered them for sale. Yonder, an old Indian minstrel stands with his harp; his grand head covered with thick white hair like that upon his chin. His sarape hangs in graceful folds, he holds his wide brimmed hat in his hand, and tells you, if you question him, he is going "to play by and by for a party going up the canal in a boat." He doesn't disdain the *real* you give him but takes it, not with an air of obsequious gratitude, but with one of lofty and graceful condescension! Not far off, an old Indian sits wrapped in a many colored sarape and surrounded by various pottery articles of quaint design while he cuts into slices the crimson tuna, which is the fruit of the Nopal, and adds it to the mess of pottage he is cooking for his own breakfast in an earthen jar set upon a bed of coals and hot ashes. A few steps further on, and we come upon a huge stone reservoir, where the water carriers are filling their earthen pitchers and jars with which, when filled and carefully adjusted, they move off at a brisk trot on their round of distribution to the different houses where they are regularly expected. Waiting at the same fountain stands a woman. Her neck and arms are bare. Her bright rebozo is knotted about her supple, uncorsetted waist. She is young and dark eyed and, as she stands there in her graceful attitude, her round arm supporting the jar poised upon her youthful head, I doubt if Jacob, in the Rachel of old beside the well of Haran, beheld a more attractive picture. Of all sorts of goods and wares and products for sale there was no end—the merchandise often being as novel and picturesque as the merchants themselves. We wandered along the white and ruined walls, yet remaining, of the old convent which dated from 1602. Through its fissured walls we could see its faded frescoes and the dimming remnants of its former splendor. Upon its crumbling dome the incautious cactus grew, and from a broken cornice long pendant boughs of a willowy tree hung down and soothingly swept the white face of the old wall which had given it room to root and grow. Suddenly we came upon an opening in the wall. There was no door, no drapery to exclude the intruder and, as we paused a moment, a pleasant voice bade us enter. We did so and found ourselves literally upon the *ground floor*, not a board nor a brick between our feet and the hard-packed earth. The apartment with walls of stone was about twenty feet square. Opposite the aperture by which we had entered stood the usual altar. It was prettily draped with moss and green branches and tinsel ornament in profusion. Behind it was a beautiful picture of the Virgin and the infant Christ which possessed undoubted merit and was of much value. It had no frame and, perhaps, had once adorned the Chapel of the very convent in the cellar of which it now hung. At one side of the room played two dusky children, while an old woman and an old man, both gray headed, looked on. In the foreground a young woman knelt before her charcoal furnace. In front of her was the low, stone, three-legged table on its three stone feet, and in her hands was her stone rolling pin with which she diligently pressed and crushed her already much crushed and pounded lime-soaked corn. Her face was bright and animated, and decidedly pretty, notwithstanding its dusky complexion. The smooth skin was without a blemish; the eyes were bright, and the teeth faultless. She had the beautifying smile of her race. Her rebozo had fallen from her head revealing a neck and shoulders of perfect symmetry, and her long, shining, black hair was braided in two plaits intertwined with strings of scarlet wool. When we began to talk with her, she laid aside her rolling pin and patted her tortillas between her small and shapely hands. Her low chemise, white and fresh and ornamented with her own needlework, displayed an exquisite bust; while she laughed and chatted with *las Americanas* with charming naiveté and modesty. We still recall the picture of the aged Indian couple; the smart children playing on the bare, earth floor; the little altar with its precious picture, its cheap candles and rude adornments; the ruined surrounding walls and the pretty *tortillera* patting her corn cakes beside her glowing charcoal furnace.

Strolling hotelward in some by-street, where, we know not and shall never know, we encountered a party of paupers taking their breakfast in the middle of the unfrequented road. There were three black-eyed boys, two girls, a middle aged woman and an old man of most picturesque type, beside a woman who knelt before a cask of pulque and dealt out her drinks. In an earthen jar, over a dull fire of charcoal, simmered and smoked a few goat's ribs. One of the girls made and cooked tortillas, which she dipped in a dish of chile near at hand, while the pulque woman on her knees before her cask of milky fluid sold it to the group around her and to the passers by, reverently and invariably making the sign of the cross over her cask before dipping from it a cup of its contents. On the further side of the way from us, up and down, walked a bright-eyed, beautiful Indian girl, apparently not more than fifteen years old, with a plump papoose hanging in the rebozo at her back. The child seemed to be her own and hung naked and content in the secure place assigned to it looking curiously about with its keen, black eyes, while its youthful mother watched us and smiled at us through unkept locks of straight black hair. We stopped and stood aside regarding with interest the pauper group so picturesquely placed beside their pulque and their pottery. How primitive were the utensils and how quaint! The bits of charcoal glowed hotly under dull, red earthen pots and jars of no newer hue and pattern than if just brought from an Egyptian Collection hundreds and hundreds of years old. The women and boys might have stepped from the canvas of some oriental picture, and the undisturbed self-possession and dignity with which they proceeded with their meal in the presence of strangers might have been a heritage from kings. As we stood silently observing them, the old man of the tribe with his thick gray locks and long white beard rose upon his bare feet, removed his tattered sombrero, and folding his ragged sarape about him as if

it were a martial cloak, with a courtly grace and deferential air said, addressing us in Spanish, "Ladies, you see before you the breakfast of the poor. It is
humble, but if you will honor us by sharing it, anything we have is entirely
at your disposition." We thanked him for his hospitality and accepted a *tortilla* much apparently to his delight. We declined, however, a savory goat's rib
but paid for and passed to him the cups of pulque proffered us. He remained
standing in his picturesque draperies of rags this Indian graybeard—wrapped
in his old sarape of many faded hues, over which fell his silvery locks. His tall
form was majestic in its pose and the whole figure worthy the pencil of a
[Gustave] Doré. When we begged him to be seated, with a gesture which
would have done credit to a prince and with an air that implied a knowledge
of the fact that "obedience is the highest courtesy," he resumed his place upon
an old kettle turned upside down; from which throne he sipped a cup of
maguey juice to our "very good healths," with as much apparent relish as if it
had been wine of a vintage as old as the history of Mount Ararat.

A *tortillera* can be found anywhere, also a pulque vendor. Goat's meat
costs but a trifle, and a few penny worth of charcoal is quite sufficient to cook
it, with the added luxury of a few *frijoles,* the black beans of the country,
which constitute a portion of most Mexican meals. Two or three caterers thus
club together. A *cocina,* or kitchen, is established in some out of the way
street, and is speedily found out and patronized by paupers who pay and
paupers who do not pay. The pulque profits are usually sufficient to induce
the proprietor to serve such as are "hungered and athirst" and utterly penni-
less without loss, though, to their credit be it said, this class are always kind
and humane to one another.

The philosophers who enjoy these meals are happy in the knowledge that
fingers were made before forks. In fact, knives, forks and spoons at such
meals would be as useless as pitchforks with which to eat cherries. The tortilla which is somewhat stiff, is rolled up; an earthen cup at hand contains
chile. Into this peppery preparation the tortilla is dipped then eaten, or, by the
tortilla, which serves every purpose, the *frijoles* or the boiled rice are scooped
up and carried to the mouth and after it has assisted everything else down
the throat, down it goes itself. It is a very convenient way of housekeeping
thus to eat up the plates with every meal. The goat's ribs are so exceedingly
spare that tooth and nail are the absolute requisites for deriving nourishment
from them and, of course, no one needs knives and forks to drink pulque. A

sharp appetite is, in fact, sufficient to carve up almost any kind of a breakfast in almost any country. The Mexican poor, who dine Gypsy fashion, in the street or fields, wherever food can be obtained, understand this and dispense with all table utensils save such as have been provided for them by nature.

We passed upon our way numbers of children belonging to the peasantry. Groups sat in doorways or rested close to the mother while she sold cakes or baked tortillas. They were odd little creatures and peculiar to Mexico as are the frijoles and tortillas. The Mexican baby could not be better if it were a rag doll. There must be soothing syrup or some mysterious sort of lullaby in the air to make these Indian infants so unfailingly "good." We never saw them romp, nor yet display peevishness and ill temper. We never heard a baby cry in Mexico and were often led to wonder if "colic" and "pins" and other ills that baby flesh is heir to were unknown in that clime. They accept any sort of position from a ride in the rebozo at the mother's back to a bed upon the bare ground with an air of serene content. They by no means have a stupid look. On the contrary, their keen black eyes seem to see everything that is going, and they display an unmistakable intelligence which later on is disguised under an aspect of apathy or a church taught gravity. The mothers display for their children a warm and demonstrative affection and, I fancy, the rod is very freely spared. Among the women of this class there are no *Houris*. A really handsome peasant woman beyond her early girlhood is a most unusual sight. Small hands and feet are not at all uncommon, and one frequently sees fine figures. The bust and shoulders and arms thanks to tortilla making are usually rounded and well developed, but pretty faces are few and far between. The season of early youth past, the Mexican woman waxes fat. Her feet being small, she does not carry her weight well then, and waddles without grace of movement. But, in her picturesque costume, with her bright eyes and fine teeth, engaged at her novel and primitive tasks, she is always with her winning smile and gentle ways, an object of interesting attractiveness.

We derived infinite amusement from the signs we read over the shop doors where the incongruity of goods sold with the sign which called attention to them seemed to indicate the acumen of mental ingenuity in this line. At *El Armería del Espíritu Santo* (the gunshop of the Holy Ghost) one can buy any kind of murderous weapon he desires. At the shoe shop of the Virgin Mary he may buy the best of brogans. At the sign of "the Angel of Peace" dueling pistols and daggers of the most approved pattern are sold, and at the sign of the flaming devil one can buy missals and rosaries. Some historical date, some Saint, some certain flower indicates to the passerby where he can find baths, bakeries, books, chapels, bridges and boats, and a very long chapter could thus be made consisting only of this droll, doorpost literature.

We found ourselves in what we dubbed the street of the shoemakers not knowing what it was called. Men, women and children were making or selling coverings of some sort for pedal extremities. A woman would stitch away at the pair in her hands with her lap full of shoes for sale. They were wonderfully cheap and looked comfortable although far from being fine or fashionable. We talked with the women and the old men, inspected old book stalls, shops and curiosities, wandered wheresoever we liked, looked at grand ruins and plazas and palaces, talked with flower vendors, mingled with the masses, invariably meeting from high and low, from rich and poor, from young and old that unfailing courtesy which is one of the distinguishing traits of the people.

We wandered into churches and libraries and found ourselves at last among the forges of the filigree workers. The stock of articles made up and the articles under process of manufacture were all in the same little shop. The forge and the finished work could all be examined at one and the same time. There were plenty of beautifully wrought objects of the most exquisite pattern. They looked like the work of Jack Frost upon a window pane. The smaller articles were inexpensive, and we bought some, then watched the Indian workman at his forge. Upon a black background which looked like a slab of charcoal his tiny, silver wires were laid. With his pincers the workman then wrought designs of artistic beauty and skill which he must have composed as he worked or which he drew from memory for no patterns were before him. He was an Indian, and two others like himself were busy in the little shop apparently soldering together the finished bits which the first had executed. It was very interesting to watch the progress of the patterns and to note the delicate, lace-like results. A well drawn butterfly with gauzy wings and tremulous antennae and tiny silver eyes was mounted in a pin to be worn in the hair. Silver flowers were similarly mounted, particularly beautiful being sprays of the lily of the valley. This shop was a curiosity in its way on account of its size. So small a place anywhere else could only have been a stall. But here there was ample room apparently for the forges and the smiths, for the goods and the customers, while the wall was not without its brilliant picture of Nuestra Señora de Guadalupe. We visited several establishments of this kind, but we found one represented all. The goods were beautiful both in silver and in gold, and the filigree workers of Mexico equal in tracery and design and in many instances surpass in elaborate finish and delicacy of detail their Italian brotherhood.

What a busy bohemian like day that was! With what pleasure we recall it. We rambled wheresoever we liked, enjoyed the sunshine, the sky, the earth, the people, with no guide save our own inclinations. Moving where we liked and stopping where we chose to, we saw much of the usually unseen portions of the great, grand city. We peeped into gay, little pulquerías where a long green fringe called tula, somewhat like our wild flag, stripped into shreds, hung over the doors, fresh and inviting, and indicating where they who thirsted after pulque might be satisfied. The shops were always clean and neat, even if those who hung about were not always immaculate as to toilet and personal cleanliness. We looked into match factories, where it was a curious sight to see the wax matches invariably used by the Mexicans turned out complete in their neat little illuminated boxes at one dollar per hundred boxes. We saw cigar manufactories, where dozens of dark-eyed *muchachas* sat rolling the precious weed. Mexican tobacco and Mexican cigars are declared, by those who claim they know, to be fully equal to some of the best brands of Havana, while they cost much less. We stepped into queer, little pawn shops, where the displayed collections formed rare heaps of curiosities, and where the invisible contents of visible packages thrust into nooks and corners led the imagination off upon many a wild goose chase. We, of course, encountered the imitative Indians who with quiet pride displayed no end of curious things of their own workmanship. Beside the featherwork and other marvelous bits of handicraft they will readily produce a perfect portrait of yourself in wax *bas relief* and clothe the figure in tiny feathers so harmonizing tints and adroitly managing light and shade that you look at yourself well pleased and feeling inclined to say "verily Solomon in all his glory was not arrayed like one of these." Some of the most wonderful work we saw were in clay upon little figures not an inch high yet perfect representatives in every respect of all that one sees in real life in the country. To examine them in detail one may use a microscope yet fail to discover an error of any kind. The birds of the region are represented in floss silk, and the donkeys, bulls, horses and cows are molded in miniature with a fidelity to nature and an artistic ability which amounts to absolute genius. Some of the larger ones are finished by drawing over the carved wooden form a bit of tender hide obtained by killing the mother and taking the pliant skin from the embryo kid or calf. This delicate covering fits itself so accurately to the figure that it seems to have been placed there by nature, and the result is an imitation of the original quite wonderful to behold. Herds of Lilliputian cattle of this description can thus be obtained of the choicest breeds at a ridiculously small cost, although orders for the European market have somewhat advanced the price.

Under the Arcades in certain streets we found stationed at intervals men whose stock in trade consisted of a stool, a wooden desk, a rude inkstand and pen and paper. These were the public scribes. For a very small consideration they turn into writing the thoughts of those who are unable to do it for themselves. They are the public confidants, though by no means confidence men. Love letters, dunning letters, political letters, business letters, letters of wrath, hate, vengeance, romance and reality—letters expressive of passing emotion, passion and the most prosy and practical phases of human existence, these pens lie in wait for, and the men on their high stools with their feet on the rungs anxiously watch for, customers, looking meanwhile like a row of fishermen waiting for nibbles.

Here and there we came upon rare and exquisite embroidery executed by the Mexican women. There were pillow slips and towels daintily wrought, and initialed handkerchiefs were decorated with needlework in black so deftly it could not be distinguished from steel engraving; while underwear and bed linen were ornamented in a manner and with a skill fully equal to the best needleworkers of France.

At last it was sunset, street lamps here and there began to be lighted as after our long walk we strolled leisurely into the grand court of our hotel. To our surprise we found a party of American friends there awaiting us in the greatest anxiety and agitation. Messengers had been sent, some in one direction, some in another in frantic haste to search for us, the general impression among them being that we were kidnaped. Our appearance with happy faces speedily destroyed any pretty tragedies their imaginations had built up, and when the breathless mercuries who had been sent out returned, we with those who expected to act as our chief mourners were off enjoying one of many charming evenings spent at the American Legation.

16

❁

Mexico City's Major Attractions

*The Tour of the Plaza. Its area. What Carlota did for it. The mention in the
fifth letter. Anecdote. The flower market. The site of the Cathedral. A field of
bones. The old tradition. The calendar stone. Don Antonio de León y Gama's
book. Dimensions of the Cathedral. Its adornments. Cost of construction. Its
chapels. Its valuable possessions. The Sagrario. The Virgin's jewels. Ashes of
Iturbide. What one remembers. Up in the towers. How the bells are rung.
Palace of Montezuma. Monte de Piedad. Count de Regla. The purpose of the
Inquisition. The plan upon which it is conducted. What may be seen there.
The* Portales de Mercaderes. *Bookstalls in the Portal de Augustín. The
beating down system. A dollar bird cage. The municipal palace. The histori-
cal drum. The oldest book in America. The National Palace. Some bits of its
history. Its size. Its cost. How occupied. Hall of the Ambassadors. Portrait of
Washington. Swords of history.*

I remember no ground upon this continent which in the same extent of area
comprises so much of ancient and modern historical interest as that occupied
by the Plaza Mayor and the buildings surrounding it in the city of Mexico.
To make what may be called the tour of the Plaza is to take a delightful little
journey, void though it may [be] of especial incident and unmarked by any
stirring adventure.

To begin with, the "square" is not square being a little more than eight
hundred feet long from north to south by six hundred feet wide from east to

west. Cortez in the famous fifth letter of his to King Carlos alludes to this spot in his description of the "one temple which far surpasses all the rest, whose architectural grandeur no human tongue is able to describe; *and within the precincts of which surrounded by a lofty wall there is room enough for a town of five hundred families.*" Some forty years ago more or less when General Winfield Scott at the head of his dragoons rode into this Plaza it was herbless and arid, a miniature desert in the heart of a great town. To Carlota, the unhappy Empress, Mexico is indebted for the blooming garden into which the square has been converted and which has made it the sweet blessing to rich and poor alike that it now is. There are wide marble paved walks, a grand fountain, trees and flowers. There is a Zócalo near the center where a fine military band plays on Sunday mornings, on feast days and on certain evenings during the week. Statues which in Maximilian's time were in his gardens at Chapultepec adorn the place and add to its many attractions. Stationary seats are numerous, and on feast nights added chairs are conveniently placed for the accommodation of the many who come to enjoy the open air concert under the stars. I remember on one occasion when we were there that we overheard a sentimental foreign youth remark to a fair Mexican, as the full moon rose, "You have be-yu-ti-ful big moons in Mexico." "Yes," was the quick retort, "and we have big fools also."

There is a handsome, airy structure on the southwest border of the Plaza which was originally the ten-pin alley constructed for Maximilian. Like the statues it was brought from the Castle to adorn the square. It stands upon a platform which is reached by several stone steps. It is roofed, and its sides have open arches ornamented with light iron work outside of which is a walk by which one may make the entire circuit of the building. In its spacious interior every morning is the greatest profusion of flowers for sale and of infinite variety. It is the flower market of Mexico and a most delightful place to visit. The vendors are all Indians; children, women, old men, young men and boys; the groups presenting aspects as varied, and characteristics as defined as the fragrant products which they sell. The flowers are wonderfully cheap, and for a dollar and a half one can purchase a cluster of pansies, Calla lilies, violets, heliotropes and roses as large around as a half bushel.

On the east side of the Plaza is situated the National Palace. On the south side is the Municipal Hall; on the west is a long row of buildings called the *Portal de Mercaderes*—or gate of shopkeepers—and also on that side is the famous *Monte de Piedad.* On the northern side is the Cathedral. Between these buildings and the Plaza itself extends on every side a wide and handsome thoroughfare; that on the north and south affording stands for street cars all lines of which center there. Let us begin with the Cathedral in making our grand tour of the Plaza. The extensive plateau of stone on which the edifice rests is elevated several feet above the streets. No other buildings, save the Sagrario, crowd about it. It is a massive and imposing structure of acknowledged architectural beauty, with two lofty towers richly ornamented. The stone cap of each tower represents an immense bell. These, with the noble dome of the building, can be seen from every part of the valley. Within the last few years the solid stone, which formerly paved the wide, open space in front of the sacred edifices, has been taken up and the ground beautifully laid out in plots of grass, winding walks circling about fountains, and statues, and beds of ever blooming flowers. This adds much to the appearance of the place and may be noted among the recent marked improvements of the city. In making this pretty bit of work about the Cathedral numerous Aztec relics were unearthed. Some were of great interest, and were added to the collection in the Museum. Others were retained to ornament the grounds from under which they were taken. A field of bones was also found, human bones telling of vast numbers slain either upon this scene of sacrifice to the Aztec gods or in that ghastly slaughter when the ancient town became the Spaniard's spoil, and the Indians lay dead by thousands beside the altars and the homes they had died in defending. They tell no tales now, and of the history of this Mexican Golgotha much remains unrevealed.

The massive pillars and ponderous chains which formerly fenced in the church property from its unconsecrated surroundings are still retained.

The cathedral is built upon the exact spot where originally stood the Great Teocalli, or ancient temple of the Aztecs, the ruins of which, with its overthrown gods and its enormous pedestals of stone were made to serve as foundations for the temple of the conquerors.[1] The site was originally in the midst of a lake. As is well known, the Aztecs were guided to the spot by a

---

1. Townsend states the traditional view here, but more recent archaeological research has demonstrated that the Spaniards actually built the Cathedral adjacent to the Great Teocalli, thus being able to utilize more easily construction stone from the Teocalli. The Cathedral does occupy the site of the Aztec Temple of the Sun, however. See Jorge E. Hardoy, *Pre-Columbian Cities* (New York: Walker and Co., 1973), 186–97.

tradition which existed among them that when their people should find the nopal piercing a rock and upon the rock an eagle resting with a writhing serpent in his beak, these they should regard as a token and a sign, and thereon build their most sacred edifice. The vision appeared in 1325. A rocky island was found in the waters of Lake Tezcuco. Through the crevices of the stone the hardy cactus had pushed itself, and upon the cactus an eagle rested with a living serpent in its mouth. The Aztecs in their pilgrimage from the north here arrested their course and founded in the midst of the lake their temple and its defenses. The centuries that have elapsed since then have obliterated not only landmarks, but water marks, the nearest water to the ancient site being now more than a league away; but the eagle and the serpent, the clustered rocks and the nopal have survived, as an emblem, the changes of time. The Spaniards adopted it as a national symbol from the Aztecs, and to this day it remains the Mexican coat of arms.

On the outer wall at the western corner of the cathedral until recently hung that relic of ancient skill and science, the Aztec calendar stone. It is a curious study, and one that excites wonder at its workmanship, when it is remembered how limited were the tools with which the sculptors wrought, that those of iron and steel were unknown to them, and that chief among their instruments were those of stone and obsidian. This calendar was dug up in the plaza in 1790. Prescott describes it as a "colossal fragment" of dark porphyry, which

> in its original dimensions as taken from the quarry, is computed to have weighed nearly fifty tons. It was transported from the mountains beyond Lake Chalco, a distance of many leagues, over a broken country intersected by water courses and canals. In crossing a bridge which traversed one of these latter, [in the capital,] the supports gave way and the huge mass was precipitated into the water, whence it was with difficulty recovered. The fact, that so enormous a fragment of porphyry could be thus safely carried for leagues, in the face of such obstacles, and without the aid of cattle,—for the Aztecs had no animals of draught,—suggests to us no mean ideas of their mechanical skill, and of their machinery; and implies a degree of cultivation, little inferior to that demanded for the geometrical and astronomical science displayed in the inscriptions of this very stone. . . . This [calendar] shows that they had the means of settling the hours of the day with precision, the periods of the

solstices and of the equinoxes, and that of the transit of the sun across the zenith of Mexico.[2]

Another writer asserts that "ten thousand men were engaged in the transportation of this enormous mass,"[3] and still another suggests that it was brought hither by the aid of mastodons, supporting his theory by the fact that remains of these animals are still occasionally found in Mexico.[4] Some writers declare the stone to be of Toltec origin, dating back to a time long anterior to the Aztec domination and a distinguished Mexican writer, *Don Antonio de León y Gama* [1735–1802], has, in a work first published in the year 1793, given a wonderfully interesting historical and chronological description of this stone.[5] But, above all the theories and speculations concerning it, which after all can be no more than speculations and theories, and which cannot all be true, the marvelous sculpture asserts itself as an authentic and visible fact, with a degree of antiquity pertaining to it which no one can dispute. It is a few inches more than twelve feet in diameter and for years was mortared into the western wall of the church at a height above the ground of about five or six feet. The old Cathedral, which is but an infant in age compared to it, seemed to clasp it to its side as a talismanic shield which should turn away the very arrows of time. It has wisely been removed out of the wind and weather to the shelter of the National Museum, where it remains an object of curiosity to the chance visitor, a study for the archeologist and a wonder to the most indifferent. The Calendar, in spite of the many vicissitudes through which it has passed, is perfect. The surrounding portions of the stone are uneven, and one edge has a piece broken off, perhaps in that

2. William Hickling Prescott, *History of the Conquest of Mexico,* 3 vols. (New York: Harper & Brothers, 1843). In the Modern Library (1936) edition, these quotations appear on pp. 71–72 and 83.

3. Prescott attributes this statement to Tezozomoc, "whose narrative, with all the accompanying prodigies is minutely transcribed by Bustamante," W. H. Prescott, *The Conquest of Mexico and the Conquest of Peru* (New York: Modern Library, 1936), 83.

4. Prescott attributes this remark to an English traveler, Charles Joseph Latrobe, *The Rambler in Mexico: MDCCCXXXIV* (London: Seely and Burnside, 1836), 145.

5. Townsend is undoubtedly referring to his *Descripción histórica y cronológica de las dos piedras que con occasión del nuevo empedrado que se está formando en la plaza principal de México, se hallaron en ella el año de 1790* (Mexico: F. de Zúñiga y Ontiveros, 1792). An English translation of this work appears in *La piedra del sol: Aztec Calendar,* by Eduardo Matos Moctezuma (Mexico: n.p., 1992).

famous tumble from the bridge while in course of transit. One cannot resist the flood of vague musings which rush upon his soul as he contemplates this stupendous monument of stone: this "graven image" of a heathen (?) people whose origin and history lie so deep in the dust of ages, and whose progress in art and literature and science, whose principles of law, religion and education must still long mystify the student in the future as they have puzzled, interested and defied the scholar, the sage and the scientist of the past. Someday, someone, who knows?, may discover a rosetta stone which shall prove to be the magic *Open Sesame* to the vast treasures which lie stored in sculptured stone and mystic temple under the ideographs of a people whose amount of culture and wisdom may then prove to be a greater source of wonder and speculation than are the secret signs and symbols which now it so securely locks away.

But, to return to the cathedral. Upon the space now so beautifully laid out as a garden just in front of the building stood, about the year 1530, the old parochial church of St. Mary of the Assumption. Although regarded as too small to serve as a cathedral, by a special order from Pope Clement VII it was dignified as such. In 1552, Philip II ordered the old building to be razed and a new one to be erected in its place, but the work was not undertaken. In 1573 a quarter of a century after the death of Cortez such had become the wealth and grandeur of New Spain that a cathedral of corresponding magnificence was desired and deemed an imperative necessity, and in that year the corner stone of the now existing temple was laid immediately adjoining the old church, the destruction of which was now begun. At the end of forty-two years the mason work of the new building was not completed—"the exterior walls had reached but half their height, and the arches and columns for the chapels of kings were only 'well advanced.'" The inundation of the city in 1629 caused the work to be entirely suspended, and it was not resumed until six years later, 1635. Two years after its recommencement it was open to public worship, although even at that time its towers were not completed. In fact these were not finished until 1791. The cathedral was formally and solemnly dedicated in December, 1677, more than a century after the laying of the corner stone. Its vast dimensions are not equaled by any ecclesiastical edifice in America and cause it to be classed with the largest cathedrals in the old world. It covers in its entirety an area five hundred feet long by four hundred and twenty-five feet wide. The cost of the structure, exclusive of the exterior decoration, amounted to nearly two millions of dollars. Upon the towers, each of which is two hundred feet high, are several fine statues of stone wrought by the Cora brothers, who were noted sculptors of the country. The interior of the building forms a Greek Cross, and is divided into five naves. The proportions are noble and the adornments magnificent. On either side of the main nave are side chapels sumptuously fitted up and shut in by elaborately carved lattices of wood with bronze gates. There are fourteen of these and six besides one of which is still called "The Chapel of the Kings," the viceroys having been buried there. Another is "The Chapel of Souls" being the burial place of Bishops—others are devoted to Saints Joseph and Lawrence; one is called "The Chapel of Good Resolves," and in "The Chapel of Forgiveness" every half hour of every day in the year mass is said. The wealth of this Cathedral in the days when Catholicism ruled the land was incalculable. Its ornaments alone were of fabulous value. There were saints in silver and in gold, quantities of priceless jewels, massive services and vessels of precious metal and pictures of inestimable price. Wars and rumors of wars have reduced the number of treasures as well as the sums in the treasury though great wealth and magnificence yet remain. The walls are crowded with pictures in rich old Spanish frames and a genuine Murillo is said to be among them, but the eye, confused among the yards and yards of colored canvas, fails to find it out if it really be there which is scarcely probable. It is not at all likely to have escaped the rapacity of those to whom troublous times offered opportunity to secure the prize. The dome is grand and adorned by a fine fresco of the Assumption of the Virgin. There are no pews, and the length of the floor from portal to opposite altar is one hundred and thirty-three Spanish yards, and the width between the columns of the chapels, being seventy-four Spanish yards, gives an impression of vast space and grandeur; the stupendous height from floor to dome adds to this effect. The choir which is one mass of elaborate carving stands near the center of the Cathedral and between it and the altar of the Kings is another altar, its canopy supported by eight polished green marble columns as smooth and bright as glass. A rich balustrade of antique bronze surrounds this and connects it with the choir. This railing is in itself a possession of immense value; a foreigner at one time offered to purchase it, proposing to replace the bronze with a balustrade of solid silver to be in all respects as elegant in finish and design as the original balustrade of bronze, and to give half a million dollars to boot.

His offer was promptly declined. About this main altar stand life-size statues of the twelve Apostles and of numerous Saints. There is also one of the Virgin, which has been deprived of a magnificent array of precious stones it once possessed which were the gift of *Carlos Quinto*. Besides this statue of *La Purissima*, it is said the church possesses two other images of the Immaculate Mother. One is that representing the Assumption wrought of the finest gold and set with gems and weighing hundreds of ounces; the other one represents the Conception, [and] is three feet in height and of solid silver. The six candlesticks upon the main altar are of solid gold and richly ornamented. The receptacle in which the Most Holy Sacrament was formerly carried on the feast of *Corpus Christi* was magnificent with two correspondingly valuable reliquaries, one of them studded with emeralds and pearls; the other, counting among its flashing gems a single sapphire of immense value. These are but a few of the still fabulous possessions of this Church which upon certain occasions produces from its regal coffers chalices, vases, altar cloths and candelabra of the richest material and rarest device. One chalice in particular is in itself a mine of wealth being encrusted with rubies, emeralds and diamonds representing, perhaps unintentionally, the national Mexican colors. The services are conducted with great pomp, ceremony and solemnity, especially when High Mass is performed under the auspices of the Archbishop.

The absence of stained glass may detract somewhat from the appearance of the interior by daylight, but at night illuminated by hundreds of wax candles the effect is brilliant, solemn and imposing. In the day, as one walks through, he will hear at almost any hour the choristers chanting in the choir and find a few humble and devout worshipers kneeling on the old wooden floor, a motley gathering always possessed of the attributes of grace, color and picturesqueness ever to be found in all gatherings in Mexico, and alas, too often that other element, uncleanliness. It is a place to which one can go day after day with ever renewed pleasure to enjoy not only the services but that material religion which is of architectural splendor, grand proportions and beautiful adornments. As a general thing, it is a matter of impossibility to convey in words any but the most vague idea of the grandeur of magnificent buildings. Save with a few, the imagination is not a good architect even when given a plan. Solomon's temple, although we learn by heart its measurements in cubic feet and know intimately most of the materials of which it is constructed, does not readily build itself and never accurately I venture to say in the fancy. We hear of carved and graven towers, of mighty domes, of rich and gilded chapels, of magnificent altars, of splendid and spacious naves, of height and breadth, of stupendous columns and soaring arches, and out of it all is gathered a dreamy vision of splendor, vastness and beauty but a really clear idea of little beyond details. The effect as a whole is lost and can only be enjoyed by personal inspection.

Immediately adjoining the Cathedral upon its eastern wall, an annex indeed of the grander edifice, is the Parish Church of the Sagrario. Its possessions are rich and many of them beautiful. It has a highly ornate facade in which, although details are finely wrought, the whole is too florid to be pleasing; so far as the Cathedral is concerned, it would be a great addition to the main structure if the Sagrario would be taken away, a case of addition by subtraction which the Mexicans, devoted as they are to their traditions and ancient landmarks, will probably never work out. I remember a picture of the Virgin which one morning attracted my attention in the Sagrario by the wonderful manner in which the jewels upon it were painted. The earrings and the necklace about the throat were rendered with a truth and perfection I never saw equaled. I stood some distance from the picture and was struck with the superiority of that portion of the work over every other part of the painting. A priest, noticing the interest I bestowed upon this canvas, beckoned me toward the small altar over which it hung. The jewels were real! Earrings of precious pearls and a necklace of the same was about the throat and suspended in the painted ears; a votive offering probably of someone tired of "the pomp and vanities." For this revelation of "high art" I dropped a trifle into the contribution box just at hand and passed through the connection door once more into the Cathedral where under the arched ceiling and lofty columns of the Royal Chapel in a marble urn are preserved the remains of the ambitious and unfortunate Don Augustín de Iturbide. Mexico holds him, whatever were his faults, in constant and honored memory. His portraits are prominent in the public halls; his sword is sacredly kept in the National Palace, and mementoes of him are displayed in the Museum. There is or was a silver baptismal font here, and also a vast one of carved cedar held sacred to the memory of some Mexican martyr—whose name I forget.

Standing within the Cathedral upon this famed and legendary spot you recall something of what you have read of the ancient temple which once stood here and the vast area it covered. You remember the solid walls which surrounded it which were eight feet in height and known as the Wall of Serpents because of the sculptured reptiles on its face. You remember the four huge battlemented gateways which were placed toward each point of the compass. You recall the great pyramid itself with the procession of priests, its stench of blood and its surmounting stone which was one mighty block of jasper and upon which were stretched the victims of the sacrifice. You see, in fancy, the altars of the sanctuary, their fires undying, their lights never extinguished. You behold the gigantic images of the war god Huitzilopochtli to whom the temple is dedicated and before which lie the reeking offerings of human hearts, smoking, warm and gory, as when torn from the lacerated bosoms of the victims. You seem to hear the beating of the great cylindrical drum made of serpents' skins, throbbing out its dreadful summons to the people, and it seems to sound the voice of the great Conquistador saying to the King: "Permit me here to erect the True Cross, and to place the images of the Virgin and her Son in your sanctuaries, and you will soon see how your false gods will shrink before them." Montezuma, as firm in his faith as Cortez is in his own, replies: "These are the gods who have led the Aztecs on to victory since they were a nation; and who send the seed time and the harvest in their seasons," and he turns away shocked and angered at the sacrilegious words he has heard, and eager to purify the temple from the profane breath and presence of the strangers who have dared to speak lightly of his Deities.

After the model of the principal one, other Teocallis stood within this same extended space on which you gaze, an area which comprised not only that now occupied by the Cathedral, but also all of that now covered by the Grand Plaza and the buildings which immediately surround it. Where the *Zócalo* now is, and where the bands play to listeners gathered about the fountains and under the trees, may have stood the one consecrated to Quetzalenatl, or, that which was circular in form, with an entrance in imitation of an immense dragon's mouth bristling with sharp fangs and kept constantly dripping with streams of human gore. Yes, here, where the children are playing, where many men of many beliefs pass and repass, where the descendants of the Montezumas kneel and pray to those "images" which Cortez set up instead of the "false gods," here was the consecrated ground of the Aztecs where the earth drank the horrifying wine of their sacrifices, whence went out the piercing cries of those in the awful agonies of death, while the torturing priests went on with their horrible ceremonies and appalling butcheries. Memory has only time to gasp with horror at these things and to turn her eyes from these visions of blood, when heathen priest and temple and altar and sacrifice are swept from the scene and give place to the Christian Church of the conqueror with its supreme powers, its iron torture stake, its blazing faggots and the trials of the inquisition.

The ancient landmarks have all disappeared. The lake is dried up, the causeways gone, the conquerors and conquered are all dead and the descendants of each mingle amicably upon the scene of former contests and opposing passions. One feels, as he wanders over this portion of the city, as if he were gazing upon a palimpsest whence the records of one race have been blotted out to write thereon the histories of another. He gazes with awe into remote chambers of antiquity. The air he breathes is full of the sounds of other days, vague echoes of a buried past, and the ground beneath his feet teems with relics of a wonderful race whose works have survived the passing of the ages and whose impress makes itself apparent in the features and characteristics of those who throng the streets about him. The heart stirs with strange emotions as one treads these places so linked with idolatry and iconoclasm, with God and godlessness, with razing and rebuilding of temples, with the downfall and establishment of faiths and with the subjection abject and complete of these who once were rulers in the land.

But come, let us away from all this. By many steps which are far from being always clean and which are deeply worn by the ascending and descending feet of generations of human beings, let us make our way to the immense towers. It is well worth the climb to see the splendid view which they command. Go slowly; remember it is necessary to be cautious in making all ascents. On the first floor of the turrets lives a family. I have seen their neat little parlor, with its pictures of saints, and its pretty altar,

"And the people—ah, the people
They that dwell up in the steeple"

father, mother, sons and daughter and the dog! There are forty-eight bells in the turrets and like all the bells in the city they are rung by hand, electric bell ringing not yet having been adopted here. Some of them are rung by attaching a rope to the great clapper which being lifted and let fall rings the bell.

The smaller ones turn over and over when rung on an axle, and it was at one time no uncommon thing for Mexican boys to ascend the towers, seize the clapper of a bell with both hands, and swing to and fro, over and under as the ringer pulled his rope, then drop unharmed down upon the stone floors of the belfries. The feat recalls the poem entitled "The Curfew shall not ring tonight," and the daring act of its devoted young heroine.

Anyone in search of a new sensation should station himself on the stairs in the turret at bell ringing time. I chanced there one day at such an hour, and fancied an earthquake would be a gentle suspiration in comparison. From below, however, or softened by distance, they had a peculiar music of their own. For Cora and me those bells never lost their first impressiveness. Were we gaily chatting at the first peal, we grew mute. Were we walking at the first stroke, we paused instinctively and our hearts seemed to bow and uncover themselves as to something holy passing by. Out upon the heights far away from the shadow of the towers where they swung, in the gorgeous Mexican twilights we would hear the steady peals take up their evening march across the quiet valley, and though bound by no religious tie to the church to which they were consecrated, we stood awed and hushed prone to do them reverence.

Just yonder, across the street and west of the Cathedral, where now are stores and dwellings and numerous places of business, once stood the magnificent Palace of Montezuma. Two blocks westward and three blocks northward, present measure, it is said to have covered. The Concordia, where we take our coffee every morning, was the southwest corner of that splendid edifice which was so vast in its proportions that upon its flat roof was ample room "for thirty knights to run their courses in a regular tourney." It was built of stone with beams of cedar and palm and other precious wood, and enriched with gold and native gems and all the barbaric splendor of the time. Amid the convulsions which attended the conquest it fell and helped to fill up and make solid the water courses which interrupted or impeded the free passage of the conqueror's troops in those last awful days, when with fire and sword the doom of the Aztec Empire was written and sealed with blood, and with torture, and with death.

Upon what was the site of the main front of that palace in *la calle del Empadrillo, número 8,* stands the National Monte de Piedad—the Mexican Bank of Loans and Pledges. It fronts the western wall of the Cathedral. It is one of the oldest edifices in the city and was built immediately after the conquest for the private residence of Cortez. Subsequently, it was occupied for a time as the palace of the Viceroys. It is a spacious building, and the house has remained unaltered since its erection. Its doors, windows, staircases, ceilings, courts, corridors, and balconies are today as they were when the early Spaniards filled the vast chambers with their presence and gazed from the wide windows out upon their new temple rising on the ruins of the old.

The Monte de Piedad was founded in 1774 by the Count de Regla, Don Pedro Romero de Terreros [1710–1781]. The pious philanthropist endowed the institution with $300,000 cash from his own private fortune and originated the plan upon which to this day it is conducted. His object was to relieve the poor and needy from the ruinous usury of the ordinary class of pawnbrokers, as well as to assist the *needy rich*—and this class is much larger than is suspected in every country. The laws and regulations of the *Monte de Piedad* permit those who need money to obtain it on the most liberal terms. The depositor receives upon his pledges, which are duly appraised, a certain sum at certain rates of interest. These rates are never lower than 3 per cent, and never higher than 12 ½ per cent *per annum*. When the depositor ceases to pay interest on the loan advanced, his pledges, whatever they may be, are retained for a period of seven months in the bank. They are then placed in the hands of special officials who appraise them, and they are exposed for sale at the appraisers' valuation for one month. If still unsold they are again valued this time at a lower figure and again displayed for sale in the salesrooms on the lower floor. The process is continued for six months with articles that do not find purchasers within that period, and if the goods are still in [the] bank at the end of the year they are sold at public auction to the highest bidder.

If they bring less than the value set upon them by the appraisers, the latter must themselves make up the deficit to the bank. If they bring more the surplus is added to the bank fund. The appraisers are men of experience and careful judgment, and it may be guessed that under these rules they are especially careful in their valuations. There are certain days in each month appointed for the sale of certain goods at public sale. One is for the sale of clothes, one for the sale of jewels, and one for the sale of miscellaneous articles. The portrait of the founder occupies a prominent place in the bank, and his name is one of the most cherished in Mexico. The profits of the institution for seventy years were paid out to secure masses for the soul of the honored originator, but those are no longer continued, and the surplus funds are devoted to the establishment of branch banks of the same kind and for which need arose, and several are in existence in different parts of the city.

The president of the bank very kindly took us through the building, and we were also shown the great vault and allowed to enter it, where we stood among immense heaps of money bags containing in silver six million, three hundred thousand dollars—hard cash—of funds belonging to the bank. The house and its contents are of the most interesting nature.

Everything is here from a slipper to a scepter, and it is a complete museum of antiquities and modern conveniences. Many things seem to have a pathos in them that reaches the heart, and all things have a voice. Here are the commonest gowns, sarapes, sandals, rebozos, sombreros, garments of little children, robes of priests, thousands of pieces of family plate, pictures, magnificent mirrors, furniture of every kind, carriages, sewing machines enough to stock a store, beautiful mosaic tables, carpets, curtains, bedsteads, statuettes, vases, bronzes and antique silver in every conceivable form, candlesticks, flagons, cups, bowls and pitchers. As a special mark of favor through the kindness of the gentleman who accompanied us, we were shown into the jewelry department, one not often opened to visitors. Here were "sermons in stones," and very precious stones they were, whatever may be said of the sermons. I do not suppose a richer or rarer collection could be seen anywhere of set jewels than are here. The most splendid pearls of wonderful size, rubies, emeralds, sapphires, diamond chains which glittered like tears, family jewels of nobility, the inheritance of kings, gems which had glittered on the white necks of happy brides brought here, perhaps, by the hands of unhappy wives—for they probably exist even in beautiful Mexico—clusters of rare old gems in brooches, necklaces, pendants and rings, ornaments for the hair, jeweled combs, bracelets, buckles; the heirlooms of ages all slumber on these shelves, each with its silent record written somewhere deep on anxious hearts. In gazing on the millions represented by the treasures in this old building, it seems as if the surges of scattered joy, want, wealth, disappointment, sorrow and despair must have found no other shore to break upon than the walls of the *Monte de Piedad*. Yet what a drop in the infinite ocean of all this it is. The institution is a source of inestimable blessing to the poor and needy and "a transaction" with the *Monte de Piedad* bears with it for no one any humiliation. It is simply like doing business with a bank, and all classes take advantage of its benefits, and all dealings are held strictly confidential. Many persons put their treasures in this stronghold for safe keeping merely, and the silver and jewels of many noted persons are thus deposited here. Among these are the jewels of Santa Anna's wife.

The "Street of San Francisco" must now be crossed, and we arrive at the Portal de Mercaderes still on the western side of the square. These *"portales"* are what we would perhaps call a long arcade, the arches opening on the street. On this walk at the outer and inner sides are established booths and stands for a great variety of things, while in the store windows may be seen displays of wonderful sombreros, sarapes, and rebozos besides the usual order of dry goods. This block has portales on its three sides. Its north side is on a portion of San Francisco Street called Calle de los Plateros, which we just crossed from the Monte de Piedad. There are located fashion stores but the portales are found alone on the west, north and this the eastern side. There are other portales in different parts of the city but none so well known as these. A walk around this block on Sunday morning is a most interesting one. The newspapers are beginning to talk against their occupancy by the numerous dealers, but to drive them away would be to deprive strangers [of] one of the novelties of Mexico, and though the presence of the vendors may offend the eyes of some of the residents, it would be well for them first to attend to those parts of the city where the olfactories of both residents and strangers cannot pass without a pocket handkerchief guard well-armed with eau de cologne, or Atkinson's white rose. The newspapers may find the portales odious, but at least they are not odorous with those offenses which are "rank and smell to Heaven." In the Portal de Mercaderes the scene presented is like a fair. There is the vendor of lottery tickets who carries the package in his hand, and proffers tickets to the passerby calling out the amount of the prize to be drawn and the day on which the drawing will take place. There is the newspaper vendor who points to his stand and politely informs you that he has *El Monitor Republicano, La Libertad, La Patria, El Siglo XIX*, etc. There is the Jew from Jerusalem with olive wood for sale. There is the strolling shopman with his stock in trade in his hands, who proffers you combs, and knives, and sundry other things. Here is the optician with all sorts of glasses, of tints so numerous that a purchaser may see through them a world of any hue he likes. There are toys and confectionery, embroideries, ribbons, wooden ware, pottery, Mexican dulces, harness and bridles, cigars, and matches, and cigarettes and shoes. Merchants great and small, the humble booth and the grand bazaar. Goods of native and foreign manufacture, fancy articles in filigree silver and gold, of native metal and native workmanship. Here are hats and hosiery, laces and *lingerie,* saddles and silks, tops and trinkets, dolls and dry goods, sarapes and sandals, rebozos and beads, pins and prints and periodicals—in short, all sorts of vendors of all sorts of things, while in the windows of the shops are displayed the great sombreros: black, white, gray, brown, fawn color and even red. They are of felt and of straw, and are stiff or soft, and are loaded on crown and on brim with silver or with gold, all embroidered or are plain, to suit all fancies, and range in price from four to fifty dollars to suit all purses.

Turning the corner you find yourself in the Portal de Augustín, and quite a different scene presents itself. Here on the inner side of the walk are stores with fancy goods and china, stores and libraries, and shops of picture dealers. On the outer edge of the walk are stands and shelves and tables, some of which are so arranged they can lock up at night, and here are the second-hand book stalls. Musty tomes, vellum bound, antique typed specimens of the literature of all nations printed in all tongues—books quaintly illustrated, books hundreds of years old, books of art, of science, of love and war—books on every subject and bound in every style attract the passerby. Here you find the antiquarian turning over faded and yellow pages, searching for the indication of a date with a magnifying glass. Here is the bookworm adding to his stores; here is the poor student bartering for a volume he covets; here is the novel reader purchasing for a trifle an armful of light literature; here are the autograph copies of books given by authors to dear friends with "affectionate regards" or with "much love" or "in memory of never-to-be-forgotten kindness," and here they lie without even the sign of having been opened by the "dear friends." Here is the rare book worth its weight in gold and here one equally precious to him who knows which may be bought for a song. It is the favorite hunting ground of book lovers of all classes, and the purchasers present as interesting a study as the printed piles over which they hover so eagerly, so anxiously, or so enthusiastically.

Around the corner once more and you come among a most motley assemblage of persons selling most motley wares. On the sidewalk's gutter side on the flagging are spread straw mats, and upon these are carefully gathered together everything, apparently, that everyone else throws away. Odds and ends of china, bits of broken glass, odd tools of every description, doorplates, knockers, spikes, nails, old bits of bronze and brass and copper and silver, packs of old cards, rusty locks without any keys and rusty keys without any locks, old pictures, curiosities, buttons, mismatched old plates, old carvings, now and then an Aztec bead or amulet or idol of stone, old candlesticks, old vases, old knives and forks, old dinner bells and convent bells, old swords, and dirks and poniards of every age and pattern, old spurs, old parchments, old scissors, old crosses, old boxes, old ornaments ripped from old clothes, old stirrups, old spoons, a multitude of things that seem of no use to anyone and sometimes a truly rare and valuable bit of old *bric-a-brac* may be found here and also old coins and ancient medals. The portales are worth visiting any morning, but the best times are Sundays and feast days, as there are certain dealers who only go there with their wares at such times. It is a boast with Americans that they always pay half the price asked them for anything in the portales. Their habit of "beating down" has become so well known among the vendors that they probably ask an American just double the price they expect to get, and they, of course, recognize a foreigner the moment they see him. We were discussing this matter the other day in our alcove at the Concordia, and Don José asserted that they would not attempt such a thing with a Mexican but would at once name to him the lowest price, aware that a Mexican could not be taken in and would not be asked two prices. At that moment came by the window a cage vendor. From his stock he selected a large cage of wire and wood very prettily made, and such as at home we pay four or five dollars for. The man held it up outside the window. "Cuanto," questioned Don José, who is a well-known Mexican. "Dos Pesos" was the reply. "How cheap!" exclaimed Cora. "Offer him one," said I. "He never would take it," said Don José, at the same time confidently holding up one finger to the vendor and saying "*un peso.*" Immediately the man made a gesture of assent, lowered the cage to the ground, and held out his hand for the money! Don José very gallantly ordered his undesired purchase sent to our hotel. Then, what was the use of a cage with no bird? Two birds we bought. Two little green parakeets. They were sold us as being very gentle and tame. They turned out to be wild and malicious and bit us ferociously. Then their great appetites required a great deal of seed; then a servant had to be paid to take care of them; then their passage had to be paid wherever we took them, and, where the expense of that dollar bird cage was going to stop became a thing that was past finding out. But, let us hie us back to the plaza from which the *Portales* have caused us to make a long detour. On the southern side is situated the *Casa de Cabildo* or Municipal Palace, where are the apartments of the *Lonja Mercantil* or Chamber of Commerce. We were taken through all the rooms and found much that was interesting and entertaining. A very handsome full-length portrait of Iturbide hung *vis-a-vis* to one of Morelos. Nearby hung a copy of the original act of Independence with the signatures. In the next room hung the portraits of all the viceroys from Mendoza to O'Donojú and those also of all the Presidents with the exception of Miramón. For some unexplained reason that was found banished to another part of the house with one of Maximilian and an unfinished one of Carlota, representing her with a hard, ambitious, haughty countenance, yet handsome withal. A drum was placed before us for inspection which seemed a very ordinary drum indeed until we learned it was the identical one which had been beaten to call the troops together when Iturbide proclaimed Independence. Then it at once became an extraordinary drum. Such is the power of association with things and events. We also had the pleasure of here examining the oldest book of records in America. The *Libro del Cabildo* is in manuscript and contains the proceedings of the first Municipal Assembly ever convened in Mexico. It is a remarkable, interesting work and was begun in 1524 a few years after the Spanish victories. It contains among other matters allusions to the great square and the mighty temple which stood upon it, and is justly guarded and regarded as one of the treasures of the city. Below these rooms the *Portales de las Flores* extend along the sidewalk devoted, as are the other Portales, to the sale of various kinds of merchandise, while the omnipresent street vendors of dulces or eatables may also be found there.

Passing on we next arrive at the National Palace on the eastern boundary of the Plaza. It is a substantial stone pile, simple but effective in appearance. It covers an immense block of ground and has a frontage of nearly seven hundred feet. It is the capitol and as such is, of course, an object of interest to all eyes both native and foreign. Its style of architecture is plainer than that of our own White House at Washington and is less ornate than that in its general interior decoration. Originally its color was a somber shade of red, but this many years ago gave place to the white garb it now wears. Several public institutions are established in it on its northern side, among them being the National Museum, the Academy of Fine Arts and the Post Office. On that side also are the rooms formerly occupied by President Juárez during those important years of change and trouble when he held the reins of government.

The capitol, though now of vaster dimensions, occupies the site of one of the ancient Aztec palaces pertaining to Montezuma. The King's houses were near the great temple of his gods. In the war of the conquest it was destroyed, and Cortez caused a new palace to be erected on its immediate site. On the ruins of the Aztec Emperor's abode rose a low, massive, turreted building of considerable extent to which Cortez himself held the right and title in 1529. The edifice belonged to the son of the Conqueror until 1562, when the King of Spain purchased it as a royal residence for his viceroys, paying for it 33,000 dollars. The viceroys found it inadequate for their regal requirements, but it remained unaltered until more than thirty years elapsed when in 1692, with other buildings, the Cortez palace was burned by the populace and remained among the wrecks of that outbreak for more than a twelvemonth when its reconstruction was begun. Buildings were of slow but substantial growth at that time. One of the portals, the one now known as *la puerta principal,* the central entrance, was completed in the time of Charles II. Another, that one [at] the southern corner, was finished in the time of Philip V, and it was more than ninety years from its beginning to completion of the edifice. Men who began work upon it as youths, grew old and died and were forgotten, and another generation filled their places and wrought their lives into the palace before it was finally finished. It was already old the day when the last stone was set, the last rivet driven, and men called it new. Its ultimate cost was 900,000 dollars. It is strong enough for a fortress, is two stories high, and at each of its upper windows is a stone balcony with an iron railing. Several turrets break the monotony of its extended front. Upon these yet remain devices which in former times indicated the purpose for which the towers were erected. In the center is the clock turret illuminated at night, and on all State occasions the national banner is unfurled there from its tall staff lending its sanction to either the solemnity or gay grandeur of the hour. The Palace contains a vast number of rooms. For Maximilian's occupation they were thoroughly renovated and fitted up in regal style. Little of that splendor now remains; it having given place to simpler taste under Republican rule though the spacious apartments remain unchanged in their grand proportions, and some of them are still sumptuous. That known as the Hall of the Ambassadors is the handsomest of all. It is three hundred feet long by twenty five feet wide. There, among the portraits of the most noted men of Mexico, hangs that of our own immortal Washington. Draped with the national colors and preserved under a glass case is the sword of Iturbide. Here is also to be seen the sword of Maximilian. Suspended on the wall in a prominent place is the original act of Mexican Independence with the autographs of its signers. In spaces between the pillars which support the galleries in letters gold on tablets of stone are preserved the names of heroes illustrious in the Nation's history whose memory and example are thus kept before the people and their rulers. It might justly be called Memorial Hall.

The three entrances on the front during the early Spanish domination represented the three principal departments into which the building was divided. Within the four great *patios* or courts were the pleasure gardens of the Viceroys, and by the great fountain in the arched and columned center court, which was circular, once stood, it is said, a beautiful bronze statue of Fame, of which no trace remains that we could discover, and which seems no longer to exist in the city. The royal chapel was there and regal reception rooms, while the palace also contained within its limits a prison and barracks where infantry and cavalry were quartered.

In later days Santa Anna resided in the palace in pomp and splendor unapproached even by his luxury loving Spanish predecessors. The magnificence of his entertainments, it is asserted, were never surpassed even if ever equaled in the most aristocratic capitals of Europe. Those events still form a theme of deep and delightful interest for society veterans who, in themselves, once represented the beauty and chivalry of the time and who are fond of recalling bygone days in Mexico.

All the offices pertaining to the government which were relegated to other quarters during Maximilian's reign, upon his overthrow were again gathered within the palace. The mails, the telegraph office, the government printing [office] are established there, besides the national institutions already alluded to, while the public work of the President and his chief officials is done there. The President, however, resides with his charming wife at his own residence a short distance from the capitol when the distinguished pair are in town.

As one walks the palace floors how the memory steps along from peak to peak of history, and from name to name connected with the old building from the days of Montezuma to the days of Díaz! What vicissitudes, in the interior, has the country passed through! What turbulence, what trials, what defeats and what triumphs have been hers! As for the city itself, that which Baron von Humboldt[6] said of it three quarters of a century ago applies to it today so far as its fine buildings, its wide and level streets, the regularity of its plan and its style of architecture are concerned. He then declared it to be "undoubtedly one of the finest cities ever built by Europeans in either hemisphere." The town upon which one gazes today contains 275,000 inhabitants.

6. Alexander von Humboldt (1769–1859) was a German scientist who made a notable journey through Spanish America, from 1799 to 1804, collecting much scientific and geographical data. The voluminous reports of his journey became an important historical source on Spanish America near the close of the colonial period. Especially popular, and translated and reprinted in many languages, was his *Political Essay on the Kingdom of New Spain,* a recent edition of which is the abridged John Black translation with an introduction by Mary Maples Dunn (1972; reprint, Norman: University of Oklahoma Press, 1988).

17

❈

Life, Dress, and Customs in the Mexican Capital

In the window of the Café Concordia. *Our alcove. A hint or two. The street dress of Mexican padres. The mantilla. La Señorita. Too much ease and too little exercise. Odors not of Araby. Drainage. A Christian association. Indian woman's dress. The rebozo. Popcorn and peanut vendors. Chances for market gardeners. Industrialists and capitalists. Labor competitors. Among the shops. Changes in the mode of shopping. Book stores. Fancy goods. High price of small things. The paper bag. Postal matter. Telegraph rates. Outskirts of town. Tints of houses. Occupations of Indians.* Moscas. Cajas. Bateas. *Sunday and feast days. Everyday street life. The cries of street vendors. Peeps at street pictures and indoor work. Contrasts of race, dress and condition. The* Lépero. *The* Pordiosero. *Pickpockets. Street nomenclature.* Cinco de Mayo. *Cemetery of San Fernando. Mode of advertising places for rent. The street of Tacuba. Its connection with the conquest. Aqueduct of San Cosme. Public gardens. Popotla. The tree of the* Noche Triste. *In old Tlacopán. What Cortez said. Alvarado's camp. Nuestra Señora de los Remedios. Her little history. Her chapel. Her miraculous powers. Her fiesta. Votive offerings. Her rival. Pestilence in a petticoat. A source of revenue to the Church. The change of habitation. Her substitute. Absence of religious pageants in public. The stolen pearl.*

It is nearly noon. Carriages begin to roll through the streets bearing their fair occupants to the great Cathedral. You can see them from the little alcove of the restaurant known as La Café Concordia where we come nearly every day for our cup of chocolate or coffee. Here is a little marble table between two benches cushioned in green plush. A broad, plate glass window affords a full view of the street San José and the facade of *La Profesa* with its flocks of pigeons among the sculptures just across the way. We come here so regularly the alcove seems especially ours, and, if by chance we find it has another occupant, we are somewhat inclined to regard him as an intruder. The alcove is not unlike a section in a Pullman sleeper, but it is more attractive. A waiter presents himself wearing a spotless white jacket and a fresh white apron which passes around him almost like a tight skirt and reaches quite to his feet. With a damask napkin, also a model of cleanliness at his belt, he covers the marble with a neat linen cloth and respectfully awaits orders. The Mexicans do not consider it good taste to serve refreshments on uncovered marble. With few exceptions, even in the *tierra caliente* they cover it with fresh damask. In the white jacket, the neat apron, the deferential attendant and the covered marble are hints which restaurants, in cities holding themselves as far more civilized than Mexico, might profit by.

A few ladies are walking to church. How pretty some of them are though beauty as a rule is not found among Mexican women. The street dress of Mexican ladies of any age is usually black. The head dress for morning church is still the mantilla. Bonnets are growing in favor, more's the pity, but the principal families still adhere to the Spanish lace mantilla. Long may they do so. Nothing in the way of a head covering could be so becoming, so coquettish, so graceful. It conceals ugliness and enhances beauty, and on none does it look better than a young Mexican girl, especially if she be pretty. She was such who this moment passed. Her bright, soft black eyes so adequate to express whatever sentiment she wishes to reveal, her complexion rich and clear, her smiling mouth revealing its exquisite teeth, her abundant hair and slender shape all were enhanced in attractiveness by the soft folds of rich, black lace drooping here, caught up there, falling about her graceful shoulders and fastened by a flower to her thick and shining braids. How can she ever be let to exchange this for the stiff and clumsy and often ugly and always awkward fashionable bonnet? How demurely she walked with her ivory prayer book in her hand and her sedate duenna at her side! How slender, how girlish, how fair! Alas!! as years increase the Mexican dame waxeth fat and unwieldy. The feet are usually very small and unfitted to bear the burden of body which the upper class of women ultimately casts upon them. Too much ease, too little exercise is the bane of a Mexicana's life, and such habits bring about the same results that "honest Jack Falstaff" was wont to declare pertained to "sighing and grief."

Have you finished your coffee? Then put your handkerchief to your nose, for you have already found out that this is a great city of great smells, and let us sally forth. Is it not a crying shame that everywhere you go, such obnoxious odors assail your nostrils? In church portals; on the broad staircase of the best public restaurants; in the vestibule of the National Theater, the most fashionable place of amusement in the city, where beauty and refinement congregate night after night and where the price of seats is high enough to exclude everything that is low; at the corners of some of the principal streets; and in a hundred places where you least expect it; you feel sure that "something is rotten in Denmark." You don't exactly know what it is, but you feel sure it is not the odor of Araby the blest, and you envy the Donkey who goes about with his nose in a bag! The drainage of Mexico is known to be bad, and the city authorities must also be "bad" at least in the sense of inefficiency, for there is uncleanliness in the streets, and inattention to hygiene generally leads one to believe the city must have fallen into the keeping of one of those political rings from which cities suffer in the United States. One can but cover his nostrils, look up at the faultless sky and afar at the crowned mountains and say, with Joaquin Miller,

"Where God has done so much for man
Will man do nought for man at all?"

The abominable effluvium is not likely to inspire a poet but this or something else wrung a pathetic appeal from Mr. Miller.[1]

Who, do you enquire as we make our way along the novel streets, are all those young, well dressed gentlemen ranged along the shady side of the *Calle de Plateros?* They are tall, fine looking men, fashionably attired and with the remarkably small feet and hands which pertain to the Mexican. That is the Young Men's Christian Association. At least, let us hope so. I do not know

1. Joaquin Miller (1837–1913) was a popular western United States poet in the late nineteenth century. See *Complete Poetical Works of Joaquin Miller* (San Francisco: Whitaker & Ray, 1902).

any more about them than you do; but you remember it is the hour when the wealth and youth and beauty of Mexico go to mass at the Cathedral. These Christian men come forth from their abiding places every day at this hour and devoutly range themselves within earshot of the cathedral *belles.*

Do you notice the dress of the Indian woman here? It is usually a blue cotton skirt reaching to the ankle with a strip of white cotton about eight inches wide sewn at the top of the blue calico. This is then attached to the belt. The skirts all seem to have been "let down." A white chemise is the only waist; the neck and arms are bare, save when covered by the rebozo. You will observe that when figures are pretty and arms plump and rounded, the rebozo has a habit of slipping off and dropping down so as to occasionally get simply knotted about the waist, where it hangs ready for use if really needed. Do you notice also that you meet *dulce* vendors and lottery ticket vendors and fruit vendors and even red balloon vendors, but you do not see a popcorn vendor nor even a peanut seller? Molasses candy? Yes, plenty of it of just the same complexion and in just such sticks as at home. Among the fruits also observe there is not a grape to be seen, and the apples are about as large as apricots and never larger; there are no pears, and although you have repeatedly been told that strawberries grow here "all the year round," we have only been able to obtain them twice, and at the entertainments to which we have been invited they have not been on the table, nor have we seen them in our morning rambles about the markets. That they grow here and are of most delicious flavor, I know by experience, but we have never seen them in abundance. Sufficient attention is not given to the cultivation of fruits and vegetables, although climate and soil should encourage and warrant it. The celery that is produced here is more like the heart of a cabbage than anything else, and the crisp, bleached stalk with its appetizing green leaves atop, so plentiful and so appreciated in the States, is here unknown. Let anyone of industrious habits come here, take a piece of ground in the outskirts of the city upon any of the general lines of railroad, devote himself to the cultivation of grapes and other fruits and fine vegetables, etc., and he will make money. The gardeners here have gotten into grooves. They are principally Indians, and the class of vegetables they bring to market are such as they have been bringing probably ever since Cortez first took a "dinner of herbs" in Mexico. Industrialists as well as capitalists are needed in this country. No one need come here with the idea that money is to be picked up in the streets, or that he has only to bring money here to find at once big paying investment for it. Moreover, there is even something besides railroads needed, for notwithstanding the locomotive is the greatest missionary in the world, like lesser missionaries it must have a people to preach to and a great deal more is necessary to the success of a railway enterprise than expectations of making a "swift thing" out of its contract and its stock. To honest workers the people of the country extend openhanded welcome. The capitalist, whether possessed of large or small means, would find plenty of room for good investments. He would feel for awhile true Christian amazement at the cheapness of native labor, then be among the first to avail himself of it! Day labor, that is white labor, could not stand up against the wonderful endurance, the low wages and the content with cheap living which characterizes Indian labor. Just as railways will for a long time find a freight rival in the donkey, so white labor will find a potent competitor in the Indian. Still, the generous soil, the various climates and the general healthfulness of the country offer enticing inducements above and beyond all that to only one with an honest purpose in his heart to pitch his tent here. There is "ample room and verge enough" for all who with honest purpose wish to undertake honest work. The small trades and the manufacture of useful little necessities afford excellent business opportunities.

But, let us move on among the shops for if straws show which way the wind blows so do shops show the tastes and habits of a community. Observe that we pass no barrooms. Such glittering generalities do not exist in this city. The gentlemen of Mexico will have the choicest wines upon their tables, but no Mexican gentleman would lend his support to a public barroom. Since the introduction of street railways their convenience has brought about a system of shopping like our own with the generality of people, but many ladies still firmly adhere to the old customs; are never seen walking on the streets after early mass, and never without some companion or duenna. These go shopping in their carriages and often, as in Havana, goods desired are brought to the carriage door and there displayed and purchased. Most of the stores are small in comparison to those in large cities in the States, but the business done *per annum* amounts in the aggregate to that of many of our largest establishments. European goods are quite as cheap as with us, but goods from the United States are very dear. The cash system prevails. Butcher, baker, grocer, dry goods merchant all are paid on the spot, and no

Mexican lady goes to bed with the specter of debt to destroy her chances of pleasant dreams. In the millinery shops are hats and bonnets of the latest Parisian style, chiefly supported, let us rejoice to hear, by Americans. *Modistes* are well up in the fashions and their prices are well up also not being lower than those of leading cities in the United States. Many prominent Mexican families import their wardrobes directly from Paris. A bridal trousseau for a young lady whose wedding we attended and whose bridal outfit we saw had imported every article from France. The duties alone upon this outfit exceeded eight thousand dollars.

In jewelry, and gold and silver ware, taste and richness are displayed, and finer jewels are rarely seen than are sold and worn in Mexico. Dealers often come from abroad to make selections from Mexican gems especially of pearls, the latter being a favorite jewel. Numbers of magnificent ones find their way into the country.

The book binderies do very superior work, and book stores are numerous and well supplied, though of fancy stationery there is but a meager display and apparently no call for it. [In] the fancy stores beautiful goods are found. Dealers find ready sale for all such wares and are obliged to employ highly cultivated taste in the selection of engravings, glass, china, carvings, bronzes and all *objets de vertée*.

The prices for small necessities are very high. A box of black pins for instance costing five cents at home here bring from 12 ½ to twenty-five cents according as one buys in a fashionable or unfashionable quarter. The confectionery stores are full of tempting *dulces,* but if a place exists (an ice cream saloon) where one may go in to take a glass of soda or a dish of ice cream, we do not find it. The paper bag is also unknown here, and I know of no place where it could be of greater use. There are paper mills in Mexico, but if the paper bag is made, it keeps itself well out of sight, for as yet we have failed to see one. Neither will you find any street boxes for postal matter, that convenience not having reached this city. The postal arrangements are as annoying here as anywhere else in the Republic. You can only buy postage stamps at the post office, and there is always difficulty in getting letters weighed and mailed. The small change can only go one way and that is into the post office department, as it is almost impossible for it to be made for the hurried individual struggling to mail his matter. The post office officials, however, are very kind and obliging and exceedingly polite. The telegraph rates are very high. It is fifty cents a word from Mexico to the United States or five dollars for ten words, and night rates are precisely the same as day rates.

If we wander to the outskirts of the town we find the houses wearing many colors, each occupant tinting his *casa* or his shop according to his fancy. Then the houses become smaller and smaller until they dwindle to mere hovels and the aspect of suburbs, unlike the greeneries which surround Orizaba, Córdoba and Jalapa, is desolate, dirty and given over to yelping dogs and the off scourings of the dissolute and degraded classes. It is quite outside of the city that the Indians who bring their produce to market have their little farm gardens and ply those petty trades which have descended to them from their Aztec forefathers. It is there you find the hunters, the pottery makers, the fishermen and basket makers, the toy builders and bird catchers and those who ply the curious trade of catching in little nets the *moscas,* a sort of mosquito which settles in swarms so dense upon the waters of the little lakes and canals that to the inexperienced eye they seem like mud lumps or sand bars protruding from the water. These find ready sale in town as bird food for the many specimens of the feathered tribe which are kept caged to adorn the extensive colonnades and corridors of the houses, and it is averred that the eggs of the mosquitoes are also collected and worked into the maize flour to add an agreeable flavor to the tortilla. The variety of small trades plied by what may be called the working class of Indians is astonishing, and their ingenuity in making something out of nothing is equally surprising. They have all the imitative powers of the Chinese coupled with a great deal of inventive genius. The little sculptures they produce out of material of a value too small to be computed are marvels of skill. From the grass under their feet they construct strong and pretty bird cages and useful mats— and the worthless garden gourds they fashion into drinking cups or *cajas* decorating them with dyes and juices in such fashion they are worthy a place in households and the cabinet of the collector. They also scoop from the traverse cutting of a large tree immense shallow basins which they paint in gay colors and use to carry fruit, or flowers or vegetables. These *Bateas* were in use by the Aztecs and very old ones, in a good state of preservation, are occasionally unearthed among the relics of Montezuma's people and re-garded as prizes among curiosity hunters. At Jalpa, in the country house of La Señora T[errero]s, two were suspended on the walls like immense plaques. They had been dug up on the lands and were made of the wood of trees of which the Conquerors found so many and left us so few.

On Sundays and on feast days the streets appear most animated. Then, every man, woman and child that can possibly do so adds a trifle to his costume or removes from it, as much as possible, what is detrimental. Even the *Léperos* on such occasions are said to turn their tattered sarapes. The church bells ring often and add their clamor to the increased activity in the plaza's booths, streets and *pulquerías,* but at night there is more dancing and drunkenness and quarreling among the lower classes than ordinary occasions.

The everyday street life is even more interesting than that of holidays. There the people themselves are seen at their various callings. From every side one hears the street cries, and although the multitude of street vendors would seem to make a Babel of the town, each has his own peculiar intonation which makes his especial cry as distinct in its nature as the article he sells. *"Pan fresco"* cries the baker. *"Chocolate muy caliente"* shrieks another, while *"patos fritos"* in pathetic contralto tones issues from the throat of the peddler of fried ducks. Then, in a piercing, nasal lament one discovers the words *"nieva nieve,"* the long, drawn out vowels impressing upon one the fact that the ice cream vendor is at hand. *"Agua fresca"* is a water carrier's cry, while the woman who calls at the gate for scraps of meat and bread utters a string of words on a rising and descending scale of notes which is a whole Irish wake in itself. You next hear a shrill female voice pitched high and sending out such agonized cries you are sure she has just sustained some great personal injury until you find she is simply informing the public that she has *"enchiladas y tamales calientitos"* to refresh the hungry. Besides things to eat and to drink, cooked and uncooked, are things to wear: shoes, hats, cravats, rebozos and also utensils of various kinds—baskets, woodenware, pottery, bridles—every conceivable commodity is thus hawked about until it seems no necessity can exist for the numerous markets, stores and groceries. Vegetables, meat, milk, poultry all come to the door to be bought. Meanwhile troops of donkeys in the middle of the street are being driven along with their loads. Indians trot hither and thither or lounge whilst waiting to be hired. Groups of dusky faces gather about a jarro of pulque and some simmering meat to share the outdoor meal. The different shops are always open. You can see the artisans at their trades. The leather worker with his thread of pita and embossing tools ornaments his saddle before your eyes, the shoe-maker nonchalantly stitches away in your presence, the *tortillera* crushes her corn uninterrupted by your halt beside her *metate* [grinding stone], and the potter proceeds to mould his clay not one whit disturbed because you closely observe him. It is the same with the jeweler and filigree worker or any man or woman whose occupation does not remove him from the ground floor.

Nowhere can be seen a more cosmopolitan populace, such mixture of races nor greater contrasts in social condition than in the teeming thorough-fares of Mexico. Secular priests and uniformed soldiers, the scion of Spanish nobility and the crippled beggar and scores of other strangely contrasted classes and conditions move here and there, jostle one another, pass and re-pass in costumes as varied as their blood distinctions. The intermingling tints, of rebozos, sarapes, Paris gowns and beggar rags, peasant *mantas* and Spanish mantillas, broadcloth and Indian blankets lend a masquerading gaiety of aspect to the street. Then there are the Léperos, as much a part of the Mexican streets as are the stones which pave them. These are idle, worth-less fellows disdaining work and proud to beg if they can be said to have any pride at all. From their numbers one might suppose the alms houses and hospitals had disgorged their inmates and let a horde of paupers, including the halt, the lame, and the blind loose upon the community. They are to Mexico what the lazzaroni are to Italy and crop up at all times and in all places. There are some who make a pretense of gaining a livelihood by the sale of lottery tickets or small wares but it is a mere mask for mendicancy. Your lépero is shrewd withal, a quick reader of physiognomy and ready to be saint or sinner whichever may best suit his purpose. He lives anyhow and anywhere, is ragged, dirty, often deformed, yet is seldom cast down but gen-erally light of heart and ready if his gains permit to "go in" for a frolic with his fellows when the business of the day is over. He is always receiving small sums but he never thinks of saving, and can live upon almost nothing. There are classes again within this class, the lowest perhaps being the *pordioseros*. These are importunate beggars who appeal to the charity of the passerby in the name of everything the latter holds dearest and holiest. As they usually begin their whining petitions with "*por Dios*" [for God's sake], they have gained the soubriquet of *pordioseros*. It is well enough whenever out-of-doors to keep one's eye upon one's valuables, purse and pocket handkerchief; for the lépero, crushed and humble though he seem, is as dexterous as any of the most light fingered gentry in the world, and regards no purse that comes within reach of his supple digits as "trash." "Beware of pickpockets" is written on the abject countenance which he tries to mask with a martyr air as he covertly glances about for a victim.

A bewildering fashion of street nomenclature exists as the same avenue takes a new name with every few blocks of buildings. In the street of San Francisco the first block is the *Calle de los Plateros,* or street of the silver-smiths, and the next block is *Calle de la Profesa,* and so on. Of course there is a street of the *Cinco de Mayo.* The honored name serves everywhere in the Republic for plazas, shops or factories, and [Ignacio] Zaragoza's victory over the French when they attacked the fort of Guadalupe at Puebla on the 5th of May, 1862, is thus kept before the people in every possible way. Its anniversary is held as a National holiday and is celebrated with military pomp, feasts, fireworks and rejoicing. If we go to the cemetery of San Fernando where slumber some of Mexico's most heroic men, we shall see the tomb of Zaragoza. This burial ground is not very large, but it is closely filled. On three sides are walls where the dead are immured by the coffins being slid flatly into niches one above another; while the center ground is filled with five distinctive tombs, some of them bearing beautiful sculptures; eminently so that of President Juárez. Not far from him slumber Generals Arteaga, and Salazar, and Miramón and Mejía, the Mexican generals who died victims of their adherence to the cause of Maximilian. There are newer and more extensive cemeteries, which are on the outskirts of the city, also adorned by handsome and very costly statuary and kept perpetually bright and blooming. They are sacred gardens where Love and Memory ever pace the peaceful paths.

As we move about the streets here and there is seen a bit of paper—newspaper or any waste scrap thrust between the outer bars of a window or iron work of a balcony. This is the customary way of announcing that a house is for rent. No written notice or printed advertisement is deemed essential, it being taken for granted that if "further particulars" are desired by anyone he will hunt them up.

The street called Tacuba was one of the three original great causeways leading out from the ancient city in the lake. It was intersected by numerous canals and had "eight bridges very large and high," the least of which, according to the description given by the Conqueror, was wide enough for ten horses to stand abreast upon, while "the street itself was lined with lofty terraces and towers." The waters which bounded it and the canals which crossed it have utterly disappeared, having been made part of the solid earth by the ultimate military measure of Cortez which was not to advance a step without destroying all houses on the line of march and "converting into solid ground whatever was water no matter how slow the operation might be." The street runs parallel with that of San Francisco passing opposite it on the northern side of the Alameda. It is broad, and like others takes a new name to itself with nearly every *manzana* or block of buildings. As of yore, handsome edifices border it on each side, the modern ones excelling those of the Aztecs in point of size and beauty. A statue of Morelos adorns it at one point, and a solid cross street intersecting it called *el puente de Alvarado* obliterates the canal across which that fair and agile Spaniard is said to have leaped. Hotly pursued and hard pressed by the victorious Aztecs, [Pedro de] Alvarado planted his spear and grasping it tightly, with one prodigious bound vaulted over the watery space which had seemed to oppose his further flight when, with Cortez and his harassed army, he made his way out of the town by this very road. Upon it then stood the palace of Guatimotzín, the ill fated young Aztec prince, destined to be the last of the Montezumas. The lights in its windows flashed upon the flying Spaniards in the terrible hours of their bloody retreat on the night of July 1, 1520. On the 24th day of the same month in the same year[2] the Spaniards succeeded in gaining complete control of the causeway, and on that day the palace of Guatimotzín was razed to the ground, and, probably, its charred timbers and demolished stone walls helped to fill the very canal over which Alvarado had made his wonderful leap. Cortez alludes to the destruction of the palace in these words, after showing that Indians from distant provinces who had been oppressed by Montezuma's rule had flocked to the Spanish standard moved by a spirit of revenge: "More than fifty thousand Indians gave us their aid that day when, marching over heaps of dead and dying, we at last gained the great street of Tacuba, and burned the house of Guatimotzín," the cacique of the city. The prince was a young man not much more than twenty years of age. In his third letter to Charles the Fifth the allusions made to this great causeway and scenes of conflict enacted upon it are frequent and its importance in his eyes is shown

2. Actually, this occurred a year later, in 1521, when the Spaniards returned to the city.

in the words, "I was extremely anxious to secure this noble road, in order that the force in the camp of Pedro de Alvarado might communicate with ours." Alvarado's camp at that time was located in the town of Tacuba at least a league distant and between it and the city of Mexico this noble road was the principal thoroughfare and the connecting link.

At the *Garita de San Cosme,* the city gate so named, we are met in the center of the street of Tacuba by the aqueduct of San Cosme which brings to the city the *agua delgada* or pure water so called to distinguish it from the *agua gorda* [thick water] which, much more impregnated with mineral properties, the Belén aqueduct brings to the city from the springs of Chapultepec terminating in the fountain known as *El Salto de Agua.* It was this aqueduct which the valiant Spanish Captains Cristobal Olid and Pedro de Alvarado destroyed in the early days of the siege and which was subsequently rebuilt by Spain. The aqueduct of San Cosme is fed by the springs of Santa Fé, near that of Amilco which filled the ancient aqueduct of the Aztecs, so constructed with double troughs of burnt earth that a constant supply of pure water was uninterrupted, one pipe carrying on the water whilst the other was being cleaned. Neither of the existing aqueducts equals that one, though their lofty arches and vast extent of masonry render them objects of interest as well as of vast sanitary importance. That of Chapultepec is more than two miles in length; that of San Cosme is brought a distance of six miles, although its actual extent of arches is not more than that of Chapultepec. This latter aqueduct terminates in the reservoir called *el Fuente de Tlaxpana* at the bridge *de la Marescala.* This reservoir is a highly ornamented structure in marble with much sculpturing and yet gloomy in appearance, producing an effect quite opposite to the cheering and beneficent purpose it was originally designed to perpetuate. The aguadors are filling their water jars from the basin of the fountain, as aguadors seem forever doing in Mexico wherever opportunity is afforded them, and so seem part and parcel of all the public waterworks.

We can traverse this historic road either by private conveyance or by streetcars, the latter charging but a trifle for a trip along its entire length. Soon after passing the Garita of San Cosme lovely residences standing in beautiful grounds are seen, and then we reach one after another the fashionable pleasure gardens which are the delightful resorts of this outdoor living people. The gardens are large, beautifully planned, adorned with large streams, rustic bridges, summer houses large and small, kiosks, pagodas and cottages. Some of the latter are simply latticed; others are wood, painted to imitate stone, and others again resemble the most primitive of rustic log cabins. Numerous games are set up about the grounds to add to their great attractiveness, and the *Grand Tivoli,* the *Tivoli Eliseo,* and the *Tivoli Ferro Carril* vie with one another in beautiful grounds and in excellence of the "Table." The restaurants at these gardens are first class, and the meals are served neatly. Many who merely take rooms in Mexico find the cheap hack hire affords them opportunity to breakfast or dine at these gardens quite as cheaply and much more delightfully than at any hotel in town.

Going on for a distance of perhaps a mile we reach a dusty, dirty, unattractive little village called Popotla. It has an old church which was erected immediately after the Conquest in front of an aged Ahuehuete which, at that time, was of gigantic dimensions. Under its mighty branches Cortez with his defeated and dispirited army found pause and shelter in their flight from the triumphant Aztecs. There, pacing backward and forward he passed a night of wretched anxiety beneath the branches of the tree which tented his beaten soldiers, a night which Cortez himself designated as *la noche triste.* The old cypress has been despoiled of its stupendous proportions by fire. This is said to have been applied by the hands of a vandal priest, or at least his emissaries, in a spirit of vengeance aroused by a decision against him of some question of rights pending between him and the alcalde of the village. Some imaginative persons claim that the foliage left upon the tree has taken the exact form of a poising eagle and the superstitious take pains to discover the outline of the out stretched wings and body of the bird and to find in the leafy shape a sign that calls for renewed awe and reverence for the tree of the *noche triste.* When Don Sebastián Lerdo de Tejada was President of the Republic, he caused a stone wall to be built around the remains of the old cypress and that again encircled by an iron fence, while in addition an ever pacing sentry keeps watch and ward over the historic tree. The greatest veneration is felt for it by the people. Money cannot buy a chip of it and the very infrequent gifts which are made of its wood the Mexicans regard as the most precious they can bestow. When [Adelaide] Ristori [Marquisa del Grillo (1822–1906)] last played in Mexico, an exquisite jewel box was made from a bit of *el arbol de la noche triste* and presented to her by the state and city authorities. From the account given by Cortez himself, but a small portion of his broken and demoralized force could have shared with him the shelter of the cypress on the sad night. He speaks of rushing across with great speed a portable bridge he had caused to be constructed and carried by forty men. It was seized by the enemy at the first point it was used, when he says "followed by five horse-men and of hundred foot I passed all the broken bridges by swimming and reached the main land." He speaks of leaving this advance and returning to the rear,

> where I found the troops hotly engaged and the amount of suffering among our people, both Spaniards and Indian allies of Tascaltecal beyond all compu-tation. Nearly all of the allies perished, together with the Spaniards and horses, while we lost besides these gold, jewels, cotton cloth and many other things including the artillery. Having collected all who were alive I sent them on before, while with three or four horse and twenty foot that dared remain with me I followed in the rear incessantly engaged with the enemy until we reached a city called Tacuba, beyond the causeway, after encountering a degree of toil and danger the extent of which God only knows.[3]

A little way beyond Popotla we find ourselves in the dusty village of Tacuba, the ancient Tlacopán. It is a small town with a large church which with its chapels and former convent stands enclosed by a high wall. There was the usual knot of mendicants in its vicinity, filthy beggars who seemed to have grown old in the same suit of clothes they had donned at maturity. It would be a relief to see in Mexico less church and more charity. Ecclesias-tical architecture seems to have swallowed up all the building material and left nothing wherewith to shelter the poor. They flaunt their rags and wretch-edness in town and country; everywhere a blot upon the land. Here, not far from the church an object of interest exists in the remnant of an ancient teocalli. It has been used and abused in the process of obtaining building material from it, and looks as much like a gravel pit as a religious monument,

3. This is quoted from Cortez's second letter to Emperor Charles V, written at Segura de la Frontera, New Spain, on October 30, 1520. Many versions have been published in Spanish and English, but I have not identified which of them Townsend may be quoting from here. A somewhat different translation may be found in the English edition of J. Bayard Morris, translator and editor, *Five Letters, 1519–1526* (1928; reprint, New York: W. W. Norton, 1962), 119–20.

but enough remains to place beyond doubt the nature and purpose of the original structure. A little digging brought to light bits of obsidian knives and arrow heads, and broken pottery the color of the ground, work still brilliant, and its darker tracery of designs perfectly distinct. Some declare it to have been only an Indian mound of unusual extent, but a gentleman who has resided long in Mexico and made its archeological remains a study, gives as his opinion that it was originally one of the terraced pyramids of the Aztecs and crowned by a temple for religious rites and ceremonies.

Tacuba, the ancient capital of the Tepanec Kingdom, is two leagues from the city of Mexico in a north westerly direction and is several miles north of Tacubaza with which village it has sometimes been confounded. Cortez always speaks of it as a city, and at the time of the conquest it, no doubt, contained a large Indian population. From it one can look down the wide road upon which the routed Spaniards battled with Indians who leaped upon them in the dark from their pursuing boats, burning to avenge the wrongs they had suffered from the invaders and the insults that had been heaped upon their altars and their gods. The Spaniards kept to the causeway, save as they were forced to swim the unbridged canals some of which were forty feet wide and from ten to twelve feet deep. The enraged Aztecs fought them from the water and on land, leaping back to the streams the moment they were hard pushed, and Cortez acknowledges that he made his way that night over a path paved with the dead bodies of his men and their allies to the city of Tacuba. Here was Pedro Alvarado's camp, and here Cortez says, "I found my people gathered in the square not knowing where to go." From there he led them out into the open fields and thence to take possession of a hill on which "there was a tower and a strong building" where he maintained his position. "God only knows," he repeats,

> the toil and danger with which this success was obtained. Of twenty four horses that remained to us, there was not one that could move freely, nor a horseman able to raise his arm, nor a foot soldier unhurt who could make any effort. In this defeat one hundred and fifty Spaniards were killed; more than two thousand Indian allies, among them the son and daughters of Montezuma, and other caciques whom I had taken prisoners, and forty five horses.[4]

4. Morris, *Five Letters,* 121.

It is in this vicinity one feels the great cypress must have stood, beneath which the wretched commander and his worn-out army halted on that night of sorrows, and not at Popotla where tradition has placed it. The hill of the tower of which Cortez gained possession was called the hill of Montezuma. It is four leagues from the city of Mexico and two leagues beyond Tacuba. The famous image of Our Lady of Remedies belongs to the *noche triste* upon which woeful night she may be said to have been born to Mexico. A wounded soldier who had brought the wooden image from home in his knapsack, a secret and sacred treasure, that night put it among the spikes of a maguey plant where, possibly, he placed it to pray before it in his dying hour. It was subsequently discovered there by an Indian who gave it into the hands of Cortez. The latter at once availed himself of it as a means by which to reanimate and arouse to new efforts his dispirited and almost broken hearted men. He proclaimed it the image of the Virgin Mary, miraculously sent from Heaven in their behalf, to heal their wounds and to secure to them the conquest they so much desired. The image was hailed with enthusiasm, and the zeal of his soldiers once more awakened, Cortez succeeded in eluding the enemies immediately about him and in finally cutting his way to the friendly province of Tlaxcala, which he entered July 8, 1520 not to return to the siege of Mexico until May 1521.

Among the very first sanctuaries erected after the Spanish occupation was one to this miraculous Virgin which had been given the title of *Nuestra Señora de los Remedios*. It was built upon the hill of Montezuma four leagues from the city of Mexico where she was first shown to the despondent army, and the original image was there enshrined in a silver maguey plant and zealously watched and guarded. It ranks in age the younger Virgin, *Nuestra Señora de Guadalupe*, who did not make herself manifest until 1531, ten years after the conquest. The church devoted to Our Lady of Remedies, though in a wild and very desolate spot, was originally a handsome structure and very handsomely adorned within. Rich Catholics could not die in peace until some valuable legacy had been bequeathed to *La Señora de los Remedios*. For a long time, in the Holy of Holies of this mountain sanctuary, the image was kept and, before the late hampering of Church pomp, she was displayed with great ceremony her satin robes white with pearls and her crown glittering with diamonds. This "graven image" is a common doll, uncommonly ugly; cut from wood and holding an equally rude figure of the infant Jesus in its arms. The main figure is about twelve inches high and bears evidence of rough usage; being battered and bruised to a degree that suggests it has been "through the wars." A superstition exists that a fatality attends whoever presumes to touch the sacred image with a view to repairing her broken features. One artist who endeavored to do so was struck blind and one or two others paid for their temerity by long suffering of some kind and others again fell ill and died after their sacrilegious designs so that all attempts to improve her appearance have been abandoned as being attended by some inevitable calamity. Upon her first establishment in *el sanctuario de Nuestra Señora de [los] Remedios* on the hill of Montezuma her fame spread with amazing rapidity among the people of the land and thousands were attracted to her shrine showering before it gifts of inestimable value as votive offerings. An annual festival was appointed in her honor which, every 28th day of August, drew throngs to that locality. The people began to gather days before the anniversary taking with them supplies of chile, tortillas, tamales, frijoles, dulces and fruits, and camped upon the grounds with no other shelter nor bed than such as the solid earth and open sky afforded. The festival is about the same as that held annually on the 12th of December in honor of Santa María de Guadalupe and like that brings together rich and poor; the former class, of course, exempt from the hardships which attend the devotion of the latter. When the long anticipated hour arrived a priest conducted religious services then displayed the miraculous image, marvelously clad, to the multitude who kneel before it with uncovered heads and adoring eyes. After that, to the sound of drums, the people moved to the altar whereon they laid offerings of flowers, or those of far greater value, while all who could afford to do so gave also wax candles, great quantities of which were consumed every year burning before the Virgin's shrine. After the offerings, feast and fireworks were enjoyed and at night monotonous dances to the monotonous music of drums, bandalons and shrill pipes kept the crowds of Indians awake and in motion until the term of the festival was announced by the priest to be at an end, when the crowd vanished much more quickly than it had gathered, leaving Our Lady to the silence and solitude of her romantic shrine. It has been the custom ever since she was duly acknowledged by the country to invoke the aid of Our Lady of Remedies in all cases of illness, of wealthy or important personages and also in all seasons of general disaster such as an epidemic of cholera, fever, or other disease. On such occasions formerly a grand procession paraded the streets with banners, flowers and especial pomp, bearing this Virgin sumptuously appareled and bejewelled to the stricken quarters, or the house of some individual sufferer. During the Spanish domination the Viceroy himself, whenever the image was borne abroad, went on foot before it; while the Lady of Remedies occupied a magnificent carriage which was driven by a Spanish nobleman of the first rank. In this way a tour of all the principal convents was made by her most Holy Highness as well as all the infected districts and private houses. At the time of the terrible inundations in the city of Mexico her aid was devoutly invoked. Alternately with Santa María de Guadalupe she was brought to the overflowed town from which, alas! the waters refused to subside for either the one or the other miraculous presence. Still, her popularity did not fail her. If there is too prolonged a dry season she is prayed to for rain; if there is too continued rain she is invoked for sunshine. She is simply the goddess of good luck and is supposed to have power to cheer the sorrowing, remove disease, banish misfortune and bring about prosperity. Where success attends her it is bruited all over the country; where failure follows invocation to her, no notice is taken of that. At one time a smallpox patient rose from his bed of convalescence too soon and went to kiss the hem of her begemmed petticoat in gratitude for his recovery. He left with her so much contagion that they who visited her after him took from her skirts the horrible disease which in this way spread throughout the city and adjacent towns with a virulence her oft and widely invoked aid had no effect upon whatsoever.

She even became a political Virgin and at one time was mingled with party funds. Having been chosen by the Spaniards during the war of Independence as their protective power, sure to secure them victory, she received from the opposing party, who had chosen Our Lady of Guadalupe, the soubriquet of *La Guachupina* as belonging to the Spaniards who are called Guachupines by the natives. The same powers supposed to be possessed by Our Lady of Remedies are ascribed, by her enthusiastic adherents, to Our Lady María of Guadalupe and the rival Virgins are appealed to by all classes in all quarters and of all conditions. Girl children without number receive at baptism the name of Maria de Guadalupe and her *fiesta* becomes their own. The day of each Lady is scrupulously honored in scores of private houses independently of the church festivals and both are appealed to in time of need with an enthusiasm of devotion and credulity pathetic in its earnestness. As the church does not disdain to charge roundly for the services of the sacred images, it derives a large income from the miracles they are engaged to perform. Thousands of dollars have been paid by the rich for a single visitation of one or the other Virgin at the sick bed of some sufferer or to some agricultural possession threatened with loss of crop or other disaster. Now that all religious pageants are forbidden in the public streets of Mexico the miraculous ministrations have to be very privately conducted. Even the Host is no longer allowed to be carried openly about, nor are priests, nor monks, nor nuns permitted to appear upon the streets in other than secular dress. The sanctuary of Our Lady of Remedies is falling into neglect and ruin on the side of its barren mountain where, it would seem, nothing was ever destined to grow save veneration for its Virgin. From the heights which rear themselves back of the edifice and from the church tower, the view commanded is one of singular grandeur and beauty. Near at hand are the rocks and hills, deep glens and savage wildernesses from among the waters of which the old aqueduct takes its way of arches out from the wild solitudes. To the east lies the whole beautiful Valley of Mexico, its city smiling on the plain, its lakes nestled in its bosom. Owing to the solitary position of *el sanctuario de Nuestra Señora de los Remedios* the genuine *noche triste* image and her vast wealth was years ago brought away from her lonely and desolate mountain shrine and deposited in the safer and secreter keeping of the Cathedral in Mexico. A lépero, meanwhile, however, under cover of paying the Virgin homage, had bitten from the hem of her garment, whilst pretending to kiss it, one of its largest and most valuable pearls. The adroit thief succeeded in making off with his booty undetected. Another image of the same size as the first, and covered with imitation jewels was placed in the stead of the *noche triste* doll, and the Indians, who were always obliged to worship her at a most respectful distance, saw her at too remote a point to enable them to discover the exchange.

18

❀

Family Life in Mexico

Pan dulce *and Mexican newspapers. A morning call. The Mexican adieu. Invitation to breakfast. A Mexican family at home. The poet Prieto. A visit of condolence. House draped in mourning. No undertakers. Notification of death. Traits. The comradeship existing between parents and children. Mexican households. Honors to the Mother-in-law. The poet Acuña. Filial reverence. Family ties. Social entertainments. The* tertulia. *Personal appearance of Mexican ladies. Habits at home. Intellectual attainments.* La Niña. *Mexican sincerity. Education of children. Young men. Love of horses. Distaste for drink. "My family." No liquor saloons. Fascinations of Paris. The Mexican bachelor. Social intercourse of young people. The duenna system. Construction of houses. Bribing a porter. Playing the bear. The Mexican Romeo and Juliet. Rules for the affianced. A vigilance committee of one. The United Signatures. Love of letters. Literary tastes. Altamarino. Natural endowments of the people. The besetting sin. Streets watered by law. Padded conversation.* Cargadores. *Coffins running about town. The burden bearers. The* aguador. *The Indian in the army—as guide, as messenger. His powers of endurance. His wages. Cruelty to animals. Diversity of race in Mexico.* Mestizos, criollos, mezclados, *Mexicanos and Mexicanos. Division of the population. Indian children. The physical powers of the women. Value of the race to Mexico. Poor payment makes poor workmen. Incitements to ambition. Mental capacity. Justice due the descendants of the Aztecs from the descendants of their conquerors. Rays of light. Propensities of porters. Mexican servants and some peculiarities.*

Our appetite, having, no doubt, been badly brought up, always rebelled at waiting for the one o'clock breakfast. At about nine A.M., after early rising and a ramble of miles about town or a ride out of it: " . . . a vague unrest and a nameless longing filled the breast," which our dusky attendant with the sanctified name always satisfied with a little more than the usual supply of coffee and pan dulce. A delightful accompaniment to the repast was the daily journals. In addition to the flowers sent us every morning, all the leading papers were left at our door "with compliments of the Editors." It was an attention highly appreciated. The Mexican newspapers as such, differ essentially from the great journals of the United States, but they are ably conducted, well edited and kept up to the Mexican standard of journalism under difficulties which would appall men less determined and devoted to the profession. We had the pleasure of meeting a number of the Editors and found them highly cultivated and most courteous gentlemen, more than one of them, in addition to his newspaper work, having made his record as a poet, essayist or novelist.

The wife of a prominent journalist called upon us one morning whose beauty of the Spanish type was enhanced by her tasteful black gown and graceful mantilla. It is with a groan of regret one views the possibility of this most becoming of all head-wear going out of fashion. How any women "to the manner born" can ever consent to exchange its bewitching grace for any millinery creation whatsoever is a mystery. Our caller was not only young and extremely beautiful, but her manners and bearing, graceful, frank, yet so dignified, were charming. She conversed fluently with those present in English, French and Spanish and, upon leaving, requested us to name an early day when we would breakfast with her. According to the custom of the people, she was "our friend," her "services at our command," her "house, her servants, all at our *disposición*." This was said in a way so winning, and with a voice so sweet that never was an empty compliment made to seem more sweetly sincere. We having accepted her invitation, she took her departure. It is the custom in Mexico to accompany the guest to the head of the grand stairway. There adieus are made. The hostess remains standing at the stairhead, and the visitor descends to the first landing; parting salutations are made. The construction of the houses probably had something to do with the origin of this practice. The hospitable Eastern habit even in country houses maintains of going a little way with the departing guest, and the city guest has a great way to go. The staircases are long and he must, besides, cross the wide patio before he gains the outer portal. It is a pleasing custom, but Cora and I found it one quite impossible for us to practice. It was such a journey to the stairhead! We had to pass through an outer room, two vestibules and all along the corridor overhanging one side of the great court, to reach the flight of steps. To take this trip and return many times a day would have incapacitated us, good pedestrians though we were, for other walking in the vale of Anahuac. Therefore, we usually parted with our guests at our parlor door; but in this instance we went through the accustomed form and were rewarded by the fair picture our visitor presented as, with her lovely face upturned, she gave us the parting salute from the landing.

As we had at her request named an early day it soon arrived and at the orthodox hour of one o'clock we were at her gates. The Porter admitted us, and we crossed the usual court and went up the usual flight of stone steps at the head of which our hostess, in a very handsome toilet, gracefully welcomed us. We were led along a corridor brilliant with blooming orchids where, in pretty bird cages, twittered and hopped about ornamental birds of the most beautiful plumage, all tame and responsive to my lady's call as she gave them a finger or a word in passing. In the drawing room we were received by our host. This apartment was handsomely furnished and very large as nearly all such rooms are in those grand old houses. At one side of the spacious apartment a grand piano was drawn up near the windows. Many objects of taste were distributed about, and a delightful air of occupation peculiar to Mexican drawing rooms lent a charm to the elegant salon. Like the French the Mexicans are fond of mirrors. Although there are no fire places nor mantels to suggest the mantel mirror, the walls are rarely found destitute of a splendid French plate glass generally of immense size superbly framed and so hung as to do its full duty in the way of multiplying lamps, reflecting beautiful objects and adding brilliancy to gay scenes of social life. Mexicans love light in their houses. They draw back their curtains and ask the sunshine and the daylight to walk in and make themselves at home. It is a rare thing to find these essential elements of health and pleasure excluded from dwellings. The Mexicans take the light as their flowers do and, like them, thrive under its influence.

The bedroom where we were shown to take off our hats was as dainty as a jewel box. Rugs lay upon the tiled floor—pictures adorned the walls and

above a pretty altar hung the portrait of the Virgin of Guadalupe. The bedstead was of polished brass. Its pillow slips worked in the most intricate pattern of Mexican "drawn work," its counterpane of dainty embroidered lace
and satin. Flowers were in all the rooms. During the space of time before
breakfast our host led us to the library. Here were many books, rare first
editions of valuable works—precious manuscripts, curios and very fine paintings. Among the latter was a Murillo and one or two by [Miguel] Cabrera,
a Mexican artist who flourished about a hundred years ago. His works are
highly prized in Mexico and very seldom found on sale. When we returned
to the salon other guests had arrived. Among them was General B——,
Señor F——z, a leading editor, and Guillermo Prieto, Mexico's well beloved
poet. We found the latter a gentle mannered man fluent and eloquent of
speech as he is graceful and fervid with his pen. He is keenly alive to the
beauty of his native land and uses the gift of the singer to chant her praises.

An Indian servant announced breakfast. Our hostess advancing took me
by the hand and all proceeded to the breakfast room which was light and
pretty and gay with flowers. I was placed at the head of the table. The host
and hostess seated themselves at its foot. Upon my left hand sat Judge C., a
learned lawyer and one eminent in literary and art circles. He was a man of
infinite jest also, and by his wit and repartee was the "life" of all gatherings
in which he took part. The other guests being happily neighbored, conversation became brisk and the repast began. Every dish served was strictly Mexican. Many of them were excellent but some, wherein *chile* did preponderate,
I was not yet enough of a salamander to enjoy. Pulque in glass decanters and
tinted crimson with the juice of the tuna and pulque flavored with pineapple
was very palatable thus cheated of its natural flavor. Judge C.'s little grandson,
a child of three years, having found his way into the room was by acclamation
voted a place at the board and his first attempt in the English language was
in his mastery of the two words in which he conveyed to us his hospitable
wish that we should "drink pulque." Fruits, dulces and a cup of Uruapam
coffee concluded the repast which had consisted of eighteen courses. In the
drawing room we had music; our hostess herself giving choice selections on
the piano, she being an accomplished musician.

After this Mexican chocolate was served whipped to a delicious frothiness
by a little wooden implement made for the purpose. After this liqueurs were
proffered and the gentlemen lighted their cigarettes. I never saw a Mexican

lady smoke. The custom had at one time been quite common but gradually fell into disuse save with a few señoras of the old nobility who still claim the privilege of an occasional smoke in the privacy of their own apartments. But, the men! After breakfast, after dinner, after everything the inevitable cigarette or cigar is lighted always with the polite prelude "by your leave ladies" but the ladies never dream of refusing "leave." Should one do so it would undoubtedly occasion great astonishment. The practice of smoking at all times and in all places loses some of its objectionable features on account of the peculiar lightness of the atmosphere which allows the fumes to pass off quickly. Consequently, the hair, beard and clothing do not retain the offensive odor of the stale tobacco nor do carpets and curtains remain scented with it for any length of time.

When the hour of departure came flowers were presented to us and one or two valuable books were given to me and a very nice piece of Mexican silver work to Cora as a souvenir. We made our adieus, but in leaving the salon succeeded, unnoticed, in leaving our gifts upon a little side table. We had heard so much of the insincerity of the Mexicans in proffering presents they never expected to have accepted that we thought the easiest way out of the dilemma was to *forget* the parcels and leave them behind. Our hostess accompanied us to the stairhead and our host went with us to the great gate of the patio. There we found, in place of the hack we had ordered to wait for us, a handsome private equipage, with liveried servants. Into this carriage we were handed and driven to our hotel, bearing away from the pretty Mexican home so embellished by taste, intellect and beauty, the impression that Love in its most beautiful guise there glorified whatever one saw, whatsoever one touched. Early the next morning a servant appeared at our door with the gifts we had not brought away, and a note couched in most kindly terms enquiring after our health, etc., etc. and trusting we had not found the little souvenirs quite unworthy of our acceptance.

An acquaintance of ours, la Señora ———, having buried from her house a remote but beloved relative, we went to pay her a visit. Her house was truly palatial in all its appointments and crossing the court and ascending the broad marble stairs we were ushered from the corridor, which was paved with marble tiles, into the grand drawing room. The mother and eldest daughter, dressed in deep black received us cordially, though gravely, and I was given the seat in the right hand corner of the sofa—the seat of honor accorded to

callers whenever possible. The beautiful furniture of the apartment upholstered in a rich light satin was all touched with crepe. Loops and festoons of
it descended from the cornices and picture frames, knots of it were on the
chairs, and a scarf of it lay across the back of the sofa. Similar ones mingled
with the curtain draperies. The deceased was spoken of by the mourners with
tears and tenderness. She had lived to be very old, but had never outlived the
love of those with whom she was connected, they said. Then they took us to
her room which she had occupied and showed us with tender reverence the
books she had loved to read, the altar where she had prayed, the bed on
which she slept and died. All things, they said, were to be kept as nearly as
possible as she liked to have them while she lived, and everywhere in the
house a tender regard for her memory was manifest. This respect for the
dead, for religion, for old age are noticeable features in the Mexican character. The office of undertaker as known in the United States and other countries is not in existence in Mexico. A family would deem it an impious and
sacrilegious act to resign the body of one beloved to any hands save their own
to be prepared for burial. Upon the death of a member the family are expected to write the announcement of it to every friend and one who does not
receive such a letter regards it a slight. Reverence for the dead and tenderness
for the living are prominent Mexican traits and all the home life of Mexico
is marked with frankness, cheerfulness and confiding affection. A spirit of
cordial sympathy among those who constitute its members is characteristic
of the Mexican family and love of kindred amounts to clannishness. Parents
and children live in close confidence with one another. There is no chilling
formality and no forbidding distances established by the elders to ensure
homage from the young. They meet upon the common ground of home to
illuminate it with mutual love, forbearance and respect. A beautiful comradeship exists between fathers and sons, and any disrespect from children to
parents is a thing almost unknown. A cordial sympathy exists between them
and confidence on the one hand is met by the most gentle consideration on
the other. Whatever the familiarity existing between them no look or word
evincing lack of tenderness, devotion and unfailing deference is seen on the
part of children toward their parents. One can scarcely imagine a young
Mexican flippantly calling his father "the old man," or "the Governor," and
alluding to his Mother as "the old lady." I knew elderly men there who had
never failed to keep fresh flowers on the grave of the mother lost in boyhood

and in many homes whence the parents had passed out forever their memory was kept so sacredly fresh the actual presence seemed scarcely absent. It is no uncommon thing to find parents, children and grandchildren comprising one household, those who marry continuing to dwell under the parental roof, the previous harmonious relations continuing undisturbed and unbroken. The Mexican family is a center around which the best and strongest emotions of the heart revolve. Its branches are bound together by the tenderest ties and the spacious houses admit of large numbers living together under the same roof, the wife that the son has brought home, and the husband of the daughter of the house. None but a Mexican poet would have ever dreamed, in his love verses, of holding out as an added source of bliss to his bride that her Mother-in-law should reside with her. Yet, [Manuel] Acuña, in a lyric where fervent passion and pathos are blended with the despair and disappointment which wrung from him one of the most touching poems of modern Mexican literature says, in addressing her who has been to him "love of his loves," star of his darkness, etc., etc., "How beautiful might our united lives have been passed beneath that roof; thou, the ever beloved one, I, the ever loving. Two with but one soul, two with but one heart, *and with us, ever, like some being divine, my Mother!*"

Yet the lines depict a common and harmonious phase of domestic life in a country where the breaking up and separation of a family is regarded as a calamity. The homes of Mexico as houses may be excelled in many lands but in all the noblest essentials of home they can be surpassed in no country. As the family circle is large, within its limits the members find those pleasures and pastimes which make them in a great measure independent of general society. Evening visits are not the custom. Parties and balls, to which the "dear five hundred" are invited are seldom given in private houses. The nearest approach to a *tertulia* or evening party is an informal reception to which the circle of kindred is invited and some chosen outsiders—if there be room! At these gatherings there is always good music, plenty of chat, parlor games and dancing. There is a general talent for music. Many deem music a necessary part of education for sons as well as daughters and one soon learns that men perform on some instrument and nearly all play the piano to some extent. In the houses of the wealthy are fine libraries and beautiful pictures and a close attention to all that makes home attractive. The keeping of anniversaries is faithfully observed in Mexico. Instead of birthdays, one's saint's day is celebrated, and where the circle of kindred is large, a *día de fiesta* of this kind is of frequent occurrence and gives occasion for holiday pastimes which are invariably made the most of. Then there are certain feasts of the church such as the *posadas* at Christmas and others which are scrupulously observed in families and carried out with no little display of wax lights and other accessories, so that the Mexican house can never be said to be dull.

The Mexican ladies have fine eyes, fine teeth, small hands and feet. The complexion is usually a clear, colorless olive, but the soft brightness of the dark eyes compensates for the lack of roses on the cheek. One does not find among them many who are very beautiful women, but their qualities of heart are of the noblest and these lending beauty of expression to the faces endow them with a liveliness which outlasts mere beauty of skin and perfection of features. Their manners are charming and they possess in a marked degree all the higher attributes of the heart, being generous, charitable and humane. They are not much given to reading, but are pleasing and vivacious in conversation and can converse in two or three languages with ease. The teaching of the elder class has been chiefly conventual, and they are highly accomplished rather than highly educated. They obey St. Paul's injunction to a much greater extent than the women of other large American cities and are "keepers at home," superintending all household affairs; the natural indolence of the Indian servants rendering strict supervision on the part of the mistress a necessity. Cleanliness, order, and love of flowers are prominent features of all the better class of Mexican houses combined with a spirit of affection, frankness and cheerfulness on the part of its inmates. The Mexican housekeeper practices a wise economy and teaches the same sterling virtue to her children. She runs up no bills, paying cash for all purchases when bought. Fully understanding the difficulty and expense with which many articles, even of the most ordinary kind, are gotten into the country, she preserves them with a care the New England housekeeper could not exceed. Where women are not wasteful, a nation is seldom found open to the charge of extravagance.

The lack of fashionable entertainments gives little opportunity for lavish expenditure in dress. The charge to which they were open some few years ago of tasteless overdressing, even in making morning calls, no longer applies to them as they have in a great measure adopted and closely conformed to the French mode. The wealthy classes possess magnificent jewels, the possession of such property being deemed a necessary adjunct to a young girl's wedding outfit and, being handed down as an heirloom in families, the accretion in the keeping of one person is often something marvelous.

Since the church has to a great measure ceased to dominate home affairs, there has been an awakening among Mexican women to a knowledge of their own intellectual capacities and weight of influence in a sphere hitherto unentered by them. Several have aspired to literary distinction with success. Others have received diplomas and positions as professors of languages, and others again have graduated as physicians. Some of the largest private seminaries in the city are ably conducted by Mexican women, and they are rapidly becoming alive to the fact that there is a wider and wiser field for them than that bounded by a convent wall and that their usefulness now finds a noble and extended scope which could never have been attained save on the hither side of nunnery gates.

The Mexicans, although their "table" is excellent and bountiful, are not as a rule addicted to the Antony-Cleopatra style of banquet in their houses. When they dissolve their pearls in vinegar it is not to swallow them. In hospitality of a nobler kind, which bestows personal attention, kindness, gives time and the best the house affords to a guest, the Mexican is unsurpassed. Besides consideration to strangers the Mexican keeps open house for his friends. When a guest chances to arrive at meal time he is bidden at once to the board and the hospitality thus extended is accepted as frankly as it is proffered. Servants reflect the manners of their employers and are attentive, soft voiced and polite. The eldest daughter of a house is called by them *la niña*, and the eldest son frequently is spoken of and addressed as *el niño*, a term which would seem to correspond to the English appellation *Childe* formerly a prefix to the Christian name during the term of minority.

Much has been said about the hollowness of the Mexican custom of saying *a su disposición de usted* and seeming to place all his possessions at the entire disposal of his guest. It is simply equivalent to our own custom of saying "make yourself perfectly at home," "you are most welcome," or "consider this house as your own." If anyone to whom we said these things should arrive at the conclusion that he therefore obtained right and title to our house and lands or could carry off our bric-a-brac, books, or pictures, he would make as grave a mistake as those who have taken *a su disposición* literally and suffered mortification from subsequent results. Although from a genuine kindness of heart the Mexicans may sometimes be hurried into promising more than they can possibly perform, I do not think they are more open to the charge of insincerity than any other people with whom politeness is a social virtue. Without it, sincere or insincere "society" could not exist.

While the daughters are kept at home under the guardianship of parents, priests and duennas, the sons of the better class are educated in Europe and given the benefit of foreign travel. Upon his return home the life of the young Mexican is one of ease and pleasure. Skilled in the arts of fencing, fire arms and horsemanship; with elegant manners, refined and luxurious tastes, several languages at his command and the usual society accomplishments his time is occupied or "killed" by visiting his estates, hunting, driving or taking part in the popular amusements of the country. If he does not choose the life of the Haciendas, he is free to adopt such pursuits as taste or education may have given him inclination for. Labor of any kind does not enter much into his scheme of life beyond the fact that if there is any to be done somebody else must be hunted up to do it. The wealthy young "swell" is fond of his horse and lavishes money on its accoutrements and his own riding costume with a prodigal hand, but it is an extravagance which has its limits, and the habit of spending a small fortune upon one fashionable repast he has not yet adopted. Neither is he addicted to the vice of tippling. Whatever other faults he may have and he has his full share, drunkenness is not among them. The serious decorum which marks the manners of Mexican men is never marred by a libelous tour of the barrooms. In fact the drinking saloon does not exist in Mexico. An American recently started one but soon failed for want of support. Wine is used upon the home tables but the public "drink" is a thing unknown.

Upon the death of the father the eldest son, even though scarcely out of his teens, becomes the head of the house. He is looked up to and deferred to in all matters of business and questions of propriety even though the actual "affairs" have to be conducted through the medium of an agent whose superior years and experience render him more fit for the responsible position. It is no uncommon thing to hear a youth of twenty speaking of "my family" and arrangements he has made for their travels, comforts and pleasures with the gravity of a patriarch. It is very rarely that he fails in any of the offices due from a good son and brother although Paris, once tasted, seldom loses its flavor for him and from time to time lures him again to its charms when, of course, he has found reason why "my family also should have a trip abroad." Such are said to be the enticements of Paris in the ranks of Mexican bachelorhood they not seldom are obliged to recover financially from a few months on the other side by a whole year of retirement upon their Mexican estates.

The social intercourse of young people is so circumscribed one marvels how opportunity for proposal and acceptance of marriage is ever found. They can seldom converse together alone, the duenna system being strictly adhered to and the young girl being invariably chaperoned both in and out of doors. A few moments seized for conversation upon going in or coming out of church, a few hastily exchanged words on the Paseo in the pauses of the drive, a chat obtained in the slow movement of the *danza* or the brief meeting in the theater or opera box constitute the opportunities for courtship. Making an evening call is something never expected of gentlemen in Mexico and a morning visit must be paid in the presence of the inevitable third party. The houses are so constructed that but one gateway admits to the street. This is always in charge of a porter who, upon the arrival of a visitor, pulls a bell rope that rings a bell upstairs thus communicating to the family that a guest has arrived. The lower floor, level with the street, is the patio or court, frequently paved with polished marble and having a fountain and flowers in the center. There are the servant quarters, the offices and the stables. The family carriages are also kept there. One crosses this square court, around which, more or less spacious, but invariably, the better class of Mexican house is built, and ascends by the only staircase to the upper floor from which there is no communication with the street save such as is afforded by the windows; the only outer door in the building being the main one below, through which all the members of the household must find ingress and egress. In large establishments these form quite a colony and young people, even if they have the disposition, have no opportunity for stolen interviews or elopements. The porter is a man whose integrity can be depended upon and he is usually faithful to the responsible position assigned him. I knew of an instance where a young cavalier gave a porter a fifty dollar note simply to convey a letter to his young mistress. The porter pocketed the money and gave the letter to the young lady openly in her mother's presence. The writer was not a favored suitor. His letter was regarded as an impertinence and its author received instead of an answer from the fair one, a challenge from her brother. But, where hearts are equally inclined, eyes are eloquent in Mexico and their language is well understood by both youths and maidens. The young men have a mode of courtship which, for what reason I never learned, is called "Playing the Bear." It consists of paying compliments and making love under a lady's window. Learning the residence of the fair one, her appearance upon her balcony is watched and waited for. The balcony is the one place to which a young girl may resort unattended. Even though the duenna may suspect the "Bear" is below, it is known he is not a climbing bear, and so he is left unmolested. So soon as the young lady appears, the Mexican Romeo passes on the opposite side of the way and, by gesture and glance conveys his respectful admiration, or his passionate devotion as the case may be. Or he stations himself directly below her balcony and the evening may favor his uttering words that she may hear. Juliet, from her elevated stand point, returns or repels her admirers' advances. If she favor the suit, the lover may be bold enough to sing, of a moonlight night, beneath her window accompanying himself on the bandalon or guitar and, sometimes, a note, a rose, or some other token of approval, falls at his feet or is let down to him by a silken cord by which same means he can return trifles in kind. In this fashion matches are often made, the high contracting parties knowing little of each other's disposition or characteristics until marriage gives ample time for the study of both. It is lovemaking under difficulties, but it is the sole little gleam of romance the rigid scrutiny of the chaperon allows to enter into *affaires du coeur* in Mexico. It is the custom for the groom to present to his bride the *corbeille,* which often includes so rich and complete an outfit very little is left for the bride herself to furnish, but even when she has become his *novia* or affianced, he can never see her out of her mother's presence. A lady who married off her eleventh daughter when we were in Mexico maintained her supervision of the last one's courtship with the same unrelaxing vigilance she had bestowed upon the first. Still, marriage and giving in marriage is as much practiced in Mexico as elsewhere and with apparently the average result of happiness.

Children in their signatures retain the surnames of both father and mother; the latter not so entirely merging her identity in that of her husband as with us. The father's name is written first, the mother's last. For instance, a member of the Aguila and Brabanta families being united in marriage, their son would sign himself, after his given name, Aguila y Brabanta.

As I have said, a Mexican lady has no reception days or evenings. Her *sala* is for her kindred, not fashionable gatherings. Home life gains, in many ways, what it loses by ignoring the social fashions inasmuch as for it are acquired, and to it are devoted those charms and accomplishments which go to make it attractive. The people cultivate and appreciate letters not only in their public halls but in their private houses. I doubt if any excel them in the choice and extent of private libraries, many of which are rich in rare works and valuable manuscripts. Their literary societies are large and gather together a high order of talent. The public libraries are rich and admirably conducted. The literary taste is high toned and refined, and its cultivation pursued with avidity.

Under those wonderful skies, and among such romantic scenes and associations, the arts should find as natural growth as the marvelous ferns and flowers, and from races so poetic in temperament, so filled with the instincts of art should spring poetry, music, sculpture and painting to be acknowledged by the nations. Ability for such pursuits is strongly developed both with high and low and is among the natural endowments of the people. Together with literature they meet cordial encouragement wheresoever displayed. In fact, from a fear of not giving native talent praise enough, the mistake is frequently made of lauding it far beyond its real deserts. But, after all, this is an error that leans to virtue's side and will right itself in time. Meanwhile, there are orators, novelists, historians, poets and artists of whom the country is justly proud and, if permanent peace but grant opportunity for the culture of native genius, Mexico will soon boast a distinct and noble literature of her own. At the head of letters there at this time stands Ignacio M. Altamarino, a scholar whose fine talents have been highly cultivated. He is of unadulterated Indian blood and proud of his descent.

Among the common classes one is constantly struck with the display of refined talent existing with those whose daily lives are passed amidst squalor, dirt and privation. Like a flower, it pushes its way to the light under the most disheartening circumstances and proves its existence amid the most incongruous surroundings. Indian musicians are readily found anywhere who perform with taste and skill not only upon wind instruments but upon the harp, guitar, bandalon and violin without the slightest knowledge of written music. They are a race of improvisators. The ear is never at fault and they possess besides an imitative skill and fine memory. Yet to the sweetest melodies words are set which are the veriest nonsense. Numbers of the songs of the people, the music of which is delightful, have accompanying ballads scarcely worthy of the sweet singer of Michigan. The assertion that words were given us to conceal thought was never more thoroughly exemplified than in these verbal jingles which are void not only of sentiment but of sense. The fact clashes with the evidence of abundant mental ability and munificence of material for the ballad making.

If one speaks to a resident foreigner in Mexico of the fine natural abilities of the people he is at once met with the retort, "yes, fine talent but too lazy to cultivate it. Never will amount to anything." A visit to the numerous studios, to the Academy of Design and other schools as well as to the workshops, stamps this as an unfair and too sweeping judgement. At the same time, it must be admitted that indolence is a characteristic pervading all ranks. The very poor are too contented with a small share of anything, even of culture. The very rich are too contented with knowing everything is within their reach. Too much contentment is a bane. The men are brave, determined, full of pluck and spirit, and throw into their sports the hardest kind of work. They cannot be accused of idleness, but their land is the land of *mañana,* and where everything is going to be done tomorrow, it is a long time in getting done. Only the strongest will can conquer the natural leaning to indolence, but there are innumerable evidences that Mexicans can and have exerted it and triumphed.

During the winter months, when the dust is a drawback to many out of door pleasures, the city streets and public avenues would be intolerable were it not for the law which obliges every man to keep the street sprinkled in front of his own door. Everyone dutifully keeps this law and in the mornings and the evenings and often at mid-day Indians are to be seen with cotton pants rolled up nearly to their thighs and barefooted, carrying a huge tin can, and often two of them, such as gardeners use. These they swing up and down, and around and about, converting themselves into peripatetic summer showers which very effectually "lay the dust." Sprinkling machines are as yet not in common use. There is a miniature one on the Paseo, a one barrel affair which makes up for its inadequacy by attaching to it several Indian *aides de camp* who run with it, watering pot in hand, and beat the machine at its own business.

In summer during the rainy season when the short sharp showers flood the city streets the same Indians earn many a *medio* by carrying pedestrians from one dry point to another. It is no uncommon sight then to see a half clad Indian bearing a well dressed personage safely through the sudden torrents.

It is a popular belief in some countries that conversation would die a natural death were it not for that general topic, the weather, which is resorted to to begin talk, to prop it when failing, and enliven it when dull. But the Mexicans do not talk upon this subject. One never hears the words "it is a fine day"—"it is cold"—etc., etc. Half the year the weather is always fine, the other half it rains every day. These being facts everybody is supposed to understand, no one pads his conversation with the weather.

Upon the streets, generally at the corners can always be found men big hatted, saraped, with leather sandals or bare feet. A leather strap hangs from the right shoulder to the hip on the left side where it is ornamented with a brass label bearing a number. These men are *cargadores* or street porters. They are for public hire as drays would be and are employed to carry anything that is moveable from a parcel to a pulpit. The furniture cart is not seen. Everything is carried from place to place on the heads and shoulders of men or on rude hand barrows with a man before and man behind trotting between the shafts. In this manner all sorts of merchandise can be seen passing through the streets and it is no uncommon thing to see a coffin going to its destination on a man's head the bearer trotting along in the blithest way beneath his ghastly burden. Of the loads carried by men who wear no brass labels the variety is also infinite. Yonder one is seen with a three story house on his back. On its lower floor are chickens, on its second great pieces of meat, on its third all sorts of vegetables. Another passes carrying sausage cases, cleansed, dried and blown up ready for filling. They are light weight but take up an immense deal of room and curled and twisted into divers curves they nearly conceal the man who is beneath them. Seen from the rear, with nothing but dusky legs and this fluffy bunch of dried cases, looking at a little distance like blond frizzettes caricatured, the bearer presents a very comical appearance. Both men and women carry immense loads, and a woman lugging a haystack on her back is one of the commonest sights; it is also one that makes the heart ache and long for the amelioration of this hard working race who, if they are not stupid as beasts, must have wonderful strength and vigor of brain and body to preserve anything of the natural intelligence with which they were originally endowed. At a very early age children begin to bend their backs for the burden which is held in place by the strap across the forehead. The head, it would seem, must be pressed out of shape, and the brain ultimately suffer. The sight is never a pleasant one, however novel it may be. Horses, much less heavily burdened in proportion to their size and strength are seen with a sort of saddle which has an iron rod fastened lengthwise upon it. Strong iron hooks are on each side of this rod and from the hooks are suspended the carcasses of butchered hogs and beeves and calves and goats and sheep. In short, it is a peripatetic market—which can be halted by any who wish to purchase from its supplies. A sheet like curtain hanging on each side is supposed to conceal the raw burden when the horse is in motion, but the white screen is constantly blowing aside and plainly advertising all which it pretends to conceal.

Another conspicuous figure in Mexican streets is a man with sandals on his feet, white cotton trousers over which are drawn overalls of blue cotton which descend a little below the knee leaving the white ones to show underneath. He wears a leather apron, a white shirt, a vest, like his apron, of brown leather, on the breast of which is his brass tag. His shirt sleeves are rolled up, his unbuttoned vest shows his shirt front open, its broad white collar turned over and his dusky chest exposed. On his head is a leather cap with a visor something like a soldier's. Across the top of his head is a leathern strap which descends below his waist in front, where it is fastened to the handle of an earthen pitcher, full of water to the brim. He steadies it by one hand on the handle, the other on the strap just above it. Across the front of his head, above the visor of the cap, is another broad band which, passing down below the shoulders is fastened to the two handles of a huge earthen jar also filled with water to the very top where a leathern lid closes the mouth. So evenly is his burden balanced, should either jar be broken the bearer would tumble down. This is the *aguador*, or water carrier, who supplies those not willing to pay the water rates or who have not water works at their residences with what they require. A belt passes around his waist to which is affixed his leather purse or pouch, and it also sustains a cushioned pad behind, which keeps the heavy stone jar from resting directly against his back. Thus harnessed and thus loaded, he is seen trotting about the streets and climbing up the tall staircases day by day, and the pittance he earns is miserably small. This dress is sometimes varied by the overalls being of leather, left open to the knee on the outer seam; but except this, and the vest being sometimes bound with a bright color, there is almost a uniform worn by these fellows, who are the most distinct in appearance of any of their class.

An iron bedstead and appurtenances, a woolen carpet, a table turned upside down and a large trunk, runs past on a brisk trot. It is a load and a pair of legs; nothing else being visible. One would not suppose anything human could be under such a burden, and be alive. There a man is seen moving under a pile of lumber; I don't know how many feet long the boards are, but they extend far beyond his head, and reach nearly to the ground behind. He is bent almost double, and the muscles in his bare legs are working like pulley ropes, and one groans for him as he silently passes by. If the curse cast upon Cain was ever felt by any people, it is by these poor Indians who not only earn their bread (and very humble bread it is, too) by the sweat of their brows, but by the wear and tear of every bone and sinew. The mule or the horse has someone to groom and stable him, but this human animal, harnessed in his leathern straps, is without care of any kind, though his patience and his wonderful powers of endurance make him, perhaps, the most truly valuable of all Mexican beasts of burden. Regarded simply as athletes they are marvels. One can see in the streets of Mexico a hundred times a day feats of strength and agility which are more wonderful than any he would pay a dollar to look at in a gas lit theater performed with a balance pole, or on a swing trapeze. A weight of eight *arrobas*, 200 pounds, and often more, is slung to the tawny shoulders of one of these dwellers in a land where "all men are free and equal" and in this way one sees acres of cabbages striding to town, the entire crop of a farm ambling gently along to market, or the product of a large poultry yard serenely marching down the road at a "double quick," so covering its Indian bearer from head to foot as to make him appear a most comical feathered nondescript. Talk of the floating gardens! They are as nothing compared to these trotting gardens which one sees everywhere.

The army is chiefly composed of Indians; only the officers being white. As soldiers, though shiftless in appearance, they are unequaled on the march and in all duties requiring endurance and fortitude. Their fighting qualities are said not to be of the highest order nor are the ranks always to be relied upon; being just as likely to go over to the victor as to share the fate of the vanquished. Whether this be truth or slander, *¿quién sabe?* A large convict element is employed in the army which in itself tends to degrade, and then perhaps it is difficult to inspire men with patriotism who have few real rights in a country save to encumber the ground. They are descendants of a race that fought well and, given homes and home interests to defend, they might prove themselves worthy sons of their Aztec sires.

As guides or messengers these Indians are remarkable. They seem to know by intuition the geography of Mexico and travel as a bird flies in the directest path. One will start off in his long, swinging trot, equipped for his journey by being nearly stripped, and accomplishes his sixteen or twenty leagues a day with ease. A few tortillas of a value almost too small to be computed supplies him with food and his earnings for the trip will amount to 50 or 60 cents.

It is well known that the regal Montezuma, in his splendid palace in Mexico, by aid of Indian runners who knew every path and pass in the apparently impassable mountains, was served regularly every day with fresh fish from the waters of the Gulf. The fleet-footed aborigine possibly made the first track for his marvelous successor the steam engine, and there is no doubt that these toilers we look upon today are the direct descendants of those historic tribes who hewed and hauled the great Calendar Stone, who erected the numerous *teocallis* in the land of the Aztec Emperor, who worked the quarries, and built the palaces of ancient kings and moved the mighty gods of granite which yet exist as monuments of human strength and skill. But, the day has come when the amelioration of the race should be thought of and taken in hand. I heard a proposal made very seriously in Mexico to establish a society for the prevention of cruelty to animals. They should begin with the Indian. Cruelty, unconscious cruelty let us believe, is constantly practiced upon him, and he is also cruel to himself. He doesn't know how to be otherwise. As for his donkey—well, if it is beaten, and overworked, and half starved, and scarcely sheltered, and insufficiently covered, and has skinned legs and a sore back, isn't it after all just as well off as he is? Shall he show to his beast a care which has never been shown to himself, and of the first principles of which he is profoundly ignorant?

The diversity of race in Mexico is almost equal to its diversity of climate. Out of a population estimated at more than ten millions only one million of pure Spanish blood is given; four millions being set down as of mixed blood, and five millions are Indians, direct descendants of the aborigines who inhabited the country at the time of the Conquest. Where the father is white, and the mother an Indian, the children of such a union are called *mestizos*. If the mother herself be a *mestiza* and the father white the offspring are called *criollos*. As in other countries the child of a white father and a negress is called a mulatto and so on to quadroons and octoroons. These are all classed under the general term *mezclado* or "mixed." From such intermingling many castes have sprung which it would be impossible to classify. As natives of the country all are Mexicans but, it is plain, *hay Mexicanos y Mexicanos* [there are Mexicans and Mexicans].

The Indians of Mexico, who comprise fully two-thirds of the population, differ essentially from the savage tribes whose names have so long existed as a terror and a vexed problem with our governmental powers. In disposition the Mexican Indians are gentle, affectionate, and tractable. In cities they are servants and burden bearers. In the country their inclinations are for pastoral pursuits and if they can rent a few acres of land, the simplest of tenements, the most patient of assistants in the way of oxen and donkeys, and the most primitive of agricultural implements, they consider themselves "well off" and are content. The scarcity of streams and springs in the country causes them to gravitate toward the neighborhood of large *haciendas* which have appropriated these few resources. There they become of the "people," of "the place," and are happy in so being. They have strong local attachments and can with difficulty be weaned away from scenes and associations among which they have once established themselves. They are so inured to hardship it has ceased to become such, and they will sleep as soundly on a bed of rocks with a stone for a pillow and arise as strong and agile as any white laborer from a comfortable couch. We consider their food to be wretched, but a hardier race cannot be found than this which thrives on it. The Mexican Indian is, generally speaking, short, sinewy and firmly built, with calves so well developed the sight is enough to make a ballet dancer go mad with envy. He will work all day like a hard tasked mule, and subsist on what would scarcely suffice for a year old American baby. They are a race of workers. One can observe them everywhere every day about their tasks, or engaged in the lighter petty trades of feather work, clay figures, etc., peculiar to them. And to so observe them speedily disabuses one's mind of the notion which has been impressed upon it of the indolence of these lower classes. That there are numbers of worthless idlers among them, such as are to be found in all classes, cannot be doubted. There are drones in every hive, but if the Indians do not work in Mexico it is a marvel how the work gets done. I spent weeks in their villages, saw them daily on their farms, saw them everywhere upon the roads, saw them engaged in building, in factory work in the shoe business and always working diligently. I stood by them at the filigree forges, at the anvils, in the carpenters' shops, in the market stalls, saw them acting the part of donkeys and drays and machines. I saw the women in the fields and in the cabins, busy always at something, even in their hours of rest with the bit of needlework in hand to pass time, and I was impressed with their patient diligence, their natural industry and the faithfulness with which they performed any work entrusted to them. Their labor is cheap and readily commanded and what is more, everyone, beyond the mere infant, can work. No one is too old, and few are too young to be at some kind of useful work. If "Labor is worship" then the Indian is a *devoté*. To consider the Indians an idle and worthless class is to do them a great injustice. They are dexterous at all trades, quick to learn and easy to manage. A marked feature among them is the usefulness of the children. They work fully as hard in proportion to their age as their elders, and seem to understand the seriousness of life and labor almost as soon as they can walk. At the haciendas one sees gangs of children performing work which would be suited apparently to well grown boys or men; and, at an age when children are usually left to tumble about and do nothing but grow, often a burden to themselves and those who have them to support, these little Indians have learned by experience that "life is earnest, life is real." It is surprising how much they can accomplish and how intelligently they work. They fill places that bigger people could not get into, and their little hands perform duties which larger ones would be too clumsy to execute. They can walk immense distances, carrying astonishingly large burdens and heavy weights, and are taught in every way, from their earliest years, to be of assistance to their elders. If they are left mentally ignorant, they are physically educated. They understand their own powers, and feet, hands, limbs, and all their five senses are acutely trained. One rarely sees an idle child and seldom one that cries. The Bible says, "There is a time to weep," but the little Indians never seem to find it. The women do women's work and men's too. They are as capable in the field as in the house, and are cheerful and reliable. They may frequently be seen performing duties which would be difficult for the hardiest men. Thus, it will be seen all the manpower of the race, to speak generically, is good and available; a fact of weight when the establishment of manufactures is to be considered.

It is asserted they will not work for any length of time; that when they have earned a few reals they will do no more until the absolute need of money rouses them to new exertion. This may be true, but it has been proven that they are capable of steady toil. 250,000 bales of cotton are manufactured annually in the country, exclusively by these native Indians; which fact favors a belief in their capacity and intelligence and also in their powers of perseverance. I remember to have seen a body of six or seven hundred Mexican Indians passing through the streets whom I at first thought were recruits or convicts, but who proved to be operatives from the cotton factories who had come to seek an interview with the President and ask for an abatement of their hours of labor. The skill, quick intelligence and patience of the operatives and other laborers proves the Indians to be an invaluable element in the mining, agricultural, pastoral and mechanical resources of the country.

A very intelligent gentleman occupying a high position as one of the officers of the Vera Cruz railroad, told me that the main part of all public works was done by the natives, that the new mole, built by the company at Vera Cruz, was chiefly constructed by them and that in building the railroad the work of one native Indian was equal to one and a half of any Irishman or German employed.

The "hands" at the haciendas and the ranchos are Indians, and one is led to wonder why these people are not encouraged to set to work on the vast tracts of land lying idle and unproductive for lack of labor which immigrants are sought for to perform. Time after time colonies have been established upon these lands, of Italians and other nationalities, only as a general thing, to prove a failure and disappointment, while the masses of people just at hand seem to be overlooked in such schemes. There is a class of producers familiar with the country and its inhabitants, the capabilities of the climate, and the soil, who speak the language, who can subsist on very little, are of hardy habits and simple tastes. Instead of getting up colonizations schemes and introducing into the land a foreign element incapable of speaking the native tongue and ignorant as to the cultivation of the native crops, why not establish these Indians on the unworked lands? To distribute them over such farms and teach them to use and understand modern agricultural implements—to establish manufactures and occupy them there, and above all to *pay them good wages* seems a missionary work which lies at the very doors of Mexican capitalists and land owners, which would result in triple benefits—

benefits to the employer, to the employee, and to the credit of the whole country. It is objected that they will steal. It has been repeatedly proved that so does the foreign farmer in Mexico whenever he gets the chance. It is said they are lazy. No doubt they sometimes are. The climate, in some districts, is enervating and it is said an American or a European set to work there does not retain his energies unimpaired for a longer period than three years. The Indian, if anyone, is able to withstand these climatic effects. One thing regarding him should be taken into consideration. Poor pay-men make poor work-men. A man who puts forth all his strength, and strains every muscle from morning till night and then only earns enough to buy a few *tortillas*, or a cup or two of *pulque*, has not much to arouse his ambition nor to make tomorrow of any especial interest to him. For him there is no more dignity in labor than in idleness. He is simply an animal who must exert himself because exertion will furnish him with a fresh mouthful of food or drink from another spring. The Negro slave used to pride himself upon the price he knew he would bring in the market, but the Mexican Indian cannot regard himself as worth anything to anybody, not even to himself. His wages for the hardest kind of work range from a real to forty, sometimes fifty cents a day. He lives in a cane hut or a mud cabin and wears the simplest kind of clothing. These are facts, yet in spite of them all, the Indian works well and willingly, and no doubt feels his ill paid labor entitles him to some hours of idleness. He is never insolent to his employer. On the contrary, his manners are invariably marked with gentle courtesy and unfailing politeness even in his intercourse with others of his own class. If paid the same wages that the immigrant would demand, would he not improve in status and condition? A man who commands good wages is worth more to a country than the man who can gain but a pittance. Good labor and good wages like gold and quicksilver have an affinity for each other. Honest pay would insure honest labor and infuse a new spirit into this much enduring race. The country will find a fruitful source of development in the elevation of the masses which will be a slow process but a sure one. As the Republic becomes more truly a Republic with peace and the continuation of a wise government, it is bound to come about; and some immediate steps have been taken toward its accomplishment. The Indians are capable of high mental cultivation. They have patience and quick intelligence, two important factors in the paths of learning. Wherever one has been given any educational chance he has risen to front rank in the nation. Mexico in her list of patriots and statesmen shows this to be a fact. Juárez was a full blooded Indian, so was Mejía, and others, connected with the developments of science and literature, are of that race. It would be noble justice in the descendants of the race who conquered the Aztecs to restore to them in some measure the rank they had attained in science, agriculture, mechanical arts, literature and refinement when Cortez turned his religious zeal toward their overthrow and subjection.

Pulque to the Mexican peasant is often as sad a betrayer as is whiskey to the Irish laborer, but this fault, with a little tact and discipline, could be easily guarded against if not entirely overcome. Philanthropy is an active virtue in Mexico and it has ample field for its labors at its very doors. These labors have been begun in the establishment of schools, and the building of railroads will aid materially as it will tend to increase wages, and increase of wages will ensure increase of self respect and from that stepping stone the impulse to go forward follows as naturally "as the sparks fly upward." The Indian needs only to be helped to earnestly help himself.

Strangers often allude to the dejected cast of countenance which these poor people have, and attribute it to their being descendants of a conquered race. But their sad faces must really be a very ancient trait for the Spaniards, upon entering the city on their mission of conquest, found the features of the natives all touched with the serious, even sad expression characteristic of the national physiognomy. For my own part, I found them like all people of small needs easily pleased and made happy with very little. They have an ever ready smile although their features have a serious cast. They are always courteous, and their voices soft and musical. They possess a natural air of dignity and grace and it is no uncommon thing to see a Mexican peasant remove his hat to friend or superior with the air of a grand Duke.

As for servants, we never had the slightest occasion to find fault with our own but the complaints we heard of them gave us reason to believe the servant question in Mexico was as much a vexed one as anywhere else. No matter how late we returned from theater or ball we found the servants of the hotel soundly asleep on a bit of matting upon the floor. When we knocked at the great portal that admitted us to the Court below, immediately the voice of Salvador from within cried, "*Que número?*" "*Siete*"—or whatever it was, when by a rope attached to the drop latch he opened the door and closed it after us never forgetting his *buenas noches niña, buenas noches Señora* as we passed by. At the top of the stairs outside our doors on the upper landing were always Augustín and Amador and Luis; the *petate* their bed, a sarape their covering, the stone floor their couch. They all slept well, were always cheerful and content much more so than servants I know of in the States who have carpeted rooms, spring mattresses, ample comfort and good wages; yet are always dissatisfied and ready to "give warning" on the slightest provocation. The street porters and others of that class, we were assured, needed to have the eighth commandment forcibly impressed upon them. Said a friend to us,

> You may call upon an Indian in the streets whom you know nothing about and whom you never saw before in your life. You may safely entrust him with any parcel no matter how valuable to be carried to any given address. You need give yourself no anxiety about its safe delivery. He will discharge his duty with the utmost fidelity. You will find your package, jewels, money, whatsoever it may contain, awaiting you although the dusky messenger in coming away has perhaps stolen the common hand bell from your table or the bright knob from your door or any other little object which chanced to meet his jackdaw propensities. A trust they scorn to betray; but, to steal small things which come in their way while discharging that trust is a constitutional frailty in which they indulge *ad libitum*. The petty pawn brokers whose shops abound in every portion of the city keep the traffic in stolen goods lively. The thief knows that in such places he can readily dispose of his spoil, and the loser, on his part, knows at once, when an article is gone, that a cruise among the pawnshops will enable him to recover his property.

But, with all this, they have their redeeming traits, and theft is the natural outcome of low wages. The civility and respectful demeanor of these peasants not only toward their superiors but among themselves is a national trait. They are faithful in their attachment to employers and are inclined to remain with one family as long as possible, proud to grow gray in the service. They learn the duties assigned them readily, rarely evincing that stupidity which characterizes servants of some other countries. They probably lie; as falsehood is the twin sister of theft and in all grades of intelligence the liar is the chief assistant of the thief. I never could bring myself to believe, however, that their faults were ineradicable and would not yield to patient care and discipline and education.

19

❀

Shrine of the Virgin of Guadalupe, Chapultepec Castle, and More

Early hours in the saddle. Morning on horseback. Courtesies. Riding equipments. Riders and grooms. The phaeton. A lake of ducks. How they are hunted. Mexico's first tramway. Las Escaleras. Breakfast. About the fields. Novel invitation to a ball. Surrounded by armed men. A fright. Compliments of the Administrator. The sanctuary of Nuestra Señora de Guadalupe. Mendicants. Votive offerings. The story of Juan Diego and the legend of the miraculous roses. Feast of the 12th of December. The wonderful well. The hill top chapel. The sailor's stone mast. Hidalgo's banner and his war cries. Signing of the treaty of peace between the United States and Mexico. Temple of Tomantzín. The Path of Penitence. The flight into Egypt. To Chapultepec. Montezuma's cypress. Its circumference and height. What may have been. A shrewd Indian. Associations with American heros. A little ghost story. The beautiful mementoes of its last imperial occupants. Out of the gates. Darkness. "Your money or your life." La Libertad.

A clatter of hoofs in the court below, a sheen of silvered sombreros, a jingle of spurs, a champing of bridle bits, laughter, gay voices, footsteps running up and down the broad stone stairs, about the wide portals a merry cavalcade gathered, and horses waiting in the patio for riders. The equestriennes were speedily ready in hats and habits, the former being the broad brimmed *sombrero* of the same style but of lighter weight than those worn by gentlemen.

The whips were the simple quince tree branch which for its flexibility was at that time all the rage.

From the first week we were in Mexico there was no day that saddled horses were not sent us in the morning with a groom bringing a note saying if we wished to ride friends were ready to accompany us. The horses, all equipped, were proof enough the proffer was no empty ceremony. A lady who owned a superb thousand dollar chestnut mare placed it three or four times a week at Cora's disposition. Every evening, when not driving with us in the larger carriage, a beautiful little vehicle with seats for two was sent to the door with its fine horses and liveried servants by someone of Señor Escandón's family and placed "entirely at our service" with a cordial hospitality such as is characteristic of the Mexicans. Flowers sent every morning to our rooms, invitations to breakfast, to dine, to visit city homes and haciendas, to attend some *fête champetre* or opera or theater in the evening, caused us to spend among that kind hearted and cultivated people days never to be forgotten. Upon this especial morning a tinge of sadness mingled with our pleasure, for we well knew the day was rapidly drawing nigh when we must say adios to all friends and all pleasures of this fair city. At an early hour horses and grooms were in the old stone court. There was Señor B. and Señor R. in full riding costume, and three grooms in all the glory of buckskin and bullion, big sombreros, chaquetas and chaparreras, and goat skin saddle cloths. Cora's horse was a beautiful creature, proudly displaying in form and motion his noble blood. At the door stood the phaeton with its cream colored ponies and servants in waiting. Into this pretty carriage I sprang and Señor T., who was going out but not coming back with us, took his place on my left. The "tiger" folded his arms and became a statue in livery in his perch behind and I gathered the reins in my fingers for I was to drive. The mounted members of the party went on before, we followed. It is a novel experience to ride through the streets of Mexico in the morning: to see the great town yawn and rub its eyes and stretch itself and gradually grow wide awake to listen to the many clamorous bells and see the streets become peopled. One hears the cries of the lard vendor, the fresh cheese and curd seller, the persuasive tones of the *tamales* maker, and the sweetmeat seller, and in all directions he sees the street merchants of other commodities appearing with their wares while the various costumes, the color and grouping delight the eye. The lottery ticket is cried and proffered on all sides; flowers, game, crockery, charcoal also, and besides these with their shrieks and cries, donkey droves appear with vegetables and haystacks, etc., etc., for the passage of which one waits lest she be swept from her seat by a crate of pottery or a load of cabbages. The basket maker, nearly covered with his light wares, jostles the sausage seller, and the sausage seller jostles the pigskin of pulque on his neighbor's shoulder, and the flower women laugh, and the group of beggars by the old wall draw their rags closer and huddle nearer to the sunny side of the old convent gate, while lines of Indian farm "hands" come trotting past from the fields, with loads of corn in husks upon their backs strapped as usual to their bowed down foreheads. The tall sheafs extend far above the head and reach within an inch or two of the ground, and as the bearers trot along the motion sets all the stalks to rustling. Looked at from the rear it seems as if the whole cornfield had gathered itself up into sheafs and started off to market by itself. Turn which way one will, all is animation and picturesque novelty. North toward Guadalupe, thence northwest toward the mountains stretched our way, the gay cavalcade before us leading on at the gentle pace all equestrians practice in Mexico, while the birds sang, the atmosphere was cool and the cloudless skies, like a dome of turquoise bent above us their brightest and serenest aspect all in odd contrast to the filth and bad odors of the suburbs by which we made our way out of town. Our path lay along a causeway elevated some feet above the meadows on either hand. The graceful arboles de Peru with their beautiful crimson berries grew upon each side affording shade to the dusty road. To the right lay a large shallow pond upon the bosom of which sat multitudes of wild ducks. The Indians "bag" them by tying a number of guns together which are "rested" and brought to bear upon the game. A simple apparatus fires them all at once and by means of this novel *metrailleuse* hundreds of birds are killed at one shot and hunting made easy. To our left was a pathway marked at regular intervals by rapidly crumbling arches of stone extending from near town to the Church of Guadalupe.

The distance between the city and the famous Cathedral of Guadalupe is but a league and the first tramway ever built to lead out of Mexico occupies a portion of the causeway and carries passengers at a real a head, about 12 1/2 cents. Many in the morning prefer the saddle and we met gay cavalcades and were joined by or passed others. Fast riding is not practiced by pleasure parties. Turning from the causeway to the left we soon passed through a beautiful avenue of poplars. Then the ponies scampered across a rustic bridge and we stopped at last at the stone gateway of an hacienda known as Las Escaleras about three leagues from the city. The great portal was quickly opened and the Administrador lifted his sombrero to the proprietor who had not visited this estate before in two years. Everything looked neat and orderly. In the patio flowers were blooming, and birds were singing in clean bright cages in the corridor. We were taken over a large portion of the estate which the owner found in satisfactory order in all its departments. We were taken to the pulque cellars where the great oxhide vats were brimming full of the beverage. Glasses were brought and we all dutifully sipped the maguey's milk. Afterward we visited the stables and a number of splendid animals were brought out for our inspection and thence we went to the granaries of wheat and corn where were the fat harvests all carefully garnered. From the granaries we went into the open fields, and herds of magnificent cattle were driven up in splendid crowds for our party to see. So numerous were these herds we began to think "the cattle on a thousand hills" were holding a congress here. Most of the choicest breeds were represented. Returning to the spacious house our host suggested to the Administrador that something to eat would not be amiss. The request had been forestalled by the Superintendent, who quietly issued orders to sundry servants quick to answer his beckoning finger. A tall, straight Indian next appeared, who in a low voice announced that breakfast was ready. We found the table very neatly spread with excellent damask, pretty china of a blue and white pattern, and plated silver knives and forks. Our excursion had been a most impromptu affair and, as I before remarked, the proprietor had not visited the hacienda for two years. Yet all things were in readiness and the breakfast was excellent. Of course bouquets were presented us. Flowers here seem to be the grace before and after meat. While we sat in the court admiring these, and the numerous plants which grew around, great, blue eyed mastiffs with ponderous paws came to make friends with us. One was called *Manito*, and looked as if he could have felled a foe at any time with one stroke of his "Big Hand." We admired these dogs and were at once with the usual Mexican courtesy offered one, or two, or three, as we might wish, but, of course, declined, with all the politeness and ceremony at our command. Then, suddenly, guns were fired. Upon my rather startled inquiry of what that meant, we were told that this was a Mexican country custom, informing neighbors and villagers, near and far, that a ball was about to be given and their presence requested. We entered a large apartment and took seats. Soon, the Indian aristocracy of the village, and the lesser peasants, came flocking in. A few wore calico "dresses" such as we see in any United States village on a holiday. The rest wore the skirt and the rebozo, and with their babies came flocking in, some seating themselves upon the chairs and sofas, and the steps of the porch, or corridor, others sat or kneeled upon the cleaned and shining floor. A band of Bandalonco and one or two violins began to play. Dusky men led forward dusky maids and dancing began. We had the *Jarabe* with all its variations, the fandango, wild choruses and wonderful steps, and other dances the names of which I could not learn. Upon the floor of the outer corridor stood a woman I longed to sketch. Tall, and of splendid proportions, she leaned against a pillar which was wreathed with vines. Her dusky face, with its great lustrous eyes, was half hidden by a blue rebozo. Her attitude was full of classic grace. In one arm she held a half year old infant clad only in the end of her own rebozo which gave the child's supple limbs most free and naked play. At her skirts clung a little one somewhat older, with great black eyes like its mother, and wonderfully thick black hair. This party looked on, joining neither in the dancing nor the pulque and refreshments which followed. About half past three, we started homeward, with many adieus and farewells wafting from dusky hands left behind. Señor B., Señor R. and Cora, with their attendant grooms, led the way on horseback. I, as in coming out, drove the pony phaeton. Don P. had said adios, so only the groom behind, and I on the seat in front, occupied the carriage. We all lingered awhile to see the Indian farmhands trotting in from the fields with loads of corn in husk upon their backs, strapped to their foreheads with the usual leathern strap.

Away went the equestrians, riders and grooms, out over the bridge, and down the great *mesquite* avenue. After them flew my ambitious ponies, eager to go, and hard to hold; but those in saddle had the start, and were well on in advance. Suddenly, over the bridge in the rear, came the clattering of many hoofs! The house was out of sight now. Meadows lay on either hand, the tall trees on each side cast dense shadows, the road was lonely. I looked back. A dozen horsemen "all saddled and bridled and fit for a fight" came dashing after us. I saw their great sombreros, their glittering jackets, their carbines and their lassoes, their knifed belts, and the glittering bridle bits. A glance sufficed. "At last!" I said to myself. "At last." Beyond my life, I had only my simple ear-rings and my watch to lose. I felt with one hand for both. They were in their places. The equestrians were far ahead; I could see the after-noon sunshine glinting on the *chaquetas* of the grooms and striking the silver buckle on Cora's hat. I uttered no word—and as I do not belong to a scream-ing family, no cry. The servant sat in his place behind and kept silence. Our pursuers dashed up. Four rode abreast of my ponies' heads, two on each side; four rode on each side of my phaeton's front wheels; four rode behind! "We are surrounded," I thought, and a pang of pity swept my heart for the pretty cream-colored ponies and the blue lined phaeton which I drove. Suddenly Don José, far in advance, turned his head. Perhaps my face was pale; if it was not it belied my courage, which was rapidly developing a white feather. The Don's horse was wheeled, and came rapidly towards me. "The Administra-dor," he said, as he drew rein at my wheel, "has shown his compliments and respects by furnishing an armed escort, which you see about you. Of course, you are not alarmed?" "Indeed," I answered stoutly, "I was just half frightened to death." Thus escorted we rode to the grand old Cathedral of Guadalupe. Here the armed rode forward, halted, and arranged themselves in open file, each rider standing, dismounted and bare-headed by his horse. Our party rode through. Señor B. turned in his saddle and spoke a few words of cour-tesy and thanks. The escort remounted and dashed away homeward, leav-ing us to inspect the famed edifice and boiling spring of "Our Lady of Guadalupe."

Leaving our horses, we went forward to inspect the famous church and its no less famous spring. We were obliged to make our way through a crowd of beggars who were of "the halt, the lame and the blind"; and who piteously besought us "In the name of the Virgin," "For the sake of our children," "In the name of God," and upon every other conceivable plea to aid them. The gentlemen bestowed alms upon them and amid profane blessings we passed through the sacred portals.

The edifice is large and handsome. It has altar adornments and balus-trades of solid silver, and numerous costly images. The choir is rich in quaint and curious carving, and this church seems to have preserved more of its original costly endowments than others we have seen.

Here, as elsewhere, we found the money changers in the temple; regular stands of merchandise being stationed at one end of the building where ro-saries, crucifixes, pamphlets, cards, and medals bearing the image of the Guadalupe Virgin, in gold, and in silver, and in plated metals, are sold. At the other side, under the strong light which poured in at the great windows, were hung the crutches cast away and canes of those who had drunk of the precious waters and been healed. Here also were dozens of votive offerings; ears of corn, the first and best fruits of the harvest; locks of hair; the dolls and toys of children; pictures, also, of the rudest kind, but touching tributes of simple faith. They represented awful accidents which had been averted, a hair breadth escape which had been made by a hasty prayer to "Our Lady" in the moment of supreme danger. Here, she had appeared and stopped a run away horse who was dragging his rider by one foot caught in the stirrup. There, she had appeared when a man nearly had his brains knocked out by a falling tree, and let him off with only a bleeding nose. Now, she came and saved a baby who almost died from eating too much jam, and then she had thwarted the designs of a band of robbers. All these facts are graphically described in the pictures or the story written underneath, and the figure of the Virgin is invariably represented as appearing at the critical moment. There is something in these crude and simple tributes, these visible expressions of a sincere and unquestionable faith, which curbs the sneer of the scoffer and checks the smile of ridicule on the lips of the unbeliever. Humble though they be, they are the honest attestations of those who have absolute faith, and who truly believe themselves to have been the recipient of especial miraculous favors by the timely invoking of this miraculous Virgin. Of course, so well known is the legend of this church, I am well aware that if I repeat it I tell "an oft told tale," yet if I do not, then I leave the place without its romance, the church without its story, and though the narrative be not new I at least am a new narrator of it.

Once upon a time—tradition has it—in the year 1531, Juan Diego, an Indian, came up this way to learn something of Christianity as taught nearby by some of the Franciscan monks. He was a native of Quatitlán and was journeying to the province of Tlaltelalco. He was ignorant, but eager to learn. Denied his own religion and that of his forefathers, he turned to the new doctrines of the Conquest, for his heart was heavy, deprived of the comfort of all pious consolation. Now, the mountain of Tepeyac was frightfully barren and desolate, but he must pass it in order to arrive at his destination. Bravely he planted his foot on rock and on hillock and trudged along. Suddenly appeared before him a vision of the Holy Virgin who bade him at once to hasten to *El Illustrísimo*, the good Bishop Don Juan Zumárraga, [the first

Bishop of Mexico], with the message that she desired to have a chapel erected in her name on the hill. The gentle Bishop would none of this, and received the announcement with undisguised incredulity. Repeated journeys of Juan Diego, and repeated messages which he brought back, failed to have any effect upon the doubting Bishop. At last, the hapless pilgrim said, "What can make thee believe? Must I bring thee some sign?" "Yes," replied the Bishop, "bring me roses from the topmost rock of Tepeyac."

Almost hopeless the Indian went upon his way. Reaching the topmost rock, barren even of a bit of moss or spear of lichen, he took his blanket from his shoulders and spread it there, then fervently prayed to the Holy Apparition. Straightway, about him sprang up in profusion the richest and most unrivaled roses. Juan Diego filled his dusty sarape. He fled down the height. He rushed into the Bishop's presence. "I come," he cried, "with the Virgin's own visible sign. On yonder rock, where never grew a shrub or flower, she has, with her own holy hands, filled this sarape with roses."

The incredulous Bishop, with a smile, opened the blanket. Not only was it filled with fragrant roses, but in their midst, upon the sarape's dingy ground, was distinctly imprinted the glorious image of the wonderful Virgin herself! The astonished Bishop no longer doubted or demurred. He at once caused the foundations of a grand Cathedral to be laid. At the first digging a wonderful spring bubbled to the surface of the ground. Wonderful, because [it was] found to possess healing powers almost miraculous, and to this day it is the resort of hundreds and hundreds of pilgrims who annually come here, often from great distance, to pray, to drink of the spring and to be healed. The anniversary of the Virgin's first appearance, the night of the 12th of December, is held as a great feast all over the country and magnificent illuminations are made in towns and hamlets in her honor, and houses during that day are decorated, to the full extent of the tenants' means and taste, with flowers and draperies and bannerets and the Virgin's colors—blue and white.

For a night or two prior to that date, Indians assemble in immense crowds at Guadalupe. They sleep upon the ground, in the open air, anywhere, and when the 12th arrives, they begin a festive dance which they keep up for several days.

Under the dome of a little temple a short distance from the church, the medicinal spring perpetually bubbles. Those who come year after year to drink of it and be healed, carry away what they can in jugs and jars and receptacles of every description. Scrofulous diseases are said to yield readily to the efforts of these waters. The well marks the spot where the Virgin first revealed herself to Juan Diego. The Church marks the scene of her second apparition. A path of stone steps, steep and rugged, leads to the very summit of the height where on Tepeyac's barren rock the glorious Virgin gave the Indian her portrait in his old sarape and the miraculous roses for the skeptical Bishop. On feast days this original blanket (!) is displayed high up above the main altar in a sacred niche assigned it. Copies of it are to be seen everywhere throughout the country from the humblest booth to the most sumptuous Halls.

She is represented in a robe of pale crimson, her hands clasped before her breast like those of Raphaelle's Mary. A dark blue mantle studded with stars covers her head and falls to the ground behind. Above the mantle is a pointed gold crown and she stands upon a crescent which a cherub supports. This is the divine picture as given by the Virgin herself to glorify and make famous forever Juan Diego's dingy Talma.

About midway between the base and the summit of the high hill of Tepeyac, on which the roses were so miraculously grown, stands a curious and costly monument in the shape of a ship's sail. It is in stone, and the votive offering of a Spanish sailor who, being threatened with shipwreck and consequent loss of many precious bars of gold and silver, vowed to the Virgin of Guadalupe that if she would spare him and save his treasure this offering should be erected in her honor, here upon this sacred spot. His prayer was granted. He brought here a part of the wooden mast of his frigate which he encased in stone and reared to her glory.

It is claimed that no church in Mexico was originally so richly endowed as this one, and its cost, independently of the upper chapel, was three millions of dollars. It possessed fabulous treasures, but revolutions have not spared it, and vandal hands have carried away pictures, jewels and plate. The Cathedral, with its bell towers in which are twenty sweet toned bells, seems ample enough to contain the entire population of the dull, uninteresting village clustered about it. This village bears the name of Guadalupe Hidalgo in honor of the patriot priest who in 1810 placed himself at the head of the movement for Independence in Mexico. At Atotonilco he took from a church a banner bearing the image of the Virgin of Guadalupe. It was the first army flag ever carried which bore the sacred figure, and the cry of Hidalgo's men was; "*Viva la Religión! Viva Nuestra Madre Santísima de Guadalupe! Viva la América y muera al mal gobierno!*" ["Long live the Religion! Long live our Most Holy Mother of Guadalupe! Long live America and death to bad government!"] In this village of Guadalupe in February 1848 was signed the treaty of peace between the United States and Mexico.

The fact that where today stands the magnificent Cathedral of *Nuestra Señora de Guadalupe* formerly stood a "heathen" temple is probably as true a reason for the existence of the present church as the miraculous revelation of the healing spring and the old tradition of the Virgin and her blanket full of roses, for, wherever Cortez found an Aztec temple, there he wrought its destruction and reared a Christian church. Either at the foot, or on the summit of this hill the Aztecs called Tepeyac, stood the temple of *Tomantzín,* one of the most beneficent of their deities. She was the goddess of the earth and its golden harvests of corn. No human victims were offered in her honor, she having manifested only a desire for game. Therefore only young pigeons, turtle doves, nightingales, and humming birds were needed to propitiate this benign power, who was the especial protectress of a tribe known as the Tetonques. As was usual with them, the Aztecs reared their temple on one of the most beautiful and commanding sites to be found, and the Spanish in turn were quick to recognize its excellence for their own splendid edifice.

As we turned our horses cityward, the long avenue shaded by its tall trees was filled with wayfarers going to or coming from the town. The old road, now on our right hand, which had attracted our attention in the morning, with its stone arches, we learned was formerly known as "The Path of Penitence." Its ruined arches originally represented small chapels or stations, fourteen in number, which commemorated fourteen notable incidents in the life of Jesus. This road extended from the Northern gate of the City, to the church doors of Guadalupe; and the time is not out of memory of the present generation when all along this way penitents by thousands crowded from the city to the shrine upon their knees, resting at these wayside chapels to pray and to meditate.

In the highway, as we rode home, a *tableau vivant* of the flight into Egypt was very well represented. A woman with her rebozo over her head and an infant in her arms was riding a small, panniered donkey which an old man, bare legged and brawny armed, led by a hemp halter along the shadowy road.

It being yet early in the day, it was decided, after we reached our rooms,

and had ridded ourselves of dust by a bath and change of garments, to drive
out to Chapultepec and see the sunset from the Castle tower. One is constantly astonishing himself in Mexico with the amount of going about and
sight-seeing he accomplishes in a day. Work of this kind which would leave
him dead with fatigue in most other places, he manages with ease in Mexico,
and goes to bed comparatively fresh, and eager to rise early next morning and
begin again what seem like decidedly herculean tasks.

We summoned two friends and called a hack. An Indian driver, gay in a
rainbow hued sarape and wearing a sombrero the brim of which was wide
enough for the eaves of a sanctuary, managed a forlorn looking span of horses
whose appearance of good-for-nothingness suggested their adaptability for
the bull ring. The streets through which we drove were broad and level
though far from being always sweet smelling and smooth, but one is apt to
forget those small discomforts in that delicious climate and under those ex-
quisitely blue skies which the snow peaks pierce and beneath which the low
hills lie down like peaceful flocks. The calla lily, that fair treasure of the conservatories at home, grew wild and luxuriant along our way soon after we had
turned into the paseo. The Mesquite tree (*el arbol de Peru*), graceful as an elm
and as drooping as a willow, tempted the wild birds with its crimson clusters
of peppery berries, and the great stone aqueduct which carries water from the
springs of Chapultepec (hill of the grasshoppers) to the city stretched along
the road its noble line of nine hundred arches, each one of which enclosed
a lovely landscape. Here and there water trickled down, cool and bright
through some broken bit of mossy masonry. Now a wild vine adorned the
solid wall, and then, delicate, frightened looking flowers trembled at the base
of some stony arch like a little family of frightened children in the presence
of some stern father. Indians with their burdens trotted to and from the
town, scampering donkeys scurried past hidden in the clouds of dust they
raised, and women with children hanging at their backs met, glanced at us,
and went by. Soon the part of the drive called *el camino de los arcos* was passed.
We reached the great iron gates. They were swung wide by the silent porter
and we drove into the grounds sacred to the memory of monarchs. Shadowy
grottoes, rocks, vines, groves, silence! Only the note of a wild bird now and
then, and the hoof beats of our own horses. At a short distance from the gate
the carriage stopped. The *cochero* opened the door. We stepped out and stood
beneath the mighty boughs of Montezuma's cypress. It is an immense, and

hoary tree; hung from its loftiest to its lowest branch with the same sort of long, gray moss which drapes the cypress of our southern swamps. That at Chapultepec is coarser and heavier, and better suited to the colossal limbs it drapes. The circumference of the trunk is a little more than 48 feet and the height is one hundred and seventy six feet. It is of the same family as the giant trees of California, though smaller than the best known of those; not having yet, perhaps, attained its full size. It is a superb object to contemplate, tall, stately, moss hung, in fact, "a perfect mausoleum," declared the irreverent punster of our party. It is the most conspicuous tree in a grove of similar ones embowering the porphyritic height which the castle crowns. Parts of its trunk on which are some protuberances measure 51 feet. It stands in proud, imposing dignity, notable amongst historic trees, sending its branches far above and beyond the spot where it first took root—when? Who can count the cycles, who enumerate the years which have since elapsed? The old ahuehuete keeps its age to itself like a woman. The grim uncompromising census-taker Death will one day find it out perhaps when some iconoclastic axe shall chop its secret from its heart or the lightning betray it with one fiery stroke. The tree of Montezuma! The tree of tradition! The king which has outlived the long line of mortal kings that has moved on to the unrevealed kingdom. What curious ceremonies, what wild revelries, what pomp and splendor has it witnessed, this tree which is a temple in itself. What gods have been worshiped beneath it. What strange people were the worshipers. What regal magnificence it has seen. What downfalls, despair and desolation. Under its refreshing shade Montezuma, the Sultan of a thousand wives, mused upon the destinies of nations who, ages before his empires, ruled the land. After his bath in the adjacent grotto with its marble basin, here he sat to smoke his gilded pipe in which was "mingled with tobacco the odorous gum of the liquid amber." The court jester may have made the monarch merry on that very spot or the death of his favorite sultana have made him sorry for an hour. Here the flower of athletic Aztec youth perhaps assembled to throw the spear, to send the arrow darting through the glade, or to seize the *maquahuitl* and rush to mimic battle for the sake of a guerdon of honor from the gentle emperor or a smile from some soft-eyed maiden of his court. Vain and idle fancies all, yet they crowd upon one under the branches of that ancient cypress as naturally as do the odors of hidden blossoms and the songs of unseen birds in those historic gardens. It is said to have been from the boughs of this same hoary *ahuehuete* that Guatimotzín, the last of the Montezumas, was suspended head downward by the avaricious Spaniards and tortured, by setting fire to oil poured upon the soles of his feet, in order to exhort from him the hiding place of supposed treasure they had failed to find in the Aztec realm. While one shudders at the cruelty, one smiles to know it availed the perpetrators nothing, as no words could be wrung from the lips of the haughty young chieftain.

We strolled along the smooth road which lies at the base of the hill and leads, by a sharp turn eastward, up a broad, smooth road made by Maximilian, up to the summit. The cypresses all along this lower road are marvels of beauty, each hung with its festoons of gray moss or *heno* (hay) as they call it in Mexico, which the slightest breeze causes to sway as softly and lightly as though it were locks of hair left there by an army of Absaloms in flight. Our coachman had remained behind as we walked on, driving his span of antique equines slowly about, a precaution said to be an absolute necessity in that climate even after so short a drive, as if left standing after exercise the horse takes pneumonia or whatever may be its equivalent in the ills that flesh is heir to. We had told him to follow us slowly and walked on among the beautiful shadiness of the place. Upon our left the noble trees towered loftily; on our right tangled thickets ascended the steep bank. The passion vine swung from the rocks and mingled with the dark hue of the myrtle, while here and there scarlet berries lent a dash of brilliant color to the somber tint, or that cosmopolitan weed the Golden Rod unsheathed itself like a flaming sword from masses of russet foliage or gray and ancient stone. Far up amongst the dense verdure of the height once stood cut from the natural rock two Aztec idols said to have been the finest pieces of sculpture which Cortez found in all the valley. His priests in their eager zeal to destroy all vestiges of the Aztec religion demolished these and today one seeks in vain for even a vestige of these old "Idylls of the King." The baths of Montezuma, his groves and gardens and royal resting places at last lay behind us. We reached the turn of the road terraced into the side of the hill and which by an easy ascent leads to the castle at the top. We waited now for our coachman to appear, whom we had supposed to be slowly following us along the level road. Shrewd Indian that! He had followed but so far "behind" that to return to summon him was equal to going on to the summit. He had saved his old horses the up hill pull and there was nothing left for us to do but to accept the situation. Fortunately the road was excellent, the grade not excessively steep, nor the distance great, so we pushed on. The splendid route by which our little band went up differed materially from the rough and rugged way which opposed itself to the Americans who stormed the heights in 1847 and we were sure of a more agreeable reception than they received. Yet, they have left memories here for their countrymen. Names seem to spring out of the rocks of Chapultepec, illustrious names which have been written in the annals of American heroes and patriots since the days of the Mexican War but who won their first soldierly honors on the soil of Mexico.

As one ascends Chapultepec every step reveals a new beauty in the landscape. A curtain seems slowly and silently rolling back from a wonderful picture. The castle crowns the ridge of the height and rests upon the exact site of the ancient palace of the Aztec kings, which building Cortez destroyed. Tradition has it that it was upon this height the Aztecs halted in their march from the north, and that from it they beheld that promised sign which led them to build their city in the waters of Tezcoco. The height has been the abode of royalty from Montezuma down to Maximilian, and probably no kingly palace in the world surpasses it in beauty, or approaches it in surrounding scenery. One recognizes at every turn the artistic instinct and poetic feeling which influenced the Aztecs when they chose the sites of their homes, their majestic temples, their gardens and their beautiful cities. Advantage of locality with regard to opposing tribes at enmity with them may have had something to do with such choice, but beauty of scenery was invariably secured with a commanding position. Chapultepec rises from the plain so isolated a height that one might easily fancy it an artificial hill reared by those undaunted and indefatigable builders who reared Cholula and the pyramids of the Sun and the Moon at old Teotihuacán. It is, however, the work of nature alone, and the grand cypresses at its base are remnants of the vast forests which covered the land when the Spaniards came and which they ruthlessly cut off for the rebuilding of the city they had destroyed. It can scarcely be doubted that the Toltecs occupied the summit of Chapultepec before Montezuma's palace walls rose thereon, for the advantages and supreme beauty of the noble eminence would not be likely to escape the intelligent appreciation of any people. The foundations of the ancient palace remain. Upon them rose the Spanish edifice which has since been the beautiful abiding place of Princes and Presidents. Each new ruler has altered the place somewhat to suit his own tastes, so that it is usually in a chronic state of repair. Workmen were busily engaged upon building and grounds as we neared the summit, and mementoes of the last imperial dwellers there, Maximilian and Carlota, were being blotted out as fast as possible.

The viceroy Count Bernardo de Gálvez upon coming into power about the year 1785 determined to make his abiding place, not as his predecessors had done in the heart of the town, but upon this superb and commanding height. The palace assumed much of its present style and proportion under his hand. His alterations, repairs, and additions with subterranean cellars and storehouses cost the Spanish government enormous sums besides arousing jealousy and suspicion. On the lovely and rocky eminence on which the castle stood, its mighty ramparts, its moats, its vast receptacles for stores and provisions, gave rise to the rumor that a fortress not a palace was in course of construction. Gálvez died leaving the work incomplete, the interior being unfinished. His beautiful and unhappy young wife, the vice queen, is said to have possessed a type of loveliness most rare in that part of the country, she being a blonde of the most exquisite type. She was universally beloved being as good as she was beautiful.[1] A superstition exists that she still haunts the scene where her husband's ambitious dreams and her own hopes of reigning in the noble palace were so sadly ended, and that often at twilight she may be seen flitting about the parapet and the castle's ever unfinished walls which the presence of her restless spirit causes to constantly fall short of completion! As we approached the summit we saw a young girl dressed in black with hair of the richest golden tint standing on the very verge of the parapet that looked toward Mexico shading her eyes with a soft dark Spanish hat which she held in her hand. She stood like a statue looking dreamily away toward the Moorish domes and turrets of the fair and glittering city. Was it the spirit of the fair vice queen herself? At our approach she turned a young face of exquisite beauty toward us for an instant, gathered her soft dark draperies about her and vanished silently somewhere within the castle, where although we followed almost immediately we saw her no more. She was, of course, some American girl, a visitor like ourselves to the ancient and storied heights; but her unexpected appearance on the parapet's very verge, her gen-

1. Gálvez's wife was Félicité de St. Maxent d'Estrehan, of Louisiana, which Gálvez had governed from 1777 to 1783.

eral resemblance to the Lady Gálvez and her swift and silent disappearance just after having listened to the ghostly tradition sent quite a creepy sensation along one's veins.

The castle crouches on its ridge of rock, long in shape rather than high, reminding one of the posture of a lion couchant. Alcoves, niches, recesses, corridors are numerous, and two lofty towers overlook leagues and leagues of land and water. The main entrance to the castle is by beautiful gates of latticed bronze. The palace, undergoing changes for the occupancy of President Díaz and his family, when finished will surpass in taste and beauty of interior decoration anything it has ever hitherto approached. No expense has been spared to make the building worthy of its site and the presence of the first lady of the land. To Casarin, a well known Mexican artist of great ability and established reputation, is due the beautiful frescoing and exquisite adornment of the elegant rooms. Each apartment is in itself a study of artistic work of this kind. A skillful use of rare woods and rich hangings has resulted in fine effects. The marqueterie floors and paneled walls show excellent work; the painting is such as those who know Casarin might expect. The work in the Eastern rooms alone with the furniture it is said will cost a quarter of a million. The bathrooms are sumptuous. Into them an abundance of water, clear as crystal, is brought from sources which supplied the Aztec emperors' magnificent marble basins before the days of Hernando Cortez. There is an infinite number of rooms both on the ground floor and above and taken for all in all I doubt if there is any building of the kind on the Western continent to equal it. It is the White House of Mexico under republican rule as it was the King's palace under a monarchical government, and, under all powers it is and will be the castle of Chapultepec on its storied height amidst its hoary ahuehuetes and its clustering associations. The noble view the eminence commands is well worth a journey across the world to see. Repairs and improvements will probably always be going on at the palace but, until such time as earth is swung out of the universe and broken up and laid aside as an out of fashion, worn out old planet, the magnificent prospect the site overlooks must remain as one of the loveliest landscapes ever beheld by human eyes. Men may build up and break down and distort or disguise many of the natural beauties of the height itself; but the valley below it, the mountains all around, the city on the plain, and the romantic and beautiful visible on every side, he can not reach to ruin with "improvements" nor hope to rival with all the appliances of modern architecture and decorative art. The meadows below were once a portion of that lake which filled so large a portion of the valley and washed the limits of the Imperial Aztec gardens at Chapultepec. It is still easy for fancy to convert them into a lake dotted with Indian barks, navigated by Indian boatmen, sailed upon by dusky maidens and their swarthy suitors, gazed upon by the mellow moon reflected in the depths of velvety water. All this is easy enough to fancy, if one prefers such an aspect to meadows green with pleasant pastures, ripe with fair harvests, tilled by sturdy husbandmen, dotted with rural homes, while cattle are heard lowing, peasants seen crossing to and fro in the twilight, lovers strolling together among the evening shadows. So, we beheld the plain. It stretched before us an illuminated page in Nature's rarest volume. The lofty aqueducts like an army of arches went marching down toward the town which lifted its domes and towers upon its ancient battle ground. Beyond it, rising almost opposite in a northeasterly direction, was the fabled hill of Tepeyac with the grand Cathedral and convent of Nuestra Señora de Guadalupe. Avenues of graceful elms and poplars, an occasional ruin, peaceful hamlets and picturesque groups [were] on the one hand, on the other the red wall of *el mocino del Rey* with their battle associations. To the south the lovely out-lying villages of Tacubaya, San Angel, San Augustín, and more distant Tlalpám with their orchards and ornamental trees and beautiful country seats of Mexican millionaires stretched away like one glorious garden while, encircling ruin, village, field, city, meadow, and lake like a guard of honor, shoulder to shoulder, stood the marble mountains which enclose this wonderful vale, their snow peaks Popocatépetl and Ixtaccihuatl receiving the levelled glance of the sun in salute. The sun went down in masses of gorgeous color. A strange sweet odor of lilies swept up to us as if the bier of the dying day were iris scented. Deeper grew the stillness about us. Birds no longer chirped. The clink of hammer and chisel no longer came up to the tower where we stood from the rock below. We descended to the terrace. We drank water from the hushed basins of cool clear fountains. We looked upon the arabesques, the frescoes, the very few mementoes yet remaining of Mexico's last emperor. We parted the vines and entered the colonnade which he designed but never finished. Here Carlota had walked. There she had trained her flowers. Yonder was her room in which her ambitious brain had fostered its dazzling dreams. We walked and looked from windows whence queens had looked and rejoiced to know that "the noblest Roman of them all" in the lovely and accomplished wife of Porfirio Díaz would soon preside here.[2]

We passed through the great banqueting hall where Maximilian gave his last grand dinner before his departure for the fatal hillsides of Querétaro, and where Juárez entertained our own William H. Seward at breakfast. How strange to think that not one of those three prominent men, President, Statesman, Emperor, whose presence that sumptuous hall had known, were now among the living. We stepped out upon the southern terrace where a pretty little Indian girl with bright cheeks and shining eyes gathered for us calla lilies which Carlota's own hand had planted. A native wild bird hung, caged and singing the national airs of Mexico, against the castle wall. Geraniums were growing of the stature of young trees. Fuchsias, like those of our own gardens seen through a magnifying glass so large were they, were abundant everywhere, while tropical plants and blossoms had been brought to adorn the spot. Carlota's love of flowers seems to have been her one passionate affection. The cold and haughty Empress wrote her memory in blossoms wherever she went. Some of the loveliest parks in Mexico are due to her and floral survivors of her day spring from the rarest roots about the tall windows of the lower floor of the palace, and adorn the marble terraces. The noble drive she planned with its avenue of graceful trees is in full view from the eastern windows and her vines and shrubs and blossoms speak, now that she is far away, of characteristics she never betrayed to the world, and clinging deep in the castle's soil, refuse to let her be forgotten. In marked contrast with the native flowers and haughty exotics, come, storming the eastern slope of the hill under the very eyes of the gorgeous palace, a battalion of Golden Rod. From Montreal to Mexico we had found this handsome wild weed growing, sending out its sturdy yellow banners from strange buttresses and foreign battlements, opposing itself to strongly defended fortresses and lending its strength to verdure ascending like a 'forlorn hope' the stoniest and most forbidding heights. Verily it is a brave little plant. It thrives beside the hovel and sleeps beside the Hall, saucy bold and independent always.

2. Díaz's wife was Carmen Romero Rubio.

The year before we had greeted it above the noisy rapids of Niagara. That day, we took off our hats and kissed our hands to its nodding pennons on the grim heights of old Chapultepec.

As we passed again through the silent and empty palace to regain the highway, whispers seemed to follow us. The roses rustled as if garments on unseen forms had brushed against them and other footsteps than our own seemed to echo on the marble floor. The ghosts of bygone ages seemed astir as if returning with the approach of night to these scenes of their ancient triumphs and trials, grandeur and glory, love, romance and chivalry:

> "O'er all there hung a shadow and a fear;
>   A sense of mystery the spirit daunted
> And said, as plain as whisper in the ear,
>   'The place is haunted!'"

Upon the lofty terrace our feet were almost on a level with the topmost boughs of Montezuma's cypress. Its moss hung branches stirred with invisible touches and shadows seemed substance. The whole valley became veiled and grew into one vast plain of gloom. The sky was an amber sea on which lay isles of amethyst, and among them floated funeral barges of dull gold, draped in purple; while down upon the western mountains rained a flood of fire. Crickets chirped in the myrtle thickets, belated birds flew to the shelter of grey bearded groves. Amid these fading splendors, these misty reminders of a long gone past we found our carriage and drove out under the stupendous cypresses among shadows growing dense about the gardens, the ancient baths, the druidical groves. The strong gates opened and clashed shut behind our departing wheels. Cora and I involuntarily stood up in the barouche to take one more look at the castle, the gardens, the grottoes, the venerable trees.

It now began to grow very dark indeed. The road was oppressingly lonely. The wayside was deserted, the broad plains unpeopled. The spirit of haste animated neither our coachman nor his horses. All of a sudden we found ourselves going slower and slower, then came to a dead halt. Now then we thought has come indeed the long promised bandits and ye ancient watchword "your money or your lives." Cora and I clasped one another's hands. We had no money about us but our lives we respected very much for merely to be alive in Mexico is worth a great deal. Señores R. and P. threw open the carriage door and sprang out. Our valiant little steeds were found standing stock still, their dejected noses over the fountain basin of La Libertad and our driver sound asleep upon his box!

Index